Charles Kingsley

Hereward

The last of the English

Charles Kingsley

Hereward
The last of the English

ISBN/EAN: 9783337111090

Printed in Europe, USA, Canada, Australia, Japan

Cover: Foto ©ninafisch / pixelio.de

More available books at **www.hansebooks.com**

HEREWARD,

THE LAST OF THE ENGLISH.

BY

CHARLES KINGSLEY,

AUTHOR OF "TWO YEARS AGO," &C.

NEW EDITION.

New York:
MACMILLAN AND CO.
1891.

CONTENTS.

	PAGE
PRELUDE	1

CHAPTER
I. How HEREWARD WAS OUTLAWED, AND WENT NORTH TO SEEK HIS FORTUNES 11
II. How HEREWARD SLEW THE BEAR 86
III. How HEREWARD SUCCORED A PRINCESS OF CORNWALL . . 46
IV. How HEREWARD TOOK SERVICE WITH RANALD, KING OF WATERFORD 62
V. How HEREWARD SUCCORED THE PRINCESS OF CORNWALL A SECOND TIME 73
VI. How HEREWARD WAS WRECKED UPON THE FLANDERS SHORE 80
VII. How HEREWARD WENT TO THE WAR AT GUISNES . . . 92
VIII. How A FAIR LADY EXERCISED THE MECHANICAL ART TO WIN HEREWARD'S LOVE 97
IX. How HEREWARD WENT TO THE WAR IN SCALDMARILAND . 102
X. How HEREWARD WON THE MAGIC ARMOR 108
XI. How THE HOLLANDERS TOOK HEREWARD FOR A MAGICIAN 119
XII. How HEREWARD TURNED BERSERK 120
XIII. How HEREWARD WON MARE SWALLOW 126
XIV. How HEREWARD RODE INTO BRUGES LIKE A BEGGAR-MAN . 133
XV. How EARL TOSTI GODWINSSON CAME TO ST. OMER . . 138
XVI. How HEREWARD WAS ASKED TO SLAY AN OLD COMRADE . 147
XVII. How HEREWARD TOOK THE NEWS FROM STANFORD BRIGG AND HASTINGS 154
XVIII. How EARL GODWIN'S WIDOW CAME TO ST. OMER 163
XIX. How HEREWARD CLEARED BOURNE OF FRENCHMEN . . 176
XX. How HEREWARD WAS MADE A KNIGHT AFTER THE FASHION OF THE ENGLISH 187
XXI. How IVO TAILLEBOIS MARCHED OUT OF SPALDING TOWN . 198
XXII. How HEREWARD SAILED FOR ENGLAND ONCE AND FOR ALL . 206

CONTENTS.

XXIII.	How Hereward gathered an Army	211
XXIV.	How Archbishop Aldred died of Sorrow . . .	226
XXV.	How Hereward found a wiser Man in England than Himself	234
XXVI.	How Hereward fulfilled his Words to the Prior of the Golden Borough	239
XXVII.	How they held a great Meeting in the Hall of Ely	258
XXVIII.	How they fought at Aldreth	263
XXIX.	How Sir Dade brought News from Ely . . .	269
XXX.	How Hereward played the Potter; and how he cheated the King	275
XXXI.	How they fought again at Aldreth	287
XXXII.	How King William took Counsel of a Churchman .	293
XXXIII.	How the Monks of Ely did after their Kind . .	305
XXXIV.	How Hereward went to the Greenwood . . .	314
XXXV.	How Abbot Thorold was put to Ransom . . .	323
XXXVI.	How Alftruda wrote to Hereward	333
XXXVII.	How Hereward lost Sword Brain-biter . . .	352
XXXVIII.	How Hereward came in to the King	356
XXXIX.	How Torfrida confessed that she had been inspired by the Devil	362
XL.	How Hereward began to get his Soul's Price .	368
XLI.	How Earl Waltheof was made a Saint . . .	379
XLII.	How Hereward got the Rest of his Soul's Price .	382
XLIII.	How Deeping Fen was drained	394

HEREWARD,

THE LAST OF THE ENGLISH.

PRELUDE.

The heroic deeds of Highlanders, both in these islands and elsewhere, have been told in verse and prose, and not more often, nor more loudly, than they deserve. But we must remember, now and then, that there have been heroes likewise in the lowland and in the fen. Why, however, poets have so seldom sung of them; why no historian, save Mr. Motley in his "Rise of the Dutch Republic," has condescended to tell the tale of their doughty deeds, is a question not difficult to answer.

In the first place, they have been fewer in number. The lowlands of the world, being the richest spots, have been generally the soonest conquered, the soonest civilized, and therefore the soonest taken out of the sphere of romance and wild adventure, into that of order and law, hard work and common sense, as well as — too often — into the sphere of slavery, cowardice, luxury, and ignoble greed. The lowland populations, for the same reasons, have been generally the first to deteriorate, though not on account of the vices of civilization. The vices of incivilization are far worse, and far more destructive of human life; and it is just because they are so, that rude tribes deteriorate physically less than polished nations. In the savage struggle for life, none but the strongest, healthiest, cunningest, have a chance of living, prospering, and propagating their race. In the civilized state, on the contrary, the weakliest and the silliest, protected by law, religion, and humanity, have chance likewise, and transmit to their offspring their own weakliness or silliness. In these islands, for instance, at the time of the Norman Conquest, the average of man was doubtless superior, both in body and mind, to the average of man now, simply because the weaklings could not have lived at all; and the rich and delicate beauty, in which the women of the Eastern Counties still surpass all other races in these isles, was doubtless far more common in proportion to the numbers of the population.

Another reason — and one which every Scot will understand — why lowland heroes "carent vate sacro," is that the lowlands and those who live in them are wanting in the poetic and romantic elements. There is in the lowland none of that background of the unknown, fantastic, magical, terrible, perpetually feeding curiosity and wonder, which still remains in the Scottish highlands; which, when it disappears from thence, will remain embalmed forever in the pages of Walter Scott. Against that half-magical background his heroes stand out in vivid relief; and justly so. It was not put there by him for stage purposes; it was there as a fact; and the men of whom he wrote were conscious of it, were moulded by it, were not ashamed of its influence. Nature among the mountains is too fierce, too strong, for man. He cannot conquer her, and she awes him. He cannot dig down the cliffs, or chain the storm-blasts; and his fear of them takes bodily shape: he begins to people the weird places of the earth with weird beings, and sees nixes in the dark linns as he fishes by night, dwarfs in the caves where he digs, half-trembling, morsels of copper and iron for his weapons, witches and demons on the snowblast which overwhelms his herd and his hut, and in the dark clouds which brood on the untrodden mountain-peak. He lives in fear: and yet, if he be a valiant-hearted man, his fears do him little harm. They may break out, at times, in witch-manias, with all their horrible suspicions, and thus breed cruelty, which is the child of fear: but on the whole they rather produce in man thoughtfulness, reverence, a sense, confused yet precious, of the boundless importance of the unseen world. His superstitions develop his imagination; the moving accidents of a wild life call out in him sympathy and pathos; and the mountaineer becomes instinctively a poet.

The lowlander, on the other hand, has his own strength, his own "virtues," or manfulnesses, in the good old sense of the word: but they are not for the most part picturesque or even poetical.

He finds out, soon enough for his weal and his bane, that he is stronger than Nature: and right tyrannously and irreverently he lords it over her, clearing, delving, diking, building, without fear or shame. He knows of no natural force greater than himself, save an occasional thunder-storm; and against that, as he grows more cunning, he insures his crops. Why should he reverence Nature? Let him use her, and eat. One cannot blame him. Man was sent into the world (so says the Scripture) to fill and subdue the earth. But he was sent into the world for other purposes, which the lowlander is but too apt to forget. With the awe of Nature, the awe of the unseer dies out in him. Meeting with no visible superior, he is apt to become not merely unpoetical and irreverent, but somewhat of a sensualist and an atheist. The sense of the beautiful dies out in him more and more. He has little or nothing around him to refine or lift up his soul; and unless he meet with a religion, and with a civilization, which can deliver him, he may sink into that dull brutality which is too common among the lowest classes of the English lowlands; and remain for generations gifted with the strength and industry of the ox, and with the courage of the lion, and, alas! with the intellect of the former, and the self-restraint of the latter.

But there may be a period in the history of a lowland race when they, too, become historic for a while. There was such a period for the men of the Eastern Counties; for they proved it by their deeds.

When the men of Wessex, the once conquering race of Britain, fell at Hastings once and for all, and struck no second blow, then the men of the Danelagh disdained to yield to the Norman invader. For seven long years they held their own, not knowing, like true Englishmen, when they were beaten; and fought on desperate, till there were none left to fight. Their bones lay white on every island in the fens; their corpses rotted on gallows beneath every Norman keep; their few survivors crawled into monasteries, with eyes picked out, or hands and feet cut off; or took to the wild wood as strong outlaws, like their successors and representatives, Robin Hood, Scarlet, and John, Adam Bell, and Clym of the Cleugh, and William of Cloudeslee. But they never really bent their necks to the Norman yoke; they kept alive in their hearts that proud spirit of personal independence, which they brought with them from the moors of Denmark and the dales of Norway; and they kept alive, too, though in abeyance for a while, those free institutions which were without a doubt the germs of our British liberty.

They were a changed folk since first they settled in that Danelagh; — since first in the days of King Beorhtric, "in the year 787, three ships of Northmen came from Hæretha land, and the King's reeve rode to the place, and would have driven them up to the King's town, for he knew not what men they were: but they slew him there and then"; and after the Saxons and Angles began to find out to their bitter bale what men they were, those fierce Vikings out of the dark northeast.

But they had long ceased to burn farms, sack convents, torture monks for gold, and slay every human being they met, in mere Berserker lust of blood. No Barnakill could now earn his nickname by entreating his comrades, as they tossed the children on their spear-points, to "Na kill the barns." Gradually they had settled down on the land, intermarried with the Angles and Saxons, and colonized all England north and east of Watling Street (a rough line from London to Chester), and the eastern lowlands of Scotland likewise. Gradually they had deserted Thor and Odin for "the White Christ"; had their own priests and bishops, and built their own minsters. The convents which the fathers had destroyed, the sons, or at least the grandsons, rebuilt; and often, casting away sword and axe, they entered them as monks themselves; and Peterborough, Ely, and above all Crowland, destroyed by them in Alfred's time with a horrible destruction, had become their holy places, where they decked the altars with gold and jewels, with silks from the far East, and furs from the far North; and where, as in sacred fortresses, they, and the liberty of England with them, made their last unavailing stand.

For a while they had been lords of all England. The Anglo-Saxon race was wearing out. The men of Wessex, priest-ridden, and enslaved by their own aristocracy, quailed before the free Norsemen, among whom was not a single serf. The God-descended line of Cerdic and Alfred was worn out. Vain, incapable, profligate kings, the tools of such prelates as Odo and Dunstan, were no match for such wild heroes as Thorkill the tall, or Olaf Trygvasson, or Swend Forkbeard. The Danes had gradually colonized, not only their own Danelagh and Northumbria, but great part of Wessex. Vast sums of Danegelt were yearly sent out of the country to buy off the fresh invasions which were perpetually threatened. Then Ethelred the Unready, Ethelred Evil-counsel, advised himself to fulfil his name, and the curse which Dunstan had pronounced against him at the baptismal font. By his counsel the men of Wessex rose against the unsuspecting Danes; and on St. Brice's eve, A. D. 1002, murdered them all with tortures, man, woman, and child. It may be that they only did to the children as the fathers had done to them: but the deed was "worse than a crime; it was a mistake." The Danes of the Danelagh and of Northumbria, their brothers of Denmark and Norway, the Orkneys and the east coast of Ireland, remained unharmed. A mighty host of Vikings poured from thence into England the very next year, under Swend Forkbeard and the great Canute; and after thirteen fearful campaigns came the great battle of Assingdown in Essex, — where " Canute had the victory; and all the English nation fought against him; and all the nobility of the English race was there destroyed."

That same year saw the mysterious death of Edmund Ironside, the last man of Cerdic's race worthy of the name. For the next twenty-five years, Danish kings ruled from the Forth to the Land's End.

A noble figure he was, that great and wise Canute, the friend of the famous Godiva, and Leofric, Godiva's husband, and Siward Biorn, the conqueror of Macbeth: trying to expiate by justice and mercy the dark deeds of his bloodstained youth; trying (and not in vain) to blend the two races over which he ruled; rebuilding the churches and monasteries which his father had destroyed; bringing back in state to Canterbury the body of Archbishop Elphege, — not unjustly called by the Saxons martyr and saint, — whom Tall Thorkill's men had murdered with beef bones and ox-skulls, because he would not give up to them the money destined for God's poor; rebuking, as every child has heard, his housecarles' flattery by setting his chair on the brink of the rising tide; and then laying his golden crown, in token of humility, on the high altar of Winchester, never to wear it more. In Winchester lie his bones unto this day, or what of them the civil wars have left: and by him lie the bones of his son Hardicanute, in whom, as in his half-brother Harold Harefoot before him, the Danish power fell to swift decay, by insolence and drink and civil war; and with the Danish power England fell to pieces likewise.

Canute had divided England into four great earldoms, each ruled, under him, by a jarl, or earl, a Danish, not a Saxon title.

At his death in 1036, the earldoms of Northumbria and East Anglia — the more strictly Danish parts — were held by a true Danish hero, Siward Biorn, alias Digre the Stout, conqueror of Macbeth, and son of the fairy bear; proving his descent, men said, by his pointed and hairy ears.

Mercia, the great central plateau of England, was held by Earl Leofric, husband of the famous Lady Godiva.

Wessex, which Canute had at first kept in his own hands, had passed into those of the furious Earl Godwin, the then ablest man in England. Possessed of boundless tact and cunning, gifted with an eloquence which seems, from the accounts remaining of it, to have been rather that of a Greek than an Englishman; himself of high — perhaps of royal — Sussex blood (for the story of his low birth seems a mere fable of his French enemies), and married first to Canute's sister, and then to his niece, he was fitted, alike by fortunes and by talents, to be the king-maker which he became.

Such a system may have worked well as long as the brain of a hero was there to overlook it all. But when that brain was turned to dust, the history of England became, till the Norman Conquest, little more than the history of the rivalries of the two great houses of Godwin and Leofric.

Leofric had the first success in king-making. He, though

bearing a Saxon name, was the champion of the Danish party and of Canute's son, or reputed son, Harold Harefoot; and he succeeded, by the help of the "Thanes north of Thames," and the "lithsmen of London," which city was more than half Danish in those days, in setting his puppet on the throne. But the blood of Canute had exhausted itself. Within seven years Harold Harefoot and Hardicanute, who succeeded him, had died as foully as they lived; and Godwin's turn had come.

He, though married to a Danish princess, and acknowledging his Danish connection by the Norse names which were borne by his three most famous sons, Harold, Sweyn, and Tostig, constituted himself the champion of the men of Wessex and the house of Cerdic. He had murdered, or at least caused to be murdered, horribly, Alfred the Etheling, King Ethelred's son and heir-apparent, when it seemed his interest to support the claims of Hardicanute against Harefoot; he now found little difficulty in persuading his victim's younger brother to come to England, and become at once his king, his son-in-law and his puppet.

Edward the Confessor, if we are to believe the monks whom he pampered, was naught but virtue and piety, meekness and magnanimity, — a model ruler of men. Such a model ruler he was, doubtless, as monks would be glad to see on every throne; because while he rules his subjects, they rule him. No wonder, therefore, that (according to William of Malmesbury) the happiness of his times (famed as he was both for miracles and the spirit of prophecy) "was revealed in a dream to Brithwin, Bishop of Wilton, who made it public"; who, meditating, in King Canute's time, on "the near extinction of the royal race of the English," was "rapt up on high, and saw St. Peter consecrating Edward king. His chaste life also was pointed out, and the exact period of his reign (twenty-four years) determined; and, when inquiring about his posterity, it was answered, 'The kingdom of the English belongs to God. After you, He will provide a king according to his pleasure.'" But those who will look at the facts will see in the holy Confessor's character little but what is pitiable, and in his reign little but what is tragical.

Civil wars, invasions, outlawry of Godwin and his sons by the Danish party; then of Alfgar, Leofric's son, by the Saxon party; the outlaws on either side attacking and plundering the English shores by the help of Norsemen, Welshmen, Irish, and Danes, — any mercenaries who could be got together; and then, — "In the same year Bishop Aldred consecrated the minster at Gloucester to the glory of God and of St. Peter, and then went to Jerusalem with such splendor as no man had displayed before him"; and so forth. The sum and substance of what was done in those "happy times" may be well described in the words of the Anglo-Saxon chronicler for the year 1058. "This year Alfgar the earl was banished; but he came in again with violence, through aid of Griffin (the king of North Wales, his brother-in-law). And this year came a fleet from Norway. It is tedious to tell how these matters went." These were the normal phenomena of a reign which seemed, to the eyes of monks, a holy and a happy one; because the king refused, whether from spite or superstition, to have an heir to the house of Cerdic, and spent his time between prayer, hunting, the seeing of fancied visions, the uttering of fancied prophecies, and the performance of fancied miracles.

But there were excuses for him. An Englishman only in name, — a Norman, not only of his mother's descent (she was aunt of William the Conqueror), but by his early education on the Continent, — he loved the Norman better than the Englishman; Norman knights and clerks filled his court, and often the high dignities of his provinces, and returned as often as expelled; the Norman-French language became fashionable; Norman customs and manners the signs of civilization; and thus all was preparing steadily for the great catastrophe, by which, within a year of Edward's death, the Norman became master of the land.

Perhaps it ought to have been so. Perhaps by no other method could England, and, with England, Scotland, and in due time Ireland, have become partakers of that classic civilization and learning, the fount whereof, for good and for evil, was Rome and the Pope of Rome: but the method was at least wicked; the actors in it tyrannous, brutal, treacherous, hypocritical; and the conquest of England by William will remain to the end of time a mighty crime, abetted — one may almost say made possible, as too many such crimes have been before and since — by the intriguing ambition of the Pope of Rome.

Against that tyranny the free men of the Danelagh and of Northumbria rose. If Edward, the descendant of Cerdic, had been little to them, William, the descendant of Rollo, was still less. That French-speaking knights should expel them from their homes, French-chanting monks from their convents, because Edward had promised the crown of England to William, his foreign cousin, or because Harold Godwinsson of Wessex had sworn on the relics of all the saints to be William's man, was contrary to their common-sense of right and reason.

So they rose and fought: too late, it may be, and without unity or purpose; and they were worsted by an enemy who had both unity and purpose; whom superstition, greed, and feudal discipline kept together, at least in England, in one compact body of unscrupulous and terrible confederates.

But theirs was a land worth fighting for, — a good land and large: from Humber mouth inland to the Trent and merry Sherwood, across to Chester and the Dee, round by Leicester and the five burghs of the Danes; eastward again to Huntingdon and Cambridge (then a poor village on the site of an old Roman town); and then northward again into the wide fens, the land of the Girvii and the Eormingas, "the children of the peat-bog," where the great central plateau of England slides into the sea, to form, from the rain and river washings of eight shires, lowlands of a fertility inexhaustible, because ever-growing to this day.

They have a beauty of their own, those great fens, even now, when they are diked and drained, tilled and fenced, — a beauty as of the sea, of boundless expanse and freedom. Much more had they that beauty eight hundred years ago, when they were still, for the most part, as God had made them, or rather was making them even then. The low rolling uplands were clothed in primeval forest: oak and ash, beech and elm, with here and there, perhaps, a group of ancient pines, ragged and decayed, and fast dying out in England even then; though lingering still in the forests of the Scotch highlands.

Between the forests were open wolds, dotted with white sheep and golden gorse; rolling plains of rich though ragged turf, whether cleared by the hand of man or by the wild fires which often swept over the hills. And between the wood and the wold stood many a Danish "town," with its clusters of low straggling buildings round the holder's house, stone or mud below, and wood above; its high dikes round tiny fields; its flocks of sheep ranging on the wold; its herds of swine in the forest; and below, a more precious possession still, — its herds of mares and colts, which fed with the cattle in the rich grass-fen.

For always, from the foot of the wolds, the green flat stretched away, illimitable, to an horizon where, from the roundness of the earth, the distant trees and islands were hulled down like ships at sea. The firm horse-fen lay, bright green, along the foot of the wold; beyond it, the browner peat, or deep fen; and among it, dark velvet alder beds, long lines of reed-rond, emerald in spring, and golden under the autumn sun; shining river-reaches; broad meres dotted with a million fowl, while the cattle waded along their edges after the rich sedge-grass, or wallowed in the mire through the hot summer's day. Here and there, too, upon the far horizon, rose a tall line of ashen trees, marking some island of firm rich soil. Here and there, too, as at Ramsey and Crowland, the huge ashes had disappeared before the axes of the monks, and a minster tower rose over the fen, amid orchards, gardens, cornfields, pastures, with here and there a tree left

standing for shade,—" Painted with flowers in the spring," with
"pleasant shores embosomed in still lakes," as the monk-chronicler of Ramsey has it, those islands seemed to such as the monk terrestrial paradises.

Overhead the arch of heaven spread more ample than elsewhere, as over the open sea; and that vastness gave, and still gives, such "effects" of cloudland, of sunrise, and sunset, as can be seen nowhere else within these isles. They might well have been star-worshippers, these Girvii, had their sky been as clear as that of the East: but they were like to have worshipped the clouds rather than the stars, according to the too universal law, that mankind worship the powers which do them harm, rather than the powers which do them good.

And therefore the Danelagh men, who feared not mortal sword or axe, feared witches, ghosts, Pucks, Will-o'-the-Wisps, werewolves, spirits of the wells and of the trees, and all dark, capricious, and harmful beings whom their fancy conjured up out of the wild, wet, and unwholesome marshes, or the dark wolf-haunted woods. For that fair land, like all things on earth, had its darker aspect. The foul exhalations of autumn called up fever and ague, crippling and enervating, and tempting, almost compelling, to that wild and desperate drinking which was the Scandinavian's special sin. Dark and sad were those short autumn days, when all the distances were shut off, and the air choked with foul brown fog and drenching rains from off the eastern sea; and pleasant the bursting forth of the keen northeast wind, with all its whirling snow-storms. For though it sent men hurrying out into the storm, to drive the cattle in from the fen, and lift the sheep out of the snow-wreaths, and now and then never to return, lost in mist and mire, in ice and snow;—yet all knew that after the snow would come the keen frost and the bright sun and cloudless blue sky, and the fenman's yearly holiday, when, work being impossible, all gave themselves up to play, and swarmed upon the ice on skates and sledges, and ran races, township against township, or visited old friends full forty miles away; and met everywhere faces as bright and ruddy as their own, cheered by the keen wine of that dry and bracing frost.

Such was the Fenland; hard, yet cheerful; rearing a race of hard and cheerful men; showing their power in old times in valiant fighting, and for many a century since in that valiant industry which has drained and embanked the land of the Girvii, till it has become a very "Garden of the Lord." And the Scotsman who may look from the promontory of Peterborough, the "golden borough" of old time; or from the tower of Crowland, while Hereward and Torfrida sleep in the ruined nave beneath;

or from the heights of that Isle of Ely which was so long the camp of refuge" for English freedom; over the labyrinth of dikes and lodes, the squares of rich corn and verdure,—will confess that the lowland, as well as the highland, can at times breed gallant men.*

* The story of Hereward (often sung by minstrels and old-wives in succeeding generations) may be found in the "Metrical Chronicle of Geoffrey Gaimar," and in the prose "Life of Hereward" (paraphrased from that written by Leofric, his house-priest), and in the valuable fragment "Of the family of Hereward." These have all three been edited by Mr. T. Wright. The account of Hereward in Ingulf seems taken, and that carelessly, from the same source as the Latin prose, "De Gestis Herewardi." A few curious details may be found in Peter of Blois's continuation of Ingulf; and more, concerning the sack of Peterborough, in the Anglo-Saxon Chronicle. I have followed the contemporary authorities as closely as I could, introducing little but what was necessary to reconcile discrepancies, or to illustrate the history, manners, and sentiments of the time.— C. K.

CHAPTER I.

HOW HEREWARD WAS OUTLAWED, AND WENT NORTH TO SEEK HIS FORTUNES.

KNOWN to all is Lady Godiva, the most beautiful as well as the most saintly woman of her day; who, "all her life, kept at her own expense thirteen poor folk wherever she went; who, throughout Lent, watched in the church at triple matins, namely, one for the Trinity, one for the Cross, and one for St. Mary; who every day read the Psalter through, and so persevered in good and holy works to her life's end,"— the "devoted friend of St. Mary, ever a virgin," who enriched monasteries without number, — Leominster, Wenlock, Chester, St. Mary's Stow by Lincoln, Worcester, Evesham; and who, above all, founded the great monastery in that town of Coventry, which has made her name immortal for another and a far nobler deed; and enriched it so much " that no monastery in England possessed such abundance of gold, silver, jewels, and precious stones," beside that most precious jewel of all, the arm of St. Augustine, which not Lady Godiva, but her friend, Archbishop Ethelnoth, presented to Coventry, "having bought it at Pavia for a hundred talents of silver and a talent of gold."*

Less known, save to students, is her husband, Leofric the great Earl of Mercia and Chester, whose bones lie by those of Godiva in that same minster of Coventry; how "his counsel was as if one had opened the Divine oracles"; very "wise," says the Anglo-Saxon Chronicle, "for God and for the world, which was a blessing to all this nation"; the greatest man, save his still greater rival, Earl Godwin, in Edward the Confessor's court.

Less known, again, are the children of that illustrious pair: Algar, or Alfgar, Earl of Mercia after his father, who died, after a short and stormy life, leaving two sons, Edwin and Morcar, the fair and hapless young earls, always spoken of together, as if they had been twins; a daughter, Aldytha, or Elfgiva, married first (according to some) to Griffin, King of North Wales, and certainly afterwards to Harold, King of England; and another, Lucia (as

* William of Malmesbury.

the Normans at least called her), whose fate was, if possible, more sad than that of her brothers.

Their second son was Hereward, whose history this tale sets forth; their third and youngest, a boy who-e name is unknown.

They had, probably, another daughter beside; married, it may be, to some son of Leofric's stanch friend old Siward Biorn, the Viking Earl of Northumberland, and conqueror of Macbeth; and the mother, may be, of the two young Siwards, the " white " and the " red," who figure in chronicle and legend as the nephews of Hereward. But this pedigree is little more than a conjecture.

Be these things as they may, Godiva was the greatest lady in England, save two: Edith, Harold's sister, the nominal wife of Edward the Confessor; and Githa, or Gyda, as her own Danes called her, Harold's mother, niece of Canute the Great. Great was Godiva; and might have been proud enough, had she been inclined to that pleasant sin. And even then (for there is a skeleton, they say, in every house) she carried that about her which might well keep her humble; namely, shame at the misconduct of Hereward, her son.

Her favorite residence, among the many manors and " villas," or farms which Leofric possessed, was neither the stately hall at Loughton by Bridgenorth, nor the statelier castle of Warwick, but the house of Bourne in South Lincolnshire, between the great woods of the Bruneswald and the great level of the fens. It may have been her own paternal dowry, and have come down to her in right of her Danish ancestors, and that great and " magnificent " Jarl Oslac, from whom she derived her all-but-royal blood. This is certain, that Leofric, her husband, went in East Anglia by the name of Leofric, Lord of Bourne; that, as Domesday Book testifies, his son Alfgar, and his grandson Morcar, held large lands there and thereabout. Alfgar's name, indeed, still lives in the village of Algar-Kirk; and Lady Godiva, and Algar after her, enriched with great gifts Crowland, the island sanctuary, and Peterborough, where Brand, either her brother or Leofric's, was a monk, and in due time an abbot.

The house of Bourne, as far as it can be reconstructed by imagination, was altogether unlike one of the tall and gloomy Norman castles which twenty years later reared their evil donjons over England. It was much more like a house in a Chinese painting; an irregular group of low buildings, almost all of one story, stone below and timber above, with high-peaked roofs, — at least in the more Danish country, — affording a separate room, or rather house, for each different need of the family. Such a one may be seen in the illuminations of the century. In the centre of the building is the hall, with door or doors opening out into the

court; and sitting thereat, at the top of a flight of steps, the lord
and lady, dealing clothes to the naked and bread to the hungry.
On one side of the hall is a chapel; by it a large room or "bower"
for the ladies; behind the hall a round tower, seemingly the strong
place of the whole house; on the other side a kitchen; and stuck
on to bower, kitchen, and every other principal building, lean-to
after lean-to, the uses of which it is impossible now to discover.
The house had grown with the wants of the family, — as many
good old English houses have done to this day. Round it would
be scattered barns and stables, in which grooms and herdsmen
slept side by side with their own horses and cattle; and outside
all, the "yard," "garth," or garden-fence, high earth-bank with
palisades on top, which formed a strong defence in time of war.
Such was most probably the "villa," "ton," or "town" of Earl
Leofric, the Lord of Bourne, the favorite residence of Godiva, —
once most beautiful, and still most holy, according to the holiness
of those old times.

Now on a day — about the year 1054 — while Earl Siward
was helping to bring Birnam wood to Dunsinane, to avenge his
murdered brother-in-law, Lady Godiva sat, not at her hall door,
dealing food and clothing to her thirteen poor folk, but in her
bower, with her youngest son, a two-years' boy, at her knee. She
was listening with a face of shame and horror to the complaint of
Herluin, Steward of Peterborough, who had fallen in that afternoon with Hereward and his crew of "housecarles."

To keep a following of stout housecarles, or men-at-arms, was
the pride as well as the duty of an Anglo-Danish Lord, as it was,
till lately, of a Scoto-Danish Highland Laird. And Hereward,
in imitation of his father and his elder brother, must needs have
his following from the time he was but fifteen years old. All the
unruly youths of the neighborhood, sons of free "holders," who
owed some sort of military service to Earl Leofric; Geri his
cousin; Winter, whom he called his brother-in-arms; the Wul-
frics, the Wulfards, the Azers, and many another wild blade, had
banded themselves round a young nobleman more unruly than
themselves. Their names were already a terror to all decent folk,
at wakes and fairs, alehouses and village sports. They atoned,
be it remembered, for their early sins by making those names in
after years a terror to the invaders of their native land: but as
yet their prowess was limited to drunken brawls and faction
fights; to upsetting old women at their work, levying black-mail
from quiet chapmen on the high road, or bringing back in triumph,
sword in hand and club on shoulder, their leader Hereward from
some duel which his insolence had provoked.

But this time, if the story of the sub-prior was to be believed,

Hereward and his housecarles had taken an ugly stride forward toward the pit. They had met him riding along, intent upon his psalter, in a lonely path of the Bruneswald, — " whereon your son, most gracious lady, bade me stand, saying that his men were thirsty and he had no money to buy ale withal, and none so likely to help him thereto as a fat priest, — for so he scandalously termed me, who, as your ladyship knows, am leaner than the minster bell-ropes, with fasting Wednesdays and Fridays throughout the year, beside the vigils of the saints, and the former and latter Lents.

" But when he saw who I was, as if inspired by a malignant spirit, he shouted out my name, and bade his companions throw me to the ground."

" Throw you to the ground?" shuddered the Lady Godiva.

" In much mire, madam. After which he took my palfrey, saying that heaven's gate was too lowly for men on horseback to get in thereat; and then my marten's fur gloves and cape which your gracious self bestowed on me, alleging that the rules of my order allowed only one garment, and no furs save catskins and such like. And lastly — I tremble while I relate, thinking not of the loss of my poor money, but the loss of an immortal soul — took from me a purse with sixteen silver pennies, which I had collected from our tenants for the use of the monastery, and said, blasphemously, that I and mine had swindled your ladyship, and therefore him, your son, out of many a fair manor ere now; and it was but fair that he should tithe the rents thereof, as he should never get the lands out of our claws again; with more of the like, which I blush to repeat, — and so left me to trudge hither in the mire."

" Wretched boy!" said the Lady Godiva, and hid her face in her hands; "and more wretched I, to have brought such a son into the world!"

The monk had hardly finished his doleful story, when there was a pattering of heavy feet, a noise of men shouting and laughing outside, and a voice, above all, calling for the monk by name, which made that good man crouch behind the curtain of Lady Godiva's bed. The next moment the door of the bower was thrown violently open, and in walked, or rather reeled, a noble lad eighteen years old. His face was of extraordinary beauty, save that the lower jaw was too long and heavy, and that his eyes wore a strange and almost sinister expression, from the fact that the one of them was gray and the other blue. He was short, but of immense breadth of chest and strength of limb; while his delicate hands and feet and long locks of golden hair marked him of most noble, and even, as he really was, of ancient royal race. He was dressed in a gaudy costume, resembling on the whole that of a Highland chieftain. His knees, wrists, and throat were tattoed in bright blue patterns; and he carried sword and dagger, a gold ring round his neck, and gold rings on his wrists. He was a lad to have gladdened the eyes of any mother: but there was no gladness in the Lady Godiva's eyes as she received him; nor had there been for many a year. She looked on him with sternness, — with all but horror; and he, his face flushed with wine, which he had tossed off as he passed through the hall to steady his nerves for the coming storm, looked at her with smiling defiance, the result of long estrangement between mother and son.

"Well, my lady," said he, ere she could speak, "I heard that this good fellow was here, and came home as fast as I could, to see that he told you as few lies as possible."

"He has told me," said she, "that you have robbed the Church of God."

"Robbed him, it may be, an old hoody crow, against whom I have a grudge of ten years' standing."

"Wretched, wretched boy! What wickedness next? Know you not, that he who robs the Church robs God himself?"

"And he who harms God's people," put in the monk from behind the chair, "harms his Maker."

"His Maker?" said the lad, with concentrated bitterness. "It would be a gay world, if the Maker thereof were in any way like unto you, who call yourselves his people. Do you remember who told them to set the peat-stack on fire under me ten years ago? Ah, ha, Sir Monk, you forget that I have been behind the screen, — that I have been a monk myself, or should have been one, if my pious lady mother here had had her will of me, as she may if she likes of that doll there at her knee. Do you forget why I left Peterborough Abbey, when Winter and I turned all your priest's books upside down in the choir, and they would have flogged us, — me, the Earl's son, — me, the Viking's son, — me, the champion, as I will be yet, and make all lands ring with the fame of my deeds, as they rung with the fame of my forefathers, before they became the slaves of monks; and how, when Winter and I got hold of the kitchen spits, and up to the top of the peat-stack, and held you all at bay there, a whole abbeyful of cowards there, against two seven years' children? It was you bade set the peat-stack alight under us, and so bring us down; and would have done it, too, had it not been for my Uncle Brand, the only man that I care for in this wide world. Do you think I have not owed you a grudge ever since that day, monk? And do you think I will not pay it? Do you think I would not have burned Peterborough minster over your head before now, had it not been for Uncle Brand's sake? See that I do not do it yet. See that when there is another Prior in Borough you do not find Hereward the Berserker smoking you out some dark night, as he would smoke a wasps' nest. And I will, by —"

"Hereward, Hereward!" cried his mother, "godless, god-forgotten boy, what words are these? Silence, before you burden your soul with an oath which the devils in hell will accept, and force you to keep!" and she sprung up, and, seizing his arm, laid her hand upon his mouth.

Hereward looked at her majestic face, once lovely, now careworn, and trembled for a moment. Had there been any tenderness in it, his history might have been a very different one; but alas! there was none. Not that she was in herself untender; but that her great piety (call it not superstition, for it was then the only form known or possible to pure and devout souls) was so outraged by this, or even by the slightest insult to that clergy whose willing slave she had become, that the only method of reclaiming the sinner had been long forgotten, in genuine horror at his sin. "Is it not enough," she went on, sternly, "that you should have become the bully and the ruffian of all the fens? — that Hereward the leaper, Hereward the wrestler, Hereward the thrower of the hammer — sports, after all, only fit for the sons of slaves — should be also Hereward the drunkard, Hereward the common fighter, Hereward the breaker of houses, Hereward the leader of mobs of boon companions which bring back to us, in shame and sorrow, the days when our heathen forefathers ravaged this land with fire and sword? Is it not enough for me that my son should be a common stabber — ?"

"Whoever called me stabber to you, lies. If I have killed men, or had them killed, I have done it in fair fight."

But she went on unheeding, — "Is it not enough, that, after having squandered on your fellows all the money that you could wring from my bounty, or win at your brutal sports, you should have robbed your own father, collected his rents behind his back, taken money and goods from his tenants by threats and blows; but that, after outraging them, you must add to all this a worse sin likewise, — outraging God, and driving me — me who have borne with you, me who have concealed all for your sake — to tell your father that of which the very telling will turn my hair to gray?"

"So you will tell my father?" said Hereward, coolly.

"And if I should not, this monk himself is bound to do so, or his superior, your Uncle Brand."

"My Uncle Brand will not, and your monk dare not."

"Then I must. I have loved you long and well; but there is one thing which I must love better than you: and that is, my conscience and my Maker."

"Those are two things, my lady mother, and not one; so you had better not confound them. As for the latter, do you not think that He who made the world is well able to defend his own property,—if the lands and houses and cattle and money which these men wheedle and threaten and forge out of you and my father are really his property, and not merely their plunder? As for your conscience, my lady mother, really you have done so many good deeds in your life, that it might be beneficial to you to do a bad one once in a way, so as to keep your soul in a wholesome state of humility."

The monk groaned aloud. Lady Godiva groaned; but it was inwardly. There was silence for a moment. Both were abashed by the lad's utter shamelessness.

"And you will tell my father?" said he again. "He is at the old miracle-worker's court at Westminster. He will tell the miracle-worker, and I shall be outlawed."

"And if you be, wretched boy, whom have you to blame but yourself? Can you expect that the king, sainted even as he is before his death, dare pass over such an atrocity towards Holy Church?"

"Blame? I shall blame no one. Pass over? I hope he will not pass over it. I only want an excuse like that for turning kempery-man,—knight-errant, as those Norman puppies call it,—like Regnar Lodbrog, or Frithiof, or Harold Hardraade; and try what man can do for himself in the world with nothing to help him in heaven and earth, with neither saint nor angel, friend or counsellor, to see to him, save his wits and his good sword. So send off the messenger, good mother mine: and I will promise you I will not have him ham-strung on the way, as some of my housecarles would do for me if I but held up my hand; and let the miracle-monger fill up the measure of his folly, by making an enemy of one more bold fellow in the world."

And he swaggered out of the room.

And when he was gone, the Lady Godiva bowed her head into her lap and wept long and bitterly. Neither her maidens nor the priest dare speak to her for nigh an hour; but at the end of that time she lifted up her head, and settled her face again, till it was like that of a marble saint over a minster door; and called for ink and paper, and wrote her letter; and then asked for a trusty messenger who should carry it up to Westminster.

"None so swift or sure," said the house steward, "as Martin Lightfoot."

Lady Godiva shook her head. "I mistrust that man," she said. "He is too fond of my poor — of the Lord Hereward."

"He is a strange one, my lady, and no one knows whence he came, and, I sometimes fancy, whither he may go either; but ever since my lord threatened to hang him for talking with my young master, he has never spoken to him, nor scarcely, indeed, to living soul. And one thing there is makes him or any man sure, as long as he is well paid; and that is, that he cares for nothing in heaven or earth save himself and what he can get."

So Martin Lightfoot was sent for. He came in straight into the lady's bedchamber, after the simple fashion of those days. He was a tall, lean, bony man, as was to be expected from his nickname, with a long hooked nose, a scanty brown beard, and a high conical head. His only garment was a shabby gray woollen tunic, which served him both as coat and kilt, and laced brogues of untanned hide. He might have been any age from twenty to forty; but his face was disfigured with deep scars and long exposure to the weather. He dropped on one knee, holding his greasy cap in his hand, and looked, not at his lady's face, but at her feet, with a stupid and frightened expression. She knew very little of him, save that her husband had picked him up upon the road as a wanderer some five years since; and that he had been employed as a doer of odd jobs and runner of messages, and that was supposed, from his taciturnity and strangeness, to have something uncanny about him.

"Martin," said the lady, "they tell me that you are a silent and a prudent man."

"That am I.
> 'Tongue speaketh bane,
> Though she herself hath nane.'"

"I shall try you: do you know your way to London?"

"Yes."

"To your lord's lodgings in Westminster?"

"Yes."

"How long shall you be going there with this letter?"

"A day and a half."

"When shall you be back hither?"

"On the fourth day."

"And you will go to my lord and deliver this letter safely?"

"Yes, your Majesty."

"Why do you call me Majesty? The King is Majesty."

"You are my Queen."

"What do you mean, man?"

"You can hang me."

"I hang thee, poor soul! Who did I ever hang, or hurt for a moment, if I could help it?"

"But the Earl may."

"He will neither hang nor hurt thee if thou wilt take this letter safely, and bring me back the answer safely."

"They will kill me."

"Who?"

"They," said Martin, pointing to the bower maidens, — young ladies of good family who stood round, chosen for their good looks, after the fashion of those times, to attend on great ladies. There was a cry of angry and contemptuous denial, not unmixed with something like laughter, which showed that Martin had but spoken the truth. Hereward, in spite of all his sins, was the darling of his mother's bower; and there was not one of the damsels but would have done anything short of murder to have prevented Martin carrying the letter.

"Silence, man!" said Lady Godiva, so sternly that Martin saw that he had gone too far. "How know'st such as thou what is in this letter?"

"Those others will know," said Martin, sullenly, without answering the last question.

"Who?"

"His housecarles outside there."

"He has promised that they shall not touch thee. But how knowest thou what is in this letter?"

"I will take it," said Martin: he held out his hand, took it and looked at it, but upside down, and without any attempt to read it.

"His own mother," said he, after a while.

"What is that to thee?" said Lady Godiva, blushing and kindling.

"Nothing: I had no mother. But God has one!"

"What meanest thou, knave? Wilt thou take the letter or no?"

"I will take it." And he again looked at it without rising off his knee. "His own father, too."

"What is that to thee, I say again?"

"Nothing: I have no father. But God's Son has one!"

"What wilt thou, thou strange man?" asked she, puzzled and half-frightened; "and how camest thou to know what is in this letter?"

"Who does not know? A city that is set on a hill cannot be hid. On the fourth day from this I will be back."

And Martin rose, and putting the letter solemnly into the purse at his girdle, shot out of the door with clenched teeth, as a man upon a fixed purpose which it would lighten his heart to carry out. He ran rapidly through the large outer hall, past the long oak table, at which Hereward and his boon companions were drinking and roistering; and as he passed the young lord he cast on him a look so full of meaning, that though Hereward knew not what the meaning was, it startled him, and for a moment softened him. Did this man who had sullenly avoided him for more than two years, whom he had looked on as a clod or a post in the field beneath his notice, since he could be of no use to him, — did this man still care for him? Hereward had reason to know better than most that there was something strange and uncanny about the man. Did he mean him well? Or had he some grudge against him, which made him undertake this journey willingly and out of spite? — possibly with the will to make bad worse. For an instant Hereward's heart misgave him. He would stop the letter at all risks. "Hold him!" he cried to his comrades.

But Martin turned to him, laid his finger on his lips, smiled kindly, and saying " You promised!" caught up a loaf from the table, slipped from among them like an eel, and darted out of the door, and out of the close. They followed him to the great gate, and there stopped, some cursing, some laughing. To give Martin Lightfoot a yard advantage was never to come up with him again. Some called for bows to bring him down with a parting shot. But Hereward forbade them; and stood leaning against the gate-post, watching him trot on like a lean wolf over the lawn, till he was lost in the great elm-woods which fringed the southern fen.

"Now, lads," said Hereward, "home with you all, and make your peace with your fathers. In this house you never drink ale again."

They looked at him, surprised.

"You are disbanded, my gallant army. As long as I could cut long thongs out of other men's hides, I could feed you like earl's sons: but now I must feed myself; and a dog over his bone wants no company. Outlawed I shall be before the week is out; and unless you wish to be outlawed too, you will obey orders, and home."

"We will follow you to the world's end," cried some.

"To the rope's end, lads: that is all you will get in my company. Go home with you, and those who feel a calling, let them turn monks; and those who have not, let them learn

> 'For to plough and to sow,
> And to reap and to mow,
> And to be a farmer's boy.'

Good night."

And he went in, and shut the great gates after him, leaving them astonished.

To take his advice, and go home, was the simplest thing to be done. A few of them on their return were soundly thrashed, and deserved it; a few were hidden by their mothers for a week, in hay-lofts and hen-roosts, till their fathers' anger had passed away. But only one turned monk or clerk, and that was Leofric the Unlucky, godson of the great earl, and poet-in-ordinary to the band.

The next morning at dawn Hereward mounted his best horse, armed himself from head to foot, and rode over to Peterborough.

When he came to the abbey-gate, he smote thereon with his lance-but, till the porter's teeth rattled in his head for fear.

"Let me in!" he shouted. "I am Hereward Leofricsson. I must see my Uncle Brand."

"O my most gracious lord!" cried the porter, thrusting his head out of the wicket, "what is this that you have been doing to our Steward?"

"The tithe of what I will do, unless you open the gate!"

"O my lord!" said the porter, as he opened it, "if our Lady and St. Peter would but have mercy on your fair face, and convert your soul to the fear of God and man —"

"She would make me as good an old fool as you. Fetch my uncle, the Prior."

The porter obeyed. The son of Earl Leofric was as a young lion among the sheep in those parts; and few dare say him nay, certainly not the monks of Peterborough; moreover, the good porter could not help being strangely fond of Hereward, — as was every one whom he did not insult, rob, or kill.

Out came Brand, a noble elder: more fit, from his eye and gait, to be a knight than a monk. He looked sadly at Hereward.

"'Dear is bought the honey that is licked off the thorn,' quoth Hending," said he.

"Hending bought his wisdom by experience, I suppose," said Hereward, "and so must I. So I am just starting out to see the world, uncle."

"Naughty, naughty boy! If we had thee safe here again for a week, we would take this hot blood out of thee, and send thee home in thy right mind."

"Bring a rod and whip me, then. Try, and you shall have your chance. Every one else has had, and this is the end of their labors."

"By the chains of St. Peter," quoth the monk, "that is just

what thou needest. Hoist thee on such another fool's back, truss thee up, and lay it on lustily, till thou art ashamed. To treat thee as a man is only to make thee a more heady blown-up ass than thou art already."

"True, most wise uncle. And therefore my still wiser parents are going to treat me like a man indeed, and send me out into the world to seek my fortunes!"

"Eh?"

"They are going to prove how thoroughly they trust me to take care of myself, by outlawing me. Eh? say I in return. Is not that an honor, and a proof that I have not shown myself a fool, though I may have a madman?"

"Outlaw you? O my boy, my darling, my pride! Get off your horse, and don't sit there, hand on hip, like a turbaned Saracen, defying God and man; but come down and talk reason to me, for the sake of St. Peter and all saints."

Hereward threw himself off his horse, and threw his arms round his uncle's neck.

"Pish! Now, uncle, don't cry, do what you will, lest I cry too. Help me to be a man while I live, even if I go to the black place when I die."

"It shall not be!" .... and the monk swore by all the relics in Peterborough minster.

"It must be. It shall be. I like to be outlawed. I want to be outlawed. It makes one feel like a man. There is not an earl in England, save my father, who has not been outlawed in his time. My brother Alfgar will be outlawed before he dies, if he has the spirit of a man in him. It is the fashion, my uncle, and I must follow it. So hey for the merry greenwood, and the long ships, and the swan's bath, and all the rest of it. Uncle, you will lend me fifty silver pennies?"

"I? I would not lend thee one, if I had it, which I have not. And yet, old fool that I am, I believe I would."

"I would pay thee back honestly. I shall go down to Constantinople to the Varangers, get my Polotaswarf* out of the Kaiser's treasure, and pay thee back five to one."

"What does this son of Belial here?" asked an austere voice.

"Ah! Abbot Leofric, my very good lord. I have come to ask hospitality of you for some three days. By that time I shall be a wolf's head, and out of the law: and then, if you will give me ten minutes' start, you may put your bloodhounds on my track, and see which runs fastest, they or I. You are a gentleman, and

---

* See "The Heimskringla," Harold Hardraade's Saga, for the meaning of this word.

a man of honor; so I trust to you to feed my horse fairly the meanwhile, and not to let your monks poison me."

The Abbot's face relaxed. He tried to look as solemn as he could; but he ended in bursting into a very great laughter, and swearing likewise.

"The insolence of this lad passes the miracles of all saints. He robs St. Peter on the highway, breaks into his abbey, insults him to his face, and then asks him for hospitality; and —"

"And gets it," quoth Hereward.

"What is to be done with him, Brand, my friend? If we turn him out —"

"Which we cannot do," said Brand, looking at the well-mailed and armed lad, "without calling in half a dozen of our men-at-arms."

"In which case there would be blood shed, and scandal made in the holy precincts."

"And nothing gained; for yield he would not till he was killed outright, which God forbid!"

"Amen. And if he stay here, he may be persuaded to repentance."

"And restitution."

"As for that," quoth Hereward (who had remounted his horse from prudential motives, and set him athwart the gateway, so that there was no chance of the doors being slammed behind him), "if either of you will lend me sixteen pence, I will pay it back to you and St. Peter before I die, with interest enough to satisfy any Jew, on the word of a gentleman and an earl's son."

The Abbot burst again into a great laughter. "Come in, thou graceless renegade, and we will see to thee and thy horse; and I will pray to St. Peter; and I doubt not he will have patience with thee, for he is very merciful; and after all, thy parents have been exceeding good to us, and the righteousness of the father, like his sins, is sometimes visited on the children."

Now, why were the two ecclesiastics so uncanonically kind to this wicked youth?

Perhaps because both the old bachelors were wishing from their hearts that they had just such a son of their own. And beside, Earl Leofric was a very great man indeed; and the wind might change; for it is an unstable world.

"Only, mind, one thing," said the naughty boy, as he dismounted, and hallooed to a lay-brother to see to his horse, — "don't let me see the face of that Herluin."

"And why? You have wronged him, and he will forgive you, doubtless, like a good Christian as he is."

"That is his concern. But if I see him, I cut off his head

And, as Uncle Brand knows, I always sleep with my sword under my pillow."

"O that such a mother should have borne such a son.' groaned the Abbot, as they went in.

On the fifth day came Martin Lightfoot, and found Hereward in Prior Brand's private cell.

"Well?" asked Hereward, coolly.

"Is he —? Is he —?" stammered Brand, and could not finish his sentence.

Martin nodded.

Hereward laughed, — a loud, swaggering, hysterical laugh.

"See what it is to be born of just and pious parents. Come, Master Trot-alone, speak out and tell us all about it. Thy lean wolf's legs have run to some purpose. Open thy lean wolf's mouth and speak for once, lest I ease thy legs for the rest of thy life by a cut across the hams. Find thy lost tongue, I say!"

"Walls have ears, as well as the wild-wood," said Martin.

"We are safe here," said the Prior; "so speak, and tell us the whole truth."

"Well, when the Earl read the letter, he turned red, and pale again, and then naught but, 'Men, follow me to the King at Westminster.' So we went, all with our weapons, twenty or more, along the Strand, and up into the King's new hall; and a grand hall it is, but not easy to get into, for the crowd of monks and beggars on the stairs, hindering honest folks' business. And there sat the King on a high settle, with his pink face and white hair, looking as royal as a bell-wether new washed; and on either side of him, on the same settle, sat the old fox and the young wolf."

"Godwin and Harold? And where was the Queen?"

"Sitting on a stool at his feet, with her hands together as if she were praying, and her eyes downcast, as demure as any cat. And so is fulfilled the story, how the sheep-dog went out to get married, and left the fox, the wolf, and the cat to guard the flock."

"If thou hast found thy tongue," said Brand, "thou art like enough to lose it again by slice of knife, talking such ribaldry of dignities. Dost not know" — and he sank his voice — "that Abbot Leofric is Earl Harold's man, and that Harold himself made him abbot?"

"I said, walls have ears. It was you who told me that we were safe. However, I will bridle the unruly one." And he went on. "And your father walked up the hall, his left hand on his sword-hilt, looking an earl all over, as he is."

"He is that," said Hereward, in a low voice.

"And he bowed; and the most magnificent, powerful, and virtuous Godwin would have beckoned him up to sit on the high settle; but he looked straight at the King, as if there were never a Godwin or a Godwinsson on earth, and cried as he stood,—

"'Justice, my Lord the King!'

"And at that the King turned pale, and said, 'Who? What? O miserable world! O last days drawing nearer and nearer! O earth, full of violence and blood! Who has wronged thee now, most dear and noble Earl?'

"'Justice against my own son.'

"At that the fox looked at the wolf, and the wolf at the fox; and if they did not smile it was not for want of will, I warrant. But your father went on, and told all his story; and when he came to your robbing master monk,—'O apostate!' cries the bell-wether, 'O spawn of Beelzebub! excommunicate him, with bell, book, and candle. May he be thrust down with Korah, Balaam, and Iscariot, to the most Stygian pot of the sempiternal Tartarus.'

"And at that your father smiled. 'That is bishops' work,' says he; 'and I want king's work from you, Lord King. Outlaw me this young rebel's sinful body, as by law you can; and leave his sinful soul to the priests,— or to God's mercy, which is like to be more than theirs.'

"Then the Queen looked up. 'Your own son, noble Earl? Think of what you are doing, and one whom all say is so gallant and so fair. O persuade him, father,—persuade him, Harold my brother,—or, if you cannot persuade him, persuade the King at least, and save this poor youth from exile.'"

"Puss Velvet-paw knew well enough," said Hereward, in a low voice, "that the way to harden my father's heart was to set Godwin and Harold on softening it. They ask my pardon from the King? I would not take it at their asking, even if my father would."

"There spoke a true Leofricsson," said Brand, in spite of himself.

"'By the —' (and Martin repeated a certain very solemn oath), said your father, 'justice I will have, my Lord King. Who talks to me of my own son? You put me into my earldom to see justice done and law obeyed; and how shall I make others keep within bound if I am not to keep in my own flesh and blood? Here is this land running headlong to ruin, because every nobleman — ay, every churl who owns a manor, if he dares — must needs arm and saddle, and levy war on his own behalf, and harry and slay the king's lieges, if he have not garlic to his roast goose every time he chooses,'— and there your father did look at Godwin, once and for all;—'and shall I let my son follow the fashion, and do his best to leave the land open and weak for Norseman, or Dane, or Frenchman, or whoever else hopes next to mount the throne of a king who is too holy to leave an heir behind him?'"

"Ahoi! Martin the silent! Where learnt you so suddenly the trade of preaching? I thought you kept your wind for your running this two years past. You would make as good a talker among the Witan as Godwin himself. You give it us all, word for word, and voice and gesture withal, as if you were King Edward's French Chancellor."

Martin smiled. "I am like Falada the horse, my lords, who could only speak to his own true princess. Why I held my tongue of late was only lest they should cut my head off for talking, as they did poor Falada's."

"Thou art a very crafty knave," said Brand, "and hast had clerk-learning in thy time, I can see, and made bad use of it. I misdoubt very much that thou art some runaway monk."

"That am I not, by St. Peter's chains!" said Martin, in an eager, terrified voice. "Lord Hereward, I came hither as your father's messenger and servant. You will see me safe out of this abbey, like an honorable gentleman!"

"I will. All I know of him, uncle, is that he used to tell me stories, when I was a boy, of enchanters, and knights, and dragons, and such like, and got into trouble for filling my head with such fancies. Now let him tell his story in peace."

"He shall; but I misdoubt the fellow very much. He talks as if he knew Latin; and what business has a foot-running slave to do that?"

So Martin went on, somewhat abashed. "'And,' said your father, 'justice I will have, and leave injustice, and the overlooking of it, to those who wish to profit thereby.'

"And at that Godwin smiled, and said to the King, 'The Earl is wise, as usual, and speaks like a very Solomon. Your Majesty must, in spite of your own tenderness of heart, have these letters of outlawry made out.'

"Then all our men murmured,—and I as loud as any. But old Surturbrand the housecarle did more; for out he stepped to your father's side, and spoke right up before the King.

"'Bonny times,' he said, 'I have lived to see, when a lad of Earl Oslac's blood is sent out of the land, a beggar and a wolf's head, for playing a boy's trick or two, and upsetting a shaveling priest! We managed such wild young colts better, we Vikings who conquered the Danelagh. If Canute had had a son like Hereward — as would to God he had had! — he would have dealt with him as old Swend Forkbeard (God grant I meet him in Valhalla, in spite of all priests!) did by Canute himself when he was young, and kicked and plunged awhile at being first bitted and saddled.'

"'What does the man say?' asked the King, for old Surturbrand was talking broad Danish.

"'He is a housecarle of mine, Lord King, a good man and true; but old age and rough Danish blood has made him forget that he stands before kings and earls.'

"'By —, Earl!' says Surturbrand, I have fought knee to knee beside a braver king than that there, and nobler earls than ever a one here; and was never afraid, like a free Dane, to speak my mind to them, by sea or land. And if the King, with his French ways, does not understand a plain man's talk, the two earls yonder do right well, and I say, — Deal by this lad in the good old fashion. Give him half a dozen long ships, and what crews he can get together, and send him out, as Canute would have done, to seek his fortune like a Viking; and if he comes home with plenty of wounds, and plenty of plunder, give him an earldom as he deserves. Do you ask your Countess, Earl Godwin, — she is of the right Danish blood, God bless her! though she is your wife, — and see if she does not know how to bring a naughty lad to his senses.'

"Then Harold the Earl said: 'The old man is right. King, listen to what he says.' And he told him all, quite eagerly."

"How did you know that? Can you understand French?"

"I am a poor idiot, give me a halfpenny," said Martin, in a doleful voice, as he threw into his face and whole figure a look of helpless stupidity and awkwardness, which set them both laughing.

But Hereward checked himself. "And you think he was in earnest?"

"As sure as there are holy crows in Crowland. But it was of no use. Your father got a parchment, with an outlandish Norman seal hanging to it, and sent me off with it that same night to give to the lawman. So wolf's head you are, my lord, and there is no use crying over spilt milk."

"And Harold spoke for me? It will be as well to tell Abbot Leofric that, in case he be inclined to turn traitor, and refuse to open the gates. Once outside them, I care not for mortal man."

"My poor boy, there will be many a one whom thou hast wronged only too ready to lie in wait for thee, now thy life is in every man's hand. If the outlawry is published, thou hadst best start to-night, and get past Lincoln before morning."

"I shall stay quietly here, and get a good night's rest; and then ride out to-morrow morning in the face of the whole shire.

No, not a word! You would not have me sneak away like a coward?"

Brand smiled and shrugged his shoulders: being very much of the same mind.

"At least, go north."

"And why north?"

"You have no quarrel in Northumberland, and the King's writ runs very slowly there, if at all. Old Siward Digre may stand your friend."

"He? he is a fast friend of my father's."

"What of that? the old Viking will like you none the less for having shown a touch of his own temper. Go to him, I say, and tell him that I sent you."

"But he is fighting the Scots beyond the Forth."

"So much the better. There will be good work for you to do. And Gislebert of Ghent is up there too, I hear, trying to settle himself among the Scots. He is your mother's kinsman; and as for your being an outlaw, he wants hard hitters and hard riders, and all is fish that comes to his net. Find him out, too, and tell him I sent you."

"You are a good old uncle," said Hereward. "Why were you not a soldier?"

Brand laughed somewhat sadly.

"If I had been a soldier, lad, where would you have looked for a friend this day? No. God has done what was merciful with me and my sins. May he do the same by thee and thine."

Hereward made an impatient movement. He disliked any word which seemed likely to soften his own hardness of heart. But he kissed his uncle lovingly on both cheeks.

"By the by, Martin, — any message from my lady mother?"

"None!"

"Quite right and pious. I am an enemy to Holy Church and therefore to her. Good night, uncle."

"Hey?" asked Brand; "where is that footman, — Martin you call him? I must have another word with him."

But Martin was gone.

"No matter. I shall question him sharply enough to-morrow, I warrant."

And Hereward went out to his lodging; while the good Prior went to his prayers.

When Hereward entered his room, Martin started out of the darkness, and followed him in. Then he shut to the door carefully, and pulled out a bag.

"There was no message from my lady: but there was this."

The bag was full of money.

"Why did you not tell me of this before?"

"Never show money before a monk."

"Villain! would you mistrust my uncle?"

"Any man with a shaven crown. St. Peter is his God and Lord and conscience; and if he saw but the shine of a penny, for St. Peter he would want it."

"And he shall have it," quoth Hereward; and flung out of the room, and into his uncle's.

"Uncle, I have money. I am come to pay back what I took from the Steward, and as much more into the bargain." And he told out eight-and-thirty pieces.

"Thank God and all his saints!" cried Brand, weeping abundantly for joy; for he had acquired, by long devotion, the *donum lachrymarum,* — that lachrymose and somewhat hysterical temperament common among pious monks, and held to be a mark of grace.

"Blessed St. Peter, thou art repaid; and thou wilt be merciful!"

Brand believed, in common with all monks then, that Hereward had robbed, not merely the Abbey of Peterborough, but, what was more, St. Peter himself; thereby converting into an implacable and internecine foe the chief of the Apostles, the rock on which was founded the whole Church.

"Now, uncle," said Hereward, "do me one good deed in return. Promise me that, if you can help it, none of my poor housecarles shall suffer for my sins. I led them into trouble. I am punished. I have made restitution, — at least to St. Peter. See that my father and mother, if they be the Christians they call themselves, forgive and forget all offences except mine."

"I will; so help me all saints and our Lord. O my boy, my boy, thou shouldst have been a king's thane, and not an outlaw!"

And he hurried off with the news to the Abbot.

When Hereward returned to his room, Martin was gone.

"Farewell, good men of Peterborough," said Hereward, as he leapt into the saddle next morning. "I had made a vow against you, and came to try you; to see whether you would force me to fulfil it or not. But you have been so kind that I have half repented of it; and the evil shall not come in the days of Abbot Leofric, nor of Brand the Prior, though it may come in the days of Herluin the Steward, if he live long enough."

"What do you mean, you incarnate fiend, only fit to worship Thor and Odin?" asked Brand.

"That I would burn Goldenborough, and Herluin the Steward within it, ere I die. I fear I shall do it: I fear I must do it. Ten years ago come Lammas, Herluin bade light the peat-stack under me. Do you recollect?"

"And so he did, the hound!" quoth Brand. "I had forgotten that."

"Little Hereward never forgets foe or friend. Ever since, on Lammas night, — hold still, horse! — I dream of fire and flame, and of Goldenborough in the glare of it. If it is written in the big book, happen it must; if not, so much the better for Goldenborough, for it is a pretty place, and honest Englishmen in it. Only see that there be not too many Frenchmen crept in when I come back, beside our French friend Herluin; and see, too, that there be not a peat-stack handy: a word is enough to wise men like you. Good by!"

"God help thee, thou sinful boy!" said the Abbot.

"Hereward, Hereward! Come back!" cried Brand.

But the boy had spurred his horse through the gateway, and was far down the road.

"Leofric, my friend," said Brand, sadly, "this is my sin, and no man's else. And heavy penance will I do for it, till that lad returns in peace."

"Your sin?"

"Mine, Abbot. I persuaded his mother to send him hither to be a monk. Alas! alas! How long will men try to be wiser than Him who maketh men?"

"I do not understand thee," quoth the Abbot. And no more he did.

It was four o'clock on a May morning, when Hereward set out to see the world, with good armor on his back, good weapon by his side, good horse between his knees, and good money in his purse. What could a lad of eighteen want more, who under the harsh family rule of those times had known nothing of a father's, and but too little of a mother's, love? He rode away northward through the Bruneswald, over the higher land of Lincolnshire, through primeval glades of mighty oak and ash, holly and thorn, swarming with game, which was as highly preserved then as now, under Canute's severe forest laws. The yellow roes stood and stared at him knee-deep in the young fern; the pheasant called his hens out to feed in the dewy grass; the blackbird and thrush sung out from every bough; the wood-lark trilled above the high oak-tops, and sank down on them as his song sank down. And Hereward rode on, rejoicing in it all. It was a fine world in the Bruneswald. What was it then outside? Not to him, as to us, a world circular, sailed round, circumscribed, mapped, botanized, zoölogized; a tiny planet about which everybody knows, or thinks they know everything: but a world infinite, magical, supernatural, — because unknown; a vast flat plain reaching no one knew whence or where, save that the mountains stood on the four corners thereof to keep it steady, and the four winds of heaven blew out of them; and in the centre, which was to him the Bruneswald, such things as he saw; but beyond, things unspeakable, — dragons, giants, rocs, orcs, witch-whales, griffins, chimeras, satyrs, enchanters, paynims, Saracen Emirs and Sultans, Kaisers of Constantinople, Kaisers of Ind and of Cathay, and beyond them again of lands as yet unknown. At the very least he could go to Brittany, to the forest of Brocheliaunde, where (so all men said) fairies might be seen bathing in the fountains, and possibly be won and wedded by a bold and dexterous knight after the fashion of Sir Gruelan.* What was there not to be seen and conquered? Where would he go? Where would he not go? For the spirit of Odin the Goer, the spirit which has sent his children round the world, was strong within him. He would go to Ireland, to the Ostmen, or Irish Danes men at Dublin, Waterford, or Cork, and marry some beautiful Irish Princess with gray eyes, and raven locks, and saffron smock, and great gold bracelets from her native hills. No; he would go off to the Orkneys, and join Bruce and Ranald, and the Vikings of the northern seas, and all the hot blood which had found even Norway too hot to hold it; and sail through witch-whales and icebergs to Iceland and Greenland, and the sunny lands which they said lay even beyond, across the all but unknown ocean. He would go up the Baltic to the Jomsburg Vikings, and fight against Lett and Esthonian heathen, and pierce inland, perhaps, through Puleyn and the bison forests, to the land from whence came the magic swords and the old Persian coins which he had seen so often in the halls of his forefathers. No; he would go South, to the land of sun and wine; and see the magicians of Cordova and Seville; and beard Mussulman hounds worshipping their Mahomets; and perhaps bring home an Emir's daughter, —

"With more gay gold about her middle,
Than would buy half Northumberlee."

Or he would go up the Straits, and on to Constantinople and the great Kaiser of the Greeks, and join the Varanger Guard, and perhaps, like Harold Hardraade in his own days, after being cast to the lion for carrying off a fair Greek lady, tear out the monster's tongue with his own hands, and show the Easterns what a Viking's son could do. And as he dreamed of the infinite world and its infinite wonders, the enchanters he might meet, the

* Wace, author of the "Roman de Rou," went to Brittany a generation later, to see tnose same fairies: but had no sport; and sang, —

"Fol i alai, fol m'en revins;
Folie quis, por fol me tins."

jewels he might find, the adventures he might essay, he held that he must succeed in all, with hope and wit and a strong arm; and forgot altogether that, mixed up with the cosmogony of an infinite flat plain called the Earth, there was joined also the belief in a flat roof above called Heaven, on which (seen at times in visions through clouds and stars) sat saints, angels, and archangels, forevermore harping on their golden harps, and knowing neither vanity nor vexation of spirit, lust nor pride, murder nor war; — and underneath a floor, the name whereof was Hell; the mouths whereof (as all men knew) might be seen on Hecla and Ætna and Stromboli; and the fiends heard within. tormenting, amid fire, and smoke, and clanking chains, the souls of the eternally lost.

As he rode on slowly though cheerfully, as a man who will not tire his horse at the beginning of a long day's journey, and knows not where he shall pass the night, he was aware of a man on foot coming up behind him at a slow, steady, loping, wolf-like trot, which in spite of its slowness gained ground on him so fast, that he saw at once that the man could be no common runner.

The man came up; and behold, he was none other than Martin Lightfoot.

"What! art thou here?" asked Hereward, suspiciously, and half cross at seeing any visitor from the old world which he had just cast off. "How gottest thou out of St. Peter's last night?"

Martin's tongue was hanging out of his mouth like a running hound's, but he seemed, like a hound, to perspire through his mouth, for he answered without the least sign of distress, without even pulling in his tongue, —

"Over the wall, the moment the Prior's back was turned. I was not going to wait till I was chained up in some rat's-hole with a half-hundred of iron on my leg, and flogged till I confessed that I was what I am not, — a runaway monk."

"And why art here?"

"Because I am going with you."

"Going with me?" said Hereward; "what can I do for thee?"

"I can do for you," said Martin.

"What?"

"Groom your horse, wash your shirt, clean your weapons, find your inn, fight your enemies, cheat your friends, — anything and everything. You are going to see the world. I am going with you."

"Thou canst be my servant? A right slippery one, I expect," said Hereward. looking down on him with some suspicion.

"Some are not the rogues they seem. I can keep my secrets and yours too."

"Before I can trust thee with my secrets, I shall expect to know some of thine," said Hereward.

Martin Lightfoot looked up with a cunning smile. "A servant can always know his master's secrets if he likes. But that is no reason a master should know his servant's."

"Thou shalt tell me thine, man, or I shall ride off and leave thee."

"Not so easy, my lord. Where that heavy horse can go, Martin Lightfoot can follow. But I will tell you one secret, which I never told to living man. I can read and write like any clerk."

"Thou read and write?"

"Ay, good Latin enough, and Irish too, what is more. And now, because I love you, and because you I will serve, willy nilly, I will tell you all the secrets I have, as long as my breath lasts, for my tongue is rather stiff after that long story about the bell-wether. I was born in Ireland, in Waterford town. My mother was an English slave, one of those that Earl Godwin's wife — not this one that is now, Gyda, but the old one, King Canute's sister — used to sell out of England by the score, tied together with ropes, boys and girls from Bristol town. Her master, my father that was (I shall know him again), got tired of her, and wanted to give her away to one of his kernes. She would not have that; so he hung her up hand and foot, and beat her that she died. There was an abbey hard by, and the Church laid on him a penance, — all that they dared get out of him, — that he should give me to the monks, being then a seven-years' boy. Well, I grew up in that abbey; they taught me my fa fa mi fa: but I liked better conning of ballads and hearing stories of ghosts and enchanters, such as I used to tell you. I'll tell you plenty more whenever you're tired. Then they made me work; and that I never could abide at all. Then they beat me every day; and that I could abide still less; but always I stuck to my book, for one thing I saw, — that learning is power, my lord; and that the reason why the monks are masters of the land is, they are scholars, and you fighting men are none. Then I fell in love (as young blood will) with an Irish lass, when I was full seventeen years old; and when they found out that, they held me down on the floor and beat me till I was wellnigh dead. They put me in prison for a month; and between bread-and-water and darkness I went nigh foolish. They let me out, thinking I could do no more harm to man or lass; and when I found out how profitable folly was, foolish I remained, at least as foolish as seemed good to me. But one night I got into the abbey church, stole therefrom that which I have with me now, and which shall serve you and me in good stead yet, — out and away aboard a ship among the buscarles, and off into the Norway sea. But after a voyage or two, so it befell, I was wrecked in the Wash by Botulfston Deeps, and, begging my way inland, met with your father, and took service with him, as I have taken service now with you."

"Now, what has made thee take service with me?"

"Because you are you."

"Give me none of your parables and dark sayings, but speak out like a man. What canst see in me that thou shouldest share an outlaw's fortune with me?"

"I had run away from a monastery, so had you; I hated the monks, so did you; I liked to tell stories, — since I found good to shut my mouth I tell them to myself all day long, sometimes all night too. When I found out you liked to hear them, I loved you all the more. Then they told me not to speak to you; I held my tongue. I bided my time. I knew you would be outlawed some day. I knew you would turn Viking and kemperyman, and kill giants and enchanters, and win yourself honor and glory; and I knew I should have my share in it. I knew you would need me some day; and you need me now, and here I am; and if you try to cut me down with your sword, I will dodge you, and follow you, and dodge you again, till I force you to let me be your man, for with you I will live and die. And now I can talk no more."

"And with me thou shalt live and die," said Hereward, pulling up his horse, and frankly holding out his hand to his new friend.

Martin Lightfoot took his hand, kissed it, licked it almost as a dog would have done. "I am your man," he said. "Amen; and true man I will prove to you, if you will prove true to me." And he dropped quietly back behind Hereward's horse, as if the business of his life was settled, and his mind utterly at rest.

"There is one more likeness between us," said Hereward, after a few minutes' thought. "If I have robbed a church, thou hast robbed one too. What is this precious spoil which is to serve me and thee in such mighty stead?"

Martin drew from inside his shirt and under his waistband a small battle-axe, and handed it up to Hereward. It was a tool the like of which in shape Hereward had seldom seen, and never its equal in beauty. The handle was some fifteen inches long, made of thick strips of black whalebone, curiously bound with silver, and butted with narwhal ivory. This handle was evidently the work of some cunning Norseman of old. But who was the maker of the blade? It was some eight inches long, with a sharp edge on one side, a sharp crooked pick on the other; of the finest steel, inlaid with strange characters in gold, the work probably of some Circassian, Tartar, or Persian; such a battle-axe as Rustum or Zohrab may have wielded in fight upon the banks of Oxus; one of those magic weapons, brought, men knew not how, out of the magic East, which were hereditary in many a Norse family and sung of in many a Norse saga.

"Look at it," said Martin Lightfoot. "There is magic on it. It must bring us luck. Whoever holds that must kill his man. It will pick a lock of steel. It will crack a mail corslet as a nuthatch cracks a nut. It will hew a lance in two at a single blow. Devils' and spirits forged it,—I know that; Virgilius the Enchanter, perhaps, or Solomon the Great, or whosoever's name is on it, graven there in letters of gold. Handle it, feel its balance; but no,—do not handle it too much. There is a devil in it, who would make you kill me. Whenever I play with it I long to kill a man. It would be so easy,—so easy. Give it me back, my lord, give it me back, lest the devil come through the handle into your palm, and possess you."

Hereward laughed, and gave him back his battle-axe. But he had hardly less doubt of the magic virtues of such a blade than had Martin himself.

"Magical or not, thou wilt not have to hit a man twice with that, Martin, my lad. So we two outlaws are both well armed; and having neither wife nor child, land nor beeves to lose, ought to be a match for any six honest men who may have a grudge against us, and sound reasons at home for running away."

And so those two went northward through the green Bruneswald, and northward again through merry Sherwood, and were not seen in that land again for many a year.

CHAPTER II.

HOW HEREWARD SLEW THE BEAR.

Of Hereward's doings for the next few months naught is known. He may very likely have joined Siward in the Scotch war. He may have looked, wondering, for the first time in his life, upon the bones of the old world, where they rise at Dunkeld out of the lowlands of the Tay; and have trembled lest the black crags of Birnam should topple on his head with all their pines. He may have marched down from that famous leaguer with the Gospatricks and Dolfins, and the rest of the kindred of Crinan (abthane or abbot, — let antiquaries decide), — of Dunkeld, and of Duncan, and of Siward, and of the outraged Sibilla. He may have helped himself to bring Birnam Wood to Dunsinane, "on the day of the Seven Sleepers," and heard Siward, when his son Asbiorn's corpse was carried into camp,* ask only, "Has he all his wounds in front?" He may have seen old Siward, after Macbeth's defeat (not death, as Shakespeare relates the story), go back to Northumbria "with such booty as no man had obtained before," — a proof, if the fact be fact, that the Scotch lowlands were not, in the eleventh century, the poor and barbarous country which some have reported them to have been.

All this is not only possible, but probable enough, the dates considered: the chroniclers, however, are silent. They only say that Hereward was in those days beyond Northumberland with Gisebert of Ghent.

Gisebert, Gislebert, Gilbert, Guibert, Goisbricht, of Ghent, who afterwards owned, by chance of war, many a fair manor about Lincoln city, was one of those valiant Flemings who settled along the east and northeast coast of Scotland in the eleventh century. They fought with the Celtic princes, and then married with their daughters; got to themselves lands "by the title-deed of the sword"; and so became — the famous "Freskin the Fleming" especially — the ancestors of the finest aristocracy, both physically and intellectually, in the world. They had their con-

---

* Shakespeare makes young Siward his son. He, too, was slain in the battle: but he was Siward's nephew.

nections, moreover, with the Norman court of Rouen, through the Duchess Matilda, daughter of their old Seigneur, Baldwin, Marquis of Flanders; their connections, too, with the English Court, through Countess Judith, wife of Earl Tosti Godwinsson, another daughter of Baldwin's. Their friendship was sought, their enmity feared, far and wide throughout the north. They seem to have been civilizers and cultivators and traders, — with the instinct of true Flemings, — as well as conquerors; they were in those very days bringing to order and tillage the rich lands of the northeast, from the Frith of Moray to that of Forth; and forming a rampart for Scotland against the invasions of Sweyn, Hardrade, and all the wild Vikings of the northern seas.

Amongst them, in those days, Gilbert of Ghent seems to have been a notable personage, to judge from the great house which he kept, and the "milites tyrones," or squires in training for the honor of knighthood, who fed at his table. Where he lived, the chroniclers report not. To them the country "ultra Northumbriam," beyond the Forth, was as Russia or Cathay, where

"Geographers on pathless downs
Put elephants for want of towns."

As indeed it was to that French map-maker who, as late as the middle of the eighteenth century (not having been to Aberdeen or Elgin), leaves all the country north of the Tay a blank, with the inscription: "*Terre inculte et sauvage, habitée par les Higlanders.*"

Wherever Gilbert lived, however, he heard that Hereward was outlawed, and sent for him, says the story. And there he lived, doubtless happily enough, fighting Highlanders and hunting deer, so that as yet the pains and penalties of exile did not press very hardly upon him. The handsome, petulant, good-humored lad had become in a few weeks the darling of Gilbert's ladies, and the envy of all his knights and gentlemen. Hereward the singer, harp-player, dancer, Hereward the rider and hunter, was in all mouths; but he himself was discontented at having as yet fallen in with no adventure worthy of a man, and looked curiously and longingly at the menagerie of wild beasts enclosed in strong wooden cages, which Gilbert kept in one corner of the great court-yard, not for any scientific purposes, but to try with them, at Christmas, Easter, and Whitsuntide, the mettle of the young gentlemen who were candidates for the honor of knighthood. But after looking over the bulls and stags, wolves and bears, Hereward settled it in his mind that there was none worthy of his steel, save one huge white bear, whom no man had yet dared to face, and whom Hereward, indeed, had never seen, hidden as he was all day within the old oven-shaped Pict's house of stone, which had been turned into his den. There was a mystery about the uncanny brute which charmed Hereward. He was said to be half-human, perhaps wholly human; to be the son of the Fairy Bear, near kinsman, if not uncle or cousin, of Siward Digre. He had, like his fairy father, iron claws; he had human intellect, and understood human speech, and the arts of war, — at least so all in the place believed, and not as absurdly as at first sight seems.

For the brown bear, and much more the white, was, among the Northern nations, in himself a creature magical and superhuman. "He is God's dog," whispered the Lapp, and called him "the old man in the fur cloak," afraid to use his right name, even inside the tent, for fear of his overhearing and avenging the insult. "He has twelve men's strength, and eleven men's wit," sang the Norseman, and prided himself accordingly, like a true Norseman, on outwitting and slaying the enchanted monster.

Terrible was the brown bear: but more terrible "the white sea-deer," as the Saxons called him; the hound of Hrymir, the whale's bane, the seal's dread, the rider of the iceberg. the sailer of the floe, who ranged for his prey under the six months' night, lighted by Surtur's fires, even to the gates of Muspelheim. To slay him was a feat worthy of Beowulf''s self; and the greatest wonder, perhaps, among all the wealth of Crowland, was the twelve white bear-skins which lay before the altars, the gift of the great Canute. How Gilbert had obtained his white bear, and why he kept him there in durance vile, was a mystery over which men shook their heads. Again and again Hereward asked his host to let him try his strength against the monster of the North. Again and again the shrieks of the ladies, and Gilbert's own pity for the stripling youth, brought a refusal. But Hereward settled it in his heart, nevertheless, that somehow or other, when Christmas time came round, he would extract from Gilbert, drunk or sober, leave to fight that bear; and then either make himself a name, or die like a man.

Meanwhile Hereward made a friend. Among all the ladies of Gilbert's household, however kind they were inclined to be to him, he took a fancy but to one, — and that was to a little girl of eight years old. Alftruda was her name. He liked to amuse himself with this child, without, as he fancied, any danger of falling in love; for already his dreams of love were of the highest and most fantastic; and an Emir's daughter, or a Princess of Constantinople, were the very lowest game at which he meant to fly. Alftruda was beautiful, too, exceedingly, and precocious, and, it may be, vain enough to repay his attentions in good earnest. Moreover she was English as he was, and royal likewise; a relation of Elfgiva, daughter of Ethelred, once King of England, who, as all know, married Uchtred, prince of Northumberland and grandfather of Gospatrick, Earl of Northumberland, and ancestor of all the Dunbars. Between the English lad then and the English maiden grew up in a few weeks an innocent friendship, which had almost become more than friendship, through the intervention of the Fairy Bear.

For as Hereward was coming in one afternoon from hunting, hawk on fist, with Martin Lightfoot trotting behind, crane and heron, duck and hare, slung over his shoulder, on reaching the court-yard gates he was aware of screams and shouts within, tumult and terror among man and beast. Hereward tried to force his horse in at the gate. The beast stopped and turned, snorting with fear; and no wonder; for in the midst of the court-yard stood the Fairy Bear; his white mane bristled up till he seemed twice as big as any of the sober brown bears which Hereward yet had seen: his long snake neck and cruel visage wreathed about in search of prey. A dead horse, its back broken by a single blow of the paw, and two or three writhing dogs, showed that the beast had turned (like too many of his human kindred) "Berserker." The court-yard was utterly empty: but from the ladies' bower came shrieks and shouts, not only of women, but of men; and knocking at the bower door, adding her screams to those inside, was a little white figure, which Hereward recognized as Alftruda's. They had barricaded themselves inside, leaving the child out; and now dared not open the door, as the bear swung and rolled towards it, looking savagely right and left for a fresh victim.

Hereward leaped from his horse, and, drawing his sword, rushed forward with a shout which made the bear turn round.

He looked once back at the child; then round again at Hereward: and, making up his mind to take the largest morsel first, made straight at him with a growl which there was no mistaking.

He was within two paces; then he rose on his hind legs, a head and shoulders taller than Hereward, and lifted the iron talons high in air. Hereward knew that there was but one spot at which to strike; and he struck true and strong, before the iron paw could fall, right on the muzzle of the monster.

He heard the dull crash of the steel; he felt the sword jammed tight. He shut his eyes for an instant, fearing lest, as in dreams, his blow had come to naught; lest his sword had turned aside, or melted like water in his hand, and the next moment would find him crushed to earth, blinded and stunned. Something tugged at his sword. He opened his eyes, and saw the huge carcass bend, reel, roll slowly over to one side dead, tearing out of his hand the sword, which was firmly fixed into the skull.

Hereward stood awhile staring at the beast like a man astonished at what he himself had done. He had had his first adventure, and he had conquered. He was now a champion in his own right,— a hero of the heroes,— one who might take rank, if he went on, beside Beowulf, Frotho, Ragnar Lodbrog, or Harald Hadraade. He had done this deed. What was there after this which he might not do? And he stood there in the fulness of his pride, defiant of earth and heaven, while in his heart arose the thought of that old Viking who cried, in the pride of his godlessness: "I never on earth met him whom I feared, and why should I fear Him in heaven? If I met Odin, I would fight with Odin. If Odin were the stronger, he would slay me; if I were the stronger, I would slay him." And there he stood, staring, and dreaming over renown to come,— a true pattern of the half-savage hero of those rough times, capable of all vices except cowardice, and capable, too, of all virtues save humility.

"Do you not see," said Martin Lightfoot's voice, close by, "that there is a fair lady trying to thank you, while you are so rude or so proud that you will not vouchsafe her one look?"

It was true. Little Alftruda had been clinging to him for five minutes past. He took the child up in his arms and kissed her with pure kisses, which for a moment softened his hard heart; then, setting her down, he turned to Martin.

"I have done it, Martin."

"Yes, you have done it; I spied you. What will the old folks at home say to this?"

"What care I?"

Martin Lightfoot shook his head, and drew out his knife.

"What is that for?" said Hereward.

"When the master kills the game, the knave can but skin it We may sleep warm under this fur in many a cold night by sea and moor."

"Nay," said Hereward, laughing; "when the master kills the game he must first carry it home. Let us take him and set him up against the bower door there, to astonish the brave knights inside." And stooping down, he attempted to lift the huge carcass; but in vain. At last, with Martin's help, he got it fairly on his shoulders, and the two dragged their burden to the bower and dashed it against the door, shouting with all their might to those within to open it.

Windows, it must be remembered, were in those days so few and far between that the folks inside had remained quite unaware of what was going on without.

The door was opened cautiously enough; and out looked, to the shame of knighthood be it said, two or three knights who had taken shelter in the bower with the ladies. Whatever they were going to say the ladies forestalled, for, rushing out across the prostrate bear, they overwhelmed Hereward with praises, thanks, and, after the straightforward custom of those days, with substantial kisses.

"You must be knighted at once," cried they. "You have knighted yourself by that single blow."

"A pity, then," said one of the knights to the others, "that he had not given that accolade to himself, instead of to the bear."

"Unless some means are found," said another, "of taking down this boy's conceit, life will soon be not worth having here."

"Either he must take ship," said a third, "and look for adventures elsewhere, or I must."

Martin Lightfoot heard those words; and knowing that envy and hatred, like all other vices in those rough-hewn times, were apt to take very startling and unmistakeable shapes, kept his eye accordingly on those three knights.

"He must be knighted,—he shall be knighted, as soon as Sir Gilbert comes home," said all the ladies' in chorus.

"I should be sorry to think," said Hereward, with the blundering mock humility of a self-conceited boy, "that I had done anything worthy of such an honor. I hope to win my spurs by greater feats than these."

A burst of laughter from the knights and gentlemen followed.

"How loud the young bantam crows after his first little scuffle!"

"Hark to him! What will he do next? Eat a dragon? Fly to the moon? Marry the Sophy of Egypt's daughter?"

This last touched Hereward to the quick, for it was just what he thought of doing; and his blood, heated enough already, beat quicker, as some one cried, with the evident intent of picking a quarrel: "That was meant for us. If the man who killed the bear has not earned knighthood, what must we be, who have not killed him? You understand his meaning, gentlemen,—don't forget it!"

Hereward looked down, and setting his foot on th bear's head, wrenched out of it the sword which he had left till now, with pardonable pride, fast set in the skull.

Martin Lightfoot, for his part, drew stealthily from his bosom the little magic axe, keeping his eye on the brain-pan of the last speaker.

The lady of the house cried "Shame!" and ordered the

knights away with haughty words and gestures, which, because they were so well deserved, only made the quarrel more deadly. Then she commanded Hereward to sheathe his sword.

He did so; and turning to the knights, said with all courtesy: "You mistake me, sirs. You were where brave knights should be, within the beleaguered fortress, defending the ladies. Had you remained outside, and been eaten by the bear, what must have befallen them, had he burst open the door? As for this little lass, whom you left outside, she is too young to requite knight's prowess by lady's love; and therefore beneath your attention, and only fit for the care of a boy like me." And taking up Alftruda in his arms, he carried her in and disappeared.

Who now but Hereward was in all men's mouths? The minstrels made ballads on him; the lasses sang his praises (says the chronicler) as they danced upon the green. Gilbert's lady would need give him the seat, and all the honors, of a belted knight, though knight he was none. And daily and weekly the valiant lad grew and hardened into a valiant man, and a courteous one withal, giving no offence himself, and not over ready to take offence at other men.

The knights were civil enough to him, the ladies more than civil; he hunted, he wrestled, he tilted; he was promised a chance of fighting for glory, as soon as a Highland chief should declare war against Gilbert, or drive off his cattle, — an event which (and small blame to the Highland chiefs) happened every six months.

No one was so well content with himself as Hereward; and therefore he fancied that the world must be equally content with him, and he was much disconcerted when Martin drew him aside one day, and whispered: "If I were my lord, I should wear a mail shirt under my coat to-morrow out hunting."

"What?"

"The arrow that can go through a deer's blade-bone can go through a man's."

"Who should harm me?"

"Any man of the dozen who eat at the same table."

"What have I done to them? If I had my laugh at them, they had their laugh at me; and we are quits."

"There is another score, my lord, which you have forgotten, and that is all on your side."

"Eh?"

"You killed the bear. Do you expect them to forgive you that, till they have repaid you with interest?"

"Pish!"

"You do not want for wit, my lord. Use it, and think. What right has a little boy like you to come here, killing bears which grown men cannot kill? What can you expect but just punishment for your insolence, — say, a lance between your shoulders while you stoop to drink, as Sigfried had for daring to tame Brunhild? And more, what right have you to come here, and so win the hearts of the ladies, that the lady of all the ladies should say, 'If aught happen to my poor boy, — and he cannot live long, — I would adopt Hereward for my own son, and show his mother what a fool some folks think her.' So, my lord, put on your mail shirt to-morrow, and take care of narrow ways, and sharp corners. For to-morrow it will be tried, that I know, before my Lord Gilbert comes back from the Highlands; but by whom I know not, and care little, seeing that there are half a dozen in the house who would be glad enough of the chance."

Hereward took his advice, and rode out with three or four knights the next morning into the fir-forest; not afraid, but angry and sad. He was not yet old enough to estimate the virulence of envy; to take ingratitude and treachery for granted. He was to learn the lesson then, as a wholesome chastener to the pride of success. He was to learn it again in later years, as an additional bitterness in the humiliation of defeat; and find out, as does many a man, that if he once fall, or seem to fall, a hundred curs spring up to bark at him, who dared not open their mouths while he was on his legs.

So they rode into the forest, and parted, each with his footman and his dogs, in search of boar and deer; and each had his sport without meeting again for some two hours or more.

Hereward and Martin came at last to a narrow gully, a murderous place enough. Huge fir-trees roofed it in, and made a night of noon. High banks of earth and great boulders walled it in right and left for twenty feet above. The track, what with pack-horses' feet, and what with the wear and tear of five hundred years' rain-fall, was a rut three feet deep and two feet broad, in which no horse could turn. Any other day Hereward would have cantered down it with merely a tightened rein. To-day he turned to Martin and said, —

"A very fit and proper place for this same treason, unless you have been drinking beer and thinking beer."

But Martin was nowhere to be seen.

A pebble thrown from the right bank struck him, and he looked up. Martin's face was peering through the heather overhead, his finger on his lips. Then he pointed cautiously, first up the pass, then down.

Hereward felt that his sword was loose in the sheath, and then griped his lance, with a heart beating, but not with fear.

The next moment he heard the rattle of a horse's hoofs behind him; looked back; and saw a knight charging desperately down the gully, his bow in hand, and arrow drawn to the head.

To turn was impossible. To stop, even to walk on, was to be ridden over and hurled to the ground helplessly. To gain the mouth of the gully, and then turn on his pursuer, was his only chance. For the first and almost the last time in his life, he struck spurs into his horse, and ran away. As he went, an arrow struck him sharply in the back, piercing the corslet, but hardly entering the flesh. As he neared the mouth, two other knights crashed their horses through the brushwood from right and left, and stood awaiting him, their spears ready to strike. He was caught in a trap. A shield might have saved him; but he had none.

He did not flinch. Dropping his reins, and driving in the spurs once more, he met them in full shock. With his left hand he hurled aside the left-hand lance, with his right he hurled his own with all his force at the right-hand foe, and saw it pass clean through the felon's chest, while his lance-point dropped, and passed harmlessly behind his knee.

So much for lances in front. But the knight behind? Would not his sword the next moment be through his brain?

There was a clatter, a crash, and looking back Hereward saw horse and man rolling in the rut, and rolling with them Martin Lightfoot. He had already pinned the felon knight's head against the steep bank, and, with uplifted axe, was meditating a pick at his face which would have stopped alike his love-making and his fighting.

"Hold thy hand," shouted Hereward. "Let us see who he is; and remember that he is at least a knight."

"But one that will ride no more to-day. I finished his horse's going as I rolled down the bank."

It was true. He had broken the poor beast's leg with a blow of the axe, and they had to kill the horse out of pity ere they left.

Martin dragged his prisoner forward.

"You?" cried Hereward. "And I saved your life three days ago!"

The knight answered nothing.

"You will have to walk home. Let that be punishment enough for you," and he turned.

"He will have to ride in a woodman's cart, if he have the luck to find one."

The third knight had fled, and after him the dead man's

horse. Hereward and his man rode home in peace, and the third knight, after trying vainly to walk a mile or two, fell and lay, and was fain to fulfil Martin's prophecy, and be brought home in a cart, to carry for years after, like Sir Lancelot, the nickname of the Chevalier de la Charette.

And so was Hereward avenged of his enemies. Judicial, even private, inquiry into the matter there was none. That gentlemen should meet in the forest and commit, or try to commit, murder on each other's bodies, was far too common a mishap in the ages of faith to stir up more than an extra gossiping and cackling among the women, and an extra cursing and threatening among the men; and as the former were all but unanimously on Hereward's side, his plain and honest story was taken as it stood.

"And now, fair lady," said Hereward to his hostess, "I must thank you for all your hospitality, and bid you farewell forever and a day."

She wept, and entreated him only to stay till her lord came back; but Hereward was firm.

"You, lady, and your good lord will I ever love; and at your service my sword shall ever be: but not here. Ill blood I will not make. Among traitors I will not dwell. I have killed two of them, and shall have to kill two of their kinsmen next, and then two more, till you have no knights left; and pity that would be. No; the world is wide, and there are plenty of good fellows in it who will welcome me without forcing me to wear mail under my coat out hunting."

And he armed himself *cap-à-pie*, and rode away. Great was the weeping in the bower, and great the chuckling in the hall: but never saw they Hereward again upon the Scottish shore.

CHAPTER III.

HOW HEREWARD SUCCORED A PRINCESS OF CORNWALL.

THE next place in which Hereward appeared was far away on the southwest, upon the Cornish shore. How he came there, or after how long, the chronicles do not say. All that shall be told is, that he went into port on board a merchant ship carrying wine, and intending to bring back tin. The merchants had told him of one Alef, a valiant "regulus" or kinglet of those parts, who was indeed a distant connection of Hereward himself, having married, as did so many of the Celtic princes, the daughter of a Danish sea-rover, of Siward's blood. They told him also that the kinglet increased his wealth, not only by the sale of tin and of red cattle, but by a certain amount of autumnal piracy in company with his Danish brothers-in-law from Dublin and Waterford; and Hereward, who believed, with most Englishmen of the East Country, that Cornwall still produced a fair crop of giants, some of them with two and even three heads, had hopes that Alef might show him some adventure worthy of his sword. He sailed in, therefore, over a rolling bar, between jagged points of black rock, and up a tide river which wandered away inland, like a land-locked lake, between high green walls of oak and ash, till they saw at the head of the tide Alef's town, nestling in a glen which sloped towards the southern sun. They discovered, besides, two ships drawn up upon the beach, whose long lines and snake-heads, beside the stoat carved on the beak-head of one and the adder on that of the other, bore witness to the piratical habits of their owner. The merchants, it seemed, were well known to the Cornishmen on shore, and Hereward went up with them unopposed; past the ugly dikes and muddy leats, where Alef's slaves were streaming the gravel for tin ore; through rich alluvial pastures spotted with red cattle, and up to Alef's town. Earthworks and stockades surrounded a little church of ancient stone, and a cluster of granite cabins thatched with turf, in which the slaves abode, and in the centre of all a vast stone barn, with low walls and high sloping roof, which contained Alef's family, treasures, fighting tail, horses, cattle, and pigs. They entered at one end between the pigsties, passed on through the cow-stalls, then through the stables, and saw before them, dim through the reek of thick peat-smoke, a long oaken table, at which sat huge dark-haired Cornishmen, with here and there among them the yellow head of a Norseman, who were Alef's following of fighting men. Boiled meat was there in plenty, barley cakes, and ale. At the head of the table, on a high-backed settle, was Alef himself, a jolly giant, who was just setting to work to drink himself stupid with mead made from narcotic heather honey. By his side sat a lovely dark-haired girl, with great gold torcs upon her throat and wrists, and a great gold brooch fastening a shawl which had plainly come from the looms of Spain or of the East, and next to her again, feeding her with titbits cut off with his own dagger, and laid on barley cake instead of a plate, sat a more gigantic personage even than Alef, the biggest man that Hereward had ever seen, with high cheek-bones, and small ferret eyes, looking out from a greasy mass of bright red hair and beard.

No questions were asked of the new-comers. They set themselves down in silence in empty places, and, according to the laws of the good old Cornish hospitality, were allowed to eat and drink their fill before they spoke a word.

"Welcome here again, friend," said Alef at last, in good enough Danish, calling the eldest merchant by name. "Do you bring wine?"

The merchant nodded.

"And you want tin?"

The merchant nodded again, and lifting his cup drank Alef's health, following it up by a coarse joke in Cornish, which raised a laugh all round.

The Norse trader of those days, it must be remembered, was none of the cringing and effeminate chapmen who figure in the stories of the Middle Ages. A free Norse or Dane, himself often of noble blood, he fought as willingly as he bought; and held his own as an equal, whether at the court of a Cornish kinglet or at that of the Great Kaiser of the Greeks.

"And you, fair sir," said Alef, looking keenly at Hereward, "by what name shall I call you, and what service can I do for you? You look more like an earl's son than a merchant, and are come here surely for other things besides tin."

"Health to King Alef," said Hereward, raising the cup. "Who I am I will tell to none but Alef's self; but an earl's son I am, though an outlaw and a rover. My lands are the breadth of my boot-sole. My plough is my sword. My treasure is my good right hand. Nothing I have, and nothing I need, save to serve noble kings and earls, and win me a champion's fame. If you have battles to fight, tell me, that I may fight them for you. If you have none, thank God for his peace; and let me eat and drink, and go in peace."

"King Alef needs neither man nor boy to fight his battle as long as Ironhook sits in his hall."

It was the red-bearded giant who spoke in a broken tongue, part Scotch, part Cornish, part Danish, which Hereward could hardly understand; but that the ogre intended to insult him he understood well enough.

Hereward had hoped to find giants in Cornwall: and behold he had found one at once; though rather, to judge from his looks, a Pictish than a Cornish giant; and, true to his reckless determination to defy and fight every man and beast who was willing to defy and fight him, he turned on his elbow and stared at Ironhook in scorn, meditating some speech which might provoke the hoped-for quarrel.

As he did so his eye happily caught that of the fair Princess. She was watching him with a strange look, admiring, warning, imploring; and when she saw that he noticed her, she laid her finger on her lip in token of silence, crossed herself devoutly, and then laid her finger on her lips again, as if beseeching him to be patient and silent in the name of Him who answered not again.

Hereward, as is well seen, wanted not for quick wit, or for chivalrous feeling. He had observed the rough devotion of the giant to the Lady. He had observed, too, that she shrank from it; that she turned away with loathing when he offered her his own cup, while he answered by a dark and deadly scowl.

Was there an adventure here? Was she in duress either from this Ironhook or from her father, or from both? Did she need Hereward's help? If so, she was so lovely that he could not refuse it. And on the chance, he swallowed down his high stomach, and answered blandly enough,—

"One could see without eyes, noble sir, that you were worth any ten common men; but as every one has not like you the luck of so lovely a lady by your side, I thought that perchance you might hand over some of your lesser quarrels to one like me, who has not yet seen so much good fighting as yourself, and enjoy yourself in pleasant company at home, as I should surely do in your place."

The Princess shuddered and turned pale; then looked at Hereward and smiled her thanks. Ironhook laughed a savage laugh.

Hereward's jest being translated into Cornish for the benefit of the company, was highly approved by all; and good humor being restored, every man got drunk save Hereward, who found the mead too sweet and sickening.

After which those who could go to bed went to bed, not as in England,* among the rushes on the floor, but in the bunks or berths of wattle which stood two or three tiers high along the wall.

The next morning as Hereward went out to wash his face and hands in the brook below (he being the only man in the house who did so), Martin Lightfoot followed him.

"What is it, Martin? Hast thou had too much of that sweet mead last night that thou must come out to cool thy head too?"

"I came out for two reasons, — first, to see fair play, in case that Ironhook should come to wash his ugly visage, and find you on all fours over the brook — you understand? And next, to tell you what I heard last night among the maids."

"And what did you hear?"

"Fine adventures, if we can but compass them. You saw that lady with the carrot-headed fellow. I saw that you saw. Well, if you will believe me, that man has no more gentle blood than I have, — has no more right to sit on the settle than I. He is a No-man's son, a Pict from Galloway, who came down with a pirate crew and has made himself the master of this drunken old Prince, and the darling of all his housecarles, and now will needs be his son-in-law whether he will or not."

"I thought as much," said Hereward; "but how didst thou find out this?"

"I went out and sat with the knaves and the maids, and listened to their harp-playing, and harp they can, these Cornish, like very elves; and then I, too, sang songs and told them stories, for I can talk their tongue somewhat, till they all blest me for a right good fellow. And then I fell to praising up old Ironhook to the women."

"Praising him up, man?"

"Ay, just because I suspected him; for the women are so contrary, that if you speak evil of a man they will surely speak good of him; but if you will only speak good of him, then you will hear all the evil of him he ever has done, and more beside. And this I heard; that the King's daughter cannot abide him, and would as lief marry a seal."

"One did not need to be told that," said Hereward, "as long as one has eyes in one's head. I will kill the fellow, and carry her off, ere four-and-twenty hours be past."

"Softly, softly, my young master. You need to be told something that your eyes would not tell you, and that is, that the poor lass is betrothed already to a son of old King Ranald the Ost-

---

* Cornwall was not then considered part of England.

man, of Waterford, son of old King Sigtryg, who ruled there when I was a boy."

"He is a kinsman of mine, then," said Hereward. "All the more reason that I should kill this ruffian."

"If you can," said Martin Lightfoot.

"If I can?" retorted Hereward, fiercely.

"Well, well, wilful heart must have its way; only take my counsel: speak to the poor young lady first, and see what she will tell you, lest you only make bad worse, and bring down her father and his men on her as well as you."

Hereward agreed, and resolved to watch his opportunity of speaking to the princess.

As they went in to the morning meal they met Alef. He was in high good humor with Hereward; and all the more so when Hereward told him his name, and how he was the son of Leofric.

"I will warrant you are," he said, "by the gray head you carry on green shoulders. No discreeter man, they say, in these isles than the old earl."

"You speak truth, sir," said Hereward, "though he be no father of mine now; for of Leofric it is said in King Edward's court, that if a man ask counsel of him, it is as though he had asked it of the oracles of God."

"Then you are his true son. young man. I saw how you kept the peace with Ironhook, and I owe you thanks for it; for though he is my good friend, and will be my son-in-law erelong, yet a quarrel with him is more than I can abide just now, and I should not like to have seen my guest and my kinsman slain in my house."

Hereward would have said that he thought there was no fear of that: but he prudently held his tongue, and having an end to gain, listened instead of talking.

"Twenty years ago, of course, I could have thrashed him as easily as —; but now I am getting old and shaky, and the man has been a great help in need. Six kings of these parts has he killed for me, who drove off my cattle, and stopped my tin works, and plundered my monks' cells too, which is worse, while I was away sailing the seas; and he is a right good fellow at heart, though he be a little rough. So be friends with him as long as you stay here, and if I can do you a service I will."

They went in to their morning meal, at which Hereward resolved to keep the peace which he longed to break, and therefore, as was to be expected, broke.

For during the meal the fair lady, with no worse intention, perhaps, than that of teasing her tyrant, fell to open praises of

Hereward's fair face and golden hair; and being insulted therefor by the Ironhook, retaliated by observations about his personal appearance, which were more common in the eleventh century than they happily are now. He, to comfort himself, drank deep of the French wine which had just been brought and broached, and then went out into the court-yard, where, in the midst of his admiring fellow-ruffians, he enacted a scene as ludicrous as it was pitiable. All the childish vanity of the savage boiled over. He strutted, he shouted, he tossed about his huge limbs, he called for a harper, and challenged all around to dance, sing, leap, fight, do anything against him: meeting with nothing but admiring silence, he danced himself out of breath, and then began boasting once more of his fights, his cruelties, his butcheries, his impossible escapes and victories; till at last, as luck would have it, he espied Hereward, and poured out a stream of abuse against Englishmen and English courage.

"Englishmen," he said, "were naught. Had he not slain three of them himself with one blow?"

"Of your mouth, I suppose," quoth Hereward, who saw that the quarrel must come, and was glad to have it done and over.

"Of my mouth?" roared Ironhook; "of my sword, man!"

"Of your mouth," said Hereward. "Of your brain were they begotten, of the breath of your mouth they were born, and by the breath of your mouth you can slay them again as often as you choose."

The joke, as it has been handed down to us by the old chroniclers, seems clumsy enough; but it sent the princess, say they, into shrieks of laughter.

"Were it not that my Lord Alef was here," shouted Ironhook, "I would kill you out of hand."

"Promise to fight fair, and do your worst. The more fairly you fight, the more honor you will win," said Hereward.

Whereupon the two were parted for the while.

Two hours afterwards, Hereward, completely armed with helmet and mail-shirt, sword and javelin, hurried across the great court-yard, with Martin Lightfoot at his heels, towards the little church upon the knoll above. The two wild men entered into the cool darkness, and saw before them, by the light of a tiny lamp, the crucifix over the altar, and beneath it that which was then believed to be the body of Him who made heaven and earth. They stopped, trembling, for a moment, bowed themselves before that, to them, perpetual miracle, and then hurried on to a low doorway to the right, inside which dwelt Alef's chaplain, one of those good Celtic priests who were supposed to represent a Christianity more ancient than, and all but independent of, the then all-absorbing Church of Rome.

The cell was such a one as a convict would now disdain to inhabit. A low lean-to roof; the slates and rafters unceiled: the stone walls and floor unplastered; ill-lighted by a hand-broad window, unglazed, and closed with a shutter at night. A truss of straw and a rug, the priest's bed, lay in a corner. The only other furniture was a large oak chest, containing the holy vessels and vestments and a few old books. It stood directly under the window for the sake of light, for it served the good priest for both table and chair; and on it he was sitting reading in his book at that minute, the sunshine and the wind streaming in behind his head, doing no good to his rheumatism of thirty years' standing.

"Is there a priest here?" asked Hereward, hurriedly.

The old man looked up, shook his head, and answered in Cornish.

"Speak to him in Latin, Martin! May be he will understand that."

Martin spoke. "My lord, here, wants a priest to shrive him, and that quickly. He is going to fight the great tyrant Ironhook, as you call him."

"Ironhook?" answered the priest in good Latin enough. "And he so young! God help him, he is a dead man! What is this,—a fresh soul sent to its account by the hands of that man of Belial? Cannot he entreat him,—can he not make peace, and save his young life? He is but a stripling, and that man, like Goliath of old, a man of war from his youth up."

"And my master," said Martin Lightfoot, proudly, "is like young David,—one that can face a giant and kill him; for he has slain, like David, his lion and his bear ere now. At least he is one that will neither make peace nor entreat the face of living man. So shrive him quickly, Master Priest, and let him be gone to his work."

Poor Martin Lightfoot spoke thus bravely only to keep up his spirits and his young lord's; for, in spite of his confidence in Hereward's prowess, he had given him up for a lost man: and the tears ran down his rugged cheeks, as the old priest, rising up and seizing Hereward's two hands in his, besought him, with the passionate and graceful eloquence of his race, to have mercy upon his own youth.

Hereward understood his meaning, though not his words.

"Tell him," he said to Martin, "that fight I must, and tell him that shrive me he must, and that quickly. Tell him how the fellow met me in the wood below just now, and would have slain me there, unarmed as I was; and how, when I told him it was a shame to strike a naked man, he told me he would give me but one hour's grace to go back, on the faith of a gentleman, for my armor and weapons, and meet him there again, to die by his hand. So shrive me quick, Sir Priest."

Hereward knelt down. Martin Lightfoot knelt down by him, and with a trembling voice began to interpret for him.

"What does he say?" asked Hereward, as the priest murmured something to himself.

"He said," quoth Martin, now fairly blubbering, "that, fair and young as you are, your shrift should be as short and as clean as David's."

Hereward was touched. "Anything but that," said he, smiting on his breast, "Mea culpa, — mea culpa, — mea maxima culpa."

"Tell him how I robbed my father."

The priest groaned as Martin did so.

"And how I mocked at my mother, and left her in a rage, without ever a kind word between us. And how I have slain I know not how many men in battle, though that, I trust, need not lay heavily on my soul, seeing that I killed them all in fair fight."

Again the priest groaned.

"And how I robbed a certain priest of his money and gave it away to my housecarles."

Here the priest groaned more bitterly still.

"O my son! my son! where hast thou found time to lay all these burdens on thy young soul?"

"It will take less time," said Martin, bluntly, "for you to take the burdens off again."

"But I dare not absolve him for robbing a priest. Heaven help him! He must go to the bishop for that. He is more fit to go on pilgrimage to Jerusalem than to battle."

"He has no time," quoth Martin, "for bishops or Jerusalem."

"Tell him," says Hereward, "that in this purse is all I have, that in it he will find sixty silver pennies, beside two strange coins of gold."

"Sir Priest," said Martin Lightfoot, taking the purse from Hereward, and keeping it in his own hand, "there are in this bag moneys."

Martin had no mind to let the priest into the secret of the state of their finances.

"And tell him," continued Hereward, "that if I fall in this battle I give him all that money, that he may part it among the poor for the good of my soul."

"Pish!" said Martin to his lord; "that is paying him for having you killed. You should pay him for keeping you alive." And without waiting for the answer, he spoke in Latin, —

"And if he comes back safe from this battle, he will give you ten pennies for yourself and your church, Priest, and therefore expects you to pray your very loudest while he is gone."

"I will pray, I will pray," said the holy man; "I will wrestle in prayer. Ah that he could slay the wicked, and reward the proud according to his deservings! Ah that he could rid me and my master, and my young lady, of this son of Belial, — this devourer of widows and orphans, — this slayer of the poor and needy, who fills this place with innocent blood, — him of whom it is written, 'They stretch forth their mouth unto the heaven, and their tongue goeth through the world. Therefore fall the people unto them, and thereout suck they no small advantage.' I will shrive him, shrive him of all save robbing the priest, and for that he must go to the bishop, if he live; and if not, the Lord have mercy on his soul."

And so, weeping and trembling, the good old man pronounced the words of absolution.

Hereward rose, thanked him, and then hurried out in silence.

"You will pray your very loudest, Priest," said Martin, as he followed his young lord.

"I will, I will," quoth he, and kneeling down began to chant that noble seventy-third Psalm, "Quam bonus Israel," which he had just so fitly quoted.

"Thou gavest him the bag, Martin?" said Hereward, as they hurried on.

"You are not dead yet. 'No pay, no play,' is as good a rule for priest as for layman."

"Now then, Martin Lightfoot, good by. Come not with me. It must never be said, even slanderously, that I brought two into the field against one; and if I die, Martin — "

"You won't die!" said Lightfoot, shutting his teeth.

"If I die, go back to my people somehow, and tell them that I died like a true earl's son."

Hereward held out his hand; Martin fell on his knees and kissed it; watched him with set teeth till he disappeared in the wood; and then started forward and entered the bushes at a different spot.

"I must be nigh at hand to see fair play," he muttered to himself, "in case any of his ruffians be hanging about. Fair play I'll see, and fair play I'll give, too, for the sake of my lord's honor, though I be bitterly loath to do it. So many times as I have been a villain when it was of no use, why may n't I be one now, when it would serve the purpose indeed? Why did we ever come into this accursed place? But one thing I will do," said he, as he ensconced himself under a thick holly, whence he could see the meeting of the combatants upon an open lawn some twenty yards away; "if that big bull-calf kills my master, and I do not jump on his back and pick his brains out with this trusty steel of mine, may my right arm —"

And Martin Lightfoot swore a fearful oath, which need not here be written.

The priest had just finished his chant of the seventy-third Psalm, and had betaken himself in his spiritual warfare, as it was then called, to the equally apposite fifty-second, "Quid gloriaris?" "Why boastest thou thyself, thou tyrant, that thou canst do mischief, whereas the goodness of God endureth yet daily?"

"Father! father!" cried a soft voice in the doorway, "where are you?"

And in hurried the Princess.

"Hide this," she said, breathless, drawing from beneath her mantle a huge sword; "hide it, where no one dare touch it, under the altar behind the holy rood: no place too secret."

"What is it?" asked the priest, springing up from his knees.

"His sword, — the Ogre's, — his magic sword, which kills whomsoever it strikes. I coaxed the wretch to let me have it last night when he was tipsy, for fear he should quarrel with the young stranger; and I have kept it from him ever since by one excuse or another; and now he has sent one of his ruffians in for it, saying, that if I do not give it up at once he will come back and kill me."

"He dare not do that," said the priest.

"What is there that he dare not?" said she. "Hide it at once; I know that he wants it to fight with this Hereward."

"If he wants it for that," said the priest, "it is too late; for half an hour is past since Hereward went to meet him."

"And you let him go? You did not persuade him, stop him? You let him go hence to his death?"

In vain the good man expostulated and explained that it was no fault of his.

"You must come with me this instant to my father, — to them; they must be parted. They shall be parted. If you dare not, I dare. I will throw myself between them, and he that strikes the other shall strike me."

And she hurried the priest out of the house, down the knoll, and across the yard. There they found others on the same errand. The news that a battle was toward had soon spread, and the men-at-arms were hurrying down to the fight; kept back, however, by Alef, who strode along at their head.

Alef was sorely perplexed in mind. He had taken, as all honest men did, a great liking to Hereward. Moreover, he was his kinsman and his guest. Save him he would if he could but how to save him without mortally offending his tyrant Ironhook he could not see. At least he would exert what little power he had, and prevent, if possible, his men-at-arms from helping their darling leader against the hapless lad.

Alef's perplexity was much increased when his daughter bounded towards him, seizing him by the arm, and hurried him on, showing by look and word which of the combatants she favored, so plainly that the ruffians behind broke into scornful murmurs. They burst through the bushes. Martin Lightfoot, happily, heard them coming, and had just time to slip away noiselessly, like a rabbit, to the other part of the cover.

The combat seemed at the first glance to be one between a grown man and a child, so unequal was the size of the combatants. But the second look showed that the advantage was by no means with Ironhook. Stumbling to and fro with the broken shaft of a javelin sticking in his thigh, he vainly tried to seize and crush Hereward in his enormous arms. Hereward, bleeding, but still active and upright, broke away, and sprang round him, watching for an opportunity to strike a deadly blow. The housecarles rushed forward with yells. Alef shouted to the combatants to desist; but ere the party could reach them, Hereward's opportunity had come. Ironhook, after a fruitless lunge, stumbled forward. Hereward leapt aside, and spying an unguarded spot below the corslet, drove his sword deep into the giant's body, and rolled him over upon the sward. Then arose shouts of fury.

"Foul play!" cried one.

And others taking up the cry, called out, "Sorcery!" and "Treason!"

Hereward stood over Ironhook as he lay writhing and foaming on the ground.

"Killed by a boy at last!" groaned he. "If I had but had my own sword, — my Brain-biter which that witch stole from me but last night!" and amid foul curses and bitter tears of shame his mortal spirit fled to its doom.

The housecarles rushed in on Hereward, who had enough to do to keep them at arm's length by long sweeps of his sword.

Alef entreated, threatened, promised a fair trial if the men would give fair play; when, to complete the confusion, the Princess threw herself upon the corpse, shrieking and tearing her hair; and to Hereward's surprise and disgust, bewailed the prowess and the virtues of the dead, calling upon all present to avenge his murder.

Hereward vowed inwardly that he would never again trust

woman's fancy or fight in woman's quarrel. He was now nigh at his wits' end; the housecarles had closed round him in a ring with the intention of seizing him; and however well he might defend his front, he might be crippled at any moment from behind: but in the very nick of time Martin Lightfoot burst through the crowd, set himself heel to heel with his master, and broke out, not with threats, but with a good-humored laugh.

"Here is a pretty coil about a red-headed brute of a Pict! Danes, Ostmen," he cried, "are you not ashamed to call such a fellow your lord, when you have such a true earl's son as this to lead you if you will?"

The Ostmen in the company looked at each other. Martin Lightfoot saw that his appeal to the antipathies of race had told, and followed it up by a string of witticisms upon the Pictish nation in general, of which the only two fit for modern ears to be set down were the two old stories, that the Picts had feet so large that they used to lie upon their backs and hold up their legs to shelter them from the sun; and that when killed, they could not fall down, but died as they were, all standing.

"So that the only foul play I can see is, that my master shoved the fellow over after he had stabbed him, instead of leaving him to stand upright there, like one of your Cornish Dolmens, till his flesh should fall off his bones."

Hereward saw the effect of Martin's words, and burst out in Danish likewise.

"Look at me!" he said; "I am Hereward the outlaw, I am the champion, I am the Berserker, I am the Viking, I am the land thief, the sea thief, the ravager of the world, the bear-slayer, the ogre-killer, the raven-fattener, the darling of the wolf, the curse of the widow. Touch me, and I will give you to the raven and to the wolf, as I have this ogre. Be my men, and follow me over the swan's road, over the whale's bath, over the long-snake's leap, to the land where the sea meets the sun, and golden apples hang on every tree; and we will freight our ships with Moorish maidens, and the gold of Cadiz and Algiers."

"Hark to the Viking! Hark to the right earl's son!" shouted some of the Danes, whose blood had been stirred many a time before by such wild words, and on whom Hereward's youth and beauty had their due effect. And now the counsels of the ruffians being divided, the old priest gained courage to step in. Let them deliver Hereward and his serving man into his custody. He would bring them forth on the morrow, and there should be full investigation and fair trial. And so Hereward and Martin, who both refused stoutly to give up their arms, were marched back into the town, locked in the little church, and left to their meditations.

Hereward sat down on the pavement and cursed the Princess. Martin Lightfoot took off his master's corslet, and, as well as the darkness would allow, bound up his wounds, which happily were not severe.

"Were I you," said he at last, "I should keep my curses till I saw the end of this adventure."

"Has not the girl betrayed me shamefully?"

"Not she. I saw her warn you, as far as looks could do, not to quarrel with the man."

"That was because she did not know me. Little she thought that I could —"

"Don't hollo till you are out of the wood. This is a night for praying rather than boasting."

"She cannot really love that wretch," said Hereward, after a pause. "You saw how she mocked him."

"Women are strange things, and often tease most where they love most."

"But such a misbegotten savage."

"Women are strange things, say I, and with some a big fellow is a pretty fellow, be he uglier than seven Ironhooks. Still, just because women are strange things, have patience, say I."

The lock creaked, and the old priest came in. Martin leapt to the open door; but it was slammed in his face by men outside with scornful laughter.

The priest took Hereward's head in his hands, wept over him, blessed him for having slain Goliath like young David, and then set food and drink before the two; but he answered Martin's questions only with sighs and shakings of the head.

"Let us eat and drink, then," said Martin, " and after that you, my lord, sleep off your wounds while I watch the door. I have no fancy for these fellows taking us unawares at night."

Martin lay quietly across the door till the small hours, listening to every sound, till the key creaked once more in the lock. He started at the sound, and seizing the person who entered round the neck, whispered, "One word, and you are dead."

"Do not hurt me," half shrieked a stifled voice; and Martin Lightfoot, to his surprise, found that he had grasped no armed man, but the slight frame of a young girl.

"I am the Princess," she whispered; "let me in."

"A very pretty hostage for us," thought Martin, and letting her go seized the key, locking the door in the inside.

"Take me to your master," she cried, and Martin led her up the church wondering, but half suspecting some further trap.

'You have a dagger in your hand," said he, holding her wrist.
"I have. If I had meant to use it, it would have been used first on you. Take it, if you like."

She hurried up to Hereward, who lay sleeping quietly on the altar-steps; knelt by him, wrung his hands, called him her champion, her deliverer.

"I am not well awake yet," said he, coldly, "and don't know whether this may not be a dream, as more that I have seen and heard seems to be."

"It is no dream. I am true. I was always true to you. Have I not put myself in your power? Am I not come here to deliver you, my deliverer?"

"The tears which you shed over your ogre's corpse seem to have dried quickly enough."

"Cruel! What else could I do? You heard him accuse me to those ruffians of having stolen his sword. My life, my father's life, were not safe a moment, had I not dissembled, and done the thing I loathed. Ah!" she went on, bitterly, "you men, who rule the world and us by cruel steel, you forget that we poor women have but one weapon left wherewith to hold our own, and that is cunning; and are driven by you day after day to tell the lie which we detest."

"Then you really stole his sword?"

"And hid it here, for your sake!" and she drew the weapon from behind the altar.

"Take it. It is yours now. It is magical. Whoever smites with it, need never smite again. Now, quick, you must be gone. But promise one thing before you go."

"If I leave this land safe, I will do it, be it what it may. Why not come with me, lady, and see it done?"

She laughed. "Vain boy, do you think that I love you well enough for that?"

"I have won you, and why should I not keep you?" said Hereward, sullenly.

"Do you not know that I am betrothed to your kinsman? And — though that you cannot know — that I love your kinsman?"

"So I have all the blows, and none of the spoil."

"Tush! you have the glory, — and the sword, — and the chance, if you will do my bidding, of being called by all ladies a true and gentle knight, who cared not for his own pleasure, but for deeds of chivalry. Go to my betrothed, — to Waterford over the sea. Take him this ring, and tell him by that token to come and claim me soon, lest he run the danger of losing me a second time, and lose me then forever; for I am in hard case here, and were it not for my father's sake, perhaps I might be weak enough, in spite of what men might say, to flee with you to your kinsman across the sea."

"Trust me and come," said Hereward. whose young blood kindled with a sudden nobleness, — "trust me, and I will treat you like my sister, like my queen. By the holy rood above I will swear to be true to you."

"I do trust you, but it cannot be. Here is money for you in plenty to hire a passage if you need: it is no shame to take it from me. And now one thing more. Here is a cord, — you must bind the hands and feet of the old priest inside, and then you must bind mine likewise."

"Never," quoth Hereward.

"It must be. How else can I explain your having got the key? I made them give me the key on the pretence that with one who had most cause to hate you, it would be safe; and when they come and find us in the morning I shall tell them how I came here to stab you with my own hands, — you must lay the dagger by me, — and how you and your man fell upon us and bound us, and you escaped. Ah! Mary Mother," continued the maiden with a sigh, "when shall we poor weak women have no more need of lying?"

She lay down, and Hereward, in spite of himself, gently bound her hands and feet, kissing them as he bound them.

"I shall do well here upon the altar steps," said she. "How can I spend my time better till the morning light than to lie here and pray?"

The old priest, who was plainly in the plot, submitted meekly to the same fate; and Hereward and Martin Lightfoot stole out, locking the door, but leaving the key in it outside. To scramble over the old earthwork was an easy matter; and in a few minutes they were hurrying down the valley to the sea, with a fresh breeze blowing behind them from the north.

"Did I not tell you, my lord," said Martin Lightfoot, "to keep your curses till you had seen the end of this adventure?"

Hereward was silent. His brain was still whirling from the adventures of the day, and his heart was very deeply touched. His shrift of the morning, hurried and formal as it had been, had softened him. His danger — for he felt how he had been face to face with death — had softened him likewise; and he repented somewhat of his vainglorious and bloodthirsty boasting over a fallen foe, as he began to see that there was a purpose more noble in life than ranging land and sea, a ruffian among ruffians, seeking for glory amid blood and flame. The idea of chivalry, of succoring the weak and the opprest, of keeping faith and honor not merely towards men who could avenge themselves, but towards women who could not; the dim dawn of purity, gentleness, and the conquest of his own fierce passions, — all these had taken root in his heart during his adventure with the fair Cornish girl. The seed was sown. Would it be cut down again by the bitter blasts of the rough fighting world, or would it grow and bear the noble fruit of "gentle very perfect knighthood"?

They reached the ship, clambered on board without ceremony, at the risk of being taken and killed as robbers, and told their case. The merchants had not completed their cargo of tin. Hereward offered to make up their loss to them if they would set sail at once; and they, feeling that the place would be for some time to come too hot to hold them, and being also in high delight, like honest Ostmen, with Hereward's prowess, agreed to sail straight for Waterford, and complete their cargo there. But the tide was out. It was three full hours before the ship could float; and for three full hours they waited in fear and trembling, expecting the Cornishmen to be down upon them in a body every moment, under which wholesome fear some on board prayed fervently who had never been known to pray before.

CHAPTER IV.

HOW HEREWARD TOOK SERVICE WITH RANALD, KING OF WATERFORD.

The coasts of Ireland were in a state of comparative peace in the middle of the eleventh century. The ships of Loghlin, seen far out at sea, no longer drove the population shrieking inland. Heathen Danes, whether fair-haired Fiongall from Norway, or brown-haired Dubgall from Denmark proper, no longer burned convents, tortured monks for their gold, or (as at Clonmacnoise) set a heathen princess, Oda, wife of Thorgill, son of Harold Harfager, aloft on the high altar to receive the homage of the conquered. The Scandinavian invaders had become Christianized, and civilized also, — owing to their continual intercourse with foreign nations, — more highly than the Irish whom they had overcome. That was easy; for early Irish civilization seems to have existed only in the convents and for the religious; and when they were crushed, mere barbarism was left behind. And now the same process went on in the east of Ireland, which went on a generation or two later in the east of Scotland. The Danes began to settle down into peaceful colonists and traders. Ireland was poor; and the convents plundered once could not be plundered again. The Irish were desperately brave. Ill-armed and almost naked, they were as perfect in the arts of forest warfare as those modern Maories whom they so much resemble; and though their black skenes and light darts were no match for the Danish swords and battle-axes which they adopted during the middle age, or their plaid trousers and felt capes for the Danish helmet and chain corslet. still an Irishman was so ugly a foe, that it was not worth while to fight with him unless he could be robbed afterwards. The Danes, who, like their descendants of Northumbria, the Lowlands, and Ulster, were canny common-sense folk, with a shrewd eye to interest, found, somewhat to their regret, that there were trades even more profitable than robbery and murder. They therefore concentrated themselves round harbors and river mouths, and sent forth their ships to all the western seas, from Dublin, Waterford, Wexford, Cork, or Limerick. Every important seaport in Ireland owes its existence to those sturdy Vikings' sons. In each of these towns they had founded a petty kingdom, which endured until, and even in some cases after, the conquest of Ireland by Henry II. and Strongbow. They intermarried in the mean while with the native Irish. Brian Boru, for instance, was so connected with Danish royalty, that it is still a question whether he himself had not Danish blood in his veins. King Sigtryg Silkbeard, who fought against him at Clontarf, was actually his step-son, — and so too, according to another Irish chronicler, was King Olaff Kvaran, who even at the time of the battle of Clontarf was married to Brian Boru's daughter, — a marriage which (if a fact) was startlingly within the prohibited degrees of consanguinity. But the ancient Irish were sadly careless on such points; and as Giraldus Cambrensis says, "followed the example of men of old in their vices more willingly than in their virtues."

More than forty years had elapsed since that famous battle of Clontarf, and since Ragnvald, Reginald, or Ranald, son of Sigtryg the Norseman, had been slain therein by Brian Boru. On that one day, so the Irish sang, the Northern invaders were exterminated, once and for all, by the Milesian hero, who had craftily used the strangers to fight his battles, and then, the moment they became formidable to himself, crushed them, till "from Howth to Brandon in Kerry there was not a threshing-floor without a Danish slave threshing thereon, or a quern without a Danish woman grinding thereat."

Nevertheless, in spite of the total annihilation of the Danish power in the Emerald isle, Ranald seemed to the eyes of men to be still a hale old warrior, ruling constitutionally — that is, with a wholesome fear of being outlawed or murdered if he misbehaved — over the Danes in Waterford; with five hundred fair-haired warriors at his back, two-edged axe on shoulder and two-edged sword on thigh. His ships drove a thriving trade with France and Spain in Irish fish, butter, honey, and furs. His workmen coined money in the old round tower of Dundory, built by his predecessor and namesake about the year 1003, which stands as Reginald's tower to this day. He had fought many a bloody battle since his death at Clontarf, by the side of his old leader Sigtryg Silkbeard. He had been many a time to Dublin to visit his even more prosperous and formidable friend; and was so delighted with the new church of the Holy Trinity, which Sigtryg and his bishop Donatus had just built, not in the Danish or Ostman town, but in the heart of ancient Celtic Dublin, (plain proof of the utter overthrow of the Danish power,) that he had determined to build a like church in honor of the Holy Trinity, in Waterford itself. A thriving, valiant old king he seemed, as he sat in his great house of pine logs under Reginald's Tower upon the quay, drinking French and Spanish wines out of horns of ivory and cups of gold; and over his head hanging, upon the wall, the huge doubled-edged axe with which, so his flatterers had whispered, Brian Boru had not slain him, but he Brian Boru.

Nevertheless, then as since, alas! the pleasant theory was preferred by the Milesian historians to the plain truth. And far away inland, monks wrote and harpers sung of the death of Ranald, the fair-haired Fiongall, and all his "mailed swarms."

One Teague MacMurrough, indeed, a famous bard of those parts, composed unto his harp a song of Clontarf, the fame whereof reached Ranald's ears, and so amused him that he rested not day or night till he had caught the hapless bard and brought him in triumph into Waterford. There he compelled him, at sword's point, to sing to him and his housecarles the Milesian version of the great historical event: and when the harper, in fear and trembling, came to the story of Ranald's own death at Brian Boru's hands, then the jolly old Viking laughed till the tears ran down his face; and instead of cutting off Teague's head, gave him a cup of goodly wine, made him his own harper thenceforth, and bade him send for his wife and children, and sing to him every day, especially the song of Clontarf and his own death; treating him very much, in fact, as English royalty, during the last generation, treated another Irish bard whose song was even more sweet, and his notions of Irish history even more grotesque, than those of Teague MacMurrough.

It was to this old king, or rather to his son Sigtryg, godson of Sigtryg Silkbeard, and distant cousin of his own, that Hereward now took his way, and told his story, as the king sat in his hall, drinking "across the fire," after the old Norse fashion. The fire of pine logs was in the midst of the hall, and the smoke went out through a louver in the roof. On one side was a long bench, and in the middle of it the king's high arm-chair; right and left of him sat his kinsmen and the ladies, and his sea-captains and men of wealth. Opposite, on the other side of the fire, was another bench. In the middle of that sat his marshal, and right and left all his housecarles. There were other benches behind, on which sat more freemen, but of lesser rank.

And they were all drinking ale, which a servant poured out of a bucket into a great bull's horn, and the men handed round to each other.

Then Hereward came in, and sat down on the end of the hindermost bench, and Martin stood behind him, till one of the ladies said,—

"Who is that young stranger, who sits behind there so humbly, though he looks like an earl's son, more fit to sit here with us on the high bench?"

"So he does," quoth King Ranald. "Come forward hither young sir, and drink."

And when Hereward came forward, all the ladies agreed that he must be an earl's son; for he had a great gold torc round his neck, and gold rings on his wrists; and a new scarlet coat, bound with gold braid; and scarlet stockings, cross-laced with gold braid up to the knee; and shoes trimmed with martin's fur; and a short blue silk cloak over all, trimmed with martin's fur likewise; and by his side, in a broad belt with gold studs, was the Ogre's sword Brain-biter, with its ivory hilt and velvet sheath; and all agreed that if he had but been a head taller, they had never seen a properer man.

"Aha! such a gay young sea-cock does not come hither for naught. Drink first, man, and tell us thy business after," and he reached the horn to Hereward.

Hereward took it, and sang,—

> "In this Braga-beaker,
> Brave Ranald I pledge;
> In good liquor, which lightens
> Long labor on oar-bench;
> Good liquor, which sweetens
> The song of the scald."

"Thy voice is as fine as thy feathers, man. Nay, drink it all. We ourselves drink here by the peg at midday; but a stranger is welcome to fill his inside all hours of the day."

Whereon Hereward finished the horn duly; and at Ranald's bidding, sat him down on the high settle. He did not remark, that as he sat down two handsome youths rose and stood behind him.

"Now then, Sir Priest," quoth the king, "go on with your story."

A priest, Irish by his face and dress, who sat on the high bench, rose, and renewed an oration which Hereward's entrance had interrupted.

"So, O great King, as says Homerus, this wise king called his earls, knights, sea-captains, and housecarles, and said unto them, 'Which of these two kings is in the right, who can tell? But mind you, that this king of the Enchanters lives far away in India, and we never heard of him more than his name; but this king Ulixes and his Greeks live hard by; and which of the two is it wiser to quarrel with, him that lives hard by or him that lives far off?' Therefore, King Ranald, says, by the mouth of my humility, the great O'Brodar, Lord of Ivark, 'Take example by

Alcinous, the wise king of Fairy, and listen not to the ambassadors of those lying villains, O'Dea Lord of Slievardagh, Maccarthy King of Cashel, and O'Sullivan Lord of Knockraffin, who all three between them could not raise kernes enough to drive off one old widow's cow. Make friends with me, who live upon your borders; and you shall go peaceably through my lands, to conquer and destroy them, who live afar off; as they deserve, the sons of Belial and Judas.'"

And the priest crost himself, and sat down. At which speech Hereward was seen to laugh.

"Why do you laugh, young sir? The priest seems to talk like a wise man, and is my guest and an ambassador."

Then rose up Hereward, and bowed to the king. "King Ranald Sigtrygsson, it was not for rudeness that I laughed, for I learnt good manners long ere I came here, but because I find clerks alike all over the world."

"How?"

"Quick at hiding false counsel under learned speech. I know nothing of Ulixes, king, nor of this O'Brodar either; and I am but a lad, as you see: but I heard a bird once in my own country who gave a very different counsel from the priest's."

"Speak on, then. This lad is no fool, my merry men all."

"There were three copses, King, in our country, and each copse stood on a hill. In the first there built an eagle, in the second there built a sparhawk, in the third there built a crow.

"Now the sparhawk came to the eagle, and said, 'Go shares with me, and we will kill the crow, and have her wood to ourselves.'

"'Humph!' says the eagle, 'I could kill the crow without your help; however, I will think of it.'

"When the crow heard that, she came to the eagle herself. 'King Eagle,' says she, 'why do you want to kill me, who live ten miles from you, and never flew across your path in my life? Better kill that little rogue of a sparhawk who lives between us, and is always ready to poach on your marches whenever your back is turned. So you will have her wood as well as your own.'

"'You are a wise crow,' said the eagle; and he went out and killed the sparhawk, and took his wood."

Loud laughed King Ranald and his Vikings all. "Well spoken, young man! We will take the sparhawk, and let the crow bide."

"Nay, but," quoth Hereward, "hear the end of the story. After a while the eagle finds the crow beating about the edge of the sparhawk's wood.

"'Oho!' says he, 'so you can poach as well as that little hook-nosed rogue?' and he killed her too.

"'Ah!' says the crow, when she lay a-dying, 'my blood is on my own head. If I had but left the sparhawk between me and this great tyrant!'

"And so the eagle got all three woods to himself."

At which the Vikings laughed more loudly than ever; and King Ranald, chuckling at the notion of eating up the hapless Irish princes one by one, sent back the priest (not without a present for his church, for Ranald was a pious man) to tell the great O'Brodar, that unless he sent into Waterford by that day week two hundred head of cattle, a hundred pigs, a hundred weight of clear honey, and as much of wax, Ranald would not leave so much as a sucking-pig alive in Ivark.

The cause of quarrel, of course, was too unimportant to be mentioned. Each had robbed and cheated the other half a dozen times in the last twenty years. As for the morality of the transaction, Ranald had this salve for his conscience,—that as he intended to do to O'Brodar, so would O'Brodar have gladly done to him, had he been living peaceably in Norway, and O'Brodar been strong enough to invade and rob him. Indeed, so had O'Brodar done already, ever since he wore beard, to every chieftain of his own race whom he was strong enough to ill-treat. Many a fair herd had he driven off, many a fair farm burnt, many a fair woman carried off a slave, after that inveterate fashion of lawless feuds which makes the history of Celtic Ireland from the earliest times one dull and aimless catalogue of murder and devastation, followed by famine and disease; and now, as he had done to others, so it was to be done to him.

"And now, young sir, who seem as witty as you are good looking, you may, if you will, tell us your name and your business. As for the name, however, if you wish to keep it to yourself, Ranald Sigtrygsson is not the man to demand it of an honest guest."

Hereward looked round and saw Teague MacMurrough standing close to him, harp in hand. He took it from him courteously enough, put a silver penny into the minstrel's hand, and running his fingers over the strings, rose and began,—

> "Outlaw and free thief,
> Landless and lawless
> Through the world fare I,
> Thoughtless of life.
> Soft is my beard, but
> Hard my Brain-biter.
> Wake, men me call, whom
> Warrior or watchman
> Never caught sleeping,
> Far in Northumberland
> Slew I the witch-bear,
> Cleaving his brain-pan,
> At one stroke I felled him."

And so forth, chanting all his doughty deeds, with such a voice and spirit joined to that musical talent for which he was afterwards so famous, till the hearts of the wild Norsemen rejoiced, and "Skall to the stranger! Skall to the young Viking!" rang through the hall.

Then showing proudly the fresh wounds on his bare arms, he sang of his fight with the Cornish ogre, and his adventure with the Princess. But always, though he went into the most minute details, he concealed the name both of her and of her father, while he kept his eyes steadily fixed on Ranald's eldest son, Sigtryg, who sat at his father's right hand.

The young man grew uneasy, red, almost angry; till at last Hereward sung, —

> "A gold ring she gave me
> Right royally dwarf-worked,
> To none will I pass it
> For prayer or for sword-stroke,
> Save to him who can claim it
> By love and by troth plight,
> Let that hero speak
> If that hero be here."

Young Sigtryg half started from his feet: but when Hereward smiled at him, and laid his finger on his lips, he sat down again. Hereward felt his shoulder touched from behind. One of the youths who had risen when he sat down bent over him, and whispered in his ear, —

"Ah, Hereward, we know you. Do you not know us? We are the twins, the sons of your sister, Siward the White and Siward the Red, the orphans of Asbiorn Siwardsson, who fell at Dunsinane."

Hereward sprang up, struck the harp again, and sang, —

> "Outlaw and free thief,
> My kinsfolk have left me,
> And no kinsfolk need I
> Till kinsfolk shall need me.
> My sword is my father,
> My shield is my mother,
> My ship is my sister,
> My horse is my brother."

"Uncle, uncle," whispered one of them, sadly, "listen now or never, for we have bad news for you and us. Your father is dead, and Earl Algar, your brother, here in Ireland, outlawed a second time."

A flood of sorrow passed through Hereward's heart. He kept it down, and rising once more, harp in hand, —

> "Hereward, king, hight I,
> Holy Leofric my father,

> In Westminster wiser
> None walked with King Edward.
> High ministers he builded,
> Pale monks he maintained.
> Dead is he, a bed-death,
> A leech-death, a priest-death,
> A straw-death, a cow's death.
> Such doom I desire not.
> To high heaven, all so softly,
> The angels uphand him,
> In meads of May flowers
> Mild Mary will meet him.
> Me, happier, the Valkyrs
> Shall waft from the war-deck,
> Shall hail from the holmgang
> Or helmet-strewn moorland.
> And sword-strokes my shrift be,
> Sharp spears be my leeches,
> With heroes' hot corpses
> High heaped for my pillow."

"Skall to the Viking!" shouted the Danes once more, at this outburst of heathendom, common enough among their half-converted race, in times when monasticism made so utter a divorce between the life of the devotee and that of the worldling that it seemed reasonable enough for either party to have their own heaven and their own hell. After all, Hereward was not original in his wish. He had but copied the death-song which his father's friend and compeer, Siward Digre, the victor of Dunsinane, had sung for himself some three years before.

All praised his poetry, and especially the quickness of his alliterations (then a note of the highest art); and the old king filling not this time the horn, but a golden goblet, bid him drain it and keep the goblet for his song.

Young Sigtryg leapt up, and took the cup to Hereward. "Such a skald," he said, "ought to have no meaner cup-bearer than a king's son."

Hereward drank it dry; and then fixing his eyes meaningly on the Prince, dropt the Princess's ring into the cup, and putting it back into Sigtryg's hand, sang,—

> "The beaker I reach back
> More rich than I took it.
> No gold will I grasp
> Of the king's, the ring-giver,
> Till, by wit or by weapon,
> I worthily win it.
> When brained by my biter
> O'Brodar lies gory,
> While over the wolf's meal
> Fair widows are wailing."

"Does he refuse my gift?" grumbled Ranald.

"He has given a fair reason," said the Prince, as he bid the ring in his bosom; "leave him to me; for my brother in arms is henceforth."

After which, as was the custom of those parts, most of them drank too much liquor. But neither Sigtryg nor Hereward drank; and the two Siwards stood behind their young uncle's seat, watching him with that intense admiration which lads can feel for a young man.

That night, when the warriors were asleep, Sigtryg and Hereward talked out their plans. They would equip two ships; they would fight all the kinglets of Cornwall at once, if need was; they would carry off the Princess, and burn Alef's town over his head, if he said nay. Nothing could be more simple than the tactics required in an age when might was right.

Then Hereward turned to his two nephews who lingered near him, plainly big with news.

"And what brings you here, lads?" He had hardened his heart, and made up his mind to show no kindness to his own kin. The day might come when they might need him; then it would be his turn.

"Your father, as we told you, is dead."

"So much the better for him, and the worse for England. And Harold and the Godwinssons, of course, are lords and masters far and wide?"

"Tosti has our grandfather Siward's earldom."

"I know that. I know, too, that he will not keep it long, unless he learns that Northumbrians are free men, and not Wessex slaves."

"And Algar our uncle is outlawed again, after King Edward had given him peaceably your father's earldom."

"And why?"

"Why was he outlawed two years ago?"

"Because the Godwinssons hate him, I suppose."

"And Algar is gone to Griffin, the Welshman, and from him on to Dublin to get ships, just as he did two years ago; and has sent us here to get ships likewise."

"And what will he do with them when he has got them? He burnt Hereford last time he was outlawed, by way of a wise deed, minster and all, with St. Ethelbert's relics on board; and slew seven clergymen: but they were only honest canons with wives at home, and not shaveling monks, so I suppose that sin was easily shrived. Well, I robbed a priest of a few pence, and was outlawed; he plunders and burns a whole minster, and is made a great earl for it. One law for the weak and one for the strong, young lads, as you will know when you are as old as I. And now I suppose he will plunder and burn more minsters, and then patch up a peace with Harold again; which I advise him strongly to do; for I warn you, young lads, and you may carry that message from me to Dublin to my good brother your uncle, that Harold's little finger is thicker than his whole body; and that, false Godwinsson as he is, he is the only man with a head upon his shoulders left in England, now that his father, and my father, and dear old Siward, whom I loved better than my father, are dead and gone."

The lads stood silent, not a little awed, and indeed imposed on, by the cynical and worldly-wise tone which their renowned uncle had assumed.

At last one of them asked, falteringly, "Then you will do nothing for us?"

"For you, nothing. Against you, nothing. Why should I mix myself up in my brother's quarrels? Will he make that white-headed driveller at Westminster reverse my outlawry? And if he does, what shall I get thereby? A younger brother's portion; a dirty ox-gang of land in Kesteven. Let him leave me alone as I leave him, and see if I do not come back to him some day, for or against him as he chooses, with such a host of Vikings' sons as Harold Hadraade himself would be proud of. By Thor's hammer, boys, I have been an outlaw but five years now, and I find it so cheery a life, that I do not care if I am an outlaw for fifty more. The world is a fine place and a wide place; and it is a very little corner of it that I have seen yet; and if you were of my mettle, you would come along with me and see it throughout to the four corners of heaven, instead of mixing yourselves up in these paltry little quarrels with which our two families are tearing England in pieces, and being murdered perchance like dogs at last by treachery, as Sweyn Godwinsson murdered Biorn."

The boys listened, wide-eyed and wide-eared. Hereward knew to whom he was speaking; and he had not spoken in vain.

"What do you hope to get here?" he went on. "Ranald will give you no ships: he will have enough to do to fight O'Brodar; and he is too cunning to thrust his head into Algar's quarrels."

"We hoped to find Vikings here, who would go to any war on the hope of plunder."

"If there be any, I want them more than you; and, what is more, I will have them. They know that they will do finer deeds with me for their captain than burning a few English homesteads. And so may you. Come with me, lads. Once and for all, come. Help me to fight O'Brodar. Then help me to another little adventure which I have on hand, — as pretty a one as ever you heard a minstrel sing, — and then we will fit out a long ship or two, and go where fate leads, — to Constantinople, if you like. What can you do better? You never will get that earldom from Tosti. Lucky for young Waltheof, your uncle if he gets it, — if he, and you too, are not murdered within seven years; for I know Tosti's humor, when he has rivals in his way — "

"Algar will protect us," said one.

"I tell you, Algar is no match for the Godwinssons. If the monk-king died to-morrow, neither his earldom nor his life would be safe. When I saw your father Asbiorn lie dead at Dunsinane, I said, 'There ends the glory of the house of the bear'; and if you wish to make my words come false, then leave England to founder and rot and fall to pieces, — as all men say she is doing, — without your helping to hasten her ruin; and seek glory and wealth too with me around the world! The white bear's blood is in your veins, lads. Take to the sea like your ancestor, and come over the swan's bath with me!"

"That we will!" said the two lads. And well they kept their word.

CHAPTER V.

HOW HEREWARD SUCCORED THE PRINCESS OF CORNWALL A SECOND TIME.

FAT was the feasting and loud was the harping in the halls of Alef the Cornishman, King of Gweek. Savory was the smell of fried pilchard and hake; more savory still that of roast porpoise; most savory of all that of fifty huge squab pies, built up of layers of apples, bacon, onions, and mutton, and at the bottom of each a squab, or young cormorant, which diffused both through the pie and through the ambient air a delicate odor of mingled guano and polecat. And the occasion was worthy alike of the smell and of the noise; for King Alef, finding that after the Ogre's death the neighboring kings were but too ready to make reprisals on him for his champion's murders and robberies, had made a treaty of alliance, offensive and defensive, with Hannibal the son of Gryll, King of Marazion, and had confirmed the same by bestowing on him the hand of his fair daughter. Whether she approved of the match or not, was asked neither by King Alef nor by King Hannibal.

To-night was the bridal-feast. To-morrow morning the church was to hallow the union, and after that Hannibal Grylls was to lead home his bride, among a gallant company.

And as they ate and drank, and harped and piped, there came into that hall four shabbily drest men, — one of them a short, broad fellow, with black elf-locks and a red beard, — and sat them down sneakingly at the very lowest end of all the benches.

In hospitable Cornwall, especially on such a day, every guest was welcome; and the strangers sat peaceably, but ate nothing, though there was both hake and pilchard within reach.

Next to them, by chance, sat a great lourdan of a Dane, as honest, brave, and stupid a fellow as ever tugged at oar; and after a while they fell talking, till the strangers had heard the reason of this great feast, and all the news of the country side.

"But whence did they come, not to know it already; for all Cornwall was talking thereof?"

"O, they came out of Devonshire, seeking service down west, with some merchant or rover, being seafaring men."

The stranger with the black hair had been, meanwhile, earnestly watching the Princess, who sat at the board's head. He saw her watching him in return, and with a face sad enough.

At last she burst into tears.

"What should the bride weep for, at such a merry wedding?" asked he of his companion.

"O, cause enough"; and he told bluntly enough the Princess's story. "And what is more," said he, "the King of Waterford sent a ship over last week, with forty proper lads on board, and two gallant holders with them, to demand her; but for all answer, they were put into the strong house, and there they lie, chained to a log, at this minute. Pity it is and shame, I hold, for I am a Dane myself; and pity, too, that such a bonny lass should go to an unkempt Welshman like this, instead of a tight smart Viking's son, like the Waterford lad."

The stranger answered nothing, but kept his eyes upon the Princess, till she looked at him steadfastly in return.

She turned pale and red again; but after a while she spoke.

"There is a stranger there; and what his rank may be I know not; but he has been thrust down to the lowest seat, in a house that used to honor strangers, instead of treating them like slaves. Let him take this dish from my hand, and eat joyfully, lest when he goes home he may speak scorn of bridegroom and bride, and our Cornish weddings."

The servant brought the dish down: he gave a look at the stranger's shabby dress, turned up his nose, and pretending to mistake, put the dish into the hand of the Dane.

"Hold, lads," quoth the stranger. "If I have ears, that was meant for me."

He seized the platter with both hands; and therewith the hands both of the Cornishman and of the Dane. There was a struggle; but so bitter was the stranger's gripe, that (says the chronicler) the blood burst from the nails of both his opponents.

He was called a "savage," a "devil in man's shape," and other dainty names; but he was left to eat his squab pie in peace.

"Patience, lads," quoth he, as he filled his mouth. "Before I take my pleasure at this wedding, I will hand my own dish round as well as any of you."

Whereat men wondered, but held their tongues.

And when the eating was over and the drinking began, the Princess rose, and came round to drink the farewell health.

With her maids behind her, and her harper before her (so was the Cornish custom), she pledged one by one each of the guests, slave as well as free, while the harper played a tune.

She came down at last to the strangers. Her face was pale, and her eyes red with weeping.

She filled a cup of wine, and one of her maids offered it to the stranger.

He put it back, courteously, but firmly. "Not from your hand," said he.

A growl against his bad manners rose straightway; and the minstrel, who (as often happened in those days) was jester likewise, made merry at his expense, and advised the company to turn the wild beast out of the hall.

"Silence, fool!" said the Princess. "Why should he know our west-country ways? He may take it from my hand, if not from hers."

And she held out to him the cup herself.

He took it, looking her steadily in the face; and it seemed to the minstrel as if their hands lingered together round the cup-handle, and that he saw the glitter of a ring.

Like many another of his craft before and since, he was a vain, meddlesome vagabond, and must needs pry into a secret which certainly did not concern him.

So he could not leave the stranger in peace: and knowing that his privileged calling protected him from that formidable fist, he never passed him by without a sneer or a jest, as he wandered round the table, offering his harp, in the Cornish fashion, to any one who wished to play and sing.

"But not to you, Sir Elf-locks: he that is rude to a pretty girl when she offers him wine, is too great a boor to understand my trade."

"It is a fool's trick," answered the stranger at last, "to put off what you must do at last. If I had but the time, I would pay you for your tune with a better one than you ever heard."

"Take the harp, then, boor!" said the minstrel, with a laugh and a jest.

The stranger took it, and drew from it such music as made all heads turn toward him at once. Then he began to sing, sometimes by himself, and sometimes his comrades, "*more Girviorum tripliciter canentes*," joined their voices in a three-man-glee.

In vain the minstrel, jealous for his own credit, tried to snatch the harp away. The stranger sang on, till all hearts were softened; and the Princess, taking the rich shawl from her shoulders, threw it over those of the stranger, saying that it was a gift too poor for such a scald.

"Scald!" roared the bridegroom (now well in his cups) from the head of the table; "ask what thou wilt, short of my bride and my kingdom, and it is thine."

"Give me, then, Hannibal Grylls, King of Marazion, the Danes who came from Ranald. of Waterford."

"You shall have them! Pity that you have asked for nothing better than such tarry ruffians!"

A few minutes after, the minstrel, bursting with jealousy and rage, was whispering in Hannibal's ear.

The hot old Punic * blood flashed up in his cheeks, and his thin Punic lips curved into a snaky smile. Perhaps the old Punic treachery in his heart; for all that he was heard to reply was, "We must not disturb the good-fellowship of a Cornish wedding."

The stranger, nevertheless, and the Princess likewise, had seen that bitter smile.

Men drank hard and long that night; and when daylight came, the strangers were gone.

In the morning the marriage ceremony was performed; and then began the pageant of leading home the bride. The minstrels went first, harping and piping; then King Hannibal, carrying his bride behind him on a pillion; and after them a string of servants and men-at-arms, leading country ponies laden with the bride's dower. Along with them, unarmed, sulky, and suspicious, walked the forty Danes, who were informed that they should go to Marazion, and there be shipped off for Ireland.

Now, as all men know, those parts of Cornwall, flat and open furze-downs aloft, are cut, for many miles inland, by long branches of tide river, walled in by woods and rocks, which rivers join at last in the great basin of Falmouth harbor; and by crossing one or more of these, the bridal party would save many a mile on their road towards the west.

So they had timed their journey by the tides: lest, finding low water in the rivers, they should have to wade to the ferry-boats waist deep in mud; and going down the steep hillside, through oak and ash and hazel copse, they entered, as many as could, a great flat-bottomed barge, and were rowed across some quarter of a mile, to land under a jutting crag, and go up again by a similar path into the woods.

So the first boat-load went up, the minstrels in front, harping and piping till the greenwood rang, King Hannibal next, with his bride, and behind him spear-men and axe-men, with a Dane between every two.

When they had risen some two hundred feet, and were in the heart of the forest, Hannibal turned, and made a sign to the men behind him.

Then each pair of them seized the Dane between them, and began to bind his hands behind his back.

---

* Hannibal, still a common name in Cornwall, is held — and not unlikely — to have been introduced there by the ancient Phœnician colonists.

"What will you do with us?"

"Send you back to Ireland,—a king never breaks his word,—but pick out your right eyes first, to show your master how much I care for him. Lucky for you that I leave you an eye apiece, to find your friend the harper, whom if I catch, I flay alive."

"You promised!" cried the Princess.

"And so did you, traitress!" and he griped her arm, which was round his waist, till she screamed. "So did you promise: but not to me. And you shall pass your bridal night in my dog-kennel, after my dog-whip has taught you not to give rings again to wandering harpers."

The wretched Princess shuddered; for she knew too well that such an atrocity was easy and common enough. She knew it well. Why should she not? The story of the Cid's Daughters and the Knights of Carrion; the far more authentic one of Robert of Belesme; and many another ugly tale of the early middle age, will prove but too certainly that, before the days of chivalry began, neither youth, beauty, nor the sacred ties of matrimony, could protect women from the most horrible outrages, at the hands of those who should have been their protectors. It was reserved for monks and inquisitors, in the name of religion and the Gospel, to continue, through after centuries, those brutalities toward women of which gentlemen and knights had grown ashamed, save when (as in the case of the Albigense crusaders) monks and inquisitors bade them torture, mutilate, and burn, in the name of Him who died on the cross.

But the words had hardly passed the lips of Hannibal, ere he reeled in the saddle, and fell to the ground, a javelin through his heart.

A strong arm caught the Princess. A voice which she knew bade her have no fear.

"Bind your horse to a tree, for we shall want him; and wait!"

Three well-armed men rushed on the nearest Cornishmen, and hewed them down. A fourth unbound the Dane, and bade him catch up a weapon, and fight for his life.

A second pair were dispatched, a second Dane freed, ere a minute was over; the Cornishmen, struggling up the narrow path toward the shouts above, were overpowered in detail by continually increasing numbers; and ere half an hour was over, the whole party were freed, mounted on the ponies, and making their way over the downs toward the west.

"Noble, noble Hereward!" said the Princess, as she sat behind him on Hannibal's horse. "I knew you from the first moment; and my nurse knew you too. Is she here? Is she safe?"

"I have taken care of that. She has done us too good service to be left here, and be hanged."

"I knew you, in spite of your hair, by your eyes."

"Yes," said Hereward. "It is not every man who carries one gray eye and one blue. The more difficult for me to go mumming when I need."

"But how came you hither, of all places in the world?"

"When you sent your nurse to me last night, to warn me that treason was abroad, it was easy for me to ask your road to Marazion; and easier too, when I found that you would go home the very way we came, to know that I must make my stand here or nowhere."

"The way you came? Then where are we going now?"

"Beyond Marazion, to a little cove, — I cannot tell its name. There lies Sigtryg, your betrothed, and three good ships of war."

"There? Why did he not come for me himself?"

"Why? Because we knew nothing of what was toward. We meant to have sailed straight up your river to your father's town, and taken you out with a high hand. We had sworn an oath, — which, as you saw, I kept, — neither to eat nor drink in your house, save out of your own hands. But the easterly wind would not let us round the Lizard; so we put into that cove, and there I and these two lads, my nephews, offered to go forward as spies, while Sigtryg threw up an earthwork, and made a stand against the Cornish. We meant merely to go back to him, and give him news. But when I found you as good as wedded, I had to do what I could while I could; and I have done it."

"You have, my noble and true champion," said she, kissing him.

"Humph!" quoth Hereward, laughing. "Do not tempt me by being too grateful. It is hard enough to gather honey, like the bees, for other folks to eat. What if I kept you myself, now I have got you?"

"Hereward!"

"O, there is no fear, pretty lady. I have other things to think of than making love to you, — and one is, how we are to get to our ships, and moreover, past Marazion town."

And hard work they had to get thither. The country was soon roused and up in arms; and it was only by wandering a three days' circuit through bogs and moors, till the ponies were utterly tired out, and left behind (the bulkier part of the dowry being left behind with them), that they made their appearance on the shore of Mount's Bay, Hereward leading the Princess in triumph upon Hannibal's horse.

After which they all sailed away for Ireland, and there, like young Beichan, —

"Prepared another wedding,
With all their hearts so full of glee."

And this is the episode of the Cornish Princess, as told by Leofric of Bourne, the cunning minstrel and warlike priest.

CHAPTER VI.

HOW HEREWARD WAS WRECKED UPON THE FLANDERS SHORE

HEREWARD had drunk his share at Sigtryg's wedding. He had helped to harry the lands of O'Brodar till (as King Ranald had threatened) there was not a sucking-pig left in Ivark, and the poor folk died of famine, as they did about every seven years; he had burst (says the chronicler) through the Irish camp with a chosen band of Berserkers, slain O'Brodar in his tent, brought off his war-horn as a trophy, and cut his way back to the Danish army,—a feat in which the two Siwards were grievously wounded; and had in all things shown himself a daring and crafty captain, as careless of his own life as of other folks'.

Then a great home-sickness had seized him. He would go back and see the old house, and the cattle-pastures, and the meres and fens of his boyhood. He would see his widowed mother. Perhaps her heart was softened to him by now, as his was toward her: and if not, he could show her that he could do without her; that others thought him a fine fellow if she did not. Hereward knew that he had won honor and glory for himself; that his name was in the mouths of all warriors and sea-rovers round the coasts as the most likely young champion of the time, able to rival, if he had the opportunity, the prowess of Harold Hardraade himself. Yes, he would go and see his mother: he would be kind if she was kind; if she were not, he would boast and swagger, as he was but too apt to do. That he should go back at the risk of his life; that any one who found him on English ground might kill him; and that many would certainly try to kill him, he knew very well. But that only gave special zest to the adventure.

Martin Lightfoot heard this news with joy.

"I have no more to do here," said he. "I have searched and asked far and wide for the man I want, and he is not on the Irish shores Some say he is gone to the Orkneys, some to Denmark. Never mind; I shall find him before I die."

"And for whom art looking?"

"For one Thord Gunlaugsson, my father."

"And what wantest with him?"

"To put this through his brain." And he showed his axe.

"Thy father's brain?"

"Look you, lord. A man owes his father naught, and his mother all. At least so hold I. 'Man that is of woman born,' say all the world; and they say right. Now, if any man hang up that mother by hands and feet, and flog her to death, is not he that is of that mother born bound to revenge her upon any man, and all the more if that man had first his wicked will of that poor mother? Considering that last, lord, I do not know but what I am bound to avenge my mother's shame upon the man, even if he had never killed her. No, lord, you need not try to talk this out of my head. It has been there nigh twenty years; and I say it over to myself every night before I sleep, lest I should forget the one thing which I must do before I die. Find him I will, and find him I shall, if there be justice in heaven above."

So Hereward asked Ranald for ships, and got at once two good vessels, as payment for his doughty deeds.

One he christened the Garpike, from her narrow build and long beak, and the other the Otter, because, he said, whatever she grappled she would never let go till she heard the bones crack. They were excellent new "snekrs," nearly eighty feet long each; with double banks for twelve oars a-side in the waist, which was open, save a fighting gangway along the sides; with high poop and forecastle decks; and with one large sail apiece, embroidered by Sigtryg's Princess and the other ladies with a huge white bear, which Hereward had chosen as his ensign.

As for men, there were fifty fellows as desperate as Hereward himself, to take service with him for that or any other quest. So they ballasted their ships with great pebbles, stowed under the thwarts, to be used as ammunition in case of boarding; and over them the barrels of ale and pork and meal, well covered with tarpaulins. They stowed in the cabins, fore and aft, their weapons, — swords, spears, axes, bows, chests of arrow-heads, leather bags of bowstrings, mail-shirts, and helmets, and fine clothes for holidays and fighting days. They hung their shields, after the old fashion, out-board along the gunwale, and a right gay show they made; and so rowed out of Waterford harbor amid the tears of the ladies and the cheers of the men.

But, as it befell, the voyage did not prosper. Hereward found his vessels under-manned, and had to sail northward for fresh hands. He got none in Dublin, for they were all gone to the Welsh marches to help Earl Alfgar and King Griffin. So he went on through the Hebrides, intending, of course, to plunder as he went: but there he got but little booty, and lost several men. So he went on again to the Orkneys, to try for fresh hands from the Norse Earl Hereof; but there befell a fresh mishap. They were followed by a whale, which they made sure was a witch-whale, and boded more ill luck; and accordingly they were struck by a storm in the Pentland Frith, and the poor Garpike went on shore on Hoy, and was left there forever and a day, her crew being hardly saved, and very little of her cargo.

However, the Otter was now not only manned, but over manned; and Hereward had to leave a dozen stout fellows in Kirkwall, and sail southward again, singing cheerily to his men, —

"Lightly the long-snake
Leaps after tempests,
Gayly the sun-gleam
Glows after rain.
In labor and daring
Lies luck for all mortals,
Foul winds and foul witch-wives
Fray women alone."

But their mishaps were not over yet. They were hardly out of Stronsay Frith when they saw the witch-whale again, following them up, rolling and spouting and breaching in most uncanny wise. Some said that they saw a gray woman on his back; and they knew — possibly from the look of the sky, but certainly from the whale's behavior — that there was more heavy weather yet coming from the northward.

From that day forward the whale never left them, nor the wild weather neither. They were beaten out of all reckoning. Once they thought they saw low land to the eastward, but what or where who could tell? and as for making it, the wind, which had blown hard from northeast, backed against the sun and blew from west; from which, as well as from the witch-whale, they expected another gale from north and round to northeast.

The men grew sulky and fearful. Some were for trying to run the witch down and break her back, as did Frithiof in like case, when hunted by a whale with two hags upon his back, — an excellent recipe in such cases, but somewhat difficult in a heavy sea. Others said that there was a doomed man on board, and proposed to cast lots till they found him out, and cast him into the sea, as a sacrifice to Ægir the wave-god. But Hereward scouted that as unmanly and cowardly, and sang, —

"With blood of my bold ones,
With bale of my comrades,
Thinks Ægir, brine-thirsty,
His throat he can slake?
Though salt spray, shrill-sounding,
Sweep in swan's-flights above us,
True heroes, troth-plighted,
Together we'll die."

At last, after many days, their strength was all but worn cut. They had long since given over rowing, and contented themselves with running under a close-reefed canvas whithersoever the storm should choose. At night a sea broke over them, and would have swamped the Otter, had she not been the best of sea-boats. But she only rolled the lee shields into the water and out again, shook herself, and went on. Nevertheless, there were three men on the poop when the sea came in, who were not there when it went out.

Wet and wild dawned that morning, showing naught but gray sea and gray air. Then sang Hereward,—

> "Cheerly, my sea-cocks
> Crow for the day-dawn.
> Weary and wet are we,
> Water beladen.
> Wetter our comrades,
> Whelmed by the witch-whale.
> Us Ægir granted
> Grudging, to Gondul,
> Doomed to die dry-shod,
> Daring the foe."

Whereat the hearts of the men were much cheered.

All of a sudden, as is the wont of gales at dawn, the clouds rose, tore up into ribbons, and with a fierce black shower or two, blew clean away; disclosing a bright blue sky, a green rolling sea, and, a few miles off to leeward, a pale yellow line, seen only as they topped a wave, but seen only too well. To keep the ship off shore was impossible; and as they drifted nearer and nearer, the line of sand-hills rose, uglier and more formidable, through the gray spray of the surf.

"We shall die on shore, but not dry-shod," said Martin. "Do any of you knights of the tar-brush know whether we are going to be drowned in Christian waters? I should like a mass or two for my soul, and shall die the happier within sight of a church-tower."

"One Dune is as like another as one pea; we may be anywhere between the Texel and Cap Gris Nez, but I think nearer the latter than the former."

"So much the worse for us," said another. "If we had gone ashore among those Frieslanders, we should have been only knocked on the head outright; but if we fall among the Frenchmen, we shall be clapt in prison strong, and tortured till we find ransom."

"I don't see that," said Martin. "We can all be drowned if we like, I suppose?"

"Drowned we need not be, if we be men," said the old sailing-master to Hereward. "The tide is full high, and that gives us one chance for our lives. Keep her head straight, and row like fiends when we are once in the surf, and then beach her up high and dry, and take what befalls after."

And what was likely to befall was ugly enough. Then, as centuries after, all wrecks and wrecked men were public prey; shipwrecked mariners were liable to be sold as slaves; and the petty counts of the French and Flemish shores were but too likely to extract ransom by prison and torture, as Guy Earl of Ponthieu would have done (so at least William Duke of Normandy hinted) by Harold Godwinsson, had not William, for his own politic ends, begged the release of the shipwrecked earl.

Already they had been seen from the beach. The country folk, who were prowling about the shore after the waifs of the storm, deserted "jetsom and lagend," and crowded to meet the richer prize which was coming in "flotsom," to become "jetsom" in its turn.

"Axe-men and bow-men, put on your harness, and be ready; but neither strike nor shoot till I give the word. We must land peaceably if we can; if not, we will die fighting."

So said Hereward, and took the rudder into his own hand. "Now then," as she rushed into the breakers, "pull together, rowers all, and with a will."

The men yelled, and sprang from the thwarts as they tugged at the oars. The sea boiled past them, surged into the waist, blinded them with spray. She grazed the sand once, twice, thrice, leaping forward gallantly each time; and then, pressed by a huge wave, drove high and dry upon the beach, as the oars snapt right and left, and the men tumbled over each other in heaps.

The peasants swarmed down like flies to a carcass; but they recoiled as there rose over the forecastle bulwarks, not the broad hats of peaceful buscarles, but peaked helmets, round red shields, and glittering axes. They drew back, and one or two arrows flew from the crowd into the ship. But at Hereward's command no arrows were shot in answer.

"Bale her out quietly; and let us show these fellows that we are not afraid of them. That is the best chance of peace."

At this moment a mounted party came down between the sand-hills; it might be, some twenty strong. Before them rode a boy on a jennet, and by him a clerk, as he seemed, upon a mule. They stopped to talk with the peasants, and then to consult among themselves.

Suddenly the boy turned from his party; and galloping down the shore, while the clerk called after him in vain, reined up his horse, fetlock deep in water, within ten yards of the ship's bows

"Yield yourselves!" he shouted, in French, as he brandished a hunting spear. "Yield yourselves, or die!"

Hereward looked at him smiling, as he sat there, keeping the head of his frightened horse toward the ship with hand and heel, his long locks streaming in the wind, his face full of courage and command, and of honesty and sweetness withal; and thought that he had never seen so fair a lad.

"And who art thou, thou pretty, bold boy?" asked Hereward, in French.

"I," said he, haughtily enough, as resenting Hereward's familiar "thou," "am Arnulf, grandson and heir of Baldwin, Marquis of Flanders, and lord of this land. And to his grace I call on you to surrender yourselves."

Hereward looked, not only with interest, but respect, upon the grandson of one of the most famous and prosperous of northern potentates, the descendant of the mighty Charlemagne himself. He turned and told the men who the boy was.

"It would be a good trick," quoth one, "to catch that young whelp, and keep him as a hostage."

"Here is what will have him on board before he can turn," said another, as he made a running noose in a rope.

"Quiet, men! Am I master in this ship or you?"

Hereward saluted the lad courteously. "Verily the blood of Baldwin of the Iron Arm has not degenerated. I am happy to behold so noble a son of so noble a race."

"And who are you, who speak French so well, and yet by your dress are neither French nor Fleming?"

"I am Harold Naemansson, the Viking; and these my men. I am here, sailing peaceably for England; as for yielding,— mine yield to no living man, but die as we are, weapon in hand. I have heard of your grandfather, that he is a just man and a bountiful; therefore take this message to him, young sir. If he have wars toward, I and my men will fight for him with all our might, and earn hospitality and ransom with our only treasure, which is our swords. But if he be at peace, then let him bid us go in peace, for we are Vikings, and must fight, or rot and die."

"You are Vikings?" cried the boy, pressing his horse into the foam so eagerly, that the men, mistaking his intent, had to be represt again by Hereward. "You are Vikings! Then come on shore, and welcome. You shall be my friends. You shall be my brothers. I will answer to my grandfather. I have longed to see Vikings. I long to be a Viking myself."

"By the hammer of Thor," cried the old master, "and thou wouldst make a bonny one, my lad."

Hereward hesitated, delighted with the boy, but by no means sure of his power to protect them.

But the boy rode back to his companions, who had by this time ridden cautiously down to the sea, and talked and gesticulated eagerly.

Then the clerk rode down and talked with Hereward.

"Are you Christians?" shouted he, before he would adventure himself near the ship.

"Christians we are, Sir Clerk, and dare do no harm to a man of God."

The Clerk rode nearer; his handsome palfrey, furred cloak, rich gloves and boots, moreover his air of command, showed that he was no common man.

"I," said he, "am the Abbot of St. Bertin of Sithiu, and tutor of yonder prince. I can bring down, at a word, against you, the Chatelain of St. Omer, with all his knights, besides knights and men-at-arms of my own. But I am a man of peace, and not of war, and would have no blood shed if I can help it."

"Then make peace," said Hereward. "Your lord may kill us if he will, or have us for his guests if he will. If he does the first, we shall kill, each of us, a few of his men before we die; if the latter, we shall kill a few of his foes. If you be a man of God, you will counsel him accordingly."

"Alas! alas!" said the Abbot, with a shudder, "that, ever since Adam's fall, sinful man should talk of nothing but slaying and being slain; not knowing that his soul is slain already by sin, and that a worse death awaits him hereafter than that death of the body of which he makes so light!"

"A very good sermon, my Lord Abbot, to listen to next Sunday morning: but we are hungry and wet and desperate just now; and if you do not settle this matter for us, our blood will be on your head, — and may be your own likewise."

The Abbot rode out of the water faster than he had ridden in, and a fresh consultation ensued, after which the boy, with a warning gesture to his companions, turned and galloped away through the sand-hills.

"He is gone to his grandfather himself, I verily believe," quoth Hereward.

They waited for some two hours, unmolested; and, true to their policy of seeming recklessness, shifted and dried themselves as well as they could, ate what provisions were unspoilt by the salt water, and, broaching the last barrel of ale, drank healths to each other and to the Flemings on shore.

At last down rode, with the boy, a noble-looking man, and behind him more knights and men-at-arms. He announced himself as Manasses, Chatelain St. Omer, and repeated the demand to surrender.

"There is no need for it," said Hereward. "We are already

that young prince's guests. He has said that we shall be his friends and brothers. He has said that he will answer to his grandfather, the great Marquis, whom I and mine shall be proud to serve. I claim the word of a descendant of Charlemagne."

"And you shall have it!" cried the boy. "Chatelain! Abbot! these men are mine. They shall come with me, and lodge in St. Bertin."

"Heaven forefend!" murmured the Abbot.

"They will be safe, at least, within your ramparts," whispered the Chatelain.

"And they shall tell me about the sea. Have I not told you how I long for Vikings; how I will have Vikings of my own, and sail the seas with them, like my Uncle Robert, and go to Spain and fight the Moors, and to Constantinople and marry the Kaiser's daughter? Come," he cried to Hereward, "come on shore, and he that touches you or your ship, touches me!"

"Sir Chatelain and my Lord Abbot," said Hereward, "you see that, Viking though I be, I am no barbarous heathen, but a French-speaking gentleman, like yourselves. It had been easy for me, had I not been a man of honor, to have cast a rope, as my sailors would have had me do, over that young boy's fair head, and haled him on board, to answer for my life with his own. But I loved him, and trusted him, as I would an angel out of heaven; and I trust him still. To him, and him only, will I yield myself, on condition that I and my men shall keep all our arms and treasure, and enter his service, to fight his foes, and his grandfather's, wheresoever they will, by land or sea."

"Fair sir," said the Abbot, "pirate though you call yourself, you speak so courtly and clerkly, that I, too, am inclined to trust you; and if my young lord will have it so, into St. Bertin I will receive you, till our lord, the Marquis, shall give orders about you and yours."

So promises were given all round; and Hereward explained the matter to the men, without whose advice (for they were all as free as himself) he could not act.

"Needs must," grunted they, as they packed up each his little valuables.

Then Hereward sheathed his sword, and leaping from the bow, came up to the boy.

"Put your hands between his, fair sir," said the Chatelain.

"That is not the manner of Vikings."

And he took the boy's right hand, and grasped it in the plain English fashion.

"There is the hand of an honest man. Come down, men, and take this young lord's hand, and serve him in the wars as I will do."

One by one the men came down; and each took Arnulf's hand,

and shook it till the lad's face grew red. But none of them bowed, or made obeisance. They looked the boy full in the face, and as they stepped back, stared round upon the ring of armed men with a smile and something of a swagger.

"These are they who bow to no man, and call no man master," whispered the Abbot.

And so they were: and so are their descendants of Scotland and Northumbria, unto this very day.

The boy sprang from his horse, and walked among them and round them in delight. He admired and handled their long-handled double axes; their short sea-bows of horn and deer-sinew; their red Danish jerkins; their blue sea-cloaks, fastened on the shoulder with rich brooches; and the gold and silver bracelets on their wrists. He wondered at their long shaggy beards, and still more at the blue patterns with which the English among them, Hereward especially, were tattooed on throat and arm and knee.

"Yes, you are Vikings, — just such as my Uncle Robert tells me of."

Hereward knew well the exploits of Robert le Frison in Spain and Greece. "I trust that your noble uncle," he asked, "is well? He was one of us poor sea-cocks, and sailed the swan's path gallantly, till he became a mighty prince. Here is a man here who was with your noble uncle in Byzant."

And he thrust forward the old master.

The boy's delight knew no bounds. He should tell him all about that in St. Bertin.

Then he rode back to the ship, and round and round her (for the tide by that time had left her high and dry), and wondered at her long snake-like lines, and carven stem and stern.

"Tell me about this ship. Let me go on board of her. I have never seen a ship inland at Mons there; and even here there are only heavy ugly busses, and little fishing-boats. No. You must be all hungry and tired. We will go to St. Bertin at once, and you shall be feasted royally. Hearken, villains!" shouted he to the peasants. "This ship belongs to the fair sir here, — my guest and friend; and if any man dares to steal from her a stave or a nail, I will have his thief's hand cut off."

"The ship, fair lord," said Hereward, "is yours, not mine. You should build twenty more after her pattern, and man them with such lads as these, and then go down to

    ' Miklagard and Spanialand,
     That lie so far on the lee, O!'

as did your noble uncle before you."

And so they marched inland, after the boy had dismounted one of his men, and put Hereward on the horse.

"You gentlemen of the sea can ride as well as sail," said the Chatelain, as he remarked with some surprise Hereward's perfect seat and hand.

"We should soon learn to fly likewise," laughed Hereward, "if there were any booty to be picked up in the clouds there overhead"; and he rode on by Arnulf's side, as the lad questioned him about the sea, and nothing else.

"Ah, my boy," said Hereward at last, "look there, and let those be Vikings who must."

And he pointed to the rich pastures, broken by strips of cornland and snug farms, which stretched between the sea and the great forest of Flanders.

"What do you mean?"

But Hereward was silent. It was so like his own native fens. For a moment there came over him the longing for a home. To settle down in such a fair fat land, and call good acres his own; and marry and beget stalwart sons, to till the old estate when he could till no more. Might not that be a better life — at least a happier one — than restless, homeless, aimless adventure? And now, just as he had had a hope of peace, — a hope of seeing his own land, his own folk, perhaps of making peace with his mother and his king, — the very waves would not let him rest, but sped him forth, a storm-tossed waif, to begin life anew, fighting he cared not whom or why, in a strange land.

So he was silent and sad withal.

"What does he mean?" asked the boy of the Abbot.

"He seems a wise man: let him answer for himself."

The boy asked once more.

"Lad! lad!" said Hereward, waking as from a dream. "If you be heir to such a fair land as that, thank God for it, and pray to Him that you may rule it justly, and keep it in peace, as they say your grandfather and your father do; and leave glory and fame and the Vikings' bloody trade to those who have neither father nor mother, wife nor land, but live like the wolf of the wood, from one meal to the next."

"I thank you for those words, Sir Harold," said the good Abbot, while the boy went on abashed, and Hereward himself was startled at his own saying, and rode silent till they crossed the drawbridge of St. Bertin, and entered that ancient fortress, so strong that it was the hiding-place in war time for all the treasures of the country, and so sacred withal that no woman, dead or alive, was allowed to defile it by her presence; so that the wife of Baldwin the Bold, ancestor of Arnulf, wishing to lie by her husband, had to remove his corpse from St. Bertin to the Abbey of Blandigni, where the Counts of Flanders lay in glory for many a generation.

The pirates entered, not without gloomy distrust, the gates of
that consecrated fortress; while the monks in their turn were
(and with some reason) considerably frightened when they were
asked to entertain as guests forty Norse rovers. Loudly did the
elder among them bewail (in Latin, lest their guests should understand
too much) the present weakness of their monastery, where
St. Bertin was left to defend himself and his monks all alone
against the wicked world outside. Far different had been their
case some hundred and seventy years before. Then St. Valeri
and St. Riquier of Ponthieu, transported thither from their own
resting-places in France for fear of the invading Northmen, had
joined their suffrages and merits to those of St. Bertin, with
such success that the abbey had never been defiled by the foot of
the heathen. But, alas! the saints, that is their bodies, after
a while became homesick; and St. Valeri appearing in a dream
to Hugh Capet, bade him bring them back to France in spite of
Arnulf, Count of those parts, who wished much to retain so valuable
an addition to his household gods.

But in vain. Hugh Capet was a man who took few denials.
With knights and men-at-arms he came, and Count Arnulf had
to send home the holy corpses with all humility, and leave St.
Bertin all alone.

Whereon St. Valeri appeared in a dream to Hugh Capet, and
said unto him, "Because thou hast zealously done what I commanded,
thou and thy successors shall reign in the kingdom of
France to everlasting generations." *

However, there was no refusing the grandson and heir of Count
Baldwin; and the hearts of the monks were comforted by hearing
that Hereward was a good Christian, and that most of his crew
had been at least baptized. The Abbot therefore took courage,
and admitted them into the hospice, with solemn warnings as to the
doom which they might expect if they took the value of a horse-nail
from the patrimony of the blessed saint. Was he less powerful
or less careful of his own honor than St. Lieven of Holthem,
who, not more than fifty years before, had struck stone-blind four
soldiers of the Emperor Henry's, who had dared, after warning,
to plunder the altar? † Let them remember, too, the fate of their
own forefathers, the heathens of the North, and the check which,
one hundred and seventy years before, they had received under
those very walls. They had exterminated the people of Walcheren;
they had taken prisoners Count Regnier; they had burnt
Ghent, Bruges, and St. Omer itself, close by; they had left naught

---

* Histoire des Comtes de Flandre, par E. le Glay. E. gestis SS. R'charii et
Walerici.
† Ibid.

between the Scheldt and the Somme, save stark corpses and blackened ruins. What could withstand them till they dared to lift audacious hands against the heavenly lord who sleeps there in Sithiu? Then they poured down in vain over the Heilig-Veld, innumerable as the locusts. Poor monks, strong in the protection of the holy Bertin, sallied out and smote them hip and thigh, singing their psalms the while. The ditches of the fortress were filled with unbaptized corpses; the piles of vine-twigs which they lighted to burn down the gates turned their flames into the Norsemen's faces at the bidding of St. Bertin; and they fled from that temporal fire to descend into that which is eternal, while the gates of the pit were too narrow for the multitude of their miscreant souls.*

So the Norsemen heard, and feared; and only cast longing eyes at the gold and tapestries of the altars, when they went in to mass.

For the good Abbot, gaining courage still further, had pointed out to Hereward and his men that it had been surely by the merits and suffrages of the blessed St. Bertin that they had escaped a watery grave.

Hereward and his men, for their part, were not inclined to deny the theory. That they had miraculously escaped, from the accident of the tide being high, they knew full well; and that St. Bertin should have done them the service was probable enough. He, of course, was lord and master in his own country, and very probably a few miles out to sea likewise.

So Hereward assured the Abbot that he had no mind to eat St. Bertin's bread, or accept his favors, without paying honestly for them; and after mass he took from his shoulders a handsome silk cloak (the only one he had), with a great Scotch Cairngorm brooch, and bade them buckle it on the shoulders of the great image of St. Bertin.

At which St. Bertin was so pleased (being, like many saints, male and female, somewhat proud after their death of the finery which they despised during life), that he appeared that night to a certain monk, and told him that if Hereward would continue duly to honor him, the blessed St. Bertin, and his monks at that place, he would, in his turn, insure him victory in all his battles by land and sea.

After which Hereward stayed quietly in the abbey certain days; and young Arnulf, in spite of all remonstrances from the Abbot, would never leave his side till he had heard from him and from his men as much of their adventures as they thought it prudent to relate.

* This gallant feat was performed in A. D. 891.

CHAPTER VII.

HOW HEREWARD WENT TO THE WAR AT GUISNES.

The dominion of Baldwin of Lille, — Baldwin the Debonair — Marquis of Flanders, and just then the greatest potentate in Europe after the Kaiser of Germany and the Kaiser of Constantinople, extended from the Somme to the Scheldt, including thus much territory which now belongs to France. His forefathers had ruled there ever since the days of the "Foresters" of Charlemagne, who held the vast forests against the heathens of the fens, and of that famous Baldwin Bras-de-fer, — who, when the foul fiend rose out of the Scheldt, and tried to drag him down, tried cold steel upon him (being a practical man), and made his ghostly adversary feel so sorely the weight of the "iron arm," that he retired into his native mud, — or even lower still.

He, like a daring knight as he was, ran off with his (so some say) early love, Judith, daughter of Charles the Bald of France, a descendant of Charlemagne himself. Married up to Ethelwulf of England, and thus stepmother of Alfred the Great, — after his death behaving, alas for her! not over wisely or well, she had verified the saying:

> "Nous revenons toujours
> À nos premiers amours,"

and ran away with Baldwin.

Charles, furious that one of his earls, a mere lieutenant and creature, should dare to marry a daughter of Charlemagne's house, would have attacked him with horse and foot, fire and sword, had not Baldwin been the only man who could defend his northern frontier against the heathen Norsemen.

The Pope, as Charles was his good friend, fulminated against Baldwin the excommunication destined for him who stole a widow for his wife, and all his accomplices.

Baldwin and Judith went straight to Rome, and told their story to the Pope.

He, honest man, wrote to Charles the Bald a letter which still remains, — alike merciful, sentimental, and politic, with its usual ingrained element of what we now call (from the old monkish word "cantare") cant. Of Baldwin's horrible wickedness there is no doubt. Of his repentance (in all matters short of amendment of life, by giving up the fair Judith), still less. But the Pope has "another motive for so acting. He fears lest Baldwin, under the weight of Charles's wrath and indignation, should make alliance with the Normans, enemies of God and the holy Church; and thus an occasion arise of peril and scandal for the people of God, whom Charles ought to rule," &c., &c., which if it happened, it would be worse for them and for Charles's own soul.

To which very sensible and humane missive (times and creeds being considered), Charles answered, after pouting and sulking, by making Baldwin *bona fide* king of all between Somme and Scheldt, and leaving him to raise a royal race from Judith, the wicked and the fair.

This all happened about A. D. 863. Two hundred years after, there ruled over that same land Baldwin the Debonair, as "Marquis of the Flamands."

Baldwin had had his troubles. He had fought the Count of Holland. He had fought the Emperor of Germany; during which war he had burnt the cathedral of Nimeguen, and did other unrighteous and unwise things; and had been beaten after all.

Baldwin had had his troubles, and had deserved them. But he had had his glories, and had deserved them likewise. He had cut the Fossé Neuf, or new dike, which parted Artois from Flanders. He had so beautified the cathedral of Lille, that he was called Baldwin of Lille to his dying day. He had married Adela, the queen countess, daughter of the King of France. He had become tutor of Philip, the young King, and more or less thereby regent of the north of France, and had fulfilled his office wisely and well. He had married his eldest son, Baldwin the Good, to the terrible sorceress Richilda, heiress of Hainault, wherefore the bridegroom was named Baldwin of Mons. He had married one of his daughters, Matilda, to William of Normandy, afterwards the Conqueror; and another, Judith, to Tosti Godwinsson, the son of the great Earl Godwin of England. She afterwards married Welf, Duke of Bavaria; whereby, it may be, the blood of Baldwin of Flanders runs in the veins of Queen Victoria.

And thus there were few potentates of the North more feared and respected than Baldwin, the good-natured Earl of Flanders.

But one sore thorn in the side he had, which other despots after him shared with him, and with even worse success in extracting it,—namely, the valiant men of Scaldmariland, which we now call Holland. Of them hereafter. At the moment of Hereward's arrival, he was troubled with a lesser thorn, the Count of Guisnes, who would not pay him up certain dues, and otherwise acknowledge his sovereignty.

Therefore when the Chatelain of St. Omer sent him word to Bruges that a strange Viking had landed with his crew, calling himself Harold Naemansson, and offering to take service with him, he returned for answer that the said Harold might make proof of his faith and prowess upon the said Count, in which, if he acquitted himself like a good knight, Baldwin would have further dealings with him.

So the Chatelain of St. Omer, with all his knights and men-at-arms, and Hereward with his sea-cocks, marched northwest up to Guisnes, with little Arnulf cantering alongside in high glee; for it was the first war that he had ever seen.

And they came to the Castle of Guisnes, and summoned the Count, by trumpet and herald, to pay or fight.

Whereon, the Count preferring the latter, certain knights of his came forth and challenged the knights of St. Omer to fight them man to man. Whereon there was the usual splintering of lances and slipping up of horses, and hewing at heads and shoulders so well defended in mail that no one was much hurt. The archers and arbalisters, meanwhile, amused themselves with shooting at the castle walls, out of which they chipped several small pieces of stone. And when they were all tired, they drew off on both sides, and went in to dinner.

At which Hereward's men, who were accustomed to a more serious fashion of fighting, stood by, mightily amused, and vowing it was as pretty a play as ever they saw in their lives.

The next day the same comedy was repeated.

"Let me go in against those knights, Sir Chatelain," asked Hereward, who felt the lust of battle tingling in him from head to heel; "and try if I cannot do somewhat towards deciding all this. If we fight no faster than we did yesterday, our beards will be grown down to our knees before we take Guisnes."

"Let my Viking go!" cried Arnulf. "Let me see him fight!" as if he had been a pet gamecock or bulldog.

"You can break a lance, fine sir, if it please you," said the Chatelain.

"I break more than lances," quoth Hereward as he cantered off.

"You," said he to his men, "draw round hither to the left; and when I drive the Frenchmen to the right, make a run for it, and get between them and the castle gate; and we will try the Danish axe against their horses' legs."

Then Hereward spurred his horse, shouting, "A bear! a

bear!" and dashed into the press; and therein did mightily, like any Turpin or Roland, till he saw lie on the ground, close to the castle gate, one of the Chatelain's knights with four Guisnes knights around him. Then at those knights he rode, and slew them every one; and mounted that wounded knight on his own horse and led him across the field, though the archers shot sore at him from the wall. And when the press of knights rode at him, his Danish men got between them and the castle, and made a stand to cover him. Then the Guisnes knights rode at them scornfully, crying,—

"What footpad churls have we here, who fancy they can face horsed knights?"

But they did not know the stuff of the Danish men; who all shouted, "A bear! a bear!" and turned the lances' points with their targets, and hewed off the horses' heads, and would have hewed off the riders' likewise, crying that the bear must be fed, had not Hereward bidden them give quarter according to the civilized fashion of France and Flanders. Whereon all the knights who were not taken rode right and left, and let them pass through in peace, with several prisoners, and him whom Hereward had rescued.

At which little Arnulf was as proud as if he had done it himself; and the Chatelain sent word to Baldwin that the new-comer was a prudhomme of no common merit; while the heart of the Count of Guisnes became as water; and his knights, both those who were captives and those who were not, complained indignantly of the unchivalrous trick of the Danes,— how villanous for men on foot, not only to face knights, but to bring them down to their own standing ground by basely cutting off their horses' heads!

To which Hereward answered, that he knew the rules of chivalry as well as any of them; but he was hired, not to joust at a tournament, but to make the Count of Guisnes pay his lord Baldwin, and make him pay he would.

The next day he bade his men sit still and look on, and leave him to himself. And when the usual "monomachy" began, he singled out the burliest and boldest knight whom he saw, rode up to him, lance point in air, and courteously asked him to come and be killed in fair fight. The knight being, says the chronicler, "magnificent in valor of soul and counsel of war, and held to be as a lion in fortitude throughout the army," and seeing that Hereward was by no means a large or heavy man, replied as courteously, that he should have great pleasure in trying to kill Hereward. On which they rode some hundred yards out of the press, calling out that they were to be left alone by both sides, for it was an honorable duel, and, turning their horses, charged.

After which act they found themselves and their horses all four in a row, sitting on their hind-quarters on the ground, amid the fragments of their lances.

"Well ridden!" shouted they both at once, as they leaped up laughing and drew their swords.

After which they hammered away at each other merrily in "the devil's smithy"; the sparks flew, and the iron rang, and all men stood still to see that gallant fight.

So they watched and cheered, till Hereward struck his man such a blow under the ear, that he dropped, and lay like a log.

"I think I can carry you," quoth Hereward, and picking him up, he threw him over his shoulder, and walked toward his men.

"A bear! a bear!" shouted they in delight, laughing at the likeness between Hereward's attitude, and that of a bear waddling off on his hind legs with his prey in his arms.

"He should have killed his bullock outright before he went to carry him. Look there!"

And the knight, awaking from his swoon, struggled violently (says Leofric) to escape.

But Hereward, though the smaller, was the stronger man; and crushing him in his arms, walked on steadily.

"Knights, to the rescue! Hoibricht is taken!" shouted they of Guisnes, galloping towards him.

"A bear! a bear! To me, Biornssons! To me, Vikings all!" shouted Hereward. And the Danes leapt up, and ran toward him, axe in hand.

The Chatelain's knights rode up likewise; and so it befell, that Hereward carried his prisoner safe into camp.

"And who are you, gallant knight?" asked he of his prisoner.

"Hoibricht, nephew of Eustace, Count of Guisnes."

"So I suppose you will be ransomed. Till then — Armorer!"

And the hapless Hoibricht found himself chained and fettered, and sent off to Hereward's tent, under the custody of Martin Lightfoot.

"The next day," says the chronicler, "the Count of Guisnes, stupefied with grief at the loss of his nephew, sent the due honor and service to his prince, besides gifts and hostages."

And so ended the troubles of Baldwin, and Eustace of Guisnes.

CHAPTER VIII.

HOW A FAIR LADY EXERCISED THE MECHANICAL ART TO WIN
HEREWARD'S LOVE.

THE fair Torfrida sat in an upper room of her mother's house in St. Omer, alternately looking out of the window and at a book of mechanics. In the garden outside, the wryneck (as is his fashion in May) was calling Pi-pi-pi among the gooseberry bushes, till the cob-walls rang again. In the book was a Latin recipe for drying the poor wryneck, and using him as a philtre which should compel the love of any person desired. Mechanics, it must be understood, in those days were considered as identical with mathematics, and those again with astrology and magic; so that the old chronicler, who says that Torfrida was skilled in "the mechanic art," uses the word in the same sense as does the author of the History of Ramsey, who tells us how a certain holy bishop of St. Dunstan's party, riding down to Corfe through the forest, saw the wicked queen-mother Elfrida (her who had St. Edward stabbed at Corfe Gate) exercising her "mechanic art," under a great tree; in plain English, performing heathen incantations; and how, when she saw that she was discovered, she tempted him to deadly sin: but when she found him proof against allurement, she had him into her bower; and there the enchantress and her ladies slew him by thrusting red-hot bodkins under his arms, so that the blessed man was martyred without any sign of wound. Of all which let every man believe as much as he list.

Torfrida had had peculiar opportunities of learning mechanics. The fairest and richest damsel in St. Omer, she had been left early by her father an orphan, to the care of a superstitious mother and of a learned uncle, the Abbot of St. Bertin. Her mother was a Provençale, one of those Arlesiennes whose dark Greek beauty still shines, like diamonds set in jet, in the doorways of the quaint old city. Gay enough in her youth, she had, like a true Southern woman, taken to superstition in her old age and spent her days in the churches, leaving Torfrida to do and learn what she would. Her nurse, moreover, was a Lapp woman, carried off in some pirating foray, and skilled in all the sorceries for which the Lapps were famed throughout the North. Her uncle, partly from good-nature, partly from a pious hope that she might "enter religion," and leave her wealth to the Church, had made her his pupil, and taught her the mysteries of books; and she had proved to be a strangely apt scholar. Grammar, rhetoric, Latin prose and poetry, such as were taught in those days, she mastered ere she was grown up. Then she fell upon romance, and Charlemagne and his Paladins, the heroes of Troy, Alexander and his generals, peopled her imagination. She had heard, too, of the great necromancer Virgilius (for into such the middle age transformed the poet), and, her fancy already excited by her Lapp nurse's occult science, she began eagerly to court forbidden lore.

Forbidden, indeed, magic was by the Church in public; but as a reality, not as an imposture. Those whose consciences were tough and their faith weak, had little scruple in applying to a witch, and asking help from the powers below, when the saints above were slack to hear them. Churchmen, even, were bold enough to learn the mysteries of nature, Algebra, Judicial Astrology, and the occult powers of herbs, stones, and animals, from the Mussulman doctors of Cordova and Seville; and, like Pope Gerbert, mingle science and magic, in a fashion excusable enough in days when true inductive science did not exist.

Nature had her miraculous powers, — how far good, how far evil, who could tell? The belief that God was the sole maker and ruler of the universe was confused and darkened by the cross-belief, that the material world had fallen under the dominion of Satan and his demons; that millions of spirits, good and evil in every degree, exercised continually powers over crops and cattle, mines and wells, storms and lightning, health and disease. Riches, honors, and royalties, too, were under the command of the powers of darkness. For that generation, which was but too apt to take its Bible in hand upside down, had somehow a firm faith in the word of the Devil, and believed devoutly his somewhat startling assertion, that the kingdoms of the world were his, and the glory of them; for to him they were delivered, and to whomsoever he would he gave them: while it had a proportionally weak faith in our Lord's answer, that they were to worship and serve the Lord God alone. How far these powers extended, how far they might be counteracted, how far lawfully employed, were questions which exercised the minds of men, and produced a voluminous literature for several centuries, till the search died out, for very weariness of failure, at the end of the seventeenth century.

The Abbot of St. Bertin, therefore, did not hesitate to keep in his private library more than one volume which he would not have willingly lent to the simple monks under his charge; nor to Torfrida either, had she not acquired so complete a command over the good old man, that he could deny her nothing.

So she read of Gerbert, Pope Silvester II., who had died only a generation back: how (to quote William of Malmesbury) "he learned at Seville till he surpassed Ptolemy with the astrolabe, Alcandrus in astronomy, and Julius Firmicus in judicial astrology; how he learned what the singing and flight of birds portended, and acquired the art of calling up spirits from hell; and, in short, whatever — hurtful or healthful — human curiosity had discovered, besides the lawful sciences of arithmetic and astronomy, music and geometry"; how he acquired from the Saracens the abacus (a counting table); how he escaped from the Moslem magician, his tutor, by making a compact with the foul fiend, and putting himself beyond the power of magic, by hanging himself under a wooden bridge so as to touch neither earth nor water; how he taught Robert, King of France, and Otto the Kaiser; how he made an hydraulic organ which played tunes by steam, which stood even then in the Cathedral of Rheims; how he discovered in the Campus Martius at Rome wondrous treasures, and a golden king and queen, golden courtiers and guards, all lighted by a single carbuncle, and guarded by a boy with a bent bow; who, when Gerbert's servant stole a golden knife, shot an arrow at that carbuncle, and all was darkness, and yells of demons.

All this Torfrida had read; and read, too, how Gerbert's brazen head had told him that he should be Pope, and not die till he had sung mass at Jerusalem; and how both had come true, — the latter in mockery; for he was stricken with deadly sickness in Rome, as he sang mass at the church called Jerusalem, and died horribly, tearing himself in pieces.

Which terrible warning had as little effect on Torfrida as other terrible warnings have on young folk, who are minded to eat of the fruit of the tree of knowledge of good and evil.

So Torfrida beguiled her lonely life in that dull town, looking out over dreary flats and muddy dikes, by a whole dream-world of fantastic imaginations, and was ripe and ready for any wild deed which her wild brain might suggest.

Pure she was all the while, generous and noble-hearted, and with a deep and sincere longing — as one soul in ten thousand has — after knowledge for its own sake; but ambitious exceedingly, and that not of monastic sanctity. She laughed to scorn the notion of a nunnery; and laughed to scorn equally the notion of marrying any knight, however much of a prudhomme, whom she had yet seen. Her uncle and Marquis Baldwin could have between them compelled her, as an orphan heiress, to marry whom they liked. But Torfrida had as yet bullied the Abbot and coaxed the Count successfully. Lances had been splintered, helmits split, and more than one life lost in her honor; but she had only, as the best safeguard she could devise, given some hint of encouragement to one Ascelin, a tall knight of St. Valeri, the most renowned bully of those parts, by bestowing on him a scrap of ribbon, and bidding him keep it against all comers. By this means she insured the personal chastisement of all other youths who dared to lift their eyes to her, while she by no means bound herself to her spadassin of St. Valeri. It was all very brutal, but so was the time; and what better could a poor lady do in days when no man's life or woman's honor was safe, unless — as too many were forced to do — she retired into a cloister, and got from the Church that peace which this world certainly could not give, and, happily, dared not take away?

The arrival of Hereward and his men had of course stirred the great current of her life, and indeed that of St. Omer, usually as stagnant as that of the dikes round its wall. Who the unknown champion was, — for his name of "Naemansson" showed that he was concealing something at least, — whence he had come, and what had been his previous exploits, busied all the gossips of the town. Would he and his men rise and plunder the abbey? Was not the Chatelain mad in leaving young Arnulf with him all day? Madder still, in taking him out to battle against the Count of Guisnes? He might be a spy, — the *avant-courrier* of some great invading force. He was come to spy out the nakedness of the land, and would shortly vanish, to return with Harold Hardraade of Norway, or Sweyn of Denmark, and all their hosts. Nay, was he not Harold Hardraade himself in disguise? And so forth. All which Torfrida heard, and thought within herself that, be he who he might, she should like to look on him, again.

Then came the news how the very first day that he had gone out against the Count of Guisnes he had gallantly rescued a wounded man. A day or two after came fresh news of some doughty deed; and then another, and another. And when Hereward returned, after a week's victorious fighting, all St. Omer was in the street to stare at him.

Then Torfrida heard enough, and, had it been possible, more than enough, of Hereward and his prowess.

And when they came riding in, the great Marquis at the head of them all, with Robert le Frison on one side of him, and on the other Hereward, looking "as fresh as flowers in May," she looked down on him out of her little lattice in the gable, and loved him, once and for all, with all her heart and soul.

And Hereward looked up at her and her dark blue eyes and dark raven locks, and thought her the fairest thing that he had ever seen, and asked who she might be, and heard; and as he heard he forgot all about the Sultan's daughter, and the Princess of Constantinople, and the Fairy of Brocheliaunde, and all the other pretty birds which were still in the bush about the wide world; and thought for many a day of naught but the pretty bird which he held — so conceited was he of his own powers of winning her — there safe in hand in St. Omer.

So he cast about to see her, and to win her love. And she cast about to see him, and win his love. But neither saw the other for a while; and it might have been better for one of them had they never seen the other again.

If Torfrida could have foreseen, and foreseen, and foreseen — why, if she were true woman, she would have done exactly what she did, and taken the bitter with the sweet, the unknown with the known, as we all must do in life, unless we wish to live and die alone.

CHAPTER IX.

HOW HLREWARD WENT TO THE WAR IN SCALDMARILAND.

IT has been shown how the Count of Guisnes had been a thorn in the side of Baldwin of Lille, and how that thorn was drawn out by Hereward. But a far sharper thorn in his side, and one which had troubled many a Count before, and was destined to trouble others afterward, was those unruly Hollanders, or Frisians, who dwelt in Scaldmariland, "the land of the meres of the Scheldt." Beyond the vast forests of Flanders, in morasses and alluvial islands whose names it is impossible now to verify, so much has the land changed, both by inundations and by embankments, by the brute forces of nature and the noble triumphs of art, dwelt a folk, poor, savage, living mostly, as in Cæsar's time, in huts raised above the sea on piles or mounds of earth; often without cattle or seedfield, half savage, half heathen, but free. Free, with the divine instinct of freedom, and all the self-help and energy which spring thereout.

They were a mongrel race; and, as most mongrel races are (when sprung from parents not too far apart in blood), a strong race; the remnant of those old Frisians and Batavians, who had defied, and all but successfully resisted, the power of Rome; mingled with fresh crosses of Teutonic blood from Frank, Sueve, Saxon, and the other German tribes, who, after the fall of the Roman Empire, had swept across the land.

Their able modern historian has well likened the struggle between Civilis and the Romans to that between William the Silent and the Spaniard. It was, without doubt, the foreshadow of their whole history. They were distinguished, above most European races, for sturdy independence, and, what generally accompanies it, sturdy common sense. They could not understand why they should obey foreign Frank rulers, whether set over them by Dagobert or by Charlemagne. They could not understand why they were to pay tithes to foreign Frank priests, who had forced on them, at the sword's point, a religion which they only half believed, and only half understood. Many a truly holy man preached to them to the best of his powers: but the cross of St. Boniface had too often to follow the sword of Charles

Martel; and for every Frisian who was converted another was killed.

"Free Frisians," nevertheless, they remained, at least in name and in their statute-book, "as long as the wind blows out of the clouds, and the world stands." The feudal system never took root in their soil.* If a Frank Count was to govern them, he must govern according to their own laws. Again and again they rebelled, even against that seemingly light rule. Again and again they brought down on themselves the wrath of their nominal sovereigns the Counts of Flanders; then of the Kaisers of Germany; and, in the thirteenth century, of the Inquisition itself. Then a crusade was preached against them as "Stadings," heretics who paid no tithes, ill-used monks and nuns, and worshipped (or were said to worship) a black cat and the foul fiend among the meres and fens. Conrad of Marpurg, the brutal Director of St. Elizabeth of Hungary, burnt them at his wicked will, extirpating it may be heresy, but not the spirit of the race. That, crushed down and seemingly enslaved, during the middle age, under Count Dirk and his descendants, still lived; destined at last to conquer. They were a people who had determined to see for themselves and act for themselves in the universe in which they found themselves; and, moreover (a necessary corollary of such a resolution), to fight to the death against any one who interfered with them in so doing.

Again and again, therefore, the indomitable spirit rose, founding free towns with charters and guilds; embanking the streams, draining the meres, fighting each other and the neighboring princes; till, in their last great struggle against the Pope and Spain, they rose once and for all,

>"Heated hot with burning fears,
>And bathed in baths of hissing tears,
>And battered with the strokes of doom
>To shape and use,"

as the great Protestant Dutch Republic.

A noble errand it had been for such a man as Hereward to help those men toward freedom, instead of helping Frank Counts to enslave them;—men of his own blood, with laws and customs like those of his own Anglo-Danes, living in a land so exactly like his own that every mere and fen and wood reminded him of the scenes of his boyhood. The very names of the two lands were alike,—"Holland," the hollow land,—the one of England, the other of Flanders.

But all this was hidden from Hereward. To do as he would be done by was a lesson which he had never been taught. If

---

* Motley. "Rise of the Dutch Republic."

men had invaded his land, he would have cried, like the Frisians whom he was going to enslave, "I am free as long as the wind blows out of the clouds!" and died where he stood. But that was not the least reason why he should not invade any other man's land, and try whether or not he, too, would die where he stood. To him these Frieslanders were simply savages, probably heathens, who would not obey their lawful lord, who was a gentleman and a Christian; besides, renown, and possibly a little plunder, might be got by beating them into obedience. He knew not what he did; and knew not, likewise, that as he had done to others, so would it be done to him.

Baldwin had at that time made over his troublesome Hollanders to his younger son Robert, the Viking whom little Arnulf longed to imitate.

Florent, Count of Holland, and vassal of the great Marquis, had just died, leaving a pretty young widow, to whom the Hollanders had no mind to pay one stiver more than they were forced. All the isles of Zeeland, and the counties of Eenham and Alost, were doing that which was right in the sight of their own eyes, and finding themselves none the worse therefor, — though the Countess Gertrude doubtless could buy fewer silks of Greece or gems of Italy. But to such a distressed lady a champion could not long be wanting; and Robert, after having been driven out of Spain by the Moors with fearful loss, and in a second attempt wrecked with all his fleet as soon as he got out of port, resolved to tempt the main no more, and leave the swan's path for that of the fat oxen and black dray-horses of Holland.

So he rushed to avenge the wrongs of the Countess Gertrude; and his father, whose good-natured good sense foresaw that the fiery Robert would raise storms upon his path, — happily for his old age he did not foresee the worst, — let him go, with his blessing.

So Robert gathered to him valiant ruffians, as many as he could find; and when he heard of the Viking who had brought Eustace of Guisnes to reason, it seemed to him that he was a man who would do his work.

So when the great Marquis came down to St. Omer to receive the homage of Count Eustace of Guisnes, Robert came thither too, and saw Hereward.

"You have done us good service, Harold Naemansson, as it pleases you to be called," said Baldwin, smiling. "But some man's son you are, if ever I saw a gallant knight earl-born by his looks as well as his deeds."

Hereward bowed.

"And for me," said Robert, "Naemansson or earl's son, here

is my Viking's welcome to all Vikings like myself." And he held out his hand.

Hereward took it.

"You failed in Galicia, beausire, only because your foes were a hundred to one. You will not fail where you are going, if (as I hear) they are but ten to one."

Robert laughed, vain and gratified.

"Then you know where I have been, and where I am going?"

"Why not? As you know well, we Vikings are all brothers, and all know each other's counsel, from ship to ship and port to port."

Then the two young men looked each other in the face, and each saw that the other was a man who would suit him.

"Skall to the Viking!" cried Robert, aping, as was his fancy, the Norse rovers' slang. "Will you come with me to Holland?"

"You must ask my young lord there," and he pointed to Arnulf. "I am his man now, by all laws of honor."

A flush of jealousy passed over Robert's face. He, haplessly for himself, thought that he had a grievance.

The rights of primogeniture — *droits d'ainesse* — were not respected in the family of the Baldwins as they should have been, had prudence and common sense had their way.

No sacred or divine right is conferred by the fact of a man's being the first-born son. If Scripture be Scripture, the "Lord's anointed" was usually rather a younger son of talent and virtue; one born, not according to the flesh, but according to the spirit, like David and Solomon. And so it was in other realms besides Flanders during the middle age. The father handed on the work — for ruling was hard work in those days — to the son most able to do it. Therefore we can believe Lambert of Aschaffenbourg when he says, that in Count Baldwin's family for many ages he who pleased his father most took his father's name, and was hereditary prince of all Flanders; while the other brothers led an inglorious life of vassalage to him.

But we can conceive, likewise, that such a method would give rise to intrigues, envyings, calumnies, murders, fratracidal civil wars, and all the train of miseries which for some years after this history made infamous the house of Baldwin, as they did many another noble house, till they were stopped by the gradual adoption of the rational rule of primogeniture.

So Robert, who might have been a daring and useful friend to his brother, had he been forced to take for granted from birth that he was nobody, and his brother everybody, — as do all younger sons of English noblemen, to their infinite benefit, — held himself to be an injured man for life, because his father called his first-born Baldwin, and promised him the succession,— which indeed he had worthily deserved, according to the laws of Mammon and this world, by bringing into the family such an heiress as Richilda and such a dowry as Mons.

But Robert, who thought himself as good as his brother,— though he was not such, save in valor,—nursed black envy in his heart. Hard it was to him to hear his elder brother called Baldwin of Mons, when he himself had not a foot of land of his own. Harder still to hear him called Baldwin the Good, when he felt in himself no title whatsoever to that epithet. Hardest of all to see a beautiful boy grow up, as heir both of Flanders and of Hainault.

Had he foreseen whither that envy would have led him; had he foreseen the hideous and fratracidal day of February 22d, 1071, and that fair boy's golden locks rolling in dust and blood,— the wild Viking would have crushed the growing snake within his bosom; for he was a knight and a gentleman. But it was hidden from his eyes. He had to "dree his weird," — to commit great sins, do great deeds, and die in his bed, mighty and honored, having children to his heart's desire, and leaving the rest of his substance to his babes. Heaven help him, and the like of him!

But he turned to young Arnulf.

" Give me your man, boy ! "

Arnulf pouted. He wanted to keep his Viking for himself, and said so.

" He is to teach me to go 'leding,' as the Norsemen call it, like you."

Robert laughed. A hint at his piratical attempts pleased his vanity, all the more because they had been signal failures.

" Lend him me, then, my pretty nephew, for a month or two, till he has conquered these Friesland frogs for me; and then, if thou wilt go leding with him — "

" I hope you may never come back," thought Robert to himself; but he did not say it.

" Let the knight go," quoth Baldwin.

" Let me go with him, then."

" No, by all saints ! I cannot have thee poked through with a Friesland pike, or rotted with a Friesland ague."

Arnulf pouted still.

" Abbot, what hast thou been at with the boy? He thinks of naught but blood and wounds, instead of books and prayers."

" He is gone mad after this — this knight."

" The Abbot," said Hereward, " knows by hearing of his ears that I bid him bide at home, and try to govern lands in peace like his father and you, Sir Marquis."

" Eh ? "

The Abbot told honestly what had passed between Hereward and the lad, as they rode to St. Bertin.

Baldwin was silent, thinking, and smiling jollily, as was the wont of the Debonair.

"You are a man of sense, beausire. Come with me," said he at last.

And he, Hereward, and Robert went into an inner room.

"Sit down on the settle by me."

"It is too great an honor."

"Nonsense, man! If I be who I am, I know enough of me to know that I need not be ashamed of having you as bench-fellow. Sit down."

Hereward obeyed of course.

"Tell me who you are."

Hereward looked out of the corner of his eyes, smiling and perplexed.

"Tell me and Robert who you are, man; and be done with it. I believe I know already. I have asked far and wide of chapmen, and merchants, and wandering knights, and pirate rascals, — like yourself."

"And you found that I was a pirate rascal?"

"I found a pirate rascal who met you in Ireland, three years since, and will swear that if you have one gray eye and one blue — "

"As he has," quoth Robert.

"That I am a wolf's head, and a robber of priests, and an Esau on the face of the earth; every man's hand against me, and mine — for I never take but what I give — against every man."

"That you are the son of my old friend Leofric of Chester; and the hottest-hearted, shrewdest-headed, hardest-handed Berserker in the North Seas. You killed Gilbert of Ghent's bear, Siward Digre's cousin. Don't deny it."

"Don't hang me, or send me to the Westminster miracle-worker to be hanged, and I will confess."

"I? Every man is welcome who comes hither with a bold hand and a strong heart. 'The Refuge for the Destitute,' they call Flanders; I suppose because I am too good-natured to turn rogues out. So do no harm to mine, and mine shall do no harm to you."

Baldwin's words were true. He found house-room for everybody, helped everybody against everybody else (as will be seen), and yet quarrelled with nobody — at least in his old age — by the mere virtue of good nature, — which blessed is the man who possesseth.

So Hereward went off to exterminate the wicked Hollanders, and avenge the wrongs of the Countess Gertrude.

CHAPTER X.

HOW HEREWARD WON THE MAGIC ARMOR.

TORFRIDA had special opportunities of hearing about Hereward; for young Arnulf was to her a pet and almost a foster-brother, and gladly escaped from the convent to tell her the news.
He had now had his first taste of the royal game of war. He had seen Hereward fight by day, and heard him tell stories over the camp-fire by night. Hereward's beauty, Hereward's prowess, Hereward's songs, Hereward's strange adventures and wanderings, were forever in the young boy's mouth; and he spent hours in helping Torfrida to guess who the great unknown might be; and then went back to Hereward, and artlessly told him of his beautiful friend, and how they had talked of him, and of nothing else; and in a week or two Hereward knew all about Torfrida; and Torfrida knew — what filled her heart with joy — that Hereward was bound to no lady-love, and owned (so he had told Arnulf) no mistress save the sword on his thigh.

Whereby there had grown up in the hearts of both the man and the maid a curiosity, which easily became the parent of love.

But when Baldwin the great Marquis came to St. Omer, to receive the homage of Eustace of Guisnes, young Arnulf had run into Torfrida's chamber in great anxiety. "Would his grandfather approve of what he had done? Would he allow his new friendship with the unknown?"

"What care I?" said Torfrida. "But if your friend wishes to have the Marquis's favor, he would be wise to trust him, at least so far as to tell his name."

"I have told him so. I have told him that you would tell him so."

"I? Have you been talking to him about me?"

"Why not?"

"That is not well done, Arnulf, to talk of ladies to men whom they do not know."

Arnulf looked up, puzzled and pained; for she spoke haughtily.

"I know naught of your new friend. He may be a low-born man, for anything that I can tell."

"He is not! He is as noble as I am. Everything he says and does — every look — shows it."

"You are young, — as you have shown by talking of me to him. But I have given you my advice"; and she moved languidly away. "Let him tell your grandfather who he is, or remain suspected."

The boy went away sadly.

Early the next morning he burst into Torfrida's room as she was dressing her hair.

"How now? Are these manners for the heir of Flanders?"

"He has told all!"

"He has!" and she started and dropt her comb.

"Pick up that comb, girl. You need not go away. I have no secrets with young gentlemen."

"I thought you would be glad to hear."

"I? What can I want in the matter, save that your grandfather should be satisfied that you are entertaining a man worthy to be your guest?"

"And he is worthy: he has told my grandfather who he is."

"But not you?"

"No. They say I must not know yet. But this I know, that they welcomed him, when he told them, as if he had been an earl's son; and that he is going with my Uncle Robert against the Frieslanders."

"And if he be an earl's son, how comes he here, wandering with rough seamen, and hiding his honest name? He must have done something of which he is ashamed."

"I shall tell you nothing," said Arnulf, pouting.

"What care I? I can find out by art magic if I like."

"I don't believe all that. Can you find out, for instance, what he has on his throat?"

"A beard."

"But what is under that beard?"

"A gôitre."

"You are laughing at me."

"Of course I am, as I shall at any one who challenges me to find out anything so silly, and so unfit."

"I shall go."

"Go then." For she knew very well that he would come back again.

"Nurse," said Torfrida to the old Lapp woman, when they were alone, "find out for me what is the name of this strange champion, and what he has beneath his beard."

"Beneath his beard?"

"Some scar, I suppose, or secret mark. I must know. You will find out for your Torfrida, will you not, nurse?"

"I will make a charm that will bring him to you, were all the icebergs of Quenland between you and him: and then you can see for yourself."

"No, no, no! not yet, nurse!" and Torfrida smiled. "Only find me out that one thing: that I must know."

And yet why she wanted to know, she could not tell herself. The old woman came back to her, ere she went to bed.

"I have found it out all, and more. I know where to get scarlet toadstools, and I put the juice in his men's ale: they are laughing and roaring now, merry-mad every one of them."

"But not he?"

"No, no. He is with the Marquis. But in madness comes out truth; and that long hook-nosed body-varlet of his has told us all."

And she told Torfrida who Hereward was, and the secret mark.

"There is a Cross upon his throat, beneath his chin, pricked in after their English fashion."

Torfrida started.

"Then,— then the spell will not work upon him; the Holy Cross will turn it off."

"It must be a great Cross and a holy one that will turn off my charms," said the old hag, with a sneer, "whatever it may do against yours. But on the back of his hand,— that will be a mark to know him by,— there is pricked a bear,— a white bear that he slew." And she told the story of the fairy bear; which Torfrida duly stored up in her heart.

"So he has the Cross on his throat," thought Torfrida to herself. "Well, if it keep off my charm, it will keep off others, that is one comfort; and one knows not what fairies or witches or evil creatures he may meet with in the forests and the fens."

The discovery of Hereward's rank did not, doubtless, lessen Torfrida's fancy for him. She was ambitious enough, and proud enough of her own lineage, to be full glad that her heart had strayed away — as it must needs stray somewhere — to the son of the third greatest man in England. As for his being an outlaw, that mattered little. He might be inlawed, and rich and powerful, any day in those uncertain, topsy-turvy times: and, for the present, his being a wolf's head only made him the more interesting to her. Women like to pity their lovers. Sometimes — may all good beings reward them for it — they love merely because they pity. And Torfrida found it pleasant to pity the insolent young coxcomb, who certainly never dreamed of pitying himself.

When Hereward went home that night, he found the Abbey

of St Bertin in horrible confusion. His men were grouped outside the gate, chattering like monkeys; the porter and the monks, from inside, entreating them, vainly, to come in and go to bed quietly.

But they would not. They vowed and swore that a great gulf had opened all down the road, and that one step more would tumble them in headlong. They manifested the most affectionate solicitude for the monks, warning them, on their lives, not to step across the threshold, or they would be swallowed (as Martin, who was the maddest of the lot, phrased it) with Korah, Dathan, and Abiram. In vain Hereward stormed; assured them that the supposed abyss was nothing but the gutter; proved the fact by kicking Martin over it. The men determined to believe their own eyes, and after a while fell asleep, in heaps, in the roadside, and lay there till morning, when they woke, declaring, as did the monks, that they had been all bewitched. They knew not — and happily the lower orders, both in England and on the Continent, do not yet know — the potent virtues of that strange fungus, with which Lapps and Samoiedes have, it is said, practised wonders for centuries past.

The worst of the matter was, that Martin Lightfoot, who had drank most of the poison, and had always been dreamy and uncanny, in spite of his shrewdness and humor, had, from that day forward, something very like a bee in his bonnet.

But before Count Robert and Hereward could collect sufficient troops for the invasion of Holland, another chance of being slain in fight arose, too tempting to be overlooked; namely, the annual tournament at Pont de l'Arche above Rouen, where all the noblest knights of Normandy would assemble, to win their honor and ladies' love by hewing at each other's sinful bodies. Thither, too, the best knights of Flanders must needs go, and with them Hereward. Though no knight, he was allowed in Flanders, as he had been in Scotland, to take his place among that honorable company. For, though he still refused the honor of knighthood, on the ground that he had, as yet, done no deed deserving thereof, he was held to have deserved it again and again, and all the more from his modesty in declining it.

So away they all went to Pont de l'Arche, a right gallant meinie: and Torfrida watched them go from the lattice window.

And when they had passed down the street, tramping and jingling and caracoling, young Arnulf ran into the house with eyes full of tears, because he was not allowed to go likewise; and with a message for Torfrida, from no other than Hereward.

"I was to tell you this and no more: that if he meets your favor in the field, he that wears it will have hard work to keep it."

Torfrida turned pale as ashes; first with wild delight, and then with wild fear.

"Ha?—does he know who— Sir Ascelin?"

"He knows well enough. Why not? Every one knows. Are you afraid that he is not a match for that great bullock?"

"Afraid? Who said I was afraid? Sir Ascelin is no bullock either; but a courteous and gallant knight."

"You are as pale as death, and so—"

"Never mind what I am," said she, putting her hands over his eyes, and kissing him again and again, as a vent for her joy.

The next few days seemed years for length: but she could wait. She was sure of him now. She needed no charms. "Perhaps," thought she, as she looked in the glass, "I was my own charm." And, indeed, she had every fair right to say so.

At last news came.

She was sitting over her books; her mother, as usual, was praying in the churches; when the old Lapp nurse came in. A knight was at the door. His name, he said, was Siward the White, and he came from Hereward.

From Hereward! He was at least alive: he might be wounded, though; and she rushed out of the chamber into the hall, looking never more beautiful; her color heightened by the quick beating of her heart; her dark hair, worn loose and long, after the fashion of those days, streaming around her and behind her.

A handsome young man stood in the door-way, armed from head to foot.

"You are Siward, Hereward's nephew?"

He bowed assent. She took him by the hands, and, after the fashion of those days, kissed him on the small space on either cheek, which was left bare between the nose-piece and the chain-mail.

"You are welcome. Hereward is—is alive?"

"Alive and gay, and all the more gay at being able to send to the Lady Torfrida by me something which was once hers, and now is hers once more."

And he drew from his bosom the ribbon of the knight of St. Valeri.

She almost snatched it from his hand, in her delight at recovering her favor.

"How— where — did he get this?"

"He saw it, in the thick of the tournament, on the helm of a knight who, he knew, had vowed to maim him or take his life; and, wishing to give him a chance of fulfilling his vow, rode him down, horse and man. The knight's Norman friends attacked us in force; and we Flemings, with Hereward at our head, beat them off, and overthrew so many, that we are almost all horsed at the Norman's expense. Three more knights, with their horses fell before Hereward's lance."

"And what of this favor?"

"He sends it to its owner. Let her say what shall be done with it."

Torfrida was on the point of saying, "He has won it; let him wear it for my sake." But she paused. She longed to see Hereward face to face; to speak to him, if but one word. If she allowed him to wear the favor, she must at least have the pleasure of giving it with her own hands. And she paused.

"And he is killed?"

"Who? Hereward?"

"Sir Ascelin."

"Only bruised; but he shall be killed, if you will."

"God forbid!"

"Then," said Siward, mistaking her meaning, "all I have to tell Hereward is, it seems, that he has wasted his blow. He will return, therefore, to the Knight of St. Valeri his horse, and, if the Lady Torfrida chooses, the favor which he has taken by mistake from its rightful owner." And he set his teeth, and could not prevent stamping on the ground, in evident passion. There was a tone, too, of deep disappointment in his voice, which made Torfrida look keenly at him. Why should Hereward's nephew feel so deeply about that favor? And as she looked, — could that man be the youth Siward? Young he was, but surely thirty years old at least. His face could hardly be seen, hidden by helmet and nose-piece above, and mailed up to the mouth below. But his long mustache was that of a grown man; his vast breadth of shoulder, his hard hand, his sturdy limbs, — these surely belonged not to the slim youth whom she had seen from her lattice riding at Hereward's side. And, as she looked, she saw upon his hand the bear of which her nurse had told her.

"You are deceiving me!" and she turned first deadly pale, and then crimson. "You — you are Hereward himself!"

"I? Pardon me, my lady. Ten minutes ago I should have been glad enough to have been Hereward. Now, I am thankful enough that I am only Siward; and not Hereward, who wins for himself contempt by overthrowing a knight more fortunate than he." And he bowed, and turned away to go.

"Hereward! Hereward!" and, in her passion, she seized him by both his hands. "I know you! I know that device upon your hand. At last! at last my hero, — my idol! How I have longed for this moment! How I have toiled for it, and not in vain! Good heavens! what am I saying?" And she tried, in her turn, to escape from Hereward's mailed arms.

"Then you do not care for that man?"

"For him? Here! take my favor, wear it before all the world, and guard it as you only can; and let them all know that Torfrida is your love."

And with hands trembling with passion, she bound the ribbon round his helm.

"Yes! I am Hereward," he almost shouted; "the Berserker, the brain-hewer, the land-thief, the sea-thief, the feeder of wolf and raven, — Aoi! Ere my beard was grown, I was a match for giants. How much more now, that I am a man whom ladies love? Many a champion has quailed before my very glance. How much more, now that I wear Torfrida's gift? Aoi!"

Torfrida had often heard that wild battle-cry of Aoi! of which the early minstrels were so fond, — with which the great poet who wrote the "Song of Roland" ends every paragraph; which has now fallen (displaced by our modern Hurrah), to be merely a sailor's call or hunter's cry. But she shuddered as she heard it close to her ears, and saw, from the flashing eye and dilated nostril, the temper of the man on whom she had thrown herself so utterly. She laid her hand upon his lips.

"Silence! silence for pity's sake. Remember that you are in a maiden's house; and think of her good fame."

Hereward collected himself instantly, and then holding her at arm's length, gazed upon her. "I was mad a moment. But is it not enough to make me mad to look at you?"

"Do not look at me so, I cannot bear it," said she, hanging down her head. "You forget that I am a poor weak girl."

"Ah! we are rough wooers, we sea-rovers. We cannot pay glozing French compliments like your knights here, who fawn on a damsel with soft words in the hall, and will kiss the dust off their queen's feet, and die for a hair of their goddess's eyebrow; and then if they catch her in the forest, show themselves as very ruffians as if they were Paynim Moors. We are rough, lady, we English: but those who trust us, find us true."

"And I can trust you?" she asked, still trembling.

"On God's cross there round your neck," and he took her crucifix and kissed it. "You only I love, you only I will love, and you will I love in all honesty, before the angels of heaven, till we be wedded man and wife. Who but a fool would soil the flower which he means to wear before all the world?"

"I knew Hereward was noble! I knew I had not trusted him in vain!"

"I kept faith and honor with the Princess of Cornwall, when I had her at my will, and shall I not keep faith and honor with you?"

"The Princess of Cornwall?" asked Torfrida.

"Do not be jealous, fair queen. I brought her safe to her betrothed; and wedded she is, long ago. I will tell you that story some day. And now — I must go."

"Not yet! not yet! I have something to — to show you."

She motioned him to go up the narrow stairs, or rather ladder, which led to the upper floor, and then led him into her chamber.

A lady's chamber was then, in days when privacy was little cared for, her usual reception room; and the bed, which stood in an alcove, was the common seat of her and her guests. But Torfrida did not ask him to sit down. She led the way onward towards a door beyond.

Hereward followed, glancing with awe at the books, parchments, and strange instruments which lay on the table and the floor.

The old Lapp nurse sat in the window, sewing busily. She looked up, and smiled meaningly. But as she saw Torfrida unlock the further door with one of the keys which hung at her girdle, she croaked out, —

"Too fast! Too fast! Trust lightly, and repent heavily."

"Trust once and for all, or never trust at all," said Torfrida, as she opened the door.

Hereward saw within rich dresses hung on perches round the wall, and chests barred and padlocked.

"These are treasures," said she, "which many a knight and nobleman has coveted. By cunning, by flattery, by threats of force even, have they tried to win what lies here, — and Torfrida herself, too, for the sake of her wealth. But thanks to the Abbot my uncle, Torfrida is still her own mistress, and mistress of the wealth which her forefathers won by sea and land far away in the East. All here is mine, — and if you be but true to me, all mine is yours. Lift the lid for me, it is too heavy for my arms."

Hereward did so; and saw within golden cups and bracelets, horns of ivory and silver, bags of coin, and among them a mail shirt and helmet, on which he fixed at once silent and greedy eyes.

She looked at his face askance, and smiled. "Yes, these are more to Hereward's taste than gold and jewels. And he shall have them. He shall have them as a proof that if Torfrida has set her love upon a worthy knight, she is at least worthy of him; and does not demand, without being able to give in return."

And she took out the armor, and held it up to him.

"This is the work of dwarfs or enchanters! This was not forged by mortal man! It must have come out of some old cavern, or dragon's hoard!" said Hereward, in astonishment at the extreme delicacy and slightness of the mail-rings, and the richness of the gold and silver with which both hauberk and helm were inlaid.

"Enchanted it is, they say; but its maker, who can tell? My ancestor won it, and by the side of Charles Martel. Listen, and I will tell you how.

"You have heard of fair Provence, where I spent my youth; the land of the sunny south; the land of the fig and the olive, the mulberry and the rose, the tulip and the anemone, and all rich fruits and fair flowers,—the land where every city is piled with temples and theatres and towers as high as heaven, which the old Romans built with their enchantments, and tormented the blessed martyrs therein."

"Heavens, how beautiful you are!" cried Hereward, as her voice shaped itself into a song, and her eyes flashed, at the remembrance of her southern home.

Torfrida was not altogether angry at finding that he was thinking of her, and not of her words.

"Peace, and listen. You know how the Paynim held that land,—the Saracens, to whom Mahound taught all the wisdom of Solomon,—as they teach us in turn," she added in a lower voice.

"And how Charles and his Paladins," [Charles Martel and Charlemagne were perpetually confounded in the legends of the time] "drove them out, and conquered the country again for God and his mother."

"I have heard—" but he did not take his eyes off her face.

"They were in the theatre at Arles, the Saracens, where the blessed martyr St. Trophimus had died in torments; they had set up there their idol of Mahound, and turned the place into a fortress. Charles burnt it over their heads: you see—I have seen—the blackened walls, the blood-stained marbles, to this day. Then they fled into the plain, and there they turned and fought. Under Mont Majeur, by the hermit's cell, they fought a summer's day, till they were all slain. There was an Emir among them, black as a raven, clad in magic armor. All lances turned from it, all swords shivered on it. He rode through the press without a wound, while every stroke of his scymitar shore off a head of horse or man. Charles himself rode at him, and smote him with his hammer. They heard the blow in Avignon, full thirty miles away. The flame flashed out from the magic armor a fathom's length, blinding all around; and when they recovered their sight, the enchanter was far away in the battle, killing as he went.

"Then Charles cried, 'Who will stop that devil, whom no steel can wound? Help us, O blessed martyr St. Trophimus, and save the soldiers of the Cross from shame!'

"Then cried Torfrid, my forefather, 'What use in crying to St. Trophimus? He could not help himself, when the Paynim burnt him: and how can he help us? A tough arm is worth a score of martyrs here.'

"And he rode at that Emir, and gript him in his arms. They both fell, and rolled together on the ground; but Torfrid never loosed his hold till he had crushed out his unbaptized soul and sent it to join Mahound in hell.

"Then he took his armor, and brought it home in triumph. But after a while he fell sick of a fever; and the blessed St. Trophimus appeared to him, and told him that it was a punishment for his blasphemy in the battle. So he repented, and vowed to serve the saint all his life. On which he was healed instantly, and fell to religion, and went back to Mont Majeur; and there he was a hermit in the cave under the rock, and tended the graves hewn in the living stone, where his old comrades, the Paladins who were slain, sleep side by side round the church of the Holy Cross. But the armor he left here; and he laid a curse upon it, that whosoever of his descendants should lose that armor in fight, should die childless, without a son to wield a sword. And therefore it is that none of his ancestors, valiant as they have been, have dared to put this harness on their backs."

And so ended a story, which Torfrida believed utterly, and Hereward likewise.

"And now, Hereward mine, dare you wear that magic armor, and face old Torfrid's curse?"

"What dare I not?"

"Think. If you lose it, in you your race must end."

"Let it end. I accept the curse."

And he put the armor on.

But he trembled as he did it. Atheism and superstition go too often hand in hand; and godless as he was, sceptical of Providence itself, and much more of the help of saint or angel, still the curse of the old warrior, like the malice of a witch or a demon, was to him a thing possible, probable, and formidable.

She looked at him in pride and exultation.

"It is yours, — the invulnerable harness! Wear it in the forefront of the battle! And if weapon wound you through it, may

I, as punishment for my lie, suffer the same upon my tender body, — a wound for every wound of yours, my knight!"*

And after that they sat side by side, and talked of love with all honor and honesty, never heeding the old hag, who crooned to herself in her barbarian tongue, —

> "Quick thaw, long frost,
> Quick joy, long pain,
> Soon found, soon lost,
> You will take your gift again."

---

* " Volo enim in meo tale quid nunc perpeti corpore semel, quicquid ear ferrei vel e metallo excederet."

CHAPTER XI.

HOW THE HOLLANDERS TOOK HEREWARD FOR A MAGICIAN.

OF this weary Holland war which dragged itself on campaign after campaign for several years, what need to tell? There was, doubtless, the due amount of murder, plunder, burning, and worse; and the final event was certain from the beginning. It was a struggle between civilized and disciplined men, armed to the teeth, well furnished with ships and military engines, against poor simple folk in "felt coats stiffened with tar or turpentine, or in very short jackets of hide," says the chronicler, "who fought by threes, two with a crooked lance and three darts each, and between them a man with a sword or an axe, who held his shield before those two; — a very great multitude, but in composition utterly undisciplined," who came down to the sea-coast, with carts and wagons, to carry off the spoils of the Flemings, and bade them all surrender at discretion, and go home again after giving up Count Robert and Hereward, with the "tribunes of the brigades," to be put to death, as valiant South Sea islanders might have done; and then found themselves as sheep to the slaughter before the cunning Hereward, whom they esteemed a magician on account of his craft and his invulnerable armor.

So at least says Leofric's paraphrast, who tells long, confused stories of battles and campaigns, some of them without due regard to chronology; for it is certain that the brave Frisians could not on Robert's first landing have "feared lest they should be conquered by foreigners, as they had heard the English were by the French," because that event had not then happened.

And so much for the war among the Meres of Scheldt.

CHAPTER XII.

HOW HEREWARD TURNED BERSERK.

TORFRIDA's heart misgave her that first night as to the effects of her exceeding frankness. Her pride in the first place was somewhat wounded; she had dreamed of a knight who would worship her as his queen, hang on her smile, die at her frown; and she had meant to bring Hereward to her feet as such a slave, in boundless gratitude; but had he not rather held his own, and brought her to his feet, by assuming her devotion as his right? And if he assumed that, how far could she trust him not to abuse his claim? Was he quite as perfect seen close as seen afar off? And now that the intoxication of that meeting had passed off, she began to remember more than one little fault which she would have gladly seen mended. Certain roughnesses of manner which contrasted unfavorably with the polish (merely external though it was) of the Flemish and Norman knights; a boastful self-sufficiency, too, which bordered on the ludicrous at whiles even in her partial eyes; which would be a matter of open laughter to the knights of the Court. Besides, if they laughed at him, they would laugh at her for choosing him. And then wounded vanity came in to help wounded pride; and she sat over the cold embers till almost dawn of day, her head between her hands, musing sadly, and half wishing that the irrevocable yesterday had never come.

But when, after a few months, Hereward returned from his first campaign in Holland, covered with glory and renown, all smiles, and beauty, and health, and good-humor, and gratitude for the magic armor which had preserved him unhurt, then Torfrida forgot all her fears, and thought herself the happiest maid alive for four-and-twenty hours at least.

And then came back, and after that again and again, the old fears. Gradually she found out that the sneers which she had heard at English barbarians were not altogether without ground. Not only had her lover's life been passed among half-brutal and wild adventurers; but, like the rest of his nation, he had never felt the influence of that classic civilization without which good manners seem, even to this day, almost beyond the reach of the white man. Those among whom she had been brought up, whether soldiers or clerks, were probably no nobler or purer at heart — she would gladly have believed them far less so — than Hereward; but the merest varnish of Roman civilization had given a charm to their manners, a wideness of range to their thoughts, which Hereward had not.

Especially when he had taken too much to drink, — which he did, after the Danish fashion, far oftener than the rest of Baldwin's men, — he grew rude, boastful, quarrelsome. He would chant his own doughty deeds, and "gab," as the Norman word was, in painful earnest, while they gabbed only in sport, and outvied each other in impossible fanfarronades, simply to laugh down a fashion which was held inconsistent with the modesty of a true knight. Bitter it was to her to hear him announcing to the company, not for the first or second time, how he had slain the Cornish giant, whose height increased by a foot at least every time he was mentioned; and then to hear him answered by some smart, smooth-shaven youth, who, with as much mimicry of his manner as he dared to assume, boasted of having slain in Araby a giant with two heads, and taken out of his two mouths the two halves of the princess whom he was devouring, which being joined together afterwards by the prayers of a holy hermit, were delivered back safe and sound to her father the King of Antioch. And more bitter still, to hear Hereward angrily dispute the story, unaware (at least at first) that he was being laughed at.

Then she grew sometimes cold, sometimes contemptuous, sometimes altogether fierce; and shed bitter tears in secret, when she was complimented on the modesty of her young savage.

But she was a brave maiden; and what was more, she loved him with all her heart. Else why endure bitter words for his sake? And she set herself to teach and train the wild outlaw into her ideal of a very perfect knight.

She talked to him of modesty and humility, the root of all virtues; of chivalry and self-sacrifice; of respect to the weak, and mercy to the fallen; of devotion to God, and awe of His commandments. She set before him the example of ancient heroes and philosophers, of saints and martyrs; and as much awed him by her learning as by the new world of higher and purer morality which was opened for the first time to the wandering Viking.

And he drank it all in. Taught by a woman who loved him, he could listen to humiliating truths, which he would have sneered at, had they come from the lips of a hermit or a priest. Often he rebelled; often he broke loose, and made her angry, and himself ashamed: but the spell was on him, — a far surer, as well as purer spell than any love-potion of which foolish Torfrida had ever dreamed, — the only spell which can really civilize man, — that of woman's tact and woman's purity.

But there were relapses, as was natural. The wine at Robert the Frison's table was often too good; and then Hereward's tongue was loosed, and Torfrida justly indignant. And one evening there came a very serious relapse, and out of which arose a strange adventure.

For one day the Great Marquis sent for his son to Bruges, ere he set out for another campaign in Holland; and made him a great feast, to which he invited Torfrida and her mother. For Adela of France, the Queen Countess, had heard so much of Torfrida's beauty, that she must needs have her as one of her bower-maidens; and her mother, who was an old friend of Adela's, of course was highly honored by such a promotion for her daughter.

So they went to Bruges, and Hereward and his men went of course; and they feasted and harped and sang; and the saying was fulfilled, —

"'T is merry in the hall
When beards wag all."

But the only beard which wagged in that hall was Hereward's; for the Flemings, like the Normans, prided themselves on their civilized and smooth-shaven chins, and laughed (behind his back) at Hereward, who prided himself on keeping his beautiful English beard, with locks of gold which, like his long golden hair, were combed and curled daily, after the fashion of the Anglo-Danes.

But Hereward's beard began to wag somewhat too fast, as he sat by Torfrida's side, when some knight near began to tell of a wonderful mare, called Swallow, which was to be found in one of the islands of the Scheldt, and was famous through all the country round; insinuating, moreover, that Hereward might as well have brought that mare home with him as a trophy.

Hereward answered, in his boasting vein, that he would bring home that mare, or aught else that he had a liking to.

"You will find it not so easy. Her owner, they say, is a mighty strong churl of a horse-breeder, Dirk Hammerhand by name; and as for cutting his throat, that you must not do; for he has been loyal to Countess Gertrude, and sent her horses whenever she needed."

"One may pick a fair quarrel with him nevertheless."

"Then you must bide such a buffet as you never abode before. They say his arm has seven men's strength; and whosoever visits him, he challenges to give and take a blow; but every man that has taken a blow as yet has never needed another."

"Hereward will have need of his magic head-piece, if he tries that adventure," quoth another.

"Ay," retorted the first speaker; "but the helmet may stand the rap well enough, and yet the brains inside be the worse."

"Not a doubt. I knew a man once, who was so strong, that he would shake a nut till the kernel went to powder, and yet never break the shell."

"That is a lie!" quoth Hereward. And so it was, and told purposely to make him expose himself.

Whereon high words followed, which Torfrida tried in vain to stop. Hereward was flushed with ire and scorn.

"Magic armor, forsooth!" cried he at last. "What care I for armor or for magic? I will wager to you" — "my armor," he was on the point of saying, but he checked himself in time — "any horse in my stable, that I go in my shirt to Scaldmariland, and bring back that mare single-handed."

"Hark to the Englishman. He has turned Berserk at last, like his forefathers. You will surely start in a pair of hose as well, or the ladies will be shamed."

And so forth, till Torfrida was purple with shame, and wished herself fathoms deep; and Adela of France called sternly from the head of the table to ask what the wrangling meant.

"It is only the English Berserker, the Lady Torfrida's champion," said some one, in his most courteous tone, "who is not yet as well acquainted with the customs of knighthood as that fair lady hopes to make him hereafter."

"Torfrida's champion?" asked Adela, in a tone of surprise, if not scorn.

"If any knight quarrels with my Hereward, he quarrels with Robert himself!" thundered Count Robert. "Silence!"

And so the matter was hushed up.

The banquet ended; and they walked out into the garden to cool their heads, and play at games, and dance.

Torfrida avoided Hereward: but he, with the foolish pertinacity of a man who knows he has had too much wine, and yet pretends to himself that he has not, would follow her, and speak to her.

She turned away more than once. At last she was forced to speak to him.

"So! You have made me a laughing-stock to these knights. You have scorned at my gifts. You have said — and before these men, too — that you need neither helm nor hauberk. Give me them back, then, Berserker as you are, and go sleep off your wine."

"That will I," laughed Hereward boisterously.

"You are tipsy," said she, "and do not know what you say."
"You are angry, and do not know what you say." Hearken, proud lass. I will take care of one thing, and that is, that you shall speak the truth."

"Did I not say that you were tipsy?"

"Pish! You said that I was a Berserker. And truth you shall speak; for baresark I go to-morrow to the war, and baresark I win that mare or die."

"That will be very fit for you."

And the two turned haughtily from each other.

Ere Torfrida went to bed that night, there was a violent knocking. Angry as she was, she was yet anxious enough to hurry out of her chamber, and open the door herself.

Martin Lightfoot stood there with a large leather case, which he flung at her feet somewhat unceremoniously.

"There is some gear of yours," said he, as it clanged and rattled on the floor.

"What do you mean, man?"

"Only that my master bid me say that he cares as little for his own life as you do." And he turned away.

She caught him by the arm:—

"What is the meaning of this? What is in this mail?"

"You should know best. If young folks cannot be content when they are well off, they will go farther and fare worse," says Martin Lightfoot. And he slipt from her grasp and fled into the night.

She took the mail to her room and opened it. It contained the magic armor.

All her anger was melted away. She cried; she blamed herself. He would be killed; his blood would be on her head. She would have carried it back to him with her own hands; she would have entreated him on her knees to take it back. But how face the courtiers? and how find him? Very probably, too, he was by that time hopelessly drunk. And at that thought she drew herself into herself, and trying to harden her heart again, went to bed, but not to sleep; and bitterly she cried as she thought over the old hag's croon:—

"Quick joy, long pain,
You will take your gift again."

It might have been five o'clock the next morning when the clarion rang down the street. She sprang up and drest herself quickly; but never more carefully or gayly. She heard the tramp of horse-hoofs. He was moving a-field early, indeed. Should she go to the window to bid him farewell? Should she hide herself in just anger?

She looked out stealthily through the blind of the little window in the gable. There rode down the street Robert le Frison in full armor, and behind him, knight after knight, a wall of shining steel. But by his side rode one bare-headed, his long yellow curls floating over his shoulders. His boots had golden spurs, a gilt belt held up his sword; but his only dress was a silk shirt and silk hose. He laughed and sang, and made his horse caracol, and tossed his lance in the air, and caught it by the point, like Taillefer at Hastings, as he passed under the window.

She threw open the blind, careless of all appearances. She would have called to him: but the words choked her; and what should she say?

He looked up boldly, and smiled.

"Farewell, fair lady mine. Drunk I was last night: but not so drunk as to forget a promise."

And he rode on, while Torfrida rushed away and broke into wild weeping.

CHAPTER XIII.

HOW HEREWARD WON MARE SWALLOW.

On a bench at the door of his high-roofed wooden house sat Dirk Hammerhand, the richest man in Walcheren. From within the house sounded the pleasant noise of slave-women, grinding and chatting at the handquern; from without, the pleasant noise of geese and fowls without number. And as he sat and drank his ale, and watched the herd of horses in the fen, he thought himself a happy man, and thanked his Odin and Thor that owing to his princely supplies of horses to Countess Gertrude, Robert the Frison and his Christian Franks had not harried him to the bare walls, as they would probably do ere all was over.

As he looked at the horses, some half-mile off, he saw a strange stir among them. They began whinnying and pawing round a four-footed thing in the midst, which might be a badger, or a wolf,—though both were very uncommon in that pleasant isle of Walcheren; but which plainly had no business there. Whereon he took up a mighty staff, and strode over the fen to see.

He found neither wolf nor badger; but to his exceeding surprise, a long lean man, clothed in ragged horse-skins, whinnying and neighing exactly like a horse, and then stooping to eat grass like one. He advanced to do the first thing which came into his head, namely to break the man's back with his staff, and ask him afterwards who he might be. But ere he could strike, the man or horse kicked up with his hind legs in his face, and then springing on to the said hind legs ran away with extraordinary swiftness some fifty yards; and then went down on all-fours and began grazing again.

"Beest thou man or devil?" cried Dirk, somewhat frightened.

The thing looked up. The face at least was human.

"Art thou a Christian man?" asked it in bad Frisian, intermixed with snorts and neighs.

"What's that to thee?" growled Dirk; and began to wish a little that he was one, having heard that the sign of the cross was of great virtue in driving away fiends.

"Thou art not Christian. Thou believest in Thor and Odin? Then there is hope."

"Hope of what?" Dirk was growing more and more frightened.

"Of her, my sister! Ah, my sister, can it be that I shall find thee at last, after ten thousand miles, and thirty years of woful wandering?"

"I have no man's sister here. At least, my wife's brother was killed —"

"I speak not of a sister in a woman's shape. Mine, alas! — O woful prince, O more woful princess! — eats the herb of the field somewhere in the shape of a mare, as ugly as she was once beautiful, but swifter than the swallow on the wing."

"I've none such here," quoth Dirk, thoroughly frightened, and glancing uneasily at mare Swallow.

"You have not? Alas, wretched me! It was prophesied to me, by the witch, that I should find her in the field of one who worshipped the old gods; for had she come across a holy priest, she had been a woman again, long ago. Whither must I wander afresh!" And the thing began weeping bitterly, and then ate more grass.

"I — that is — thou poor miserable creature," said Dirk, half pitying, half wishing to turn the subject, "leave off making a beast of thyself awhile, and tell me who thou art."

"I have made no beast of myself, most noble Earl of the Frisians, for so you doubtless are. I was made a beast of, — a horse of, by an enchanter of a certain land, and my sister a mare."

"Thou dost not say so?" quoth Dirk, who considered such an event quite possible.

"I was a prince of the county of Alboronia, which lies between Cathay and the Mountains of the Moon, as fair once as I am foul now, and only less fair than my lost sister; and, by the enchantments of a cruel magician, we became what we are."

"But thou art not a horse, at all events?"

"Am I not? Thou knowest, then, more of me than I do of myself," — and it ate more grass. "But hear the rest of my story. My hapless sister was sold away, with me, to a merchant; but I, breaking loose from him, fled until I bathed in a magic fountain. At once I recovered my man's shape, and was rejoicing therein, when out of the fountain rose a fairy more beautiful than an elf, and smiled upon me with love.

"She asked me my story, and I told it. And when it was told, 'Wretch!' she cried, 'and coward, who hast deserted thy sister in her need. I would have loved thee, and made thee immortal as myself; but now thou shalt wander, ugly, and eating grass, clothed in the horse-hide which has just dropped from thy limbs, till thou shalt find thy sister, and bring her to bathe, like thee, in this magic well.'"

"All good spirits help us! And you are really a prince?"

"As surely," cried the thing, with a voice of sudden rapture, "as that mare is my sister"; and he rushed at marc Swallow. "I see, I see, my mother's eyes, my father's nose —"

"He must have been a chuckle-headed king that, then," grinned Dirk to himself. "The mare's nose is as big as a buck-basket. But how can she be a princess, man, — prince, I mean? she has a foal running by her here."

"A foal?" said the thing, solemnly. "Let me behold it. Alas, alas, my sister! Thy tyrant's threat has come true, that thou shouldst be his bride whether thou wouldst or not. I see, I see in the features of thy son his hated lineaments."

"Why he must be as like a horse, then, as your father. But this will not do, Master Horse-man; I know that foal's pedigree better than I do my own."

"Man, man, simple, though honest! Hast thou never heard of the skill of the enchanter of the East? How they transform their victims at night back again into human shape, and by day into the shape of beasts again?"

"Yes — well — I know that —"

"And do you not see how you are deluded? Every night, doubt not, that mare and foal take their human shape again; and every night, perhaps, that foul enchanter visits in your fen, perhaps in your very stable, his wretched and perhaps unwilling bride."

"An enchanter in my stable? That is an ugly guest. But no. I've been into the stables fifty times, to see if that mare was safe. Mare was mare, and colt was colt, Mr. Prince, if I have eyes to see."

"And what are eyes against enchantments? The moment you opened the door, the spell was cast over them again. You ought to thank your stars that no worse has happened yet; that the enchanter, in fleeing, has not wrung your neck as he went out, or cast a spell on you, which will fire your barns, lame your geese, give your fowls the pip, your horses the glanders, your cattle the murrain, your children the St. Vitus' dance, your wife the creeping palsy, and yourself the chalk-stones in all your fingers."

"The Lord have mercy on me! If the half of this be true, I will turn Christian. I will send for a priest, and be baptized to-morrow!"

"O my sister, my sister! Dost thou not know me? Dost thou answer my caresses with kicks? Or is thy heart, as well as thy body, so enchained by that cruel necromancer, that thou preferest to be his, and scornest thine own salvation, leaving me to eat grass till I die?"

"I say, Prince, — I say, — What would you have a man to do? I bought the mare honestly, and I have kept her well. She can't say aught against me on that score. And whether she be princess or not, I'm loath to part with her."

"Keep her then, and keep with her the curse of all the saints and angels. Look down, ye holy saints" (and the thing poured out a long string of saints' names), "and avenge this Catholic princess, kept in bestial durance by an unbaptized heathen! May his—"

"Don't! don't!" roared Dirk. "And don't look at me like that" (for he feared the evil eye), "or I'll brain you with my staff!"

"Fool, if I have lost a horse's figure, I have not lost his swiftness. Ere thou couldst strike, I should have run a mile and back, to curse thee afresh." And the thing ran round him, and fell on all-fours again, and ate grass.

"Mercy, mercy! And that is more than I ever asked yet of man. But it is hard," growled he, "that a man should lose his money, because a rogue sells him a princess in disguise."

"Then sell her again; sell her, as thou valuest thy life, to the first Christian man thou meetest. And yet no. What matters? Ere a month be over, the seven years' enchantment will have passed, and she will return to her own shape, with her son, and vanish from thy farm, leaving thee to vain repentance, and so thou wilt both lose thy money and get her curse. Farewell, and my malison abide with thee."

And the thing, without another word, ran right away, neighing as it went, leaving Dirk in a state of abject terror.

He went home. He cursed the mare, he cursed the man who sold her, he cursed the day he saw her, he cursed the day he was born. He told his story with exaggerations and confusions in plenty to all in the house; and terror fell on them likewise. No one, that evening, dare go down into the fen to drive the horses up; and Dirk got very drunk, went to bed, and trembled there all night (as did the rest of the household), expecting the enchanter to enter on a flaming fire-drake, at every howl of the wind.

The next morning, as Dirk was going about his business with a doleful face, casting stealthy glances at the fen, to see if the mysterious mare was still there, and a chance of his money still left, a man rode up to the door.

He was poorly clothed, with a long rusty sword by his side A broad felt hat, long boots, and a haversack behind his saddle.

showed him to be a traveller, seemingly a horse-dealer; for there followed him, tied head and tail, a brace of sorry nags.

"Heaven save all here," quoth he, making the sign of the cross. "Can any good Christian give me a drink of milk?"

"Ale, if thou wilt," said Dirk. "But what art thou, and whence?"

On any other day, he would have tried to coax his guest into trying a buffet with him for his horse and clothes; but this morning his heart was heavy with the thought of the enchanted mare, and he welcomed the chance of selling her to the stranger.

"We are not very fond of strangers about here, since these Flemings have been harrying our borders. If thou art a spy, it will be worse for thee."

"I am neither spy nor Fleming; but a poor servant of the Lord Bishop of Utrecht's, buying a garron or two for his lordship's priests. As for these Flemings, may St. John Baptist save from them both me and you. Do you know of any man who has horses to sell hereabouts?"

"There are horses in the fen yonder," quoth Dirk, who knew that churchmen were likely to give a liberal price, and pay in good silver.

"I saw them as I rode up. And a fine lot they are; but of too good a stamp for my short purse, or for my holy master's riding, — a fat priest likes a quiet nag, my master."

"Humph. Well, if quietness is what you need, there is a mare down there, a child might ride her with a thread of wool. But as for price, — and she has a colt, too, running by her."

"Ah?" quoth the horseman. "Well, your Walcheren folk make good milk, that's certain. A colt by her? That's awkward. My Lord does not like young horses; and it would be troublesome, too, to take the thing along with me."

The less anxious the dealer seemed to buy, the more anxious grew Dirk to sell; but he concealed his anxiety, and let the stranger turn away, thanking him for his drink.

"I say!" he called after him. "You might look at her as you ride past the herd."

The stranger assented, and they went down into the fen, and looked over the precious mare, whose feats were afterwards sung by many an English fireside, or in the forest, beneath the hollins green, by such as Robin Hood and his merry men. The ugliest, as well as the swiftest, of mares, she was, say the old chroniclers; and it was not till the stranger had looked twice at her, that he forgot her great chuckle head, greyhound-flanks, and drooping hind-quarters, and began to see the great length of those same quarters, — the thighs let down into the hocks, the arched loin, the extraordinary girth through the saddle, the sloping shoulder, the long arms, the flat knees, the large, well-set hoofs, and all the other points which showed her strength and speed, and justified her fame.

"She might carry a big man like you through the mud," said he, carelessly, "but as for pace, one cannot expect that with such a chuckle head. And if one rode her through a town, the boys would call after one, 'All head and no tail.' Why, I can't see her tail for her quarters, it is so ill set on."

"Ill set on, or none," said Dirk, testily; "don't go to speak against her pace till you have seen it. Here, lass!"

Dirk was, in his heart, rather afraid of the princess; but he was comforted when she came up to him like a dog.

"She's as sensible as a woman," said he; and then grumbled to himself, "may be she knows I mean to part with her."

"Lend me your saddle," said he to the stranger.

The stranger did so; and Dirk mounting galloped her in a ring. There was no doubt of her powers, as soon as she began to move.

"I hope you won't remember this against me, madam," said Dirk, as soon as he got out of the stranger's hearing. "I can't do less than sell you to a Christian. And certainly I have been as good a master to you as if I'd known who you were; but if you wish to stay with me you've only to kick me off, and say so, and I'm yours to command."

"Well, she can gallop a bit," said the stranger, as Dirk pulled her up and dismounted; "but an ugly brute she is nevertheless, and such a one as I should not care to ride, for I am a gay man among the ladies. However, what is your price?"

Dirk named twice as much as he would have taken.

"Half that, you mean." And the usual haggle began.

"Tell thee what," said Dirk at last, "I am a man who has his fancies; and this shall be her price; half thy bid, and a box on the ear."

The demon of covetousness had entered Dirk's heart. What if he got the money, brained or at least disabled the stranger, and so had a chance of selling the mare a second time to some fresh comer?

"Thou art a strange fellow," quoth the horse-dealer. "But so be it."

Dirk chuckled. "He does not know," thought he, "that he has to do with Dirk Hammerhand," and he clenched his fist in anticipation of his rough joke.

"There," quoth the stranger, counting out the money carefully, "is thy coin. And there — is thy box on the ear."

And with a blow which rattled over the fen, he felled Dirk Hammerhand to the ground.

He lay senseless for a moment, and then looked wildly round. His jaw was broken.

"Villain!" groaned he. "It was I who was to give the buffet, not thou!"

"Art mad?" asked the stranger, as he coolly picked up the coins, which Dirk had scattered in his fall. "It is the seller's business to take, and the buyer's to give."

And while Dirk roared for help in vain he leapt on mare Swallow and rode off shouting, "Aha! Dirk Hammerhand! So you thought to knock a hole in my skull, as you have done to many a better man than yourself. He is a lucky man who never meets his match, Dirk. I shall give your love to the Enchanted Prince, my faithful serving-man, whom they call Martin Lightfoot.

Dirk cursed the day he was born. Instead of the mare and colt, he had got the two wretched garrons which the stranger had left, and a face which made him so tender of his own teeth, that he never again offered to try a buffet with a stranger.

CHAPTER XIV.

HOW HEREWARD RODE INTO BRUGES LIKE A BEGGAR-MAN.

The spring and summer had passed, and the autumn was almost over, when great news came to the Court of Bruges, where Torfrida was now a bower-maiden.

The Hollanders had been beaten till they submitted; at least for the present. There was peace, at least for the present, through all the isles of Scheldt; and more than all, the lovely Countess Gertrude had resolved to reward her Champion by giving him her hand, and the guardianship of her lands and the infant son.

And Hereward?

From him, or of him, there was no word. That he was alive and fighting, was all the messenger could say.

Then Robert came back to Bruges, with a gallant retinue, leading home his bride. And there met him his father and mother, and his brother of Mons, and Richilda the beautiful and terrible sorceress, — who had not yet stained her soul with those fearful crimes which she had expiated by fearful penances in after years, when young Arnoul, the son for whom she had sold her soul, lay dead through the very crimes by which she had meant to make him a mighty prince. And Torfrida went out with them to meet Count Robert, and looked for Hereward, till her eyes were ready to fall out of her head. But Hereward was not with them.

"He must be left behind, commanding the army," thought she. "But he might have sent one word!"

There was a great feast that day, of course; and Torfrida sat thereat: but she could not eat. Nevertheless she was too proud to let the knights know what was in her heart; so she chatted and laughed as gayly as the rest, watching always for any word of Hereward. But none mentioned his name.

The feast was long; the ladies did not rise till nigh bedtime; and then the men drank on.

They went up to the Queen-Countess's chamber; where a solemn undressing of that royal lady usually took place.

The etiquette was this. The Queen-Countess sat in her chair

of state in the midst, till her shoes were taken off, and her hair dressed for the night. Right and left of her, according to their degrees, sat the other great ladies; and behind each of them, where they could find places, the maidens.

It was Torfrida's turn to take off the royal shoes; and she advanced into the middle of the semicircle, slippers in hand.

"Stop there!" said the Countess-Queen.

Whereat Torfrida stopped, very much frightened.

"Countesses and ladies," said the mistress. "There are, in Provence and the South, what I wish there were here in Flanders, — Courts of Love, at which all offenders against the sacred laws of Venus and Cupid are tried by an assembly of their peers, and punished according to their deserts."

Torfrida turned scarlet.

"I know not why we, countesses and ladies, should have less knowledge of the laws of love than those gayer dames of the South, whose blood runs — to judge by her dark hair — in the veins of yon fair maid."

There was a silence. Torfrida was the most beautiful woman in the room; more beautiful than even Richilda the terrible: and therefore there were few but were glad to see her — as it seemed — in trouble.

Torfrida's mother began whimpering, and praying to six or seven saints at once. But nobody marked her, — possibly not even the saints; being preoccupied with Torfrida.

"I hear, fair maid, — for that you are that I will do you the justice to confess, — that you are old enough to be married this four years since."

Torfrida stood like a stone, frightened out of her wits, plentiful as they were.

"Why are you not married?"

There was, of course, no answer.

"I hear that knights have fought for you; lost their lives for you."

"I did not bid them," gasped Torfrida, longing that the floor would open, and swallow up the Queen-Countess and all her kin and followers, as it did for the enemies of the blessed Saint Dunstan, while he was arguing with them in an upper room at Calne.

"And that the knight of St. Valeri, to whom you gave your favor, now lies languishing of wounds got in your cause."

"I — I did not bid him fight," gasped Torfrida, now wishing that the floor would open and swallow up herself.

"And that he who overthrew the knight of St. Valeri, — to whom you gave that favor, and more —"

"I gave him nothing a maiden might not give," cried Torfrida, so fiercely that the Queen-Countess recoiled somewhat.
"I never said that you did, girl. Your love you gave him. Can you deny that?"

Torfrida laughed bitterly : her Southern blood was rising.

"I put my love out to nurse, instead of weaning it, as many a maiden has done before me. When my love cried for hunger and cold, I took it back again to my own bosom : and whether it has lived or died there, is no one's matter but my own."

"Hunger and cold? I hear that him to whom you gave your love you drove out to the cold, bidding him go fight in his bare shirt, if he wished to win your love."

"I did not. He angered me — he —" and Torfrida found herself in the act of accusing Hereward.

She stopped instantly.

"What more, Majesty? If this be true, what more may not be true of such a one as I? I submit myself to your royal grace."

"She has confessed. What punishment, ladies, does she deserve? Or, rather, what punishment would her cousins of Provence inflict, did we send her southward, to be judged by their Courts of Love?"

One lady said one thing, one another. Some spoke cruelly, some worse than cruelly ; for they were coarse ages, the ages of faith ; and ladies said things then in open company which gentlemen would be ashamed to say in private now.

"Marry her to a fool," said Richilda, at last, bitterly.

"That is too common a misfortune," answered the lady of France. "If we did no more to her, she might grow as proud as her betters."

Adela knew that her daughter-in-law considered her husband a fool; and was somewhat of the same opinion, though she hated Richilda.

"No," said she; "we will do more. We will marry her to the first man who enters the castle."

Torfrida looked at her mistress to see if she were mad. But the Countess-Queen was serene and sane. Then Torfrida's southern heat and northern courage burst forth.

"You — marry — me — to —" said she, slowly, with eyes so fierce, and lips so vivid, that Richilda herself quailed.

There was a noise of shouting and laughing in the court below, which made all turn and listen.

The next moment a serving-man came in, puzzled and inclined to laugh.

"May it please your Majesty, here is the strangest adventure.

There is ridden into the castle-yard a beggar-man, with scarce a shirt to his back, on a great ugly mare, with a foal running by her, and a fool behind him, carrying lance and shield. And he says that he is come to fight any knight of the Court, ragged as he stands, for the fairest lady in the Court, be she who she may, if she have not a wedded husband already."

"And what says my Lord Marquis?"

"That it is a fair challenge, and a good adventure; and that fight he shall, if any man will answer his defiance."

"And I say, tell my Lord the Marquis, that fight he shall not: for he shall have the fairest maiden in this Court for the trouble of carrying her away; and that I, Adela of France, will give her to him. So let that beggar dismount, and be brought up hither to me."

There was silence again. Torfrida looked round her once more, to see whether or not she was dreaming, and whether there was one human being to whom she could appeal. Her mother sat praying and weeping in a corner. Torfrida looked at her with one glance of scorn, which she confessed and repented, with bitter tears, many a year after, in a foreign land; and then turned to bay with the spirit of her old Paladin ancestor, who choked the Emir at Mont Majeur.

Married to a beggar! It was a strange accident; and an ugly one; and a great cruelty and wrong. But it was not impossible, hardly improbable, in days when the caprice of the strong created accidents, and when cruelty and wrong went for nothing, even with very kindly honest folk. So Torfrida faced the danger, as she would have faced that of a kicking horse, or a flooded ford; and like the nut-brown bride,

> "She pulled out a little penknife,
> That was both keen and sharp,"

and considered that the beggar-man could wear no armor, and that she wore none either. For if she succeeded in slaying that beggar-man, she might need to slay herself after, to avoid being — according to the fashion of those days — burnt alive.

So when the arras was drawn back, and that beggar-man came into the room, instead of shrieking, fainting, hiding, or turning, she made three steps straight toward him, looking him in the face like a wild-cat at bay. Then she threw up her arms; and fell upon his neck.

It was Hereward himself. Filthy, ragged: but Hereward.

His shirt was brown with gore, and torn with wounds; and through its rents showed more than one hardly healed scar. His hair and beard was all in elf-locks; and one heavy cut across the head had shorn not only hair, but brain-pan, very close. Moreover, any nose, save that of Love, might have required perfume.

But Hereward it was; and regardless of all beholders, she lay upon his neck, and never stirred nor spoke.

"I call you to witness, ladies," cried the Queen-Countess, "that I am guiltless. She has given herself to this beggar-man of her own free will. What say you?" And she turned to Torfrida's mother.

Torfrida's mother only prayed and whimpered.

"Countesses and Ladies," said the Queen-Countess, "there will be two weddings to-morrow. The first will be that of my son Robert and my pretty Lady Gertrude here. The second will be that of my pretty Torfrida and Hereward."

"And the second bride," said the Countess Gertrude, rising and taking Torfrida in her arms, "will be ten times prettier than the first. There, sir, I have done all you asked of me. Now go and wash yourself."

* * * * * *

"Hereward," said Torfrida, a week after, "and did you really never change your shirt all that time?"

"Never. I kept my promise."

"But it must have been very nasty."

"Well, I bathed now and then."

"But it must have been very cold."

"I am warm enough now."

"But did you never comb your hair, neither?"

"Well, I won't say that. Travellers find strange bed-fellows. But I had half a mind never to do it at all, just to spite you."

"And what matter would it have been to me?"

"O, none. It is only a Danish fashion we have of keeping clean."

"Clean! You were dirty enough when you came home. How silly you were! If you had sent me but one word!"

"You would have fancied me beaten, and scolded me all over again. I know your ways now, Torfrida."

CHAPTER XV.

HOW EARL TOSTI GODWINSSON CAME TO ST. OMER.

THE winter passed in sweet madness; and for the first time in her life, Torfrida regretted the lengthening of the days, and the flowering of the primroses, and the return of the now needless wryneck; for they warned her that Hereward must forth again, to the wars in Scaldmariland, which had broken out again, as was to be expected, as soon as Count Robert and his bride had turned their backs.

And Hereward, likewise, for the first time in his life, was loath to go to war. He was, doubtless, rich enough in this world's goods. Torfrida herself was rich, and seems to have had the disposal of her own property, for her mother is not mentioned in connection therewith. Hereward seems to have dwelt in her house at St. Omer as long as he remained in Flanders. He had probably amassed some treasure of his own by the simple, but then most aristocratic, method of plunder. He had, too, probably, grants of land in Holland from the Frison, the rents whereof were not paid as regularly as might be. Moreover, as "*Magister Militum*," "Master of the Knights," he had, it is likely, pay as well as honor. And he approved himself worthy of his good fortune. He kept forty gallant housecarles in his hall all the winter, and Torfrida and her lasses made and mended their clothes. He gave large gifts to the Abbey of St. Bertin; and had masses sung for the souls of all whom he had slain, according to a rough list which he furnished, — bidding the monks not to be chary of two or three masses extra at times, as his memory was short, and he might have sent more souls to purgatory than he had recollected. He gave great alms at his door to all the poor. He befriended, especially, all shipwrecked and needy mariners, feeding and clothing them, and begging their freedom as a gift from Baldwin. He feasted the knights of the neighborhood, who since his Baresark campaign, had all vowed him the most gallant of warriors, and since his accession of wealth, the most courteous of gentlemen; and so all went merrily, as it is written, "As long as thou doost well unto thyself, men will speak well of thee."

So he would have fain stayed at home at St. Omer; but he

was Robert's man, and his good friend likewise; and to the wars he must go forth once more; and for eight or nine weary months Torfrida was alone: but very happy, for a certain reason of her own.

At last the short November days came round; and a joyful woman was fair Torfrida, when Martin Lightfoot ran into the hall, and throwing himself down on the rushes like a dog, announced that Hereward and his men would be home before noon, and then fell fast asleep.

There was bustling to and fro of her and her maids; decking of the hall in the best hangings; strewing of fresh rushes, to the dislodgement of Martin; setting out of square tables, and stoops and mugs thereon; cooking of victuals, broaching of casks; and above all, for Hereward's self, heating of much water, and setting out, in the inner chamber, of the great bath-tub and bath-sheet, which was the special delight of a hero fresh from the war.

And by midday the streets of St. Omer rang with clank and tramp and trumpet-blare, and in marched Hereward and all his men, and swung round through the gateway into the court, where Torfrida stood to welcome them, as fair as day, a silver stirrup-cup in her hand. And while the men were taking off their harness and dressing their horses, she and Hereward went in together, and either took such joy of the other, that a year's parting was forgot in a minute's meeting.

"Now," cried she, in a tone half of triumph, half of tenderness, "look there!"

"A cradle? And a baby?"

"Your baby."

"Is it a boy?" asked Hereward, who saw in his mind's eye a thing which would grow and broaden at his knee year by year, and learn from him to ride, to shoot, to fight. "Happy for him if he does not learn worse from me," thought Hereward, with a sudden movement of humility and contrition, which was surely marked in heaven; for Torfrida marked it on earth.

But she mistook its meaning.

"Do not be vexed. It is a girl."

"Never mind!" as if it was a calamity over which he was bound to comfort the mother. "If she is half as beautiful as you look at this moment, what splintering of lances there will be about her! How jolly, to see the lads hewing at each other, while our daughter sits in the pavilion, as Queen of Love!"

Torfrida laughed. "You think of nothing but fighting, bear of the North Seas."

"Every one to his trade. Well, yes, I am glad that it is a girl."

"I thought you seemed vexed. Why did you cross yourself?"

"Because I thought to myself, how unfit I was to bring up a boy to be such a knight as — as you would have him; how likely I was, ere all was over, to make him as great a ruffian as myself."

"Hereward! Hereward!" and she threw her arms round his neck for the tenth time. "Blessed be you for those words! Those are the fears which never come true, for they bring down from heaven the grace of God, to guard the humble and contrite heart from that which it fears."

"Ah, Torfrida, I wish I were as good as you!"

"Now — my joy and my life, my hero and my skald — I have great news for you, as well as a little baby. News from England."

"You, and a baby over and above, are worth all England to me."

"But listen: Edward the king is dead!"

"Then there is one fool less on earth; and one saint more, I suppose, in heaven."

"And Harold Godwinsson is king in his stead. And he has married your niece Aldytha, and sworn friendship with her brothers."

"I expected no less. Well, every dog has his day."

"And his will be a short one. William of Normandy has sworn to drive him out."

"Then he will do it. And so the poor little Swan-neck is packed into a convent, that the houses of Godwin and Leofric may rush into each other's arms, and perish together! Fools, fools, fools! I will hear no more of such a mad world. My queen, tell me about your sweet self. What is all this to me? Am I not a wolf's head, and a landless man?"

"O my king, have not the stars told me that you will be an earl and a ruler of men, when all your foes are wolves' heads as you are now? And the weird is coming true already. Tosti Godwinsson is in the town at this moment, an outlaw and a wolf's head himself."

Hereward laughed a great laugh.

"Aha! Every man to his right place at last. Tell me about that, for it will amuse me. I have heard naught of him since he sent the king his Hereford thralls' arms and legs in the pickle-barrels; to show him, he said, that there was plenty of cold meat on his royal demesnes."

"You have not heard, then, how he murdered in his own chamber at York, Gamel Ormsson and Ulf Dolfinsson?"

"That poor little lad? Well, a gracious youth was Tosti, ever since he went to kill his brother Harold with teeth and claws, like a wolf; and as he grows in years, he grows in grace. But what said Ulf's father and the Gospatricks?"

"Dolfin and young Gospatrick were I know not where. But old Gospatrick came down to Westminster, to demand law for his grandnephew's blood."

"A silly thing of the old Thane, to walk into the wolf's den."

"And so he found. He was stabbed there, three days after Christmas-tide, and men say that Queen Edith did it, for love of Tosti, her brother. Then Dolfin and young Gospatrick took to the sea, and away to Scotland: and so Tosti rid himself of all the good blood in the North, except young Waltheof Siwardsson, whose turn, I fear, will come next."

"How comes he here, then?"

"The Northern men rose at that, killed his servant at York, took all his treasures, and marched down to Northampton, plundering and burning. They would have marched on London town, if Harold had not met them there from the king. There they cried out against Tosti, and all his taxes, and his murders, and his changing Canute's laws, and would have young Morcar for their earl. A tyrant they would not endure. Free they were born and bred, they said, and free they would live and die. Harold must needs do justice, even on his own brother."

"Especially when he knows that that brother is his worst foe."

"Harold is a better man than you take him for, my Hereward. But be that as it may, Morcar is earl, and Tosti outlawed, and here in St. Omer, with wife and child."

"My nephew Earl of Northumbria! As I might have been, if I had been a wiser man."

"If you had, you would never have found me."

"True, my queen! They say Heaven tempers the wind to the shorn lamb; but it tempers it too, sometimes, to the hobbled ass; and so it has done by me. And so the rogues have fallen out, and honest men may come by their own. For, as the Northern men have done by one brother, so will the Eastern men do by the other. Let Harold see how many of those fat Lincolnshire manors, which he has seized into his own hands, he holds by this day twelve months. But what is all this to me, my queen, while you and I can kiss, and laugh the world to scorn?"

"This to you, beloved, that, great as you are, Torfrida must have you greater still; and out of all this coil and confusion you may win something, if you be wise."

"Sweet lips, be still, and let us love instead of plotting."

"And this, too — you shall not stop my mouth — that Harold Godwinsson has sent a letter to you."

"Harold Godwinsson is my very good lord," sneered Hereward.

"And this it said, with such praises and courtesies concerning you, as made thy wife's heart beat high with pride: 'If Hereward Leofricsson will come home to England, he shall have his rights in law again, and his manors in Lincolnshire, and a thanesship in East Anglia, and manors for his men-at-arms; and if that be not enough, he shall have an earldom, as soon as there is one to give.'"

"And what says to that, Torfrida, Hereward's queen?"

"You will not be angry if I answered the letter for you?"

"If you answered it one way, — no. If another, — yes."

Torfrida trembled. Then she looked Hereward full in the face with her keen clear eyes.

"Now shall I see whether I have given myself to Hereward in vain, body and soul, or whether I have trained him to be my true and perfect knight."

"You answered, then," said Hereward, "thus — "

"Say on," said she, turning her face away again.

"Hereward Leofricsson tells Harold Godwinsson that he is his equal, and not his man; and that he will never put his hands between the hands of a son of Godwin. An Etheling born, a king of the house of Cerdic, outlawed him from his right, and none but an Etheling born shall give him his right again."

"I said it, I said it. Those were my very words!" and Torfrida burst into tears, while Hereward kissed her, almost fawned upon her, calling her his queen, his saga-wife, his guardian angel.

"I was sorely tempted," sobbed she. "Sorely. To see you, rich and proud, upon your own lands, an earl may be, — may be, I thought at whiles, a king. But it could not be. It did not stand with honor, my hero, — not with honor."

"Not with honor. Get me gay garments out of the chest, and let us go in royally, and royally feast my jolly riders."

"Stay awhile," said she, kissing his head as she combed and curled his long golden locks; and her own raven ones, hardly more beautiful, fell over them and mingled with them. "Stay awhile, my pride. There is another spell in the wind, stirred up by devil or witch-wife, and it comes from Tosti Godwinsson."

"Tosti, the cold-meat butcher? What has he to say to me?"

"This, — 'If Hereward will come with me to William of Normandy, and help us against Harold, the perjured, then will William do for him all that Harold would have done, and more beside.'"

"And what answered Torfrida?"

"It was not so said to me that I could answer. I had it by a side-wind, through the Countess Judith." *

"And she had it from her sister, Matilda."

"And she, of course, from Duke William, himself."

"And what would you have answered, if you had answered, pretty one?"

"Nay, I know not. I cannot be always queen. You must be king sometimes."

Torfrida did not say that this latter offer had been a much sorer temptation than the former.

"And has not the base-born Frenchman enough knights of his own, that he needs the help of an outlaw like me?"

"He asks for help from all the ends of the earth. He has sent that Lanfranc to the Pope; and there is talk of a sacred banner, and a crusade against England."

"The monks are with him, then?" said Hereward. "That is one more count in their score. But I am no monk. I have shorn many a crown, but I have kept my own hair as yet, you see."

"I do see," said she, playing with his locks. "But, — but he wants you. He has sent for Angevins, Poitevins, Bretons, Flemings, — promising lands, rank, money, what not. Tosti is recruiting for him here in Flanders now. He will soon be off to the Orkneys, I suspect, or to Sweyn in Denmark, after Vikings."

"Here? Has Baldwin promised him men?"

"What could the good old man do? He could not refuse his own son-in-law. This, at least, I know, that a messenger has gone off to Scotland, to Gilbert of Ghent, to bring or send any bold Flemings who may prefer fat England to lean Scotland."

"Lands, rank, money, eh? So he intends that the war should pay itself — out of English purses. What answer would you have me make to that, wife mine?"

"The Duke is a terrible man. What if he conquers? And conquer he will."

"Is that written in your stars?"

"It is, I fear. And if he have the Pope's blessing, and the Pope's banner — Dare we resist the Holy Father?"

"Holy step-father, you mean; for a step-father he seems to prove to merry England. But do you really believe that an old man down in Italy can make a bit of rag conquer by saying a few prayers at it? If I am to believe in a magic flag, give me Harold Hardraade's Landcyda, at least, with Harold and his Norsemen behind it."

* Tosti's wife, Earl Baldwin's daughter, sister of Matilda, William the Conqueror's wife.

"William's French are as good as those Norsemen, man for man; and horsed withal, Hereward."

"That may be," said he, half testily, with a curse on the tanner's grandson and his French popinjays, "and our Englishmen are as good as any two Norsemen, as the Norse themselves say." He could not divine, and Torfrida hardly liked to explain to him the glamour which the Duke of Normandy had cast over her, as the representative of chivalry, learning, civilization, a new and nobler life for men than the world had yet seen; one which seemed to connect the young races of Europe with the wisdom of the ancients and the magic glories of old Imperial Rome.

"You are not fair to that man," said she, after a while. "Hereward, Hereward, have I not told you how, though body be strong, mind is stronger? That is what that man knows; and therefore he has prospered. Therefore his realms are full of wise scholars, and thriving schools, and fair minsters, and his men are sober, and wise, and learned like clerks —"

"And false like clerks, as he is himself. Schoolcraft and honesty never went yet together, Torfrida —"

"Not in me?"

"You are not a clerk, you are a woman, and more, you are an elf, a goddess; there is none like you. But hearken to me. This man is false. All the world knows it."

"He promises, they say, to govern England justly as King Edward's heir, according to the old laws and liberties of the realm."

"Of course. If he does not come as the old monk's heir, how does he come at all? If he does not promise our — their, I mean, for I am no Englishman — laws and liberties, who will join him? But his riders and hirelings will not fight for nothing. They must be paid with English land, and English land they will have, for they will be his men, whoever else are not. They will be his darlings, his housecarles, his hawks to sit on his fist and fly at his game; and English bones will be picked clean to feed them. And you would have me help to do that, Torfrida? Is that the honor of which you spoke so boldly to Harold Godwinsson?"

Torfrida was silent. To have brought Hereward under the influence of William was an old dream of hers. And yet she was proud at the dream being broken thus. And so she said "You are right. It is better for you, — it is better than to be William's darling, and the greatest earl in his court, — to feel that you are still an Englishman. Promise me but one thing, that you will make no fierce or desperate answer to the Duke."

"And why not answer the tanner as he deserves?"

"Because my art, and my heart too, tells me that your fortunes and his are linked together. I have studied my tables, but they would not answer. Then I cast lots in Virgilius—"

"And what found you there?" asked he, anxiously

"I opened at the lines,—

"Pacem me exanimis et Martis sorte peremptis
Oratis? Equidem et vivis concedere vellem."

"And what means that?"

"That you may have to pray him to pity the slain; and have for answer, that their lands may be yours if you will but make peace with him. At least, do not break hopelessly with that man. Above all, never use that word concerning him which you used just now; the word which he never forgives. Remember what he did to them of Alençon, when they hung raw hides over the wall, and cried, 'Plenty of work for the tanner!'"

"Let him pick out the prisoners' eyes, and chop off their hands, and shoot them into the town from mangonels,—he must go far and thrive well ere I give him a chance of doing that by me."

"Hereward, Hereward, my own! Boast not, but fear God. Who knows, in such a world as this, to what end we may come? Night after night I am haunted with spectres, eyeless, handless—"

"This is cold comfort for a man just out of hard fighting in the ague-fens!"

She threw her arms round him, and held him as if she would never let him go.

"When you die, I die. And you will not die: you will be great and glorious, and your name will be sung by skald and minstrel through many a land, far and wide. Only be not rash. Be not high-minded. Promise me to answer this man wisely. The more crafty he is, the more crafty must you be likewise."

"Let us tell this mighty hero, then," said Hereward,—trying to laugh away her fears, and perhaps his own,—"that while he has the Holy Father on his side, he can need no help from a poor sinful worm like me."

"Hereward, Hereward!"

"Why, is there aught about hides in that?"

"I want,—I want an answer which may not cut off all hope in case of the worst."

"Then let us say boldly, 'On the day that William is King of all England, Hereward will come and put his hands between his, and be his man.'"

That message was sent to William at Rouen. He laughed—

"It is a fair challenge from a valiant man. The day shall come when I will claim it."

Tosti and Hereward passed that winter in St. Omer, living in the same street, passing each other day by day, and never spoke a word one to the other.

Robert the Frison heard of it, and tried to persuade Hereward.

"Let him purge himself of the murder of Ulf, the boy, son of my friend Dolfin; and after that, of Gamel, son of Orm; and after that, again, of Gospatrick, my father's friend, whom his sister slew for his sake; and then an honest man may talk with him. Were he not my good lord's brother-in-law, as he is, more's the pity, I would challenge him to fight à l'outrance, with any weapons he might choose."

"Heaven protect him in that case," quoth Robert the Frison.

"As it is, I will keep the peace. And I will see that my men keep the peace, though there are Scarborough and Bamborough lads among them, who long to cut his throat upon the streets. But more I will not do."

So Tosti sulked through the winter at St. Omer, and then went off to get help from Sweyn, of Denmark, and failing that, from Harold Hardraade of Norway. But how he sped there must be read in the words of a cunninger saga-man than this chronicler, even in those of the "Icelandic Homer," Snorro Sturleson.

CHAPTER XVI.

HOW HEREWARD WAS ASKED TO SLAY AN OLD COMRADE.

IN those days Hereward went into Bruges, to Marquis Baldwin, about his business. And as he walked in Bruges street, he met an old friend, Gilbert of Ghent.

He had grown somewhat stouter, and somewhat grayer, in the last ten years: but he was as hearty as ever; and as honest, according to his own notions of honesty.

He shook Hereward by both hands, clapt him on the back, swore with many oaths, that he had heard of his fame in all lands, that he always said that he would turn out a champion and a gallant knight, and had said it long before he killed the bear. As for killing it, it was no more than he expected, and nothing to what Hereward had done since, and would do yet.

Wherefrom Hereward opined that Gilbert had need of him.

They chatted on: Hereward asking after old friends, and sometimes after old foes, whom he had long since forgiven; for though he always avenged an injury, he never bore malice for one; a distinction less common now than then, when a man's honor, as well as his safety, depended on his striking again, when he was struck.

"And how is little Alftruda? Big she must be now?" asked he at last.

"The fiend fly away with her,— or rather, would that he had flown away with her, before ever I saw the troublesome little jade. Big? She is grown into the most beautiful lass that ever was seen,— which is, what a young fellow like you cares for; and more trouble to me than all my money, which is what an old fellow like me cares for. It is partly about her that I am over here now. Fool that I was, ever to let an Etheliza* into my house"; and Gilbert swore a great deal.

"How was she an Etheliza?" asked Hereward, who cared nothing about the matter. "And how came she into your house? I never could understand that, any more than how the bear came there."

---

* A princess of the royal blood of Cerdic, and therefore of Edward the Confessor.

"Ah! As to the bear, I have my secrets, which I tell no one. He is dead and buried, thanks to you."

"And I sleep on his skin every night."

"You do, my little Champion? Well, warm is the bed that is well earned. But as for her; — see here, and I'll tell you. She was Gospatrick's ward, and kinswoman, — how, I do not rightly know. But this I know, that she comes from Uchtred, the earl whom Canute slew, and that she is heir to great estates in Northumberland.

"Gospatrick, that fought at Dunsinane?"

"Yes, not the old Thane, his uncle, whom Tosti has murdered; but Gospatrick, King Malcolm's cousin, Dolfin's father. Well, she was his ward. He gave me her to keep, for he wanted her out of harm's way — the lass having a bonny dower, lands and money — till he could marry her up to one of his sons. I took her; of course I was not going to do other men's work for naught; so I would have married her up to my poor boy, if he had but lived. But he would not live, as you know. Then I would have married her to you, and made you my heir, I tell you honestly, if you had not flown off, like a hot-headed young springald, as you were then."

"You were very kind. But how is she an Etheliza?"

"Etheliza? Twice over. Her father was of high blood among those Saxons; and if not, are not all the Gospatricks Ethelings? Their grandmother, Uchtred's wife, was Ethelred, Evil-Counsel's daughter, King Edward of London's sister; and I have heard that this girl's grandfather was their son, — but died young, — or was killed with his father. Who cares?"

"Not I," quoth Hereward.

"Well — he wants to marry her to Dolfin, his eldest son."

"Why, Dolfin had a wife when I was at Dunsinane."

"But she is dead since, and young Ulf, her son, murdered by Tosti last winter."

"I know."

"Whereon Gospatrick sends to me for the girl and her dowry. What was I to do? Give her up? Little it is, lad, that I ever gave up, after I had it once in my grip, or I should be a poorer man than I am now. Have and hold, is my rule. What should I do? What I did. I was coming hither on business of my own, so I put her on board ship, and half her dower, — where the other half is, I know; and man must draw me with wild horses, before he finds out; — and came here to my kinsman, Baldwin, to see if he had any proper young fellow to whom we might marry the lass, and so go shares in her money and the family connection. Could a man do more wisely?"

"Impossible," quoth Hereward.

"But see how a wise man is lost by fortune. When I come here, whom should I find but Dolfin himself? The dog had scent of my plan, all the way from Dolfinston there, by l'cebles. He hunts me out, the hungry Scotch wolf; rides for Leith, takes ship, and is here to meet me, having accused me before Baldwin as a robber and ravisher, and offers to prove his right to the jade on my body in single combat."

"The villain!" quoth Hereward. "There is no modesty left on earth, nor prudence either. To come here, where he might have stumbled on Tosti, who murdered his son, and I would surely do the like by him, himself. Lucky for him that Tosti is off to Norway on his own errand."

"Modesty and prudence? None now-a-days, young sire; nor justice either, I think; for when Baldwin hears us both — and I told my story as cannily as I could — he tells me that he is very sorry for an old vassal and kinsman, and so forth, — but I must either disgorge or fight."

"Then fight," quoth Hereward.

"'Per se aut per campioneem,' — that's the old law, you know."

"Not a doubt of it."

"Look you, Hereward. I am no coward, nor a clumsy man of my hands."

"He is either fool or liar who says so."

"But see. I find it hard work to hold my own in Scotland now. Folks don't like me, or trust me; I can't say why."

"How unreasonable!" quoth Hereward.

"And if I kill this youth, and so have a blood-feud with Gospatrick, I have a hornet's nest about my ears. Not only he and his sons, — who are masters of Scotch Northumberland,* — but all his cousins; King Malcolm, and Donaldbain, and, for aught I know, Harold and the Godwinssons, if he bid them take up the quarrel. And beside, that Dolfin is a big man. If you cross Scot and Saxon, you breed a very big man. If you cross again with a Dane or a Norseman, you breed a giant. His grandfather was a Scots prince, his grandmother an English Etheliza, his mother a Norse princess, as you know, — and how big he is, you should remember. He weighs half as much again as I, and twice as much as you."

"Butchers count by weight, and knights by courage," quoth Hereward.

"Very well for you, who are young and active; but I take

* Between Tweed and Forth.

him to be a better man than that ogre of Cornwall, whom they say you killed."

"What care I? Let him be twice as good, I'd try him."

"Ah! I knew you were the old Hereward still. Now hearken to me. Be my champion. You owe me a service, lad. Fight that man, challenge him in open field. Kill him, as you are sure to do. Claim the lass, and win her,—and then we will part her dower. And (though it is little that I care for young lasses' fancies), to tell you truth, she never favored any man but you."

Hereward started at the snare which had been laid for him; and then fell into a very great laughter.

"My most dear and generous host: you are the wiser, the older you grow. A plan worthy of Solomon! You are rid of Sieur Dolfin without any blame to yourself."

"Just so."

"While I win the lass, and, living here in Flanders, am tolerably safe from any blood-feud of the Gospatricks."

"Just so."

"Perfect: but there is only one small hinderance to the plan; and that is—that I am married already."

Gilbert stopped short, and swore a great oath.

"But," he said, after a while, "does that matter so much after all?"

"Very little, indeed, as all the world knows, if one has money enough, and power enough."

"And you have both," they say.

"But, still more unhappily, my money is my wife's."

"Peste!"

"And more unhappily still, I am so foolishly fond of her, that I would sooner have her in her smock, than any other woman with half England for a dower."

"Then I suppose I must look out for another champion."

"Or save yourself the trouble, by being—just as a change—an honest man."

"I believe you are right," said Gilbert, laughing; "but it is hard to begin so late in life."

"And after one has had so little practice."

"Aha! Thou art the same merry dog of a Hereward. Come along. But could we not poison this Dolfin, after all?"

To which proposal Hereward gave no encouragement.

"And now, my très beau sire, may I ask you, in return, what business brings you to Flanders?"

"Have I not told you?"

"No, but I have guessed. Gilbert of Ghent is on his way to William of Normandy."

"Well. Why not?"

"Why not?—certainly. And has brought out of Scotland a few gallant gentlemen, and stout housecarles of my acquaintance."

Gilbert laughed.

"You may well say that. To tell you the truth, we have flitted, bag and baggage. I don't believe that we have left a dog behind."

"So you intend to 'colonize' in England, as the learned clerks would call it? To settle; to own land; and enter, like the Jews of old, into goodly houses which you builded not, farms which you tilled not, wells which you digged not, and orchards which you planted not?"

"Why, what a clerk you are! That sounds like Scripture."

"And so it is. I heard it in a French priest's sermon, which he preached here in St. Omer a Sunday or two back, exhorting all good Catholics, in the Pope's name, to enter upon the barbarous land of England, tainted with the sin of Simon Magus, and expel thence the heretical priests, and so forth, promising them that they should have free leave to cut long thongs out of other men's hides."

Gilbert chuckled.

"You laugh. The priest did not; for after sermon I went up to him, and told him how I was an Englishman, and an outlaw, and a desperate man, who feared neither saint nor devil; and if I heard such talk as that again in St. Omer, I would so shave the speaker's crown that he should never need razor to his dying day."

"And what is that to me?" said Gilbert, in an uneasy, half-defiant tone; for Hereward's tone had been more than half-defiant.

"This. That there are certain broad lands in England, which were my father's, and are now my nephews' and my mother's, and some which should by right be mine. And I advise you, as a friend, not to make entry on those lands, lest Hereward in turn make entry on you. And who is he that will deliver you out of my hand?"

"God and his Saints alone, thou fiend out of the pit!" quoth Gilbert, laughing. But he was growing warm, and began to tutoyer Hereward.

"I am in earnest, Gilbert of Ghent, my good friend of old time."

"I know thee well enough, man. Why in the name of all glory and plunder art thou not coming with us? They say William has offered thee the earldom of Northumberland."

"He has not. And if he has, it is not his to give. And if it were, it is by right neither mine nor my nephews', but Waltheof Siwardsson's. Now hearken unto me; and settle it in your mind, thou and William both, that your quarrel is against none but Harold and the Godwinssons, and their men of Wessex; but that if you go to cross the Watling street, and meddle with the free Danes, who are none of Harold's men —"

"Stay. Harold has large manors in Lincolnshire, and so has Edith his sister; and what of them, Sir Hereward?"

"That the man who touches them, even though the men on them may fight on Harold's side, had better have put his head into a hornet's nest. Unjustly were they seized from their true owners by Harold and his fathers; and the holders of them will owe no service to him a day longer than they can help; but will, if he fall, demand an earl of their own race, or fight to the death."

"Best make young Waltheof earl, then."

"Best keep thy foot out of them, and the foot of any man for whom thou carest. Now, good by. Friends we are, and friends let us be."

"Ah, that thou wert coming to England!"

"I bide my time. Come I may, when I see fit. But whether I come as friend or foe depends on that of which I have given thee fair warning."

So they parted for the time.

It will be seen hereafter how Gilbert took his own advice about young Waltheof, but did not take Hereward's advice about the Lincoln manors.

In Baldwin's hall that day Hereward met Dolfin; and when the magnificent young Scot sprang to him, embraced him, talked over old passages, complimented him on his fame, lamented that he himself had won no such honors in the field, Hereward felt much more inclined to fight for him than against him.

Presently the ladies entered from the bower inside the hall. A buzz of expectation rose from all the knights, and Alftruda's name was whispered round.

She came in, and Hereward saw at the first glance that Gilbert had for once in his life spoken truth. So beautiful a girl he had never beheld; and as she swept down toward him he for one moment forgot Torfrida, and stood spell-bound like the rest.

Her eye caught his. If his face showed recognition, hers showed none. The remembrance of their early friendship, of her deliverance from the monster, had plainly passed away.

"Fickle, ungrateful things, these women," thought Hereward.

She passed him close. And as she did so, she turned her head and looked him full in the face one moment, haughty and cold.

"So you could not wait for me?" said she, in a quiet whisper, and went on straight to Dolfin, who stood trembling with expectation and delight.

She put her hand into his.

"Here stands my champion," said she.

"Say, here kneels your slave," cried the Scot, dropping to the pavement a true Highland knee. Whereon forth shrieked a bagpipe, and Dolfin's minstrel sang, in most melodious Gaelic, —

"Strong as a horse's hock, shaggy as a stag's brisket,
Is the knee of the young torrent-leaper, the pride of the house of Crinan.
It bent not to Macbeth the accursed, it bends not even to Malcolm the Anointed,
But it bends like a harebell — who shall blame it? — before the breath of beauty."

Which magnificent effusion being interpreted by Hereward for the instruction of the ladies, procured for the red-headed bard more than one handsome gift.

A sturdy voice arose out of the crowd.

"The fair lady, my Lord Count, and knights all, will need no champion as far as I am concerned. When one sees so fair a pair together, what can a knight say, in the name of all knighthood, but that the heavens have made them for each other, and that it were sin and shame to sunder them?"

The voice was that of Gilbert of Ghent, who, making a virtue of necessity, walked up to the pair, his weather-beaten countenance wreathed into what were meant for paternal smiles.

"Why did you not say as much in Scotland, and save me all this trouble?" pertinently asked the plain-spoken Scot.

"My Lord Prince, you owe me a debt for my caution. Without it, the poor lady had never known the whole fervency of your love; or these noble knights and yourself the whole evenness of Count Baldwin's justice."

Alftruda turned her head away half contemptuously; and as she did so, she let her hand drop listlessly from Dolfin's grasp, and drew back to the other ladies.

A suspicion crossed Hereward's mind. Did she really love the Prince? Did those strange words of hers mean that she had not yet forgotten Hereward himself?

However, he said to himself that it was no concern of his, as it certainly was not: went home to Torfrida, told her everything that had happened, laughed over it with her, and then forgot Alftruda, Dolfin, and Gilbert, in the prospect of a great campaign in Holland.

CHAPTER XVII.

HOW HEREWARD TOOK THE NEWS FROM STANFORD BRIGG AND HASTINGS.

AFTER that, news came thick and fast.

News of all the fowl of heaven flocking to the feast of the great God, that they might eat the flesh of kings, and captains, and mighty men, and horses, and them that sit on them, and the flesh of all men, both bond and free.

News from Rome, how England, when conquered, was to be held as a fief of St. Peter, and spiritually, as well as temporarily, enslaved. News how the Gonfanon of St. Peter, and a ring with a bit of St. Peter himself enclosed therein, had come to Rouen, to go before the Norman host, as the Ark went before that of Israel.

Then news from the North. How Tosti had been to Sweyn, and bid him come back and win the country again, as Canute his uncle had done; and how the cautious Dane had answered that he was a much smaller man than Canute, and had enough to hold his own against the Norsemen, and could not afford to throw for such high stakes as his mighty uncle.

Then how Tosti had been to Norway, to Harold Hardraade, and asked him why he had been fighting fifteen years for Denmark, when England lay open to him. And how Harold of Norway had agreed to come; and how he had levied one half of the able-bodied men in Norway; and how he was gathering a mighty fleet at Solundir, in the mouth of the Sogne Fiord. Of all this Hereward was well informed; for Tosti came back again to St. Omer, and talked big. But Hereward and he had no dealings with each other. But at last, when Tosti tried to entice some of Hereward's men to sail with him, Hereward sent him word that if he met him, he would kill him in the streets.

Then Tosti, who (though he wanted not for courage) knew that he was no match for Hereward, went off to Bruges, leaving his wife and family behind, gathered sixty ships at Ostend, went off to the Isle of Wight, and forced the landsfolk to give him money and food. And then Harold of England's fleet, which was watching the coast against the Normans, drove him away and he sailed off north, full of black rage against his brother

Harold and all Englishmen, and burned, plundered, and murdered, along the coast of Lincolnshire, out of brute spite to the Danes who had expelled him.

Then came news how he had got into the Humber; how Earl Edwin and his Northumbrians had driven him out; and how he went off to Scotland to meet Harold of Norway; and how he had put his hands between Harold's, and become his man.

And all the while the Norman camp at St. Pierre-sur-Dive grew and grew; and all was ready, if the wind would but change.

And so Hereward looked on, helpless, and saw these two great storm-clouds growing, — one from north, and one from south, — to burst upon his native land.

Two invasions at the same moment of time; and these no mere Viking raids for plunder, but deliberate attempts at conquest and colonization, by the two most famous captains of the age. What if both succeeded? What if the two storm-clouds swept across England, each on its own path, and met in the midst, to hurl their lightnings into each other? A fight between William of Normandy and Harold of Norway, on some moorland in Mercia, — it would be a battle of giants; a sight at which Odin and the Gods of Valhalla would rise from their seats, and throw away the mead-horn, to stare down on the deeds of heroes scarcely less mighty than themselves. Would that neither might win! Would that they would destroy and devour, till there was none left of Frenchmen or of Norwegians!

So sung Hereward, after his heathen fashion; and his housecarles applauded the song. But Torfrida shuddered.

"And what will become of the poor English in the mean time?"

"They have brought it on themselves," said Hereward, bitterly. "Instead of giving the crown to the man who should have had it, — to Sweyn of Denmark, — they let Godwin put it on the head of a drivelling monk; and as they sowed, so will they reap."

But Hereward's own soul was black within him. To see these mighty events passing as it were within reach of his hand, and he unable to take his share in them, — for what share could he take? That of Tosti Godwinsson against his own nephews? That of Harold Godwinsson, the usurper? That of the tanner's grandson against any man? Ah that he had been in England! Ah that he had been where he might have been, — where he ought to have been but for his own folly, — high in power in his native land, — perhaps a great earl; perhaps commander of all the armies of the Danelagh. And bitterly he cursed his youthful sins as he rode to and fro almost daily to the port of Calais, asking for news, and getting often only too much.

For now came news that the Norsemen had landed in Humber that Edwin and Morcar were beaten at York; that Hardraade and Tosti were masters of the North.

And with that, news that, by the virtue of the relics of St. Valeri, which had been brought out of their shrine to frighten the demons of the storm, and by the intercession of the blessed St Michael, patron of Normandy, the winds had changed, and William's whole armament had crossed the Channel, landed upon an undefended shore, and fortified themselves at Pevensey and Hastings.

And then followed a fortnight of silence and torturing suspense.

Hereward could hardly eat, drink, sleep, or speak. He answered Torfrida's consolations curtly and angrily, till she betook herself to silent caresses, as to a sick animal. But she loved him all the better for his sullenness; for it showed that his English heart was wakening again, sound and strong.

At last news came. He was down, as usual, at the port. A ship had just come in from the northward. A man just landed stood on the beach gesticulating, and calling in an unknown tongue to the bystanders, who laughed at him, and seemed inclined to misuse him.

Hereward galloped down the beach.

"Out of the way, villains! Why man, you are a Norseman!"

"Norseman am I, Earl, Thord Gunlaugsson is my name, and news I bring for the Countess Judith (as the French call her) that shall turn her golden hair to snow, — yea, and all fair lasses' hair from Lindesness to Loffoden!"

"Is the Earl dead?"

"And Harold Sigurdsson!"

Hereward sat silent, appalled. For Tosti he cared not. But Harold Sigurdsson, Harold Hardraade, Harold the Viking, Harold the Varanger, Harold the Lionslayer, Harold of Constantinople, the bravest among champions, the wisest among kings, the cunningest among minstrels, the darling of the Vikings of the north; the one man whom Hereward had taken for his pattern and his ideal, the one man under whose banner he would have been proud to fight — the earth seemed empty, if Harold Hardraade were gone.

"Thord Gunlaugsson," cried he, at last, "or whatever be thy name, if thou hast lied to me, I will draw thee with wild horses."

"Would God that I did lie! I saw him fall with an arrow through his throat. Then Jarl Tosti took the Land-ravager and held it up till he died. Then Eystein Orre took it, coming up hot from the ships. And then he died likewise. Then they all died. We would take no quarter. We threw off our mail, and fought baresark, till all were dead together." *

"How camest thou, then, hither?"

"Styrkar the marshal escaped in the night, and I with him, and a few more. And Styrkar bade me bring the news to Flanders, to the Countess, while he took it to Olaf Haroldsson, who lay off in the ships."

"And thou shalt take it. Martin! get this man a horse. A horse, ye villains, and a good one, on your lives!"

"And Tosti is dead?"

"Dead like a hero. Harold offered him quarter, — offered him his earldom, they say: even in the midst of battle: but he would not take it. He said he was the Sigurdsson's man now, and true man he would be!"

"Harold offered him — what art babbling about? Who fought you?"

"Harold Godwinsson, the king."

"Where?"

"At Stanford Brigg, by York Town."

"Harold Godwinsson slew Harold Sigurdsson? After this wolves may eat lions!"

"The Godwinsson is a gallant fighter, and a wise general, or I had not been here now."

"Get on thy horse, man!" said he, scornfully and impatiently, "and gallop, if thou canst."

"I have ridden many a mile in Ireland, Earl, and have not forgotten my seat."

"Thou hast, hast thou?" said Martin; "thou art Thord Gunlaugsson of Waterford."

"That am I. How knowest thou me, man?"

"I am of Waterford. Thou hadst a slave lass once, I think; Mew: they called her Mew, her skin it was so white."

"What's that to thee?" asked Thord, turning on him savagely.

"Why, I meant no harm. I saw her at Waterford when I was a boy, and thought her a fair lass enough, that is all."

And Martin dropped into the rear. By this time they were at the gates of St. Omer.

As they rode side by side, Hereward got more details of the fight.

"I knew it would fall out so. I foretold it!" said Thord. "I had a dream. I saw us come to English land, and fight; and I saw the banners floating. And before the English army was a

* For the details of this battle, see Skorro Sturleson, or the admirable description in Bulwer's "Harold."

great witchwife, and rode upon a wolf, and he had a corpse in his bloody jaws. And when he had eaten one up, she threw him another, till he had swallowed all."

"Did she throw him thine?" asked Martin, who ran holding by the stirrup.

"That did she, and eaten I saw myself. Yet here I am alive."

"Then thy dreams were naught."

"I do not know that. The wolf may have me yet."

"I fear thou art fey." *

"What the devil is it to thee if I be?"

"Naught. But be comforted. I am a necromancer; and this I know by my art, that the weapon that will slay thee was never forged in Flanders here."

"There was another man had a dream," said Thord, turning from Martin angrily. "He was standing in the king's ship, and he saw a great witchwife with a fork and a trough stand on the island. And he saw a fowl on every ship's stem, a raven, or else an eagle, and he heard the witchwife sing an evil song."

By this time they were in St. Omer.

Hereward rode straight to the Countess Judith's house. He never had entered it yet, and was likely to be attacked if he entered it now. But when the door was opened, he thrust in with so earnest and sad a face that the servants let him pass, but not without growling and motions as of getting their weapons.

"I come in peace, my men, I come in peace: this is no time for brawls. Where is the steward, or one of the Countess's ladies? Tell her, madam, that Hereward waits her commands, and entreats her, in the name of St. Mary and all Saints, to vouchsafe him one word in private."

The lady hurried into the bower. The next moment Judith hurried out into the hall, her fair face blanched, her fair eyes wide with terror.

Hereward fell on his knee.

"What is this? It must be bad news if you bring it."

"Madam, the grave covers all feuds. Earl Tosti was a very valiant hero; and would to God that we had been friends!"

She did not hear the end of the sentence, but fell back with a shriek into the women's arms.

Hereward told them all that they needed to know of that fratricidal strife; and then to Thord Gunlaugsson, —

"Have you any token that this is true? Mind what I warned you, if you lied!"

"This have I, Earl and ladies," and he drew from his bosom a

* Prophesying his own death.

reliquary. "Ulf the marshal took this off his neck, and bade me give it to none but his lady. Therefore, with your pardon, Sir Earl, I did not tell you that I had it, not knowing whether you were an honest man."

"Thou hast done well, and an honest man thou shalt find me. Come home, and I will feed thee at my own table; for I have been a sea-rover and a Viking myself."

They left the reliquary with the ladies, and went.

"See to this good man, Martin."

"That will I, as the apple of my eye."

And Hereward went into Torfrida's room.

"I have news, news!"

"So have I."

"Harold Hardraade is slain, and Tosti too!"

"Where? how?"

"Harold Godwinsson slew them by York."

"Brother has slain brother? O God that died on cross!" murmured Torfrida, "when will men look to thee, and have mercy on their own souls? But, Hereward, I have news, — news more terrible by far. It came an hour ago. I have been dreading your coming back."

"Say on. If Harold Hardraade is dead, no worse can happen."

"But Harold Godwinsson is dead!"

"Dead! Who next? William of Normandy? The world seems coming to an end, as the monks say it will soon." *

"A great battle has been fought at a place they call Heathfield."

"Close by Hastings? Close to the landing-place? Harold must have flown thither back from York. What a captain the man is, after all."

"Was. He is dead, and all the Godwinssons, and England lost."

If Torfrida had feared the effect of her news, her heart was lightened at once as Hereward answered haughtily, —

"England lost? Sussex is not England, nor Wessex either, any more than Harold was king thereof. England lost? Let the tanner try to cross the Watling street, and he will find out that he has another stamp of Englishmen to deal with."

"Hereward, Hereward, do not be unjust to the dead. Men say — the Normans say — that they fought like heroes."

"I never doubted that; but it makes me mad — as it does all Eastern and Northern men — to hear these Wessex churls and Godwinssons calling themselves all England."

---

* There was a general rumor abroad that the end of the world was at hand, that the "one thousand years" of prophecy had expired.

Torfrida shook her head. To her, as to most foreigners, Wessex and the southeast counties were England; the most civilized, the most Norman; the seat of royalty; having all the prestige of law, and order, and wealth. And she was shrewd enough to see, that as it was the part of England which had most sympathy with Norman civilization, it was the very part where the Norman could most easily gain and keep his hold. The event proved that Torfrida was right: but all she said was, "It is dangerously near to France, at least."

"It is that. I would sooner see 100,000 French north of the Humber, than 10,000 in Kent and Sussex, where he can hurry over supplies and men every week. It is the starting-point for him, if he means to conquer England piecemeal."

"And he does."

"And he shall not!" and Hereward started up, and walked to and fro. "If all the Godwinssons be dead, there are Leofricssons left, I trust, and Siward's kin, and the Gospatricks in Northumbria. Ah? Where were my nephews in the battle? Not killed too, I trust?"

"They were not in the battle."

"Not with their new brother-in-law? Much he has gained by throwing away the Swan-neck, like a base hound as he was, and marrying my pretty niece. But where were they?"

"No man knows clearly. They followed him down as far as London, and then lingered about the city, meaning no man can tell what: but we shall hear — and I fear hear too much — before a week is over."

"Heavens! this is madness, indeed. This is the way to be eaten up one by one! Neither to do the thing, nor leave it alone. If I had been there! If I had been there —"

"You would have saved England, my hero!" and Torfrida believed her own words.

"I don't say that. Besides, I say that England is not lost. But there were but two things to do: either to have sent to William at once, and offered him the crown, if he would but guarantee the Danish laws and liberties to all north of the Watling street; and if he would, fall on the Godwinssons themselves, by fair means or foul, and send their heads to William."

"Or what?"

"Or have marched down after him, with every man they could muster, and thrown themselves on the Frenchman's flank in the battle; or between him and the sea, cutting him off from France; or — O that I had but been there, what things could I have done! And now these two wretched boys have fooled away their only chance —"

"Some say that they hoped for the crown themselves.
"Which? — not both? Vain babies!" And Hereward laughed bitterly. "I suppose one will murder the other next, in order to make himself the stronger by being the sole rival to the tanner. The midden cock, sole rival to the eagle! Boy Waltheof will set up his claim next, I presume, as Siward's son; and then Gospatrick, as Ethelred Evil-Counsel's great-grandson; and so forth, and so forth, till they all eat each other up, and the tanner's grandson eats the last. What care I? Tell me about the battle, my lady, if you know aught. That is more to my way than their statecraft."

And Torfrida told him all she knew of the great fight on Heathfield Down — which men call Senlac — and the Battle of Hastings. And as she told it in her wild, eloquent fashion, Hereward's face reddened, and his eyes kindled. And when she told of the last struggle round the Dragon* standard; of Harold's mighty figure in the front of all, hewing with his great double-headed axe, and then rolling in gore and agony, an arrow in his eye; of the last rally of the men of Kent; of Gurth, the last defender of the standard, falling by William's sword, the standard hurled to the ground, and the Popish Gonfanon planted in its place, — then Hereward's eyes, for the first and last time for many a year, were flushed with noble tears; and springing up he cried: "Honor to the Godwinssons! Honor to the Southern men! Honor to all true English hearts! Why was I not there to go with them to Valhalla?"

Torfrida caught him round the neck. "Because you are here, my hero, to free your country from her tyrants, and win yourself immortal fame."

"Fool that I am, I verily believe I am crying."

"Those tears," said she, as she kissed them away, "are more precious to Torfrida than the spoils of a hundred fights, for they tell me that Hereward still loves his country, still honors virtue, even in a foe."

And thus Torfrida — whether from woman's sentiment of pity, or from a woman's instinctive abhorrence of villany and wrong, — had become there and then an Englishwoman of the English, as she proved by strange deeds and sufferings for many a year.

* I have dared to differ from the excellent authorities who say that the standard was that of "A Fighting Man"; because the Bayeux Tapestry represents the last struggle as in front of a Dragon standard, which must be — as is to be expected — the old standard of Wessex, the standard of English Royalty. That Harold had also a "Fighting Man" standard, and that it was sent by William to the Pope, there is no reason to doubt. But if the Bayeux Tapestry be correct, the fury of the fight for the standard would be explained. It would be a fight for the very symbol of King Edward's dynasty.

K

"Where is that Norseman, Martin?" asked Hereward that night ere he went to bed. "I want to hear more of poor Hardraade."

"You can't speak to him now, master. He is sound asleep this two hours; and warm enough, I will warrant."

"Where?"

"In the great green bed with blue curtains, just above the kitchen."

"What nonsense is this?"

"The bed where you and I shall lie some day; and the kitchen which we shall be sent down to, to turn our own spits, unless we mend our manners mightily."

Hereward looked at the man. Madness glared in his eyes, unmistakably.

"You have killed him!"

"And buried him, cheating the priests."

"Villain!" cried Hereward, seizing him.

"Take your hands off my throat, master. He was only my father."

Hereward stood shocked and puzzled. After all, the man was "No-man's-man," and would not be missed; and Martin Lightfoot, letting alone his madness, was as a third hand and foot to him all day long.

So all he said was, "I hope you have buried him well and safely?"

"You may walk your bloodhound over his grave, to-morrow, without finding him."

And where he lay, Hereward never knew. But from that night Martin got a trick of stroking and patting his little axe, and talking to it as if it had been alive.

CHAPTER XVIII.

HOW EARL GODWIN'S WIDOW CAME TO ST. OMER.

It would be vain to attempt even a sketch of the reports which came to Flanders from England during the next two years, or of the conversation which ensued thereon between Baldwin and his courtiers, or Hereward and Torfrida. Two reports out of three were doubtless false, and two conversations out of three founded on those false reports.

It is best, therefore, to interrupt the thread of the story, by some small sketch of the state of England after the battle of Hastings; that so we may, at least, guess at the tenor of Hereward and Torfrida's counsels.

William had, as yet, conquered little more than the South of England: hardly, indeed, all that; for Herefordshire, Worcestershire, and the neighboring parts, which had belonged to Sweyn, Harold's brother, were still insecure; and the noble old city of Exeter, confident in her Roman walls, did not yield till two years after, in A. D. 1068.

North of his conquered territory, Mercia stretched almost across England, from Chester to the Wash, governed by Edwin and Morcar, the two fair grandsons of Leofric, the great earl, and sons of Alfgar. Edwin called himself Earl of Mercia, and held the Danish burghs. On the extreme northwest, the Roman city of Chester was his; while on the extreme southeast (as Domesday book testifies), Morcar held large lands round Bourne, and throughout the south of Lincolnshire, besides calling himself the Earl of Northumbria. The young men seemed the darlings of the half-Danish northmen. Chester, Coventry, Derby, Nottingham, Leicester, Stamford, a chain of fortified towns stretching across England, were at their command; Blethyn, Prince of North Wales, was their nephew.

Northumbria, likewise, was not yet in William's hands. Indeed, it was in no man's hands, since the free Danes, north of the Humber, had expelled Tosti, Harold's brother, putting Morcar in his place, and helped that brother to slay him at Stanford Brigg. Morcar, instead of residing in his earldom of Northumbria, had made one Oswulf his deputy; but he had rivals enough. There was Gospatrick, claiming through his grandfather, Uchtred, and strong in the protection of his cousin Malcolm, King of Scotland; there was young Waltheof, "the forest thief," who had been born to Siward Biorn in his old age, just after the battle of Dunsinane; a fine and gallant young man, destined to a swift and sad end.

William sent to the Northumbrians one Copsi, a Thane of mark and worth, as his procurator, to expel Oswulf. Oswulf and the land-folk answered by killing Copsi, and doing, every man, that which was right in his own eyes.

William determined to propitiate the young earls. Perhaps he intended to govern the centre and north of England through them, as feudal vassals, and hoped, meanwhile, to pay his Norman conquerors sufficiently out of the forfeited lands of Harold, and those who had fought by his side at Hastings. It was not his policy to make himself, much less to call himself, the Conqueror of England. He claimed to be its legitimate sovereign, deriving from his cousin, Edward the Confessor; and whosoever would acknowledge him as such had neither right nor cause to fear. Therefore he sent for the young earls. He courted Waltheof, and more, really loved him. He promised Edwin his daughter in marriage. Some say it was Constance, afterwards married to Alan Fergant of Brittany; but it may, also, have been the beautiful Adelaide, who, none knew why, early gave up the world, and died in a convent. Be that as it may, the two young people saw each, and loved each other at Rouen, whither William took Waltheof, Edwin, and his brother; as honored guests in name, in reality as hostages, likewise.

With the same rational and prudent policy, William respected the fallen royal families, both of Harold and of Edward; at least, he warred not against women; and the wealth and influence of the great English ladies was enormous. Edith, sister of Harold, and widow of the Confessor, lived in wealth and honor at Winchester. Gyda, Harold's mother, retained Exeter and her land. Aldytha,* or Elfgiva, sister of Edwin and Morcar, niece of Hereward, and widow, first of Griffin of Wales, and then of Harold lived rich and safe in Chester. Godiva, the Countess, owned, so antiquarians say, manors from Cheshire to Lincolnshire, which would be now yearly worth the income of a great duke. Agatha, the Hungarian, widow of Edmund the outlaw, dwelt at Romsey, in Hampshire, under William's care. Her son, Edward Etheling, the rightful heir of England, was treated by William not only with courtesy, but with affection; and allowed to rebel, when he did rebel, with impunity. For the descendant of

* See her history, told as none other can tell it, in Bulwer's "Harold."

R

Rollo, the heathen Viking, had become a civilized, chivalrous, Christian knight. His mighty forefather would have split the Etheling's skull with his own axe. A Frank king would have shaved the young man's head, and immersed him in a monastery. An eastern sultan would have thrust out his eyes, or strangled him at once. But William, however cruel, however unscrupulous, had a knightly heart, and somewhat of a Christian conscience; and his conduct to his only lawful rival is a noble trait amid many sins.

So far all went well, till William went back to France; to be likened, not as his ancestors, to the gods of Valhalla, or the barbarous and destroying Viking of mythic ages, but to Cæsar, Pompey, Vespasian, and the civilized and civilizing heroes of classic Rome.

But while he sat at the Easter feast at Fécamp, displaying to Franks, Flemings, and Bretons, as well as to his own Normans, the treasures of Edward's palace at Westminster, and more English wealth than could be found in the whole estate of Gaul; while he sat there in his glory, with his young dupes, Edwin, Morcar, and Waltheof by his side, having sent Harold's banner in triumph to the Pope, as a token that he had conquered the Church as well as the nation of England, and having founded abbeys as thank-offerings to Him who had seemed to prosper him in his great crime: at that very hour the handwriting was on the wall, unseen by man; and he and his policy and his race were weighed in the balance, and found wanting.

For now broke out in England that wrong-doing, which endured as long as she was a mere appanage and foreign farm of Norman kings, whose hearts and homes were across the seas in France. Fitz-Osbern, and Odo the warrior-prelate, William's half-brother, had been left as his regents in England. Little do they seem to have cared for William's promise to the English people that they were to be ruled still by the laws of Edward the Confessor, and that where a grant of land was made to a Norman, he was to hold it as the Englishman had done before him, with no heavier burdens on himself, but with no heavier burdens on the poor folk who tilled the land for him. Oppression began, lawlessness, and violence; men were ill-treated on the highways; and women — what was worse — in their own homes; and the regents abetted the ill-doers. "It seems," says a most impartial historian,* "as if the Normans, released from all authority, all restraint, all fear of retaliation, determined to reduce the English nation to servitude, and drive them to despair."

* The late Sir F. Palgrave.

In the latter attempt they succeeded but too soon; in the former, they succeeded at last: but they paid dearly for their success.

Hot young Englishmen began to emigrate. Some went to the court of Constantinople, to join the Varanger guard, and have their chance of a Polotaswarf like Harold Hardraade. Some went to Scotland to Malcolm Canmore, and brooded over return and revenge. But Harold's sons went to their father's cousin; to Sweyn — Swend — Sweno Ulfsson, and called on him to come and reconquer England in the name of his uncle Canute the Great; and many an Englishman went with them.

These things Gospatrick watched, as earl (so far as he could make any one obey him in the utter subversion of all order) of the lands between Forth and Tyne. And he determined to flee, ere evil befell him, to his cousin Malcolm Canmore, taking with him Marlesweyn of Lincolnshire, who had fought, it is said, by Harold's side at Hastings, and young Waltheof of York. But, moreover, having a head, and being indeed, as his final success showed, a man of ability and courage, he determined on a stroke of policy, which had incalculable after-effects on the history of Scotland. He persuaded Agatha the Hungarian, Margaret and Christina her daughters, and Edgar the Etheling himself, to flee with him to Scotland. How he contrived to send them messages to Romsey, far south in Hampshire; how they contrived to escape to the Humber, and thence up to the Forth; this is a romance in itself, of which the chroniclers have left hardly a hint. But the thing was done; and at St. Margaret's Hope, as tradition tells, the Scottish king met, and claimed as his unwilling bride, that fair and holy maiden who was destined to soften his fierce passions, to civilize and purify his people, and to become — if all had their just dues — the true patron saint of Scotland.

Malcolm Canmore promised a mighty army; Sweyn, a mighty fleet. And meanwhile, Eustace of Boulogne, the Confessor's brother-in-law, himself a Norman, rebelled at the head of the down-trodden men of Kent; and the Welshmen were harrying Herefordshire with fire and sword, in revenge for Norman ravages.

But as yet the storm did not burst. William returned, and with him something like order. He conquered Exeter; he destroyed churches and towns to make his New Forest. He brought over his Queen Matilda with pomp and great glory; and with her, the Bayeux tapestry which she had wrought with her own hands; and meanwhile Sweyn Ulfsson was too busy threatening Olaf Haroldsson, the new king of Norway, to sail for England; and the sons of King Harold of England had to seek help

from the Irish Danes, and ravaging the country round Bristol, be
beaten off by the valiant burghers with heavy loss.

So the storm did not burst; and need not have burst, it may
be, at all, had William kept his plighted word. But he would
not give his fair daughter to Edwin. His Norman nobles, doubtless, looked upon such an alliance as debasing to a civilized lady
In their eyes, the Englishman was a barbarian; and though the
Norman might well marry the Englishwoman, if she had beauty
or wealth, it was a dangerous precedent to allow the Englishman
to marry the Norman woman, and that woman a princess. Beside, there were those who coveted Edwin's broad lands; Roger
de Montgomery, who already (it is probable) held part of them
as Earl of Shrewsbury, had no wish to see Edwin the son-in-law
of his sovereign. Be the cause what it may, William faltered,
and refused; and Edwin and Morcar left the Court of Westminster in wrath. Waltheof followed them, having discovered — what
he was weak enough continually to forget again — the treachery
of the Norman. The young earls went off, one midlandward, one
northward. The people saw their wrongs in those of their earls
and the rebellion burst forth at once, the Welsh under Blethyn,
and the Cumbrians under Malcolm and Donaldbain, giving their
help in the struggle.

It was the year 1069. A more evil year for England than
even the year of Hastings.

The rebellion was crushed in a few months. The great general
marched steadily north, taking the boroughs one by one, storm-
ing, massacring young and old, burning, sometimes, whole towns,
and leaving, as he went on, a new portent, a Norman donjon —
till then all but unseen in England — as a place of safety for his
garrisons. At Oxford (sacked horribly, and all but destroyed),
at Warwick (destroyed utterly), at Nottingham, at Stafford, at
Shrewsbury, at Cambridge, on the huge barrow which overhangs
the fen; and at York itself, which had opened its gates, trembling, to the great Norman strategist; at each doomed free borough rose a castle, with its tall square tower within, its bailey
around, and all the appliances of that ancient Roman science of
fortification, of which the Danes, as well as the Saxons, knew
nothing. Their struggle had only helped to tighten their bonds;
and what wonder? There was among them neither unity nor
plan nor governing mind and will. Hereward's words had come
true. The only man, save Gospatrick, who had a head in England, was Harold Godwinsson: and he lay in Waltham Abbey,
while the monks sang masses for his soul.

Edwin, Morcar, and Waltheof trembled before a genius superior to their own, — a genius, indeed, which had not its equal

then in Christendom. They came in and begged grace of the king. They got it. But Edwin's earldom was forfeited, and he and his brother became, from thenceforth, desperate men.

Malcolm of Scotland trembled likewise, and asked for peace. The clans, it is said, rejoiced thereat, having no wish for a war which could buy them neither spoil nor land. Malcolm sent ambassadors to William, and took that oath of fealty to the " Basileus of Britain," which more than one Scottish king and kinglet had taken before, — with the secret proviso (which, during the Middle Ages, seems to have been thoroughly understood in such cases by both parties), that he should be William's man just as long as William could compel him to be so, and no longer.

Then came cruel and unjust confiscations. Ednoth the standard-bearer had fallen at Bristol, fighting for William against the Haroldssons, yet all his lands were given away to Normans. Edwin and Morcar's lands were parted likewise; and — to specify cases which bear especially on the history of Hereward — Oger the Briton got many of Morcar's manors round Bourne, and Gilbert of Ghent many belonging to Marlesweyn about Lincoln city. And so did that valiant and crafty knight find his legs once more on other men's ground, and reappears in monkish story as "the most devout and pious earl, Gilbert of Ghent."

What followed, Hereward heard not from flying rumors; but from one who had seen and known and judged of all.*

For one day, about this time, Hereward was riding out of the gate of St. Omer, when the porter appealed to him. Begging for admittance were some twenty women, and a clerk or two; and they must needs see the chatelain. The chatelain was away. What should he do?

Hereward looked at the party, and saw, to his surprise, that they were Englishwomen, and two of them women of rank, to judge from the rich materials of their travel-stained and tattered garments. The ladies rode on sorry country garrons, plainly hired from the peasants who drove them. The rest of the women had walked; and weary and footsore enough they were.

"You are surely Englishwomen?" asked he of the foremost, as he lifted his cap.

The lady bowed assent, beneath a heavy veil.

"Then you are my guests. Let them pass in." And Hereward threw himself off his horse, and took the lady's bridle.

"Stay," she said, with an accent half Wessex, half Danish. "I seek the Countess Judith, if it will please you to tell me where she lives."

* For Gyda's coming to St. Omer that year, see Ordericus Vitalis.

"The Countess Judith, lady, lives no longer in St. Omer. Since her husband's death, she lives with her mother at Bruges."

The lady made a gesture of disappointment.

"It were best for you, therefore, to accept my hospitality, till such time as I can send you and your ladies on to Bruges."

"I must first know who it is who offers me hospitality?"

This was said so proudly, that Hereward answered proudly enough in return, —

"I am Hereward Leofricsson, whom his foes call Hereward the outlaw; and his friends, Hereward the master of knights."

She started, and threw her veil back, looking intently at him. He, for his part, gave but one glance, and then cried, —

"Mother of Heaven! You are the great Countess!"

"Yes, I was that woman once, if all be not a dream. I am now I know not what, seeking hospitality — if I can believe my eyes and ears — of Godiva's son."

"And from Godiva's son you shall have it, as though you were Godiva's self. God so deal with my mother, madam, as I will deal with you."

"His father's wit, and his mother's beauty!" said the great Countess, looking upon him. "Too, too like my own lost Harold!"

"Not so, my lady. I am a dwarf compared to him." And Hereward led the garron on by the bridle, keeping his cap in hand, while all wondered who the dame could be, before whom Hereward the champion would so abase himself.

"Leofric's son does me too much honor. He has forgotten, in his chivalry, that I am Godwin's widow."

"I have not forgotten that you are Sprakaleg's daughter, and niece of Canute, king of kings. Neither have I forgotten that you are an English lady, in times in which all English folk are one, and all old English feuds are wiped away."

"In English blood. Ah! if these last words of yours were true, as you, perhaps, might make them true, England might be saved even yet."

"Saved?"

"If there were one man in it, who cared for aught but himself."

Hereward was silent and thoughtful.

He had sent Martin back to his house, to tell Torfrida to prepare bath and food; for the Countess Gyda, with all her train, was coming to be her guest. And when they entered the court, Torfrida stood ready.

"Is this your lady?" asked Gyda, as Hereward lifted her from her horse.

8

"I am his lady, and your servant," said Torfrida, bowing.

"Child! child! Bow not to me. Talk not of servants to a wretched slave, who only longs to crawl into some hole and die, forgetting all she was and all she had."

And the great Countess reeled with weariness and woe, and fell upon Torfrida's neck.

A tall veiled lady next her helped to support her; and between them they almost carried her through the hall, and into Torfrida's best guest-chamber.

And there they gave her wine, and comforted her, and let her weep awhile in peace.

The second lady had unveiled herself, displaying a beauty which was still brilliant, in spite of sorrow, hunger, the stains of travel, and more than forty years of life.

"She must be Gunhilda," guessed Torfrida to herself, and not amiss.

She offered Gyda a bath, which she accepted eagerly, like a true Dane.

"I have not washed for weeks. Not since we sat starving on the Flat-Holme there, in the Severn sea. I have become as foul as my own fortunes: and why not? It is all of a piece. Why should not beggars beg unwashed?"

But when Torfrida offered Gunhilda the bath she declined.

"I have done, lady, with such carnal vanities. What use in cleansing that body which is itself unclean, and whitening the outside of this sepulchre? If I can but cleanse my soul fit for my heavenly Bridegroom, the body may become — as it must at last — food for worms."

"She will needs enter religion, poor child," said Gyda; "and what wonder?"

"I have chosen the better part, and it shall not be taken from me."

"Taken! taken! Hark to her! She means to mock me, the proud nun, with that same 'taken.'"

"God forbid, mother!"

"Then why say taken, to me from whom all is taken? — husband, sons, wealth, land, renown, power, — power which I loved, wretch that I was, as well as husband and as sons. Ah God! the girl is right. Better to rot in the convent, than writhe in the world. Better never to have had, than to have had and lost."

"Amen!" said Gunhilda. "'Blessed are the barren, and they that never gave suck,' saith the Lord."

"No! not so!" cried Torfrida. "Better, Countess, to have had and lost, than never to have had at all. The glutton was right, swine as he was, when he said that not even Heaven could take from him the dinners he had eaten. How much more we, if we say, not even Heaven can take from us the love wherewith we have loved. Will not our souls be richer thereby, through all eternity?"

"In Purgatory?" asked Gunhilda.

"In Purgatory, or where else you will. I love my love; and though my love prove false, he has been true; though he trample me under foot, he has held me in his bosom; though he kill me, he has lived for me. What I have had will still be mine, when that which I have shall fail me."

"And you would buy short joy with lasting woe?"

"That would I, like a brave man's child. I say,—The present is mine, and I will enjoy it, as greedily as a child. Let the morrow take thought for the things of itself.—Countess, your bath is ready."

Nineteen years after, when the great conqueror lay, tossing with agony and remorse, upon his dying bed, haunted by the ghosts of his victims, the clerks of St. Saviour's in Bruges city were putting up a leaden tablet (which remains, they say, unto this very day) to the memory of one whose gentle soul had gently passed away. " Charitable to the poor, kind and agreeable to her attendants, courteous to strangers, and only severe to herself," Gunhilda had lingered on in a world of war and crime; and had gone, it may be, to meet Torfrida beyond the grave, and there finish their doubtful argument.

The Countess was served with food in Torfrida's chamber. Hereward and his wife refused to sit, and waited on her standing.

"I wish to show these saucy Flemings," said he, "that an English princess is a princess still in the eyes of one more nobly born than any of them."

But after she had eaten, she made Torfrida sit before her on the bed, and Hereward likewise; and began to talk; eagerly, as one who had not unburdened her mind for many weeks; and eloquently too, as became Sprakaleg's daughter and Godwin's wife.

She told them how she had fled from the storm of Exeter, with a troop of women, who dreaded the brutalities of the Normans.*
How they had wandered up through Devon, found fishers' boats at Watchet in Somersetshire, and gone off to the little desert island of the Flat-Holme, in hopes of there meeting with the Irish fleet,

---

* To do William justice, he would not allow his men to enter the city while they were blood-hot ; and so prevented, as far as he could, the excesses which Gyda had feared.

which her sons, Edmund and Godwin, were bringing against the West of England. How the fleet had never come, and they had starved for many days; and how she had bribed a passing merchantman to take her and her wretched train to the land of Baldwin the Débonnaire, who might have pity on her for the sake of his daughter Judith, and Tosti her husband who died in his sins.

And at his name, her tears began to flow afresh; fallen in his overweening pride, — like Sweyn, like Harold, like herself —

"The time was, when I would not weep. If I could, I would not. For a year, lady, after Senlac, I sat like a stone. I hardened my heart like a wall of brass, against God and man. Then, there upon the Flat-Holme, feeding on shell-fish, listening to the wail of the sea-fowl, looking outside the wan water for the sails which never came, my heart broke down in a moment. And I heard a voice crying, 'There is no help in man, go thou to God.' And I answered, That were a beggar's trick, to go to God in need, when I went not to him in plenty. No. Without God I planned, and without Him I must fail. Without Him I went into the battle, and without Him I must bide the brunt. And at best, Can He give me back my sons? And I hardened my heart again like a stone, and shed no tear till I saw your fair face this day."

"And now!" she said, turning sharply on Hereward, "what do you do here? Do you not know that your nephews' lands are parted between grooms from Angers and scullions from Normandy?"

"So much the worse for both them and the grooms."

"Sir?"

"You forget, lady, that I am an outlaw."

"But do you not know that your mother's lands are seized likewise?"

"She will take refuge with her grandsons, who are, as I hear, again on good terms with their new master, showing thereby a most laudable and Christian spirit of forgiveness."

"On good terms? Do you not know, then, that they are fighting again, outlaws, and desperate at the Frenchman's treachery? Do you not know that they have been driven out of York, after defending the city street by street, house by house? Do you not know that there is not an old man or a child in arms left in York; and that your nephews, and the few fighting men who were left, went down the Humber in boats, and north to Scotland, to Gospatrick and Waltheof? Do you not know that your mother is left alone — at Bourne, or God knows where — to endure at the hands of Norman ruffians what thousands more endure?"

Hereward made no answer, but played with his dagger.

"And do you not know that England is ready to burst into a blaze, if there be one man wise enough to put the live coal into the right place? That Sweyn Ulffson, his kinsman, or Osbern, his brother, will surely land there within the year with a mighty host? And that if there be one man in England of wit enough. and knowledge enough of war, to lead the armies of England, the Frenchman may be driven into the sea — Is there any here who understands English?"

"None but ourselves."

"And Canute's nephew sit on Canute's throne?"

Hereward still played with his dagger.

"Not the sons of Harold, then?" asked he, after a while.

"Never! I promise you that — I, Countess Gyda, their grandmother."

"Why promise me, of all men, O great lady?"

"Because — I will tell you after. But this I say, my curse on the grandson of mine who shall try to seize that fatal crown, which cost the life of my fairest, my noblest, my wisest, my bravest!"

Hereward bowed his head, as if consenting to the praise of Harold. But he knew who spoke; and he was thinking within himself: "Her curse may be on him who shall seize, and yet not on him to whom it is given."

"All that they, young and unskilful lads, have a right to ask is, their father's earldoms and their father's lands. Edwin and Morcar would keep their earldoms as of right. It is a pity that there is no lady of the house of Godwin, whom we could honor by offering her to one of your nephews, in return for their nobleness in giving Aldytha to my Harold. But this foolish girl here refuses to wed —"

"And is past forty," thought Hereward to himself.

"However, some plan to join the families more closely together might be thought of. One of the young earls might marry Judith here.* Waltheof would have Northumbria, in right of his father, and ought to be well content, — for although she is somewhat older than he, she is peerlessly beautiful, — to marry your niece Aldytha." †

"And Gospatrick?"

"Gospatrick," she said, with a half-sneer, "will be as sure, as he is able, to get something worth having for himself out of any medley. Let him have Scotch Northumbria, if he claim it. He is a Dane, and our work will be to make a Danish England once and forever."

* Tosti's widow, daughter of Baldwin of Flanders.
† Harold's widow.

"But what of Sweyn's gallant holders and housecarles, who are to help to do this mighty deed?"

"Senlac left gaps enough among the noblemen of the South, which they can fill up, in the place of the French scum who now riot over Wessex. And if that should not suffice, what higher honor for me, or for my daughter the Queen-Dowager, than to devote our lands to the heroes who have won them back for us?"

Hereward hoped inwardly that Gyda would be as good as her word; for her greedy grasp had gathered to itself, before the Battle of Hastings, no less than six-and-thirty thousand acres of good English soil.

"I have always heard," said he, bowing, "that if the Lady Gyda had been born a man, England would have had another all-seeing and all-daring statesman, and Earl Godwin a rival, instead of a helpmate. Now I believe what I have heard."

But Torfrida looked sadly at the Countess. There was something pitiable in the sight of a woman ruined, bereaved, seemingly hopeless, portioning out the very land from which she was a fugitive; unable to restrain the passion for intrigue, which had been the toil and the bane of her sad and splendid life.

"And now," she went on, "surely some kind saint brought me, even on my first landing, to you of all living men."

"Doubtless the blessed St. Bertin, beneath whose shadow we repose here in peace," said Hereward, somewhat dryly.

"I will go barefoot to his altar to-morrow, and offer my last jewel," said Gunhilda.

"You," said Gyda, without noticing her daughter, "are, above all men, the man who is needed." And she began praising Hereward's valor, his fame, his eloquence, his skill as a general and engineer; and when he suggested, smiling, that he was an exile and an outlaw, she insisted that he was all the fitter from that very fact. He had no enemies among the nobles. He had been mixed up in none of the civil wars and blood feuds of the last fifteen years. He was known only as that which he was, the ablest captain of his day,— the only man who could cope with William, the only man whom all parties in England would alike obey.

And so, with flattery as well as with truth, she persuaded, if not Hereward, at least Torfrida, that he was the man destined to free England once more; and that an earldom — anything which he chose to ask — would be the sure reward of his assistance.

"Torfrida," said Hereward that night, "kiss me well; for you will not kiss me again for a while."

"What?"

" I am going to England to-morrow."

" Alone ? "

" Alone. I and Martin to spy out the land ; and a lozen or so of housecarles to take care of the ship in harbor."

" But you have promised to fight the Viscount of Pinkney."

" I will be back again in time for him. Not a word, — I must go to England, or go mad."

" But Countess Gyda? Who will squire her to Bruges?"

" You, and the rest of my men. You must tell her all. She has a woman's heart, and will understand. And tell Baldwin I shall be back within the month, if I am alive on land or water."

" Hereward, Hereward, the French will kill you ! "

" Not while I have your armor on. Peace, little fool! Are you actually afraid for Hereward at last ?"

" O heavens! when am I not afraid for you!" and she cried herself to sleep upon his bosom. But she knew that it was the right, and knightly, and Christian thing to do.

Two days after, a long ship ran out of Calais, and sailed away north and east.

CHAPTER XIX.

HOW HEREWARD CLEARED BOURNE OF FRENCHMEN.

It may have been well, a week after, that Hereward rode from the direction of Boston, with Martin running at his heels.

As Hereward rode along the summer wold the summer sun sank low, till just before it went down he came to an island of small enclosed fields, high banks, elm-trees, and a farm inside, one of those most ancient holdings of the South and East Counts, still to be distinguished, by their huge banks and dikes full of hedgerow timber, from the more modern corn-lands outside, which were in Hereward's time mostly common pasture-lands.

"This should be Azerdun," said he; "and there inside, as I live, stands Azer getting in his crops. But who has he with him?"

With the old man were some half-dozen men of his own rank; some helping the serfs with might and main; one or two standing on the top of the banks, as if on the lookout; but all armed *cap-à-pie.*

"His friends are helping him to get them in," quoth Martin, "for fear of the rascally Normans. A pleasant and peaceable country we have come back to."

"And a very strong fortress are they holding," said Hereward, "against either Norman horsemen or Norman arrows. How to dislodge those six fellows without six times their number, I do not see. It is well to recollect that."

And so he did; and turned to use again and again, in after years, the strategetic capabilities of an old-fashioned English farm.

Hereward spurred his horse up to the nearest gate, and was instantly confronted by a little fair-haired man, as broad as he was tall, who heaved up a long "twybill," or double axe, and bade him, across the gate, go to a certain place.

"Little Winter, little Winter, my chuck, my darling, my mad fellow, my brother-in-arms, my brother in robbery and murder, are you grown so honest in your old age that you will not know Hereward the wolf's-head?"

"Hereward!" shrieked the doughty little man. "I took you

for an accursed Norman in those outlandish clothes"; and lifting up no little voice, he shouted, —

"Hereward is back, and Martin Lightfoot at his heels!"

The gate was thrown open, and Hereward all but pulled off his horse. He was clapped on the back, turned round and round, admired from head to foot, shouted at by old companions of his boyhood, naughty young housecarles of his old troop, now settled down into honest thriving yeomen, hard working and hard fighting, who had heard again and again, with pride, his doughty doings over sea. There was Winter, and Gwenoch, and Gery, Hereward's cousin, — ancestor, it may be, of the ancient and honorable house of that name, and of those parts; and Duti and Outi, the two valiant twins; and Ulfard the White, and others, some of whose names, and those of their sons, still stand in Domesday-book.

"And what," asked Hereward, after the first congratulations were over, "of my mother? What of the folk at Bourne?"

All looked each at the other, and were silent.

"You are too late, young lord," said Azer.

"Too late?"

"The Norman" — Azer called him what most men called him then — "has given it to a man of Gilbert of Ghent's, — his butler, groom, cook, for aught I know."

"To Gilbert's man? And my mother?"

"God help your mother, and your young brother, too. We only know that three days ago some five-and-twenty French marched into the place."

"And you did not stop them?"

"Young sir, who are we to stop an army? We have enough to keep our own. Gilbert, let alone the villain Ivo of Spalding, can send a hundred men down on us in four-and-twenty hours."

"Then I," said Hereward in a voice of thunder, "will find the way to send two hundred down on him"; and turning his horse from the gate, he rode away furiously towards Bourne.

He turned back as suddenly, and galloped into the field.

"Lads! old comrades! will you stand by me if I need you? Will you follow Hereward, as hundreds have followed him already, if he will only go before?"

"We will, we will."

"I shall be back ere morning. What you have to do, I will tell you then."

"Stop and eat, but for a quarter of an hour."

Then Hereward swore a great oath, by oak and ash and thorn, that he would neither eat bread nor drink water while there was a Norman left in Bourne.

"A little ale, then, if no water," said Azer.

Hereward laughed, and rode away.

"You will not go single-handed against all those ruffians," shouted the old man after him. "Saddle, lads, and go with him, some of you, for very shame's sake."

But when they galloped after Hereward, he sent them back. He did not know yet, he said, what he would do. Better that they should gather their forces, and see what men they could afford him, in case of open battle. And he rode swiftly on.

When he came within the lands of Bourne it was dark.

"So much the better," thought Hereward. "I have no wish to see the old place till I have somewhat cleaned it out."

He rode slowly into the long street between the overhanging gables. At the upper end he could see the high garden walls of his mother's house, and rising over them the great hall, its narrow windows all ablaze with light. With a bitter growl he rode on, trying to recollect a house where he could safely lodge. Martin pointed one out.

"Old Viking Surturbrand, the housecarle, did live there, and maybe lives there still."

"We will try." And Martin knocked at the door.

The wicket was opened, but not the door; and through the wicket window a surly voice asked who was there.

"Who lives here?"

"Perry, son of Surturbrand. Who art thou who askest?"

"An honest gentleman and his servant, looking for a night's lodging."

"This is no place for honest folk."

"As for that, we don't wish to be more honest than you would have us; but lodging we will pay for, freely and well."

"We want none of your money"; and the wicket was shut.

Martin pulled out his axe, and drove the panel in.

"What are you doing? We shall rouse the town," said Hereward.

"Let be; these are no French, but honest English, and like one all the better for a little horse-play."

"What didst do that for?" asked the surly voice again. "Were it not for those rascal Frenchmen up above, I would come out and split thy skull for thee."

"If there be Frenchmen up above," said Martin, in a voice of feigned terror, "take us in for the love of the Virgin and all the saints, or murdered we shall be ere morning light."

"You have no call to stay in the town, man, unless you like."

Hereward rode close to the wicket, and said in a low voice, "I am a nobleman of Flanders, good sir, and a sworn foe to all

French. My horse is weary, and cannot make a step forward and if you be a Christian man, you will take me in and let me go off safe ere morning light."

"From Flanders?" And the man turned and seemed to consult those within. At length the door was slowly opened, and Perry appeared, his double axe over his shoulder.

"If you be from Flanders, come in for mercy; but be quick, ere those Frenchmen get wind of you."

Hereward went in. Five or six men were standing round the long table, upon which they had just laid down their double axes and javelins. More than one countenance Hereward recognized at ônce. Over the peat-fire in the chimney-corner sat a very old man, his hands upon his knees, as he warmed his bare feet at the embers. He started up at the noise, and Hereward saw at once that it was old Surturbrand, and that he was blind.

"Who is it? Is Hereward come?" asked he, with the dull, dreamy voice of age.

"Not Hereward, father," said some one, "but a knight from Flanders."

The old man dropped his head upon his breast again with a querulous whine, while Hereward's heart beat high at hearing his own name. At all events he was among friends; and approaching the table he unbuckled his sword and laid it down among the other weapons. "At least," said he, "I shall have no need of thee as long as I am here among honest men."

"What shall I do with my master's horse?" asked Martin. "He can't stand in the street to be stolen by drunken French horseboys."

"Bring him in at the front door, and out at the back," said Perry. "Fine times these, when a man dare not open his own yard-gate."

"You seem to be all besieged here," said Hereward. "How is this?"

"Besieged we are," said the man; and then, partly to turn the subject off, "Will it please you to eat, noble sir?"

Hereward ate and drank: while his hosts eyed him, not without some lingering suspicion, but still with admiration and some respect. His splendid armor and weapons, as well as the golden locks which fell far below his shoulders, and conveniently hid a face which he did not wish yet to have recognized, showed him to be a man of the highest rank; while the palm of his small hand, as hard and bony as any woodman's, proclaimed him to be no novice of a fighting man. The strong Flemish accent which both he and Martin Lightfoot had assumed prevented the honest Englishmen from piercing his disguise. They watched him, while he in turn watched them, struck by their uneasy looks and sullen silence.

"We are a dull company," said he after a while, courteously enough. "We used to be told in Flanders that there were none such stout drinkers and none such jolly singers as you gallant men of the Danelagh here."

"Dull times make dull company," said one, "and no offence to you, Sir Knight."

"Are you such a stranger," asked Perry, "that you do not know what has happened in this town during the last three days?"

"No good, I will warrant, if you have Frenchmen in it."

"Why was not Hereward here?" wailed the old man in the corner. "It never would have happened if he had been in the town."

"What?" asked Hereward, trying to command himself.

"What has happened," said Perry, "makes a free Englishman's blood boil to tell of. Here, Sir Knight, three days ago, comes in this Frenchman with some twenty ruffians of his own, and more of one Taillebois's, too, to see him safe; says that this new king, this base-born Frenchman, has given away all Earl Morcar's lands, and that Bourne is his; kills a man or two; upsets the women; gets drunk, ruffles, and roisters; breaks into my lady's bower, calling her to give up her keys, and when she gives them, will have all her jewels too. She faces them like a brave Princess, and two of the hounds lay hold of her, and say that she shall ride through Bourne as she rode through Coventry. The boy Godwin — he that was the great Earl's godson, our last hope, the last of our house — draws sword on them; and he, a boy of sixteen summers, kills them both out of hand. The rest set on him, cut his head off, and there it sticks on the gable spike of the hall to this hour. And do you ask, after that, why free Englishmen are dull company?"

"And our turn will come next," growled somebody. "The turn will go all round; no man's life or land, wife or daughters, will be safe soon for these accursed Frenchmen, unless, as the old man says, Hereward comes back."

Once again the old man wailed out of the chimney-corner: "Why did they ever send Hereward away? I warned the good Earl, I warned my good lady, many a time, to let him sow his wild oats and be done with them; or they might need him some day when they could not find him! He was a lad! He was a lad!" and again he whined, and sank into silence.

Hereward heard all this dry-eyed, hardening his heart into a great resolve.

"This is a dark story," said he calmly, "and it would behoove me as a gentleman to succor this distressed lady, did I but know how. Tell me what I can do now, and I will do it."

"Your health!" cried one. "You speak like a true knight."

"And he looks the man to keep his word, I'll warrant him," spoke another.

"He does," said Perry, shaking his head; "but if anything could have been done, sir, be sure we would have done it: but all our armed men are scattered up and down the country, each taking care, as is natural, of his own cattle and his own women. There are not ten men-at-arms in Bourne this night; and, what is worse, sir, as you know, who seem to have known war as well as me, there is no man to lead them."

Here Hereward was on the point of saying, "And what if I led you?" On the point too of discovering himself: but he stopped short.

Was it fair to involve this little knot of gallant fellows in what might be a hopeless struggle, and have all Bourne burned over their heads ere morning by the ruffian Frenchmen? No; his mother's quarrel was his own private quarrel. He would go alone and see the strength of the enemy; and after that, may be, he would raise the country on them: or — and half a dozen plans suggested themselves to his crafty brain as he sat brooding and scheming: then, as always, utterly self-confident.

He was startled by a burst of noise outside, — music, laughter, and shouts.

"There," said Perry, bitterly, "are those Frenchmen, dancing and singing in the hall with my Lord Godwin's head above them!" And curses bitter and deep went round the room. They sat sullen and silent it may be for an hour or more; only moving when, at some fresh outbreak of revelry, the old man started from his doze and asked if that was Hereward coming.

"And who is this Hereward of whom you speak?" said Hereward at last.

"We thought you might know him, Sir Knight, if you come from Flanders, as you say you do," said three or four voices in a surprised and surly tone.

"Certainly I know such a man, if he be Hereward the wolf's-head, Hereward the outlaw, as they call him. And a good soldier he is, though he be not yet made a knight; and married, too, to a rich and fair lady. I served under this Hereward a few months ago in the Friesland War, and know no man whom I would sooner follow."

"Nor I neither," chimed in Martin Lightfoot from the other end of the table.

"Nor we," cried all the men-at-arms at once, each vying with the other in extravagant stories of their hero's prowess, and in asking the knight of Flanders whether they were true or not.

To avoid offending them, Hereward was forced to confess to a great many deeds which he had never done: but he was right glad to find that his fame had reached his native place, and that he could count on the men if he needed them.

"But who is this Hereward," said he, "that he should have to do with your town here?"

Half a dozen voices at once told him his own story.

"I always heard," said he, dryly, "that that gentleman was of some very noble kin; and I will surely tell him all that has befallen here as soon as I return to Flanders."

At last they grew sleepy, and the men went out and brought in bundles of sweet rush, and spread them against the wall, and prepared to lie down, each his weapon by his side. And when they were lain down, Hereward beckoned to him Perry and Martin Lightfoot, and went out into the back yard, under the pretence of seeing to his horse.

"Perry Surturbrandsson," said he, "you seem to be an honest man, as we in foreign parts hold all the Danelager to be. Now it is fixed in my mind to go up, and my servant, to your hall, and see what those French upstarts are about. Will you trust me to go, without my fleeing back here if I am found out, or in any way bringing you to harm by mixing you up in my private matters? And will you, if I do not come back, keep for your own the horse which is in your stable, and give moreover this purse and this ring to your lady, if you can find means to see her face to face; and say thus to her, — that he that sent that purse and ring may be found, if he be alive, at St. Omer, with Baldwin, Count of Flanders; and that if he be dead, as he is like enough to be, his trade being naught but war, she will still find at St. Omer a home and wealth and friends, till these evil times be overpast?"

As Hereward had spoken with some slight emotion, he had dropped unawares his assumed Flemish accent, and had spoken in broad burly Lincolnshire; and therefore it was that Perry, who had been staring at him by the moonlight all the while, said, when he was done, tremblingly, —

"Either you are Hereward, or you are his fetch. You speak like Hereward, you look like Hereward. Just what Hereward would be now, you are. You are my lord, and you cannot deny it."

"Perry, if you know me, speak of me to no living soul, save to your lady my mother; and let me and my serving-man go free out of your yard-gate. If I ask you before morning to open it again to me, you will know that there is not a Frenchman left in the Hall of Bourne."

Perry threw his arms around him, and embraced him silently.

"Get me only," said Hereward, "some long woman's gear and black mantle, if you can, to cover this bright armor of mine."

Perry went off in silence as one stunned, — brought the mantle, and let them out of the yard-gate. In ten minutes more, the two slipping in by well-known paths, stood under the gable of the great hall. Not a soul was stirring outside. The serfs were al cowering in their huts like so many rabbits in their burrows, listening in fear to the revelry of their new tyrants. The night was dark: but not so dark but that Hereward could see between him and the sky his brother's long locks floating in the breeze.

"That I must have down, at least," said he, in a low voice.

"Then here is wherewithal," said Martin Lightfoot, as he stumbled over something. "The drunken villains have left the ladder in the yard."

Hereward got up the ladder, took down the head and wrapped it in the cloak, and ere he did so kissed the cold forehead. How he had hated that boy! Well, at least he had never wilfully harmed him, — or the boy him either, for that matter. And now he had died like a man, killing his foe. He was of the true old blood after all. And Hereward felt that he would have given all that he had, save his wife or his sword-hand, to have that boy alive again, to pet him, and train him, and teach him to fight at his side.

Then he slipped round to one of the narrow unshuttered win dows and looked in. The hall was in a wasteful blaze of light, — a whole month's candles burning in one night. The table was covered with all his father's choicest plate; the wine was running waste upon the floor; the men were rolling at the table in every stage of drunkenness; the loose women, camp-followers, and such like, almost as drunk as their masters; and at the table head, most drunk of all, sat, in Earl Leofric's seat, the new Lord of Bourne.

Hereward could scarce believe his eyes. He was none other than Gilbert of Ghent's stout Flemish cook, whom he had seen many a time in Scotland. Hereward turned from the window in disgust; but looked again as he heard words which roused his anger still more.

For in the open space nearest the door stood a gleeman, a dancing, harping, foul-mouthed fellow, who was showing off ape's tricks, jesting against the English, and shuffling about in mock· eries of English dancing. At some particularly coarse jest of his, the new Lord of Bourne burst into a roar of admiration.

"Ask what thou wilt, fellow, and thou shalt have it. Thou wilt find me a better master to thee than ever was Morcar, the English barbarian."

The scoundrel, say the old chroniclers, made a request concerning Hereward's family which cannot be printed here.

Hereward ground his teeth. "If thou livest till morning light," said he, "I will not."

The last brutality awoke some better feeling in one of the girls, — a large coarse Fleming, who sat by the new lord's side. "Fine words," said she, scornfully enough, "for the sweepings of Norman and Flemish kennels. You forget that you left one of this very Leofric's sons behind in Flanders, who would besom all out if he was here before the morning's dawn."

"Hereward?" cried the cook, striking her down with a drunken blow; "the scoundrel who stole the money which the Frisians sent to Count Baldwin, and gave it to his own troops? We are safe enough from him at all events; he dare not show his face on this side the Alps, for fear of the gallows."

Hereward had heard enough. He slipped down from the window to Martin, and led him round the house.

"Now then, down with the ladder quick, and dash in the door. I go in: stay thou outside. If any man passes me, see that he pass not thee."

Martin chuckled a ghostly laugh as he helped the ladder down. In another moment the door was burst in, and Hereward stood upon the threshold. He gave one war-shout, — his own terrible name, — and then rushed forward. As he passed the gleeman, he gave him one stroke across the loins; the wretch fell shrieking.

And then began a murder, grim and great. They fought with ale-cups, with knives, with benches: but, drunken and unarmed, they were hewn down like sheep. Fourteen Normans, says the chronicler, were in the hall when Hereward burst in. When the sun rose there were fourteen heads upon the gable. Escape had been impossible. Martin had laid the ladder across the door; and the few who escaped the master's terrible sword, stumbled over it, to be brained by the man's not less terrible axe.

Then Hereward took up his brother's head, and went in to his mother.

The women in the bower opened to him. They had seen all that passed from the gallery above, which, as usual, hidden by a curtain, enabled the women to watch unseen what passed in the hall below.

The Lady Godiva sat crouched together, all but alone, — for her bower-maidens had fled or been carried off long since, — upon a low stool beside a long dark thing covered with a pall. Sc utterly crushed was she, that she did not even lift up her head as Hereward entered.

He placed his ghastly burden reverently beneath the pall, and then went and knelt before his mother.

For a while neither spoke a word. Then the Lady Godiva suddenly drew back her hood, and dropping on her knees, threw her arms round Hereward's neck, and wept till she could weep no more.

"Blessed strong arms," sobbed she at last, "around me! To feel something left in the world to protect me; something left in the world which loves me."

"You forgive me, mother?"

"You forgive me? It was I, I who was in fault, — I, who should have cherished you, my strongest, my bravest, my noblest, — now my all."

"No, it was all my fault; and on my head is all this misery. If I had been here, as I ought to have been, all this might have never happened."

"You would only have been murdered too. No: thank God you were away; or God would have taken you with the rest. His arm is bared against me, and His face turned away from me. All in vain, in vain! Vain to have washed my hands in innocency, and worshipped Him night and day. Vain to have builded minsters in his honor, and heaped the shrines of his saints with gold. Vain to have fed the hungry, and clothed the naked, and washed the feet of his poor, that I might atone for my own sins, and the sins of my house. This is His answer. He has taken me up, and dashed me down: and naught is left but, like Job, to abhor myself and repent in dust and ashes — of I know not what."

"God has not deserted you. See, He has sent you me!" said Hereward, wondering to find himself, of all men on earth, preaching consolation.

"Yes, I have you! Hold me. Love me. Let me feel that one thing loves me upon earth. I want love; I must have it: and if God, and his mother, and all the saints, refuse their love, I must turn to the creature, and ask it to love me, but for a day."

"Forever, mother."

"You will not leave me?"

"If I do, I come back, to finish what I have begun."

"More blood? O God! Hereward, not that! Let us return good for evil. Let us take up our crosses. Let us humble ourselves under God's hand, and flee into some convent, and there die praying for our country and our kin."

"Men must work, while women pray. I will take you to a minster. — to Peterborough."

"No, not to Peterborough!"

"But my Uncle Brand is abbot there, they tell me, now this four years; and that rogue Herluin, prior in his place."

"He is dying,—dying of a broken heart, like me. And the Frenchman has given his abbey to one Thorold, the tyrant of Malmesbury,— a Frenchman like himself. No, take me where I shall never see a French face. Take me to Crowland—and him with me—where I shall see naught but English faces, and hear English chants, and die a free Englishwoman under St. Guthlac's wings."

"Ah!" said Hereward, bitterly, "St. Guthlac is a right Englishman, and will have some sort of fellow-feeling for us; while St. Peter, of course, is somewhat too fond of Rome and those Italian monks. Well,—blood is thicker than water; so I hardly blame the blessed Apostle."

"Do not talk so, Hereward."

"Much the saints have done for us, mother, that we are to be so very respectful to their high mightinesses. I fear, if this Frenchman goes on with his plan of thrusting his monks into our abbeys, I shall have to do more even for St. Guthlac than ever he did for me. Do not say more, mother. This night has made Hereward a new man. Now, prepare"— and she knew what he ment — "and gather all your treasures; and we will start for Crowland to-morrow afternoon."

CHAPTER XX.

HOW HEREWARD WAS MADE A KNIGHT AFTER THE FASHION OF THE ENGLISH.

A WILD night was that in Bourne. All the folk, free and unfree, man and woman, out on the streets, asking the meaning of those terrible shrieks, followed by a more terrible silence.

At last Hereward strode down from the hall, his drawn sword in his hand.

"Silence, good folks, and hearken to me, once for all. There is not a Frenchman left alive in Bourne. If you be the men I take you for, there shall not be one left alive between Wash and Humber. Silence, again!" as a fierce cry of rage and joy arose, and men rushed forward to take him by the hand, women to embrace him. "This is no time for compliments, good folks, but for quick wit and quick blows. For the law we fight, if we do fight; and by the law we must work, fight or not. Where is the lawman of the town?"

"I was lawman last night, to see such law done as there is left," said Perry. "But you are lawman now. Do as you will. We will obey you."

"You shall be our lawman," shouted many voices.

"I! Who am I? Out-of-law, and a wolf's-head."

"We will put you back into your law, — we will give you your lands in full husting."

"Never mind a husting on my behalf. Let us have a husting, if we have one, for a better end than that. Now, men of Bourne, I have put the coal in the bush. Dare you blow the fire till the forest is aflame from south to north? I have fought a dozen of Frenchmen. Dare you fight Taillebois and Gilbert of Ghent, with William, Duke of Normandy, at their back? Or will you take me, here as I stand, and give me up to them as an outlaw and a robber, to feed the crows outside the gates of Lincoln? Do it, if you will. It will be the wiser plan, my friends. Give me up to be judged and hanged, and so purge yourselves of the villanous murder of Gilbert's cook, — your late lord and master."

"Lord and master! We are free men!" shouted the bolders, or yeomen gentlemen. "We hold our lands from God and the sun."

"You are our lord!" shouted the socmen, or tenants. "Who but you? We will follow, if you will lead!"

"Hereward is come home!" cried a feeble voice behind. "Let me come to him. Let me feel him."

And through the crowd, supported by two ladies, tottered the mighty form of Surturbrand, the blind Viking.

"Hereward is come!" cried he, as he folded his master's son in his arms. "Hoi! he is wet with blood! Hoi! he smells of blood! Hoi! the ravens will grow fat now, for Hereward is come home!"

Some would have led the old man away; but he thrust them off fiercely.

"Hoi! come wolf! Hoi! come kite! Hoi! come erne from off the fen! You followed us, and we fed you well, when Swend Forkbeard brought us over the sea. Follow us now, and we will feed you better still, with the mongrel Frenchers who scoff at the tongue of their forefathers, and would rob their nearest kinsman of land and lass. Hoi! Swend's men! Hoi! Canute's men! Vikings' sons, Sea-cocks' sons, Berserkers' sons all! Split up the war-arrow, and send it round, and the curse of Odin on every man that will not pass it on! A war-king to-morrow, and Hildur's game next day, that the old Surturbrand may fall like a freeholder, axe in hand, and not die like a cow, in the straw which the Frenchman has spared him."

All men were silent, as the old Viking's voice, cracked and feeble when he began, gathered strength from rage, till it rang through the still night-air like a trumpet-blast.

The silence was broken by a long wild cry from the forest, which made the women start, and catch their children closer to them. It was the howl of a wolf.

"Hark to the witch's-horse! Hark to the son of Fenris, how he calls for meat! Are ye your fathers' sons, ye men of Bourne? They never let the gray beast call in vain."

Hereward saw his opportunity and seized it. There were those in the crowd, he well knew, as there must needs be in all crowds, who wished themselves well out of the business; who shrank from the thought of facing the Norman barons, much more the Norman king; who were ready enough, had the tide of feeling begun to ebb, of blaming Hereward for rashness, even though they might not have gone so far as to give him up to the Normans; who would have advised some sort of compromise, pacifying half-measure, or other weak plan for escaping present danger, by delivering themselves over to future destruction. But three out of four there were good men and true. The savage chant of the old barbarian might have startled them somewhat, for they were tolerably orthodox Christian folk. But there was sense as well as spirit in its savageness; and they growled applause, as he ceased. But Hereward heard, and cried,—

"The Viking is right! So speaks the spirit of our fathers, and we must show ourselves their true sons. Send round the war-arrow, and death to the man who does not pass it on! Better die bravely together than falter and part company, to be hunted down one by one by men who will never forgive us as long as we have an acre of land for them to seize. Perry, son of Surturbrand, you are the lawman. Put it to the vote!"

"Send round the war-arrow!" shouted Perry himself; and if there was a man or two who shrank from the proposal they found it prudent to shout as loudly as did the rest.

Ere the morning light, the war-arrow was split into four splinters, and carried out to the four airts, through all Kesteven. If the splinter were put into the house-father's hand, he must send it on at once to the next freeman's house. If he were away, it was stuck into his house-door, or into his great chair by the fireside, and woe to him if, on his return, he sent it not on likewise. All through Kesteven went that night the arrow-splinters, and with them the whisper, "Hereward is come again!" And before midday there were fifty well-armed men in the old camping-field outside the town, and Hereward haranguing them in words of fire.

A chill came over them, nevertheless, when he told them that he must return at once to Flanders.

"But it must be," he said. He had promised his good lord and sovereign, Baldwin of Flanders, and his word of honor he must keep. Two visits he must pay, ere he went; and then to sea. But within the year, if he were alive on ground, he would return, and with him ships and men, it might be with Sweyn and all the power of Denmark. Only let them hold their own till the Danes should come, and all would be well. And whenever he came back, he would set a light to three farms that stood upon a hill, whence they could be seen far and wide over the Bruneswold and over all the fen; and then all men might know for sure that Hereward was come again.

"And nine-and-forty of them," says the chronicler, "he chose to guard Bourne," seemingly the lands which had been his nephew Morcar's, till he should come back and take them for himself. Godiva's lands, of Witham Toft and Mainthorpe, Gery his cousin should hold till his return, and send what he could off them to his mother at Crowland.

Then they went down to the water and took barge, and laid the corpse therein; and Godiva and Hereward sat at the dead lad's head; and Winter steered the boat, and Gwenoch took the stroke-oar.

And they rowed away for Crowland, by many a mere and many an ea; through narrow reaches of clear brown glassy water; between the dark-green alders; between the pale-green reeds; where the coot clanked, and the bittern boomed, and the sedge-bird, not content with its own sweet song, mocked the song of all the birds around; and then out into the broad lagoons, where hung motionless, high overhead, hawk beyond hawk, buzzard beyond buzzard, kite beyond kite, as far as eye could see. Into the air, as they rowed on, whirred up the great skeins of wild fowl innumerable, with a cry as of all the bells of Crowland, or all the hounds of Bruneswold; and clear above all the noise sounded the wild whistle of the curlews, and the trumpet-note of the great white swan. Out of the reeds, like an arrow, shot the peregrine, singled one luckless mallard from the flock, caught him up, struck him stone dead with one blow of his terrible heel, and swept his prey with him into the reeds again.

"Death! death! death!" said Lady Godiva, as the feathers fluttered down into the boat and rested on the dead boy's pall. "War among man and beast, war on earth, war in air, war in the water beneath," as a great pike rolled at his bait, sending a shoal of white fish flying along the surface. "And war, says holy writ, in heaven above. O Thou who didst die to destroy death, when will it all be over?"

And thus they glided on from stream to stream, until they came to the sacred isle of "the inheritance of the Lord, the soil of St. Mary and St. Bartholomew; the most holy sanctuary of St. Guthlac and his monks; the minster most free from worldly servitude; the special almshouse of the most illustrious kings; the sole place of refuge for any one in all tribulations; the perpetual abode of the saints; the possession of religious men, especially set apart by the Common Council of the kingdom; by reason of the frequent miracles of the most holy Confessor, an ever fruitful mother of camphire in the vineyards of Engedi; and, by reason of the privileges granted by the kings, a city of grace and safety to all who repent."

As they drew near, they passed every minute some fisher's log canoe, in which worked with net or line the criminal who had saved his life by fleeing to St. Guthlac, and becoming his man henceforth; the slave who had fled from his master's cruelty and here and there in those evil days, the master who had fled from the cruelty of Normans, who would have done to him as he had done to others. But all old grudges were put away there They had sought the peace of St. Guthlac; and therefore they must keep his peace, and get their living from the fish of the five rivers, within the bounds whereof was peace, as of their own quiet streams; for the Abbot and St. Guthlac were the only lords thereof, and neither summoner nor sheriff of the king, or armed force of knight or earl, could enter there.

At last they came to Crowland minster,— a vast range of high-peaked buildings, founded on piles of oak and hazel driven into the fen, — itself built almost entirely of timber from the Bruneswold; barns, granaries, stables, workshops, stranger's hall, — fit for the boundless hospitality of Crowland,— infirmary, refectory, dormitory, library, abbot's lodgings, cloisters; and above, the great minster towering up, a steep pile, half wood, half stone, with narrow round-headed windows and leaden roofs; and above all the great wooden tower, from which, on high days, chimed out the melody of the seven famous bells, which had not their like in English land. Guthlac, Bartholomew, and Bettelm were the names of the biggest, Turketul and Tatwin of the middle, and Pega and Bega of the smallest. So says Ingulf, who saw them a few years after pouring down on his own head in streams of melted metal. Outside the minster walls were the cottages of the corodiers, or laboring folk; and beyond them again the natural park of grass, dotted with mighty oaks and ashes; and, beyond all those, cornlands of inexhaustible fertility, broken up by the good Abbot Egelric some hundred years before, from which, in times of dearth, the monks of Crowland fed the people of all the neighboring fens.

They went into the great court-yard. All men were quiet, yet all men were busy. Baking and brewing, carpentering and tailoring in the workshops, reading and writing in the cloister, praying and singing in the church, and teaching the children in the school-house. Only the ancient sempects — some near upon a hundred and fifty years old — wandered where they would, or basked against a sunny wall, like autumn flies, with each a young monk to guide him, and listen to his tattle of old days. For, said the laws of Turketul the good, "Nothing disagreeable about the affairs of the monastery shall be mentioned in their presence. No person shall presume in any way to offend them; but with the greatest peace and tranquillity they shall await their end."

So, while the world outside raged, and fought, and conquered, and plundered, they within the holy isle kept up some sort of order, and justice, and usefulness, and love to God and man. And about the yards, among the feet of the monks, hopped the sacred ravens, descendants of those who brought back the gloves at St. Guthlac's bidding ; and overhead, under all the eaves, built the sacred swallows, the descendants of those who sat and sang upon St. Guthlac's shoulders; and when men marvelled thereat, he the holy man replied: " Know that they who live the holy life draw nearer to the birds of the air, even as they do to the angels in heaven."

And Lady Godiva called for old Abbot Ulfketyl, the good and brave, and fell upon his neck, and told him all her tale; and Ulfketyl wept upon her neck, for they were old and faithful friends.

And they passed into the dark, cool church, where in the crypt under the high altar lay the thumb of St. Bartholomew, which old Abbot Turketul used to carry about, that he might cross himself with it in times of danger, tempest, and lightning; and some of the hair of St. Mary, Queen of Heaven, in a box of gold; and a bone of St. Leodegar of Aquitaine ; and some few remains, too, of the holy bodies of St. Guthlac; and of St. Bettelm, his servant; and St. Tatwin, who steered him to Crowland; and St. Egbert, his confessor; and St. Cissa the anchorite; and of the most holy virgin St. Etheldreda ; and many more. But little of them remained since Sigtryg and Bagsac's heathen Danes had heaped them pellmell on the floor, and burned the church over them and the bodies of the slaughtered monks.

The plunder which was taken from Crowland on that evil day lay, and lies still, with the plunder of Peterborough and many a minster more, at the bottom of the Nene, at Huntingdon Bridge. But it had been more than replaced by the piety of the Danish kings and nobles ; and above the twelve white bearskins which lay at the twelve altars blazed, in the light of many a wax candle, gold and jewels inferior only to those of Peterborough and Coventry.

And there in the nave they buried the lad Godwin, with chant and dirge; and when the funeral was done Hereward went up toward the high altar, and bade Winter and Gwenoch come with him. And there he knelt, and vowed a vow to God and St. Guthlac and the Lady Torfrida his true love, never to leave from slaying while there was a Frenchman left alive on English ground.

And Godiva and Ulfketyl heard his vow, and shuddered ; but they dared not stop him, for they, too, had English hearts.

And Winter and Gwenoch heard it, and repeated it word for word.

Then he kissed his mother, and called Winter and Gwenoch. and went forth. He would be back again, he said, on the third day

Then those three went to Peterborough, and asked for Abbot Brand. And the monks let them in; for the fame of their deed had passed through the forest, and all the French had fled.

And old Brand lay back in his great arm-chair, his legs all muffled up in furs, for he could get no heat; and by him stood Herluin the prior, and wondered when he would die, and Thorold take his place, and they should drive out the old Gregorian chants from the choir, and have the new Norman chants of Robert of Fécamp, and bring in French-Roman customs in all things, and rule the English boors with a rod of iron.

And old Brand knew all that was in his heart, and looked up like a patient ox beneath the butcher's axe, and said, "Have patience with me, Brother Herluin, and I will die as soon as I can, and go where there is neither French nor English, Jew nor Gentile, bond or free, but all are alike in the eyes of Him who made them."

But when he saw Hereward come in, he cast the mufflers off him, and sprang up from his chair, and was young and strong in a moment, and for a moment.

And he threw his arms round Hereward, and wept upon his neck, as his mother had done. And Hereward wept upon his neck, though he had not wept upon his mother's.

Then Brand held him at arms' length, or thought he held him, for he was leaning on Hereward, and tottering all the while; and extolled him as the champion, the warrior, the stay of his house, the avenger of his kin, the hero of whom he had always prophesied that his kin would need him, and that then he would not fail.

But Hereward answered him modestly and mildly, —

"Speak not so to me and of me, Uncle Brand. I am a very foolish, vain, sinful man, who have come through great adventures, I know not how, to great and strange happiness, and now again to great and strange sorrows; and to an adventure greater and stranger than all that has befallen me from my youth up until now. Therefore make me not proud, Uncle Brand, but keep me modest and lowly, as befits all true knights and penitent sinners; for they tell me that God resists the proud, and giveth grace to the humble. And I have that to do which do I cannot, unless God and his saints give me grace from this day forth."

Brand looked at him, astonished; and then turned to Herluin.

"Did I not tell thee, prior? This is the lad whom you called graceless and a savage; and see, since he has been in foreign lands, and seen the ways of knights, he talks as clerkly as a Frenchman, and as piously as any monk."

"The Lord Hereward," said Herluin, "has doubtless learned much from the manners of our nation which he would not have learned in England. I rejoice to see him returned so Christian and so courtly a knight."

"The Lord Hereward, Prior Herluin, has learnt one thing in his travels, — to know somewhat of men and the hearts of men, and to deal with them as they deserve of him. They tell me that one Thorold of Malmesbury, — Thorold of Fécamp, the minstrel, he that made the song of Rowland, — that he desires this abbey."

"I have so heard, my lord."

"Then I command, — I, Hereward, Lord of Bourne! — that this abbey be held against him and all Frenchmen, in the name of Swend Ulfsson, king of England, and of me. And he that admits a Frenchman therein, I will shave his crown for him so well, that he shall never need razor more. This I tell thee; and this I shall tell your monks before I go. And unless you obey the same, my dream will be fulfilled; and you will see Goldenbregh in a light low, and burning yourselves in the midst thereof."

"Swend Ulfsson? Swend of Denmark? What words are these?" cried Brand.

"You will know within six months, uncle."

"I shall know better things, my boy, before six months are out."

"Uncle, uncle, do not say that."

"Why not? If this mortal life be at best a prison and a grave, what is it worth now to an Englishman?"

"More than ever; for never had an Englishman such a chance of showing English mettle, and winning renown for the English name. Uncle, you must do something for me and my comrades ere we go."

"Well, boy?"

"Make us knights."

"Knights, lad? I thought you had been a belted knight this dozen years?"

"I might have been made a knight by many, after the French fashion, many a year agone. I might have been knight when I slew the white bear. Ladies have prayed me to be knighted again and again since. Something kept me from it. Perhaps" (with a glance at Herluin) "I wanted to show that an English squire could be the rival and the leader of French and Flemish knights."

"And thou hast shown it, brave lad!" said Brand, clapping his great hands.

"Perhaps I longed to do some mighty deed at last, which would give me a right to go to the bravest knight in all Christendom, and say, 'Give me the accolade, then! Thou only art worthy to knight as good a man as thyself.'"

"Pride and vainglory," said Brand, shaking his head.

"But now I am of a sounder mind. I see now why I was kept from being knighted, — till I had done a deed worthy of a true knight; till I had mightily avenged the wronged, and mightily succored the oppressed; till I had purged my soul of my enmity against my own kin, and could go out into the world a new man, with my mother's blessing on my head."

"But not of the robbery of St. Peter," said Herluin. The French monk wanted not for moral courage, — no French monk did in those days. And he proved it by those words.

"Do not anger the lad, Prior; now, too, above all times, when his heart is softened toward the Lord."

"He has not angered me. The man is right. Here, Lord Abbot and Sir Prior, is a chain of gold, won in the wars. It is worth fifty times the sixteen pence which I stole, and which I repaid double. Let St. Peter take it, for the sins of me and my two comrades, and forgive. And now, Sir Prior, I do to thee what I never did for mortal man. I kneel, and ask thy forgiveness. Kneel, Winter! Kneel, Gwenoch!" And Hereward knelt.

Herluin was of double mind. He longed to keep Hereward out of St. Peter's grace. He longed to see Hereward dead at his feet; not because of any personal hatred, but because he foresaw in him a terrible foe to the Norman cause. But he wished, too, to involve Abbot Brand as much as possible in Hereward's "rebellions" and "misdeeds," and above all, in the master-offence of knighting him; for for that end, he saw, Hereward was come. Moreover, he was touched with the sudden frankness and humility of the famous champion. So he answered mildly, —

"Verily, thou hast a knightly soul. May God and St. Peter so forgive thee and thy companions as I forgive thee, freely and from my heart."

"Now," cried Hereward, "a boon! a boon! Knight me and these my fellows, Uncle Brand, this day."

Brand was old and weak, and looked at Herluin.

"I know," said Hereward, "that the French look on us English monk-made knights as spurious and adulterine, unworthy of the name of knight. But, I hold — and what churchman will gainsay me? — that it is nobler to receive sword and belt from a man of God than from a man of blood like one's self; the fittest to consecrate the soldier of an earthly king, is the soldier of Christ, the King of kings." *

"He speaks well," said Herluin. "Abbot, grant him his boon."

"Who celebrates high mass to-morrow?"

"Wilton the priest, the monk of Ely," said Herluin, aloud. "And a very dangerous and stubborn Englishman," added he to himself.

* Almost word for word from the "Life of Hereward."

"Good. Then this night you shall watch in the church. To-morrow, after the Gospel, the thing shall be done as you will."

That night two messengers, knights of the Abbot, galloped from Peterborough. One to Ivo Taillebois at Spalding, to tell him that Hereward was at Peterborough, and that he must try to cut him off upon the Egelric's road, the causeway which one of the many Abbots Egelric had made, some thirty years before, through Deeping Fen to Spalding, at an enormous expense of labor and of timber. The other knight rode south, along the Roman road to London, to tell King William of the rising of Kesteven, and all the evil deeds of Hereward and of Brand.

And old Brand slept quietly in his bed, little thinking on what errands his prior had sent his knights.

Hereward and his comrades watched that night in St. Peter's church. Oppressed with weariness of body, and awe of mind, they heard the monks drone out their chants through the misty gloom; they confessed the sins — and they were many — of their past wild lives. They had to summon up within themselves courage and strength henceforth to live, not for themselves, but for the fatherland which they hoped to save. They prayed to all the heavenly powers of that Pantheon which then stood between man and God, to help them in the coming struggle; but ere the morning dawned, they were nodding, unused to any long strain of mind.

Suddenly Hereward started, and sprang up, with a cry of fire.

"What? Where?" cried his comrades, and the monks who ran up.

"The minster is full of flame. No use! too late! you cannot put it out! It must burn."

"You have been dreaming," said one.

"I have not," said Hereward. "Is it Lammas night?"

"What a question! It is the vigil of the Nativity of St. Peter and St. Paul."

"Thank heaven! I thought my old Lammas night's dream was coming true at last."

Herluin heard, and knew what he meant.

After which Hereward was silent, filled with many thoughts.

The next morning, before the high mass, those three brave men walked up to the altar; laid thereon their belts and swords; and then knelt humbly at the foot of the steps till the Gospel was finished.

Then came down from the altar Wilton of Ely, and laid on each man's bare neck the bare blade, and bade him take back his sword in the name of God and of St. Peter and St. Paul, and use it like a true knight, for a terror and punishment to evil-doers, and a defence for women and orphans, and the poor and the oppressed, and the monks the servants of God.

And then the monks girded each man with his belt and sword once more. And after mass was sung, they rose and went forth, each feeling himself — and surely not in vain — a bet'er man.

At least this is certain, that Hereward would say to his dying day, how he had often proved that none would fight so well as those who had received their sword from God's knights the monks. And therefore he would have, in after years, almost all his companions knighted by the monks; and brought into Ely with him that same good custom which he had learnt at Peterborough, and kept it up as long as he held the isle.

So says the chronicler Leofric, the minstrel and priest.

It was late when they got back to Crowland. The good Abbot received them with a troubled face.

"As I feared, my Lord, you have been too hot and hasty. The French have raised the country against you."

"I have raised it against them, my lord. But we have news that Sir Frederick — "

"And who may he be?"

"A very terrible Goliath of these French; old and crafty, a brother of old Earl Warrenne of Norfolk, whom God confound. And he has sworn to have your life, and has gathered knights and men-at-arms at Lynn in Norfolk."

"Very good; I will visit him as I go home, Lord Abbot. Not a word of this to any soul."

"I tremble for thee, thou young David."

"One cannot live forever, my lord. Farewell."

A week after, a boatman brought news to Crowland, how Sir Frederick was sitting in his inn at Lynn, when there came in one with a sword, and said: "I am Hereward. I was told that thou didst desire, greatly, to see me; therefore I am come, being a courteous knight," and therewith smote off his head. And when the knights and others would have stopped him, he cut his way through them, killing some three or four at each stroke, himself unhurt; for he was clothed from head to foot in magic armor and whosoever smote it, their swords melted in their hands. And so, gaining the door, he vanished in a great cloud of sea-fowl, that cried forever, "Hereward is come home again!"

And after that, the fen-men said to each other, that all the birds upon the meres cried nothing, save "Hereward is come home again!"

And so, already surrounded with myth and mystery, Hereward flashed into the fens and out again, like the lightning brand, destroying as he passed. And the hearts of all the French were turned to water; and the land had peace from its tyrants for many days.

CHAPTER XXI.

HOW IVO TAILLEBOIS MARCHED OUT OF SPALDING TOWN.

A PROUD man was Ivo Taillebois, as he rode next morning out of Spalding town, with hawk on fist, and hound at heel, and a dozen men-at-arms at his back, who would, on due or undue cause shown, hunt men while he hunted game.

An adventurer from Anjou, brutal, ignorant, and profligate, — low-born, too (for his own men whispered, behind his back, that he was no more than his name hinted, a wood-cutter's son), he still had his deserts. Valiant he was, cunning, and skilled in war. He and his troop of Angevine ruttiers had fought like tigers by William's side, at Hastings; and he had been rewarded with many a manor, which had been Earl Algar's, and should now have been Earl Edwin's, or Morcar's, or, it may be, Hereward's own.

"A fat land and fair," said he to himself; "and, after I have hanged a few more of these barbarians, a peaceful fief enough to hand down to the lawful heirs of my body, if I had one. I must marry. Blessed Virgin! this it is to serve and honor your gracious majesty, as I have always done according to my poor humility. Who would have thought that Ivo Taillebois would ever rise so high in life as to be looking out for a wife, — and that a lady, too?"

Then thought he over the peerless beauties of the Lady Lucia, Edwin and Morcar's sister, almost as fair as that hapless aunt of hers, — first married (though that story is now denied) to the wild Griffin, Prince of Snowdon, and then to his conqueror, and (by complicity) murderer, Harold, the hapless king. Eddeva faira, Eddeva pulcra, stands her name in Domesday-book even now, known, even to her Norman conquerors, as the Beauty of her time, as Godiva, her mother, had been before her. Scarcely less beautiful was Lucia, as Ivo had seen her at William's court, half captive and half guest: and he longed for her; love her he could not. "I have her father's lands," quoth he; "what more reasonable than to have the daughter, too? And have her I will, unless the Mamzer, in his present merciful and politic mood, makes a Countess of her, and marries her up to some Norman coxcomb, with a long pedigree, — invented the year before last. If he does throw away his daughter on that Earl Edwin, in his fancy for petting and patting these savages into good humor, he is not likely to throw away Edwin's sister on a Taillebois. Well, I must put a spoke in Edwin's wheel. It will not be difficult to make him, or Morcar, or both of them, traitors. We must have a rebellion in these parts. I will talk about it to Gilbert of Ghent. We must make these savages desperate, and William furious, or he will be soon giving them back their lands, beside asking them to Court: and then, how are valiant knights, like us, who have won England for him, to be paid for their trouble? No, no. We must have a rebellion, and a confiscation, and then, when English lasses are going cheap, perhaps the Lady Lucia may fall to my share."

And Ivo Taillebois kept his word; and without difficulty, for he had many to help him. To drive the English to desperation, and get a pretext for seizing their lands, was the game which the Normans played, and but too well.

As he rode out of Spalding town, a man was being hanged on the gallows there permanently provided.

That was so common a sight, that Ivo would not have stopped, had not a priest, who was comforting the criminal, ran forward, and almost thrown himself under the horse's feet.

"Mercy, good my Lord, in the name of God and all his saints!"

Ivo went to ride on.

"Mercy!" and he laid hands on Ivo's bridle. "If he took a few pike out of your mere, remember that the mere was his, and his father's before him; and do not send a sorely tempted soul out of the world for a paltry pike."

"And where am I to get fish for Lent, Sir Priest, if every rascal nets my waters, because his father did so before him? Take your hand off my bridle, or, par le splendeur Dex" (Ivo thought it fine to use King William's favorite oath), "I will hew it off."

The priest looked at him, with something of honest English fierceness in his eyes, and dropping the bridle, muttered to himself in Latin: "The bloodthirsty and deceitful man shall not live out half his days. Nevertheless my trust shall be in Thee, O Lord!"

"What art muttering, beast? Go home to thy wife" (wife was by no means the word which Ivo used) "and make the most of her, before I rout out thee and thy fellow-canons, and put in good monks from Normandy in the place of your drunken English swine. Hang him!" shouted he, as the by-standers fell on their knees before the tyrant, crouching in terror, every woman for her husband, every man for wife and daughter. "And hearken, you fen-frogs all. Who touches pike or eel, swimming or wading fowl, within these meres of mine, without my leave, I will hang him as I hanged this man, — as I hanged four brothers in a row on Wrokesham bridge but yesterday."

"Go to Wrokesham bridge and see," shouted a shrill cracked voice from behind the crowd.

All looked round; and more than one of Ivo's men set up a yell, the hangman loudest of all.

"That's he, the heron, again! Catch him! Stop him! Shoot him!"

But that was not so easy. As Ivo pushed his horse through the crowd, careless of whom he crushed, he saw a long lean figure flying through the air seven feet aloft, with his heels higher than his head, on the further side of a deep broad ditch; and on the nearer side of the same one of his best men lying stark, with a cloven skull.

"Go to Wrokesham!" shrieked the lean man, as he rose and showed a ridiculously long nose, neck, and legs, — a type still not uncommon in the fens, — a quilted leather coat, a double-bladed axe slung over his shoulder by a thong, a round shield at his back, and a pole three times as long as himself, which he dragged after him, like an unwieldy tail.

"The heron! the heron!" shouted the English.

"Follow him, men, heron or hawk!" shouted Ivo, galloping his horse up to the ditch, and stopping short at fifteen feet of water.

"Shoot, some one! Where are the bows gone?"

The heron was gone two hundred yards, running, in spite of his pole, at a wonderful pace, before a bow could be brought to bear. He seemed to expect an arrow; for he stopped, glanced his eye round, threw himself flat on his face, with his shield, not over his body, but over his bare legs; sprang up as the shaft stuck in the ground beside him, ran on, planted his pole in the next dike, and flew over it.

In a few minutes he was beyond pursuit; and Ivo turned, breathless with rage, to ask who he was.

"Alas, sir! he is the man who set free the four men at Wrokesham Bridge last night."

"Set free! Are they not hanged and dead?"

"We — we dare not tell you. But he came upon us —"

"Single-handed, you cowards?"

"Sir, he is not a man, but a witch or a devil. He asked us what we did there. One of our men laughed at his long neck and legs, and called him heron. 'Heron I am,' says he, 'and strike like a heron, right at the eyes'; and with that he cuts the man over the face with his axe, and laid him dead, and then another, and another.'

"Till you all ran away, villains!"

"We gave back a step,—no more. And he freed one of those four, and he again the rest; and then they all set on us, and went to hang us in their own stead."

"When there were ten of you, I thought?"

"Sir, as we told you, he is no mortal man, but a fiend."

"Beasts, fools! Well, I have hanged this one, at least!" growled Ivo, and then rode sullenly on.

"Who is this fellow?" cried he to the trembling English.

"Wulfric Raher, Wulfric the Heron, of Wrokesham in Norfolk."

"Aha! And I hold a manor of his," said Ivo to himself. "Look you, villains, this fellow is in league with you."

A burst of abject denial followed. "Since the French,—since Sir Frederick, as they call him, drove him out of his Wrokesham lands, he wanders the country, as you see: to-day here, but Heaven only knows where he will be to-morrow."

"And finds, of course, a friend everywhere. Now march!" And a string of threats and curses followed.

It was hard to see why Wulfric should not have found friends; as he was simply a small holder, or squire, driven out of house and land, and turned adrift on the wide world, for the offence of having fought in Harold's army at the battle of Hastings. But to give him food or shelter was, in Norman eyes, an act of rebellion against the rightful King William; and Ivo rode on, boiling over with righteous indignation, along the narrow drove which led toward Deeping.

A pretty lass came along the drove, driving a few sheep before her, and spinning as she walked.

"Whose lass are you?" shouted Ivo.

"The Abbot's of Crowland, please your lordship," said she, trembling.

"Much too pretty to belong to monks. Chuck her up behind you, one of you."

The shrieking and struggling girl was mounted behind a horseman and bound, and Ivo rode on.

A woman ran out of a turf-hut on the drove side, attracted by the girl's cries. It was her mother.

"My lass! Give me my lass, for the love of St. Mary and all saints!" and she clung to Ivo's bridle.

He struck her down, and rode on over her.

A man cutting sedges in a punt in the lode alongside looked up at the girl's shrieks, and leapt on shore, scythe in hand.

"Father! father!" cried she.

"I'll rid thee, lass, or die for it," said he, as he sprang up the drove-dike and swept right and left at the horses' legs

The men recoiled. One horse went down, lamed for life; another staggered backwards into the further lode, and was drowned. But an arrow went through the brave serf's heart, and Ivo rode on, cursing more bitterly than ever, and comforted himself by flying his hawks at a covey of patridges.

Soon a group came along the drove which promised fresh sport to the man-hunters: but as the foremost person came up, Ivo stopped in wonder at the shout of, —

"Ivo! Ivo Taillebois! Halt and have a care! The English are risen, and we are all dead men!"

The words were spoken in French; and in French Ivo answered, laughing, —

"Thou art not a dead man yet it seems, Sir Robert; art going on pilgrimage to Jerusalem, that thou comest in this fashion? Or dost mean to return to Anjou as bare as thou camest out of it?"

For Sir Robert had, like Edgar, "reserved himself a blanket, else had we all been shamed."

But very little more did either he, his lady, and his three children wear, as they trudged along the drove, in even poorer case than that

> Robert of Coningsby,
> Who came out of Normandy,
> With his wife Tiffany,
> And his maid Manpas,
> And his dog Hardigras.

"For the love of heaven and all chivalry, joke me no jokes, Sir Ivo, but give me and mine clothes and food! The barbarians rose on us last night, — with Azer, the ruffian who owned my lands, at their head, and drove us out into the night as we are, bidding us carry the news to you, for your turn would come next. There are forty or more of them in West Deeping now, and coming eastward, they say, to visit you, and, what is more than all, Hereward is come again."

"Hereward!" cried Ivo, who knew that name well.

Whereon Sir Robert told him the terrible tragedy of Bourne.

"Mount the lady on a horse, and wrap her in my cloak. Get that dead villain's clothes for Sir Robert as we go back. Put your horses' heads about and ride for Spalding."

"What shall we do with the lass?"

"We cannot be burdened with the jade. She has cost us two good horses already. Leave her in the road, bound as she is, and let us see if St. Guthlac her master will come and untie her."

So they rode back. Coming from Deeping two hours after, Azer and his men found the girl on the road, dead.

"Another count in the long score," quoth Azer. But when, in two hours more, they came to Spalding town, they found all the folk upon the street, shouting and praising the host of Heaven. There was not a Frenchman left in the town.

For when Ivo returned home, ere yet Sir Robert and his family were well clothed and fed, there galloped into Spalding from the north Sir Ascelin, nephew and man of Thorold, would-be Abbot of Peterborough, and one of the garrison of Lincoln, which was then held by Hereward's old friend, Gilbert of Ghent.

"Not bad news, I hope," cried Ivo, as Ascelin clanked into the hall. "We have enough of our own. Here is all Kesteven, as the barbarians call it, risen, and they are murdering us right and left."

"Worse news than that, Ivo Taillebois," ("Sir," or "Sieur," Ascelin was loath to call him, being himself a man of family and fashion; and holding the nouveaux venus in deep contempt,) — "worse news than that: the North has risen again, and proclaimed Prince Edgar, King."

"A king of words! What care I, or you, as long as The Mamzer, God bless him! is a king of deeds?"

"They have done their deeds, though, too. Gospatrick and Merlesweyn are back out of Scotland. They attacked Robert de Comines* at Durham, and burnt him in his own house. There was but one of his men got out of Durham to tell the news. And now they have marched on York; and all the chiefs, they say, have joined them, — Archill the Thane, and Edwin and Morcar, and Waltheof too, the young traitors."

"Blessed Virgin!" cried Ivo, "thou art indeed gracious to thy most unworthy knight!"

"What do you mean?"

"You will see some day. Now, I will tell you but one word. When fools make hay, wise men can build ricks. This rebellion, — if it had not come of itself, I would have roused it. We wanted it, to cure William of this just and benevolent policy of his, which would have ended in sending us back to France as poor as we left it. Now, what am I expected to do? What says Gilbert of Ghent, the wise man of Lic — nic — what the pest do you call that outlandish place, which no civilized lips can pronounce?"

---

* Ancestor of the Comyns of Scotland.

"Lic-nic-cole?" replied Ascelin, who, like the rest of the French, never could manage to say Lincoln.

"He says, 'March to me, and with me to join the king at York.'"

"Then he says well. These fat acres will be none the leaner, if I leave the English slaves to crop them for six months. Men! arm and horse Sir Robert of Deeping. Then arm and horse yourselves. We march north in half an hour, bag and baggage, scrip and scrippage. You are all bachelors, like me, and travel light. So off with you!"

"Sir Ascelin, you will eat and drink?"

"That will I."

"Quick, then, butler! and after that pack up the Englishman's plate-chest, which we inherited by right of fist, — the only plate and the only title-deeds I ever possessed."

"Now, Sir Ascelin," — as the three knights, the lady, and the poor children ate their fastest, — "listen to me. The art of war lies in this one nutshell, — to put the greatest number of men into one place at one time, and let all other places shift. To strike swiftly, and strike heavily. That is the rule of our liege lord, King William; and by it he will conquer England, or the world, if he will; and while he does that, he shall never say that Ivo Taillebois stayed at home to guard his own manors while he could join his king, and win all the manors of England once and for all."

"Pardieu! whatever men may say of thy lineage or thy virtues, they cannot deny this, — that thou art a most wise and valiant captain."

"That am I," quoth Taillebois, too much pleased with the praise to care about being tutoyé by younger men. "As for my lineage, my lord the king has a fellow-feeling for upstarts; and the woodman's grandson may very well serve the tanner's. Now, men! is the litter ready for the lady and children? I am sorry to rattle you about thus, madame, but war has no courtesies; and march I must."

And so the French went out of Spalding town.

"Don't be in a hurry to thank your saints!" shouted Ivo to his victims. "I shall be back this day three months; and then you shall see a row of gibbets all the way from here to Deeping, and an Englishman hanging on every one."

CHAPTER XXII.

HOW HEREWARD SAILED FOR ENGLAND ONCE AND FOR ALL.

So Hereward fought the Viscount of Pinkney, who had the usual luck which befell those who crossed swords with him, and plotted meanwhile with Gyda and the Countess Judith. Abbot Egelsin sent them news from King Sweyn in Denmark; soon Judith and Tosti's two sons went themselves to Sweyn, and helped the plot and the fitting out of the armament. News they had from England in plenty, by messengers from Queen Matilda to the sister who was intriguing to dethrone her husband, and by private messengers from Durham and from York.

Baldwin, the *débonnaire* marquis, had not lived to see this fruit of his long efforts to please everybody. He had gone to his rest the year before; and now there ruled in Bruges his son, Baldwin the Good, "Count Palatine," as he styled himself, and his wife Richilda, the Lady of Hainault.

They probably cared as little for the success of their sister Matilda as they did for that of their sister Judith; and followed out — Baldwin at least — the great marquis's plan of making Flanders a retreat for the fugitives of all the countries round.

At least, if (as seems) Sweyn's fleet made the coast of Flanders its rendezvous and base of operations against King William, Baldwin offered no resistance.

So the messengers came, and the plots went on. Great was the delight of Hereward and the ladies when they heard of the taking of Durham and York; but bitter their surprise and rage when they heard that Gospatrick and the Confederates had proclaimed Edgar Atheling king.

"Fools! they will ruin all!" cried Gyda. "Do they expect Swend Ulfsson, who never moved a finger yet, unless he saw that it would pay him within the hour, to spend blood and treasure in putting that puppet boy upon the throne instead of himself?"

"Calm yourself, great Countess," said Hereward, with a smile. "The man who puts him on the throne will find it very easy to take him off again when he needs."

"Pish!" said Gyda. "He must put him on the throne first. And how will he do that? Will the men of the Danelagh, much less the Northumbrians, ever rally round an Atheling of Cerdic's house? They are raising a Wessex army in Northumbria; a southern army in the north. There is no real loyalty there toward the Atheling, not even the tie of kin, as there would be to Swend. The boy is a mere stalking-horse, behind which each of these greedy chiefs expects to get back his own lands; and if they can get them back by any other means, well and good. Mark my words, Sir Hereward, that cunning Frenchman will treat with them one by one, and betray them one by one, till there is none left."

How far Gyda was right will be seen hereafter. But a less practised diplomat than the great Countess might have speculated reasonably on such an event.

At least, let this be said, that when historians have complained of the treachery of King Swend Ulfsson and his Danes, they have forgotten certain broad and simple facts.

Swend sailed for England to take a kingdom which he believed to be his by right; which he had formerly demanded of William. When he arrived there, he found himself a mere cat's-paw for recovering that kingdom for an incapable boy, whom he believed to have no right to the throne at all.

Then came darker news. As Ivo had foreseen, and as Ivo had done his best to bring about, William dashed on York, and drove out the Confederates with terrible slaughter; profaned the churches, plundered the town. Gospatrick and the earls retreated to Durham; the Atheling, more cautious, to Scotland.

Then came a strange story, worthy of the grown children who, in those old times, bore the hearts of boys with the ferocity and intellect of men.

A great fog fell on the Frenchmen as they struggled over the Durham moors. The doomed city was close beneath them; they heard Wear roaring in his wooded gorge. But a darkness, as of Egypt, lay upon them: "neither rose any from his place."

Then the Frenchmen cried: "This darkness is from St. Cuthbert himself. We have invaded his holy soil. Who has not heard how none who offend St. Cuthbert ever went unpunished? how palsy, blindness, madness, fall on those who dare to violate his sanctuary?"

And the French turned and fled from before the face of St. Cuthbert; and William went down to Winchester angry and sad, and then went off to Gloucestershire; and hunted — for, whatever befell, he still would hunt — in the forest of Dean.

And still Swend and his Danes had not sailed; and Hereward walked to and fro in his house, impatiently, and bided his time.

In July, Baldwin died. Arnoul, the boy, was Count of Flanders, and Richilda, his sorceress-mother, ruled the land in his name. She began to oppress the Flemings; not those of French Flanders, round St. Omer, but those of Flemish Flanders, toward the north. They threatened to send for Robert the Frison to right them.

Hereward was perplexed. He was Robert the Frison's friend, and old soldier. Richilda was Torfrida's friend; so was, still more, the boy Arnoul; which party should he take? Neither, if he could help it. And he longed to be safe out of the land.

And at last his time came. Martin Lightfoot ran in, breathless, to tell how the sails of a mighty fleet were visible from the Dunes.

"Here?" cried Hereward. "What are the fools doing down here, wandering into the very jaws of the wolf? How will they land here? They were to have gone straight to the Lincolnshire coast. God grant this mistake be not the first of dozens!"

Hereward went into Torfrida's bower.

"This is an evil business. The Danes are here, where they have no business, instead of being off Scheldtmouth, as I entreated them. But go we must, or be forever shamed. Now, true wife, are you ready? Dare you leave home and kin and friends, once and for all, to go, you know not whither, with one who may be a gory corpse by this day week?"

"I dare," said she.

So they went down to Calais by night, with Torfrida's mother, and all their jewels, and all they had in the world. And their housecarles went with them, forty men, tried and trained, who had vowed to follow Hereward round the world. And there were two long ships ready, and twenty good mariners in each. So when the Danes made the South Foreland the next morning, they were aware of two gallant ships bearing down on them, with a great white bear embroidered on their sails.

A proud man was Hereward that day, as he sailed into the midst of the Danish fleet, and up to the royal ships, and shouted: "I am Hereward the Berserker, and I come to take service under my rightful lord, Sweyn, king of England."

"Come on board, then; we know you well, and right glad we are to have Hereward with us."

And Hereward laid his ship's bow upon the quarter of the royal ship (to lay alongside was impossible, for fear of breaking oars), and came on board.

"And thou art Hereward?" asked a tall and noble warrior.

"I am. And thou art Swend Ulfsson, the king?"

"I am Earl Osbiorn, his brother."

"Then, where is the king?"

"He is in Denmark, and I command his fleet; and with me are Canute and Harold, Sweyn's sons, and earls and bishops enough for all England."

This was spoken in a somewhat haughty tone, in answer to the look of surprise and disappointment which Hereward had, unawares, allowed to pass over his face.

"Thou art better than none," said Hereward. "Now, hearken, Osbiorn the Earl. Had Swend been here, I would have put my hand between his, and said in my own name, and that of all the men in Kesteven and the fens, Swend's men we are, to live and die! But now, as it is, I say, for me and them, thy men we are, to live and die, as long as thou art true to us."

"True to you I will be," said Osbiorn.

"Be it so," said Hereward. "True we shall be, whatever betide. Now, whither goes Earl Osbiorn, and all his great meinie?"

"We purpose to try Dover."

"You will not take it. The Frenchman has strengthened it with one of his accursed keeps, and without battering-engines you may sit before it a month."

"What if I asked you to go in thither yourself, and try the mettle and the luck which, they say, never failed Hereward yet?"

"I should say that it was a child's trick to throw away against a paltry stone wall the life of a man who was ready to raise for you in Lincolnshire and Cambridgeshire, five times as many men as you will lose in taking Dover."

"Hereward is right," said more than one Earl. "We shall need him in his own country."

"If you are wise, to that country you yourselves will go. It is ready to receive you. This is ready to oppose you. You are attacking the Frenchman at his strongest point instead of his weakest. Did I not send again and again, entreating you to cross from Scheldtmouth to the Wash, and send me word that I might come and raise the Fen-men for you, and then we would all go north together?"

"I have heard, ere now," said Earl Osbiorn, haughtily, "that Hereward, though he be a valiant Viking, is more fond of giving advice than of taking it."

Hereward was about to answer very fiercely. If he had, no one would have thought any harm, in those plain-spoken times. But he was wise; and restrained himself, remembering that Torfrida was there, all but alone, in the midst of a fleet of savage men; and that beside, he had a great deed to do, and must do it as he could. So he answered,—

"Osbiorn the Earl has not, it seems, heard this of Hereward that because he is accustomed to command, he is also accustomed to obey. What thou wilt do, do, and bid me do. He that quarrels with his captain cuts his own throat and his fellows' too."

"Wisely spoken!" said the earls; and Hereward went back to his ship.

"Torfrida," said he, bitterly, "the game is lost before it is begun."

"God forbid, my beloved! What words are these?"

"Swend — fool that he is with his over-caution, — always the same! — has let the prize slip from between his fingers. He has sent Osbiorn instead of himself."

"But why is that so terrible a mistake?"

"We do not want a fleet of Vikings in England, to plunder the French and English alike. We want a king, a king, a king!" and Hereward stamped with rage. "And instead of a king, we have this Osbiorn, — all men know him, greedy and false and weak-headed. Here he is going to be beaten off at Dover; and then, I suppose, at the next port; and so forth, till the whole season is wasted, and the ships and men lost by driblets. Pray for us to God and his saints, Torfrida, you who are nearer to Heaven than I; for we never needed it more."

And Osbiorn went in; tried to take Dover; and was beaten off with heavy loss.

Then the earls bade him take Hereward's advice. But he would not.

So he went round the Foreland, and tried Sandwich, — as if, landing there, he would have been safe in marching on London, in the teeth of the *élite* of Normandy.

But he was beaten off there, with more loss. Then, too late, he took Hereward's advice, — or, rather, half of it, — and sailed north; but only to commit more follies.

He dared not enter the Thames. He would not go on to the Wash; but he went into the Orwell, and attacked Ipswich, plundering right and left, instead of proclaiming King Sweyn, and calling the Danish folk around him. The Danish folk of Suffolk rose, and, like valiant men, beat him off; while Hereward lay outside the river mouth, his soul within him black with disappointment, rage, and shame. He would not go in. He would not fight against his own countrymen. He would not help to turn the whole plan into a marauding raid. And he told Earl Osbiorn so so fiercely, that his life would have been in danger, had not the force of his arm been as much feared as the force of his name was needed.

N

At last they came to Yarmouth. Osbiorn would needs land there, and try Norwich.

Hereward was nigh desperate: but he hit upon a plan. Let Osbiorn do so, if he would. He himself would sail round to the Wash, raise the Fen-men, and march eastward at their head through Norfolk to meet him. Osbiorn himself could not refuse so rational a proposal. All the earls and bishops approved loudly; and away Hereward went to the Wash, his heart well-nigh broken, foreseeing nothing but evil.

CHAPTER XXIII.

HOW HEREWARD GATHERED AN ARMY.

THE voyage round the Norfolk coast was rough and wild. Torfrida was ill, the little girl was ill; the poor old mother was so ill that she could not even say her prayers. Packed uncomfortably under the awning on the poop, Torfrida looked on from beneath it upon the rolling water-waste, with a heart full of gloomy forebodings, and a brain whirling with wild fancies. The wreaths of cloud were gray witches, hurrying on with the ship to work her woe; the low red storm-dawn was streaked with blood; the water which gurgled all night under the lee was alive with hoarse voices; and again and again she started from fitful slumber to clasp the child closer to her, or look up for comfort to the sturdy figure of her husband, as he stood, like a tower of strength, steering and commanding, the long night through.

Yes; on him she could depend. On his courage, on his skill. And as for his love, had she not that utterly? And what more did woman need?

But she was going, she scarce knew whither; and she scarce knew for what. At least, on a fearful adventure, which might have a fearful end. She looked at the fair child, and reproached herself for a moment; at the poor old mother, whining and mumbling, her soft southern heart quite broken by the wild chill northern sea-breeze; and reproached herself still more. But was it not her duty? Him she loved, and his she was; and him she must follow, over sea and land, till death; and if possible, beyond death again forever. For his sake she would slave. For his sake she would be strong. If ever there rose in her a homesickness, a regret for leaving Flanders, and much more for that sunnier South where she was born, he at least should never be saddened or weakened by one hint of her sadness and weakness. And so it befell that, by the time they made the coast, she had (as the old chronicler says) "altogether conquered all womanly softness."

And yet she shuddered at the dreary mud-creek into which they ran their ships, at the dreary flats on which they landed shivering, swept over by the keen northeast wind. A lonely land,

and within, she knew not what of danger, it might be of hideous death.

But she would be strong. And when they were all landed, men, arms, baggage, and had pitched the tents which the wise Hereward had brought with them, she rose up like a queen, and took her little one by the hand, and went among the men, and spoke:—

"Housecarles and mariners! you are following a great captain, upon a great adventure. How great he is, you know as well as I. I have given him myself, my wealth, and all I have, and have followed him I know not whither, because I trust him utterly. Men, trust him as I trust him, and follow him to the death."

"That will we!"

"And, men, I am here among you, a weak woman, trying to be brave for his sake — and for yours. Be true to me, too, as I have been true to you. For your sake have I worked hard day and night, for many a year. For you I have baked and brewed and cooked, like any poor churl's wife. Is there a garment on your backs which my hands have not mended? Is there a wound on your limbs which my hands have not salved? O, if Torfrida has been true to you, promise me this day that you will be true men to her and hers; that if— which Heaven forbid!— aught should befall him and me, you will protect this my poor old mother, and this my child, who has grown up among you all, — a lamb brought up within the lions' den. Look at her, men, and promise me, on the faith of valiant soldiers, that you will be lions on her behalf, if she shall ever need you. Promise me, that if you have but one more stroke left to strike on earth, you will strike it to defend the daughter of Hereward and Torfrida from cruelty and shame."

The men answered by a shout which rolled along the fen, and startled the wild-fowl up from far-off pools. They crowded round their lady; they kissed her hands; they bent down and kissed their little playmate, and swore — one by God and his apostles, and the next by Odin and Thor — that she should be a daughter to each and every one of them, as long as they could grip steel in hand.

Then (says the chronicler) Hereward sent on spies, to see whether the Frenchmen were in the land, and how folks fared at Holbeach, Spalding, and Bourne.

The two young Siwards, as knowing the country and the folk, pushed forward, and with them Martin Lightfoot, to bring back news.

Martin ran back all the way from Holbeach, the very first day, with right good news. There was not a Frenchman in the town. Neither was there, they said, in Spalding. Ivo Taillebois was still away at the wars, and long might he stay.

So forward they marched, and everywhere the landsfolk were tilling the ground in peace ; and when they saw that stout array, they hurried out to meet the troops, and burdened them with food, and ale, and all they needed.

And at Holbeach, and at Spalding, Hereward split up the wararrow, and sent it through Kesteven, and south into the Cambridge fens, calling on all men to arm and come to him at Bourne, in the name of Waltheof and Morcar the earls.

And at every farm and town he blew the war-horn, and summoned every man who could bear arms to be ready, against the coming of the Danish host from Norwich. And so through all the fens came true what the wild-fowl said upon the meres, that Hereward was come again.

And when he came to Bourne, all men were tilling in peace. The terror of Hereward had fallen on the Frenchmen, and no man had dared to enter on his inheritance, or to set a French foot over the threshold of that ghastly hall, over the gable whereof still grinned the fourteen heads ; on the floor whereof still spread the dark stains of blood.

Only Geri dwelt in a corner of the house, and with him Leofric the Unlucky, once a roistering housecarle of Hereward's youth, now a monk of Crowland, and a deacon, whom Lady Godiva had sent thither that he might take care of her poor. And there Geri and Leofric had kept house, and told sagas to each other over the beech-log fire night after night ; for all Leofric's study was, says the chronicler, " to gather together for the edification of his hearers all the acts of giants and warriors out of the fables of the ancients or from faithful report, and commit them to writing, that he might keep England in mind thereof." Which Leofric was afterwards ordained priest, probably in Ely, by Bishop Egalwin of Durham ; and was Hereward's chaplain for many a year.

Then Hereward, as he had promised, set fire to the three farms close to the Bruneswold ; and all his outlawed friends, lurking in the forest, knew by that signal that Hereward was come again.

So they cleansed out the old house : though they did not take down the heads from off the gable ; and Torfrida went about it, and about it, and confessed that England was, after all, a pleasant place enough. And they were as happy, it may be, for a week or two, as ever they had been in their lives.

" And now," said Torfrida, " while you see to your army, I must be doing ; for I am a lady now, and mistress of great estates. So I must be seeing to the poor."

"But you cannot speak their tongue."

"Can I not? Do you think that in the face of coming to England and fighting here, and plotting here, and being, may be, an earl's countess, I have not made Martin Lightfoot teach me your English tongue, till I can speak it as well as you? I kept that hidden as a surprise for you, that you might find out, when you most needed, how Torfrida loved you."

"As if I had not found out already! O woman! woman! I verily believe that God made you alone, and left the Devil to make us butchers of men."

Meanwhile went round through all the fens, and north into the Bruneswold, and away again to Lincoln and merry Sherwood, that Hereward was come again. And Gilbert of Ghent, keeping Lincoln Castle for the Conqueror, was perplexed in mind, and looked well to gates and bars and sentinels; for Hereward sent him at once a message, that forasmuch as he had forgotten his warning in Bruges street, and put a rascal cook into his mother's manors, he should ride Odin's horse on the highest ash in the Bruneswold.

On which Gilbert of Ghent, inquiring what Odin's horse might be, and finding it to signify the ash-tree whereon, as sacred to Odin, thieves were hanged by Danes and Norse, made answer,—

That he Gilbert had not put his cook into Bourne, nor otherwise harmed Hereward or his. That Bourne had been seized by the king himself, together with Earl Morcar's lands in those parts, as all men knew. That the said cook so pleased the king with a dish of stewed eel-pout, which he served up to him at Cambridge, and which the king had never eaten before, that the king begged the said cook of him Gilbert and took him away; and that after, so he heard, the said cook had begged the said manors of Bourne of the king, without the knowledge or consent of him Gilbert. That he therefore knew naught of the matter. That if Hereward meant to keep the king's peace, he might live in Bourne till Doomsday, for aught he Gilbert cared. But that if he and his men meant to break the king's peace, and attack Lincoln city, he Gilbert would nail their skins to the door of Lincoln Cathedral, as they used to do by the heathen Danes in old time. And that, therefore, they now understood each other.

At which Hereward laughed, and said that they had done that for many a year.

And now poured into Bourne from every side brave men and true,— some great holders dispossessed of their land; some the sons of holders who were not yet dispossessed; some Morcar's men, some Edwin's, who had been turned out by the king.

To him came "Guenoch and Alutus Grogan, foremost in all

valor and fortitude, tall and large, and ready for work," and with them their three nephews, Godwin Gille, "so called because he was not inferior to that Godwin Guthlacsson who is preached much in the fables of the ancients," and Donti and Outi,* the twins, alike in face and manners; and Godric, the knight of Corby, nephew of the Count of Warwick; and Tosti of Davenesse, his kinsman; and Azer Vass, whose father had possessed Lincoln Tower; and Leofwin Moue,† — that is, the scythe, so called, "because when he was mowing all alone, and twenty country folk set on him with pitchforks and javelins, he slew and wounded almost every one, sweeping his scythe among them as one that moweth"; and Wluncus the Black-face, so called because he once blackened his face with coal, and came unknown among the enemy, and slew ten of them with one lance; and "Turbertin, a great-nephew (surely a mistake) of Earl Edwin"; and Leofwin Prat (perhaps the ancestor of the ancient and honorable house of Pratt of Ryston), so called from his "Prat" or craft, because he had oft escaped cunningly when taken by the enemy, having more than once killed his keepers; and the steward of Drayton; and Thurkill the outlaw, Hereward's cook; and Oger, Hereward's kinsman; and "Winter and Linach," two very famous ones; and Ranald, the butler of Ramsay Abbey, — "he was the standard-bearer"; and Wulfric the Black and Wulfric the White; and Hugh the Norman, a priest; and Wulfard, his brother; and Tosti and Godwin of Rothwell; and Alsin; and Hekill; and Hugh the Breton, who was Hereward's chaplain, and Whishaw, his brother, "a magnificent" knight, which two came with him from Flanders; and so forth; — names merely of whom naught is known, save, in a few cases, from Domesday-book, the manors which they held. But honor to their very names. Honor to the last heroes of the old English race.

These valiant gentlemen, with the housecarles whom, more or fewer, they would bring with them, constituted a formidable force, as after years proved well. But having got his men, Hereward's first care was, doubtless, to teach them that art of war of which they, like true Englishmen, knew nothing.

The art of war has changed little, if at all, by the introduction of gunpowder. The campaigns of Hannibal and Cæsar succeeded by the same tactics as those of Frederic or Wellington; and so, as far as we can judge, did those of the master-general of his age, William of Normandy.

But of those tactics the English knew nothing. Their armies were little more than tumultuous levies, in which men marched

* Named in Domesday-book (?).
† Probably the Leofwin who had lands in Bourne.

and fought under local leaders, often divided by local jealousies
The commissariats of the armies seem to have been so worthless,
that they had to plunder friends as well as foes as they went
along; and with plunder came every sort of excess: as when the
northern men marching down to meet Harold Godwinsson, and
demand young Edwin as their earl, laid waste, seemingly out of
mere brute wantonness, the country round Northampton, which
must have been in Edwin's earldom, or at least in that of his
brother Morcar. And even the local leaders were not over-well
obeyed. The reckless spirit of personal independence, especially
among the Anglo-Danes, prevented anything like discipline, or
organized movement of masses, and made every battle degenerate
into a confusion of single combats.

But Hereward had learned that art of war, which enabled the
Norman to crush, piecemeal, with inferior numbers, the vast but
straggling levies of the English. His men, mostly outlaws and
homeless, kept together by the pressure from without, and free
from local jealousies, resembled rather an army of professional
soldiers than a country *posse comitatus.* And to the discipline
which he instilled into them; to his ability in marching and ma-
nœuvring troops; to his care for their food and for their transport, possibly, also, to his training them in that art of fighting on
horseback in which the men of Wessex, if not the Anglo-Danes
of the East, are said to have been quite unskilled, — in short, to
all that he had learned, as a mercenary, under Robert the Frison,
and among the highly civilized warriors of Flanders and Normandy, must be attributed the fact, that he and his little army
defied, for years, the utmost efforts of the Normans, appearing
and disappearing with such strange swiftness, and conquering
against such strange odds, as enshrouded the guerila captain in
an atmosphere of myth and wonder, only to be accounted for, in
the mind of Normans as well as English, by the supernatural
counsels of his sorceress wife.

But Hereward grew anxious and more anxious, as days and
weeks went on, and yet there was no news of Osbiorn and his
Danes at Norwich. Time was precious. He had to march his
little army to the Wash, and then transport it by boats — no
easy matter — to Lynn in Norfolk, as his nearest point of attack.
And as the time went on, Earl Warren and Ralph de Guader
would have gathered their forces between him and the Danes,
and a landing at Lynn might become impossible. Meanwhile
there were bruits of great doings in the north of Lincolnshire.
Young Earl Waltheof was said to be there, and Edgar the
Atheling with him; but what it portended, no man knew.
Morcar was said to have raised the centre of Mercia, and to be

near Stafford; Edwin to have raised the Welsh, and to be at Chester with Alfgiva, his sister, Harold Godwinsson's widow And Hereward sent spies along the Roman Watling Street — the only road, then, toward the northwest of England — and spies northward along the Roman road to Lincoln. But the former met the French in force near Stafford, and came back much faster than they went. And the latter stumbled on Gilbert of Ghent, riding out of Lincoln to Sleaford, and had to flee into the fens, and came back much slower than they went.

At last news came. For into Bourne stalked Walfric the Heron, with axe and bow, and leaping-pole on shoulder, and an evil tale he brought.

The Danes had been beaten utterly at Norwich. Ralph de Guader and his Frenchmen had fought like lions. They had killed many Danes in the assault on the castle. They had sallied out on them as they recoiled, and driven them into the river, drowning many more. The Danes had gone down the Yare again, and out to sea northward, no man knew whither. He, the Heron, prowling about the fenlands of Norfolk to pick off straggling Frenchmen and looking out for the Danes, had heard all the news from the landsfolk. He had watched the Danish fleet along the shore as far as Blakeney. But when they came to the isle, they stood out to sea, right northwest. He, the Heron, believed that they were gone for Humber Mouth.

After a while, he had heard how Hereward was come again and sent round the war-arrow, and thought that a landless man could be in no better company; wherefore he had taken boat, and come across the deep fen. And there he was, if they had need of him.

"Need of you?" said Hereward, who had heard of the deed at Wrokesham Bridge. "Need of a hundred like you. But this is bitter news."

And he went in to ask counsel of Torfrida, ready to weep with rage. He had disappointed, deceived his men. He had drawn them into a snare. He had promised that the Danes should come. How should he look them in the face?

"Look them in the face? Do that at once — now — without losing a moment. Call them together and tell them all. If their hearts are stanch, you may do great things without the traitor earl. If their hearts fail them, you would have done nothing with them worthy of yourself, had you had Norway as well as Denmark at your back. At least, be true with them, as your only chance of keeping them true to you."

"Wise, wise wife," said Hereward, and went out and called

10

his band together, and told them every word, and all that had passed since he left Calais Straits.

"And now I have deceived you, and entrapped you, and I have no right to be your captain more. He that will depart in peace, let him depart, before the Frenchmen close in on us on every side and swallow us up at one mouthful."

Not a man answered.

"I say it again: He that will depart, let him depart."

They stood thoughtful.

Ranald, the Monk of Ramsay, drove the White-Bear banner firm into the earth, tucked up his monk's frock, and threw his long axe over his shoulder, as if preparing for action.

Winter spoke at last.

"If all go, there are two men here who stay, and fight by Hereward's side as long as there is a Frenchman left on English soil; for they have sworn an oath to Heaven and to St. Peter, and that oath will they keep. What say you, Gwenoch, knighted with us at Peterborough?"

Gwenoch stepped to Hereward's side.

"None shall go!" shouted a dozen voices. "With Hereward we will live and die. Let him lead us to Lincoln, to Stafford, where he will. We can save England for ourselves without the help of Danes."

"It is well for one at least of you, gentlemen, that you are in this pleasant mind," quoth Ranald the monk.

"Well for all of us, thou valiant purveyor of beef and beer."

"Well for one. For the first man that had turned to go, I would have brained him with this axe."

"And now, gallant gentlemen," said Hereward, "we must take new counsel, as our old has failed. Whither shall we go? For stay here, eating up the country, we must not do."

"They say that Waltheof is in Lindsay, raising the landsfolk. Let us go and join him."

"We can, at least, find what he means to do. There can be no better counsel. Let us march. Only we must keep clear of Lincoln as yet. I hear that Gilbert has a strong garrison there, and we are not strong enough yet to force it."

So they rode north, and up the Roman road toward Lincoln, sending out spies as they went; and soon they had news of Waltheof,— news, too, that he was between them and Lincoln.

"Then the sooner we are with him, the better, for he will find himself in trouble erelong, if old Gilbert gets news of him. So run your best, footmen, for forward we must get."

And as they came up the Roman road, they were aware of a great press of men in front of them, and hard fighting toward

Some of the English would have spurred forward at once. But Hereward held them back with loud reproaches. "Will you forget all I have told you in the first skirmish, like so many dogs when they see a bull? Keep together for five minutes more, the pot will not be cool before we get our sup of it. I verily believe that it is Waltheof, and that Gilbert has caught him already."

As he spoke, one part of the combatants broke up, and fled right and left; and a knight in full armor galloped furiously down the road right at them, followed by two or three more.

"Here comes some one very valiant, or very much afeared," said Hereward, as the horseman rode right upon him, shouting, —

"I am the King!"

"The King?" roared Hereward, and dropping his lance, spurred his horse forward, kicking his feet clear of the stirrups. He caught the knight round the neck, dragged him over his horse's tail, and fell with him to the ground.

The armor clashed; the sparks flew from the old gray Roman flints; and Hereward, rolling over once, rose, and knelt upon his prisoner.

"William of Normandy, yield or die!"

The knight lay still and stark.

"Ride on!" roared Hereward from the ground. "Ride at them, and strike hard! You will soon find out which is which. This booty I must pick for myself. What are you at?" roared he, after his knights. "Spread off the road, and keep your line, as I told you, and don't override each other! Curse the hot-headed fools! The Normans will scatter them like sparrows. Run on, men-at-arms, to stop the French if we are broken. And don't forget Guisnes field and the horses' legs. Now, King, are you come to life yet?"

"You have killed him," quoth Leofric the deacon, whom Hereward had beckoned to stop with him.

"I hope not. Lend me a knife. He is a much slighter man than I fancied," said Hereward, as they got his helmet off.

And when it was off, both started and stared. For they had uncovered, not the beetling brow, Roman nose, and firm curved lip of the Ulysses of the middle age, but the face of a fair lad, with long straw-colored hair, and soft blue eyes staring into vacancy.

"Who are you?" shouted Hereward, saying very bad words, "who come here aping the name of king?"

"Mother! Christina! Margaret! Waltheof Earl!" moaned the lad, raising his head and letting it fall again.

"It is the Atheling!" cried Leofric.

Hereward rose, and stood over the boy.

"Ah! what was I doing to handle him so tenderly? I took him for the Mamzer, and thought of a king's ransom."

"Do you call that tenderly? You have nigh pulled the boy's head off."

"Would that I had! Ah," went on Hereward, apostrophizing the unconscious Atheling,—"ah, that I had broken that white neck once and for all! To have sent thee feet foremost to Winchester, to lie by thy grandfathers and great-grandfathers, and then to tell Norman William that he must fight it out henceforth, not with a straw malkin like thee, which the very crows are not afraid to perch on, but with a cock of a very different hackle,— Sweyn Ulfsson, King of Denmark."

And Hereward drew Brain-biter.

"For mercy's sake! you will not harm the lad?"

"If I were a wise man now, and hard-hearted as wise men should be, I should — I should — " and he played the point of the sword backwards and forwards, nearer and nearer to the lad's throat.

"Master! master!" cried Leofric, clinging to his knees; "by all the saints! What would the Blessed Virgin say to such a deed!"

"Well, I suppose you are right. And I fear what my lady at home might say; and we must not do anything to vex her, you know. Well, let us do it handsomely, if we must do it. Get water somewhere, in his helmet. No, you need not linger. I will not cut his throat before you come back."

Leofric went off in search of water, and Hereward knelt with the Atheling's head on his knee, and on his lip a sneer at all things in heaven and earth. To have that lad stand between him and all his projects, and to be forced, for honor's sake, to let him stand!

But soon his men returned, seemingly in high glee, and other knights with them.

"Hey, lads!" said he, "I aimed at the falcon and shot the goose. Here is Edgar Atheling prisoner. Shall we put him to ransom?"

"He has no money, and Malcolm of Scotland is much too wise to lend him any," said some one. And some more rough jokes passed.

"Do you know, sirs, that he who lies there is your king?" asked a very tall and noble-looking knight.

"That do we not," said Hereward, sharply. "There is no king in England this day, as far as I know. And there will be none north of the Watling Street, till he be chosen in full husting, and anointed at York, as well as Winchester or London

We have had one king made for us in the last forty years, and we intend to make the next ourselves."

"And who art thou, who talkest so bold of king-making?"

"And who art thou, who askest so bold who I am?"

"I am Waltheof Siwardsson, the Earl, and yon is my army behind me."

"And I am Hereward Leofricsson, the outlaw, and yon is my army behind me."

If the two champions had flown at each other's throats, and their armies had followed their example, simply as dogs fly at each other, they know not why, no one would have been astonished in those unhappy times.

But it fell not out upon that wise; for Waltheof, leaping from his horse, pulled off his helmet, and seizing Hereward by both hands, cried, —

"Blessed is the day which sees again in England Hereward, who has upheld throughout all lands and seas the honor of English chivalry!"

"And blessed is the day in which Hereward meets the head of the house of Siward where he should be, at the head of his own men, in his own earldom. When I saw my friend, thy brother Osbiorn, brought into the camp at Dunsinane with all his wounds in front, I wept a young man's tears, and said, 'There ends the glory of the White-Bear's house!' But this day I say, the White-Bear's blood is risen from the grave in Waltheof Siwardsson, who with his single axe kept the gate of York against all the army of the French; and who shall keep against them all England, if he will be as wise as he is brave."

Was Hereward honest in his words? Hardly so. He wished to be honest. As he looked upon that magnificent young man, he hoped and trusted that his words were true. But he gave a second look at the face, and whispered to himself: "Weak, weak. He will be led by priests; perhaps by William himself. I must be courteous; but confide I must not."

The men stood round, and looked with admiration on the two most splendid Englishmen then alive. Hereward had taken off his helmet likewise, and the contrast between the two was as striking as the completeness of each of them in his own style of beauty. It was the contrast between the slow-hound and the deer-hound; each alike high bred; but the former, short, sturdy, cheerful, and sagacious; the latter tall, stately, melancholy, and not over wise withal.

Waltheof was a full head and shoulders taller than Hereward, — one of the tallest men of his generation, and of a strength which would have been gigantic, but for the too great length of neck and limb, which made him loose and slow in body, as he was somewhat loose and slow in mind. An old man's child, although that old man was as one of the old giants, there was a vein of weakness in him, which showed in the arched eyebrow, the sleepy pale blue eye, the small soft mouth, the lazy voice, the narrow and lofty brain over a shallow brow. His face was not that of a warrior, but of a saint in a painted window; and to his own place he went, and became a saint, in his due time. But that he could outgeneral William, that he could even manage Gospatrick and his intrigues Hereward expected as little as that his own nephews Edwin and Morcar could do it.

"I have to thank you, noble sir," said Waltheof, languidly, "for sending your knights to our rescue when we were really hard bestead, — I fear much by our own fault. Had they told me whose men they were, I should not have spoken to you so roughly as I fear I did."

"There is no offence. Let Englishmen speak their minds, as long as English land is above sea. But how did you get into trouble, and with whom?"

Waltheof told him how he was going round the country, raising forces in the name of the Atheling, when, as they were straggling along the Roman road, Gilbert of Ghent had dashed out on them from a wood, cut their line in two, driven Waltheof one way, and the Atheling another, and that the Atheling had only escaped by riding, as they saw, for his life.

"Well done, old Gilbert!" laughed Hereward. "You must beware, my Lord Earl, how you venture within reach of that old bear's paw?"

"Bear? By the by, Sir Hereward," asked Waltheof, whose thoughts ran loosely right and left, "why is it that you carry the white bear on your banner?"

"Do you not know? Your house ought to have a blood-feud against me. I slew your great-uncle, or cousin, or some other kinsman, at Gilbert's house in Scotland long ago; and since then I sleep on his skin every night, and carry his picture in my banner all day."

"Blood-feuds are solemn things," said Waltheof, frowning. "Karl killed my grandfather Aldred at the battle of Settrington, and his four sons are with the army at York now —"

"For the love of all saints and of England, do not think of avenging that! Every man must now put away old grudges, and remember that he has but one foe, — William and his Frenchmen."

"Very nobly spoken. But those sons of Karl — and I think you said you had killed a kinsman of mine?"

"It was a bear, Lord Earl, a great white bear. Cannot you understand a jest? Or are you going to take up the quarrels of all white bears that are slain between here and Iceland? You will end by burning Crowland minster then, for there are twelve of your kinsmen's skins there, which Canute gave forty years ago."

"Burn Crowland minster? St. Guthlac and all saints forbid." said Waltheof, crossing himself devoutly.

"Are you a monk-monger into the bargain, as well as a dolt? A bad prospect for us, if you are," said Hereward to himself.

"Ah, my dear Lord King!" said Waltheof, "and you are recovering?"

"Somewhat," said the lad, sitting up, "under the care of this kind knight."

"He is a monk, Sir Atheling, and not a knight," said Hereward. "Our fenmen can wear a mail-shirt as easily as a frock, and handle a twybill as neatly as a breviary."

Waltheof shook his head. "It is contrary to the canons of Holy Church."

"So are many things that are done in England just now. Need has no master. Now, Sir Earl and Sir Atheling, what are you going to do?"

Neither of them, it seemed, very well knew. They would go to York if they could get there, and join Gospatrick and Merlesweyn. And certainly it was the most reasonable thing to be done.

"But if you mean to get to York, you must march after another fashion than this," said Hereward. "See, Sir Earl, why you were broken by Gilbert; and why you will be broken again, if this order holds. If you march your men along one of these old Roman streets — By St. Mary! these Romans had more wits than we; for we have spoilt the roads they left us, and never made a new one of our own —"

"They were heathens and enchanters," — and Waltheof crossed himself.

"And conquered the world. Well, — if you march along one of these streets, you must ride as I rode, when I came up to you. You must not let your knights go first, and your men-at-arms straggle after in a tail a mile long, like a scratch pack of hounds, all sizes but except each others'. You must keep your footmen on the high street, and make your knights ride in two bodies, right and left, upon the wold, to protect their flanks and baggage."

"But the knights won't. As gentlemen, they have a right to the best ground."

"Then they may go to — whither they will go, if the French

come upon them. If they are on the flanks, and you are attacked then they can charge in right and left on the enemy's flank, while the footmen make a stand to cover the wagons."

"Yes, — that is very good; I believe that is your French fashion?"

"It is the fashion of common-sense, like all things which succeed."

"But, you see, the knights would not submit to ride in the mire."

"Then you must make them. What else have they horses for, while honester men than they trudge on foot?"

"Make them?" said Waltheof, with a shrug and a smile. "They are all free gentlemen, like ourselves."

"And, like ourselves, will come to utter ruin, because every one of them must needs go his own way."

"I am glad," said Waltheof, as they rode along, "that you called this my earldom. I hold it to be mine of course, in right of my father; but the landsfolks, you know, gave it to your nephew Morcar."

"I care not to whom it is given. I care for the man who is on it, to raise these landsfolk and make them fight. You are here: therefore you are earl."

"Yes, the powers that be are ordained by God."

"You must not strain that text too far, Lord Earl; for the only power that is, whom I see in England — worse luck for it! — is William the Mamzer."

"So I have often thought."

"You have? As I feared!" (To himself:) "The pike will have you next, gudgeon!"

"He has with him the Holy Father at Rome, and therefore the blessed Apostle St. Peter of course. And is a man right, in the sight of Heaven, who resists them? I only say it. But where a man looks to the salvation of his own soul, he must needs think thereof seriously, at least."

"O, are you at that?" thought Hereward. "*Tout est perdu.* The question is, Earl," said he aloud, "simply this: How many men can you raise off this shire?"

"I have raised — not so many as I could wish. Harold and Edith's men have joined me fairly well; but your nephew, Morcar's —"

"I can command them. I have half of them here already."

"Then, — then we may raise the rest?"

"That depends, my Lord Earl, for whom we fight!"

"For whom? — I do not understand."

"Whether we fight for that lad, Child Edgar, or for Sweyn of Denmark, the rightful king of England."

"Sweyn of Denmark! Who should be the rightful king but the heir of the blessed St. Edward?"

"Blessed old fool! He has done harm to us enough on earth, without leaving his second-cousins' aunts' malkins to harm us after he is in Heaven."

"Sir Hereward, Sir Hereward, I fear thou art not as good a Christian as so good a knight should be."

"Christian or not, I am as good a one as my neighbors. I am Leofric's son. Leofric put Harthacanute on the throne, and your father, who was a man, helped him. You know what has befallen England since we Danes left the Danish stock at Godwin's bidding, and put our necks under the yoke of Wessex monks and monk-mongers. You may follow your father's track or not, as you like. I shall follow my father's, and fight for Sweyn Ulfsson, and no man else."

"And I," said Waltheof, "shall follow the anointed of the Lord."

"The anointed of Gospatrick and two or three boys!" said Hereward. "Knights! Turn your horses' heads. Right about face, all! We are going back to the Bruneswold, to live and die free Danes."

And to Waltheof's astonishment, who had never before seen discipline, the knights wheeled round; the men-at-arms followed them; and Waltheof and the Atheling were left to themselves on Lincoln Heath.

10*

CHAPTER XXIV.

HOW ARCHBISHOP ALDRED DIED OF SORROW.

In the tragedies of the next few months Hereward took no part; but they must be looked at near, in order to understand somewhat of the men who were afterwards mixed up with him for weal or woe.

When William went back to the South, the confederates, Child Edgar the Atheling, Gospatrick, and their friends, had come south again from Durham. It was undignified; a confession of weakness. If a Norman had likened them to mice coming out when the cat went away, none could blame him. But so they did; and Osbiorn and his Danes, landing in Humber-mouth, " were met " (says the Anglo-Saxon chronicle) " by Child Edgar and Earl Waltheof and Merlesweyn, and Earl Gospatrick with the men of Northumberland, riding and marching joyfully with an immense army"; not having the spirit of prophecy, or foreseeing those things which were coming on the earth.

To them repaired Edwin and Morcar, the two young Earls, Arkill and Karl, " the great Thanes," or at least the four sons of Karl, — for accounts differ, — and what few else of the northern nobility Tosti had left unmurdered.

The men of Northumberland received the Danes with open arms. They would besiege York. They would storm the new Norman Keep. They would proclaim Edgar king at York.

In that Keep sat two men, one of whom knew his own mind, the other did not. One was William Malet, knight, one of the heroes of Hastings, a noble Norman, and chatelain of York Castle. The other was Archbishop Aldred.

Aldred seems to have been a man like too many more, — pious and virtuous and harmless enough, and not without worldly prudence; but his prudence was of that sort which will surely swim with the stream, and " honor the powers that be," if they be but prosperous enough. For after all, if success be not God, it is like enough to Him in some men's eyes to do instead. So Archbishop Aldred had crowned Harold Godwinsson, when Harold's star was in the ascendant. And who but Archbishop Aldred should crown William, when his star had cast Harold's down from heaven?

He would have crowned Satanas himself, had he only proved himself king *de facto* — as he asserts himself to be *de jure* — of this wicked world.

So Aldred, who had not only crowned William, but supported his power north of Humber by all means lawful, sat in York Keep, and looked at William Malet, wondering what he would do.

Malet would hold it to the last. As for the new Keep, it was surely impregnable. The old walls — the Roman walls on which had floated the flag of Constantine the Great — were surely strong enough to keep out men without battering-rams, balistas, or artillery of any kind. What mattered Osbiorn's two hundred and forty ships, and their crews of some ten or fifteen thousand men? What mattered the tens of thousands of Northern men, with Gospatrick at their head? Let them rage and rob round the walls. A messenger had galloped in from William in the Forest of Dean, to tell Malet to hold out to the last. He had galloped out again, bearing for answer, that the Normans could hold York for a year.

But the Archbishop's heart misgave him, as from north and south at once came up the dark masses of two mighty armies, broke up into columns, and surged against every gate of the city at the same time. They had no battering-train to breach the ancient walls; but they had — and none knew it better than Aldred — hundreds of friends inside, who would throw open to them the gates.

One gate he could command from the Castle tower. His face turned pale as he saw a mob of armed townsmen rushing down the street towards it; a furious scuffle with the French guards; and then, through the gateway, the open champaign beyond, and a gleaming wave of axes, helms, and spears, pouring in, and up the street.

" The traitors!" he almost shrieked, as he turned and ran down the ladder to tell Malet below.

Malet was firm, but pale as Aldred.

" We must fight to the last," said he, as he hurried down, commanding his men to sally at once *en masse* and clear the city.

The mistake was fatal. The French were entangled in the narrow streets. The houses, shut to them, were opened to the English and Danes; and, overwhelmed from above, as well as in front, the greater part of the Norman garrison perished in the first fight. The remnant were shut up in the Castle. The Danes and English seized the houses round, and shot from the windows at every loophole and embrasure where a Norman showed himself.

" Shoot fire upon the houses!" said Malet.

" You will not burn York? O God! is it come to this?"

"And why not York town, or York minster, or Rome itself, with the Pope inside it, rather than yield to barbarians?"

Archbishop Aldred went into his room, and lay down on his bed. Outside was the roar of the battle; and soon, louder and louder, the roar of flame. This was the end of his time-serving and king-making. And he said many prayers, and beat his breast; and then called to his chaplain for blankets, for he was very cold. "I have slain my own sheep!" he moaned, "slain my own sheep!"

His chaplain hapt him up in bed, and looked out of the window at the fight. There was no lull, neither was there any great advantage on either side. Only from the southward he could see fresh bodies of Danes coming across the plain.

"The carcass is here, and the eagles are gathered together. Fetch me the holy sacrament, Chaplain, and God be merciful to an unfaithful shepherd."

The chaplain went.

"I have slain my own sheep!" moaned the archbishop. "I have given them up to the wolves, — given my own minster, and all the treasures of the saints; and — and — I am very cold."

When the chaplain came back with the blessed sacrament, Archbishop Aldred was more than cold; for he was already dead and stiff.

But William Malet would not yield. He and his Normans fought, day after day, with the energy of despair. They asked leave to put forth the body of the archbishop; and young Waltheof, who was a pious man, insisted that leave should be given.

So the archbishop's coffin was thrust forth of the castle-gate, and the monks from the abbey came and bore it away, and buried it in the Cathedral church.

And then the fight went on, day after day, and more and more houses burned, till York was all aflame. On the eighth day the minster was in a light low over Archbishop Aldred's new-made grave. All was burnt, — minster, churches, old Roman palaces, and all the glories of Constantine the Great and the mythic past.

The besiegers, hewing and hammering gate after gate, had now won all but the Keep itself. Then Malet's heart failed him. A wife he had, and children; and for their sake he turned coward and fled by night, with a few men-at-arms, across the burning ruins.

Then into what once was York the confederate Earls and Thanes marched in triumph, and proclaimed Edgar king, — a king of dust and ashes.

And where were Edwin and Morcar the meanwhile? It is not told. Were they struggling against William at Stafford, or helping Edric the Wild and his Welshmen to besiege Chester? Probably they were aiding the insurrection, — if not at these two points, still at some other of their great earldoms of Mercia and Chester. They seemed to triumph for a while: during the autumn of 1069 the greater part of England seemed lost to William. Many Normans packed up their plunder and went back to France; and those whose hearts were too stout to return showed no mercy to the English, even as William showed none. To crush the heart of the people by massacres and mutilations and devastations was the only hope of the invader; and thoroughly he did his work whenever he had a chance.

CHAPTER XXV.

HOW HEREWARD FOUND A WISER MAN IN ENGLAND THAN HIMSELF.

THERE have been certain men so great, that he who describes them in words, much more pretends to analyze their inmost feelings, must be a very great man himself, or incur the accusation of presumption. And such a great man was William of Normandy, — one of those unfathomable master-personages who must not be rashly dragged on any stage. The genius of a Bulwer, in attempting to draw him, took care, with a wise modesty, not to draw him in too much detail, — to confess always that there was much beneath and behind in William's character which none, even of his contemporaries, could guess. And still more modest than Bulwer is this chronicler bound to be.

But one may fancy, for once in a way, what William's thoughts were, when they brought him the evil news of York. For we know what his acts were; and he acted up to his thoughts.

Hunting he was, they say, in the forest of Dean, when first he heard that all England, north of the Watling Street, had broken loose, and that he was king of only half the isle.

Did he — as when, hunting in the forest of Rouen, he got the news of Harold's coronation — play with his bow, stringing and unstringing it nervously, till he had made up his mighty mind? Then did he go home to his lodge, and there spread on the rough oak board a parchment map of England, which no child would deign to learn from now, but was then good enough to guide armies to victory, because the eyes of a great general looked upon it?

As he pored over the map, by the light of bog-deal torch or rush candle, what would he see upon it?

Three separate blazes of insurrection, from northwest to east, along the Watling Street.

At Chester, Edric, "the wild Thane," who, according to Domesday-book, had lost vast lands in Shropshire; Algitha, Harold's widow, and Blethwallon and all his Welsh, — "the white mantles," swarming along Chester streets, not as usually, to tear and ravage like the wild-cats of their own rocks, but fast friends by blood of Algitha, once their queen on Penmaenmawr.* Edwin, the young Earl, Algitha's brother, Hereward's nephew, — he must be with them too, if he were a man.

Eastward, round Stafford, and the centre of Mercia, another blaze of furious English valor. Morcar, Edwin's brother, must be there, as their Earl, if he too was a man.

Then in the fens and Kesteven. What meant this news, that Hereward of St. Omer was come again, and an army with him? That he was levying war on all Frenchmen, in the name of Sweyn, King of Denmark and of England? He is an outlaw, a desperado, a boastful swash-buckler, thought William, it may be, to himself. He found out, in after years, that he had mistaken his man.

And north, at York, in the rear of those three insurrections lay Gospatrick, Waltheof, and Merlesweyn, with the Northumbrian host. Durham was lost, and Comyn burnt therein. But York, so boasted William Malet, could hold out for a year. He should not need to hold out for so long.

And last, and worst of all, hung on the eastern coast the mighty fleet of Sweyn, who claimed England as his of right. The foe whom he had part feared ever since he set foot on English soil, a collision with whom had been inevitable all along, was come at last; but where would he strike his blow?

William knew, it may be, that the Danes had been defeated at Norwich; he knew, doubt it not (for his spies told him everything), that they had purposed entering the Wash. To prevent a junction between them and Hereward was impossible. He must prevent a junction between them and Edwin and Morcar's men.

He determined, it seems — for he did it — to cut the English line in two, and marched upon Stafford as its centre.

So it seems; for all records of these campaigns are fragmentary, confused, contradictory. The Normans fought, and had no time to write history. The English, beaten and crushed, died and left no sign. The only chroniclers of the time are monks. And little could Ordericus Vitalis, or Florence of Worcester, or he of Peterborough, faithful as he was, who filled up the sad pages of the Anglo-Saxon Chronicle, — little could they see or understand of the masterly strategy which was conquering all England for Norman monks, in order that they, following the army like black ravens, might feast themselves upon the prey which others won for them. To them, the death of an abbot, the

* See the admirable description of the tragedy of Penmaenmawr, in Bulwar's 'Harold.''

squabbles of a monastery, the journey of a prelate to Rome, are more important than the manœuvres which decided the life and freedom of tens of thousands.

So all we know is, that William fell upon Morcar's men at Stafford, and smote them with a great destruction; rolling the fugitives west and east, toward Edwin, perhaps, at Chester, certainly toward Hereward in the fens.

At Stafford met him the fugitives from York, Malet, his wife, and children, with the dreadful news that the Danes had joined Gospatrick, and that York was lost.

William burst into fiendish fury. He accused the wretched men of treason. He cut off their hands, thrust out their eyes, threw Malet into prison, and stormed on north.

He lay at Pontefract for three weeks. The bridges over the Aire were broken down. But at last he crossed and marched on York.

No man opposed him. The Danes were gone down to the Humber. Gospatrick and Waltheof's hearts had failed them, and they had retired before the great captain.

Florence, of Worcester, says that William bought Earl Osbiorn off, giving him much money, and leave to forage for his fleet along the coast, and that Osbiorn was outlawed on his return to Denmark.

Doubtless William would have so done if he could. Doubtless the angry and disappointed English raised such accusations against the earl, believing them to be true. But is not the simpler cause of Osbiorn's conduct to be found in this plain fact? He had sailed from Denmark to put Sweyn, his brother, on the throne. He found, on his arrival, that Gospatrick and Waltheof had seized it in the name of Edgar Atheling. What had he to do more in England, save what he did? — go out into the Humber, and winter safely there, waiting till Sweyn should come with reinforcements in the spring?

Then William had his revenge. He destroyed, in the language of Scripture, "the life of the land." Far and wide the farms were burnt over their owners' heads, the growing crops upon the ground; the horses were houghed, the cattle driven off; while of human death and misery there was no end. Yorkshire, and much of the neighboring counties, lay waste, for the next nine years. It did not recover itself fully till several generations after.

The Danes had boasted that they would keep their Yule at York. William kept his Yule there instead. He sent to Winchester for the regalia of the Confessor; and in the midst of the blackened ruins, while the English, for miles around, wandered starving in the snows, feeding on carrion, on rats and mice, and, at last, upon each other's corpses, he sat in his royal robes, and gave away the lands of Edwin and Morcar to his liegemen. And thus, like the Romans, from whom he derived both his strategy and his civilization, he "made a solitude and called it peace."

He did not give away Waltheof's lands; and only part of Gospatrick's. He wanted Gospatrick; he loved Waltheof, and wanted him likewise.

Therefore, through the desert which he himself had made, he forced his way up to the Tees a second time, over snow-covered moors; and this time St. Cuthbert had sent no fog, being satisfied, presumably, with William's orthodox attachment to St. Peter and Rome; so the Conqueror treated quietly with Waltheof and Gospatrick, who lay at Durham.

Gospatrick got back his ancestral earldom from Tees to Tyne, and paid down for it much hard money and treasure; bought it, in fact, he said.

Waltheof got back his earldom, and much of Morcar's. From the fens to the Tees was to be his province.

And then, to the astonishment alike of Normans and English, and it may be, of himself, he married Judith, the Conqueror's niece; and became, once more, William's loved and trusted friend — or slave.

It seems inexplicable at first sight. Inexplicable, save as an instance of that fascination which the strong sometimes exercise over the weak.

Then William turned southwest. Edwin, wild Edric the dispossessed Thane of Shropshire, and the wilder Blethwallon and his Welshmen, were still harrying and slaying. They had just attacked Shrewsbury. William would come upon them by a way they thought not of.

So over the backbone of England, by way, probably, of Halifax, or Huddersfield, through pathless moors and bogs, down towards the plains of Lancashire and Cheshire, he pushed over and on. His soldiers from the plains of sunny France could not face the cold, the rain, the bogs, the hideous gorges, the valiant peasants, — still the finest and shrewdest race of men in all England, — who set upon them in wooded glens, or rolled stones on them from the limestone crags. They prayed to be dismissed, to go home.

"Cowards might go back," said William; "he should go on." If he could not ride, he would walk. Whoever lagged, he would be foremost. And, cheered by his example, the army at last debouched upon the Cheshire flats.

Then he fell upon Edwin, as he had fallen upon Morcar. He

drove the wild Welsh through the pass of Mold, and up into their native hills. He laid all waste with fire and sword for many a mile, as Domesday-book testifies to this day. He strengthened the walls of Chester, and trampled out the last embers of rebellion; he went down south to Salisbury, King of England once again.

Why did he not push on at once against the one rebellion left alight, — that of Hereward and his fenmen?

It may be that he understood him and them. It may be that he meant to treat with Sweyn, as he had done, if the story be true, with Osbiorn. It is more likely that he could do no more; that his army, after so swift and long a campaign, required rest. It may be that the time of service of many of his mercenaries was expired. Be that as it may, he mustered them at Old Sarum, — the Roman British burgh which still stands on the down side, and rewarded them, according to their deserts, from the lands of the conquered English.

How soon Hereward knew all this, or how he passed the winter of 1070 – 71, we cannot tell. But to him it must have been a winter of bitter perplexity.

It was impossible to get information from Edwin; and news from York was almost as impossible to get, for Gilbert of Ghent stood between him and it.

He felt himself now pent in, all but trapped. Since he had set foot last in England ugly things had risen up, on which he had calculated too little, — namely, Norman castles. A whole ring of them in Norfolk and Suffolk cut him off from the south. A castle at Cambridge closed the south end of the fens; another at Bedford, the western end; while Lincoln Castle to the north, cut him off from York.

His men did not see the difficulty; and wanted him to march towards York, and clear all Lindsay and right up to the Humber.

Gladly would he have done so, when he heard that the Danes were wintering in the Humber.

"But how can we take Lincoln Castle without artillery, or even a battering-ram?"

"Let us march past it then, and leave it behind."

"Ah, my sons," said Hereward, laughing sadly, "do you suppose that the Mamzer spends his time — and Englishmen's life and labor — in heaping up those great stone mountains, that you and I may walk past them? They are put there just to prevent our walking past, unless we choose to have the garrison sallying out to attack our rear, and cut us off from home, and carry off our women into the bargain, when our backs are turned."

The English swore, and declared that they had never thought of that.

"No. We drink too much ale this side of the Channel, to think of that, — or of anything beside."

"But," said Leofwin Prat, "if we have no artillery, we can make some."

"Spoken like yourself, good comrade. If we only knew how."

"I know," said Torfrida. "I have read of such things in books of the ancients, and I have watched them making continually, — I little knew why, or that I should ever turn engineer."

"What is there that you do not know?" cried they all at once. And Torfrida actually showed herself a fair practical engineer.

But where was iron to come from? Iron for catapult springs, iron for ram heads, iron for bolts and bars?

"Torfrida," said Hereward, "you are wise. Can you use the divining-rod?

"Why, my knight?"

"Because there might be iron ore in the wolds; and if you could find it by the rod, we might get it up and smelt it."

Torfrida said humbly that she would try; and walked with the divining-rod between her pretty fingers for many a mile in wood and wold, wherever the ground looked red and rusty. But she never found any iron.

"We must take the tires off the cart-wheels," said Leofwin Prat.

"But how will the carts do without? For we shall want them if we march."

"In Provence, where I was born, the wheels of the carts are made out of one round piece of wood. Could we not cut out wheels like them?" asked Torfrida.

"You are the wise woman, as usual," said Hereward.

Torfrida burst into a violent flood of tears, no one knew why.

There came over her a vision of the creaking carts, and the little sleek oxen, dove-colored and dove-eyed, with their canvas mantles tied neatly on to keep off heat and flies, lounging on with their light load of vine and olive twigs beneath the blazing southern sun. When should she see the sun once more? She looked up at the brown branches overhead, howling in the December gale, and down at the brown fen below, dying into mist and darkness as the low December sun died down; and it seemed as if her life was dying down with it. There would be no more sun, and no more summers, for her upon this earth.

None certainly for her poor old mother. Her southern blood

was chilling more and more beneath the bitter sky of Kesteven. The fall of the leaf had brought with it rheumatism, ague, and many miseries. Cunning old leech-wives treated the French lady with tonics, mugwort, and bogbean, and good wine enow. But, like David of old, she got no heat; and before Yule-tide came, she had prayed herself safely out of this world, and into the world to come. And Torfrida's heart was the more light when she saw her go.

She was absorbed utterly in Hereward and his plots. She lived for nothing else; and clung to them all the more fiercely, the more desperate they seemed.

So that small band of gallant men labored on, waiting for the Danes, and trying to make artillery and take Lincoln Keep. And all the while — so unequal is fortune when God so wills — throughout the Southern Weald, from Hastings to Hind-head, every copse glared with charcoal-heaps, every glen was burrowed with iron diggings, every hammer-pond stamped and gurgled night and day, smelting and forging English iron, wherewith the Frenchmen might slay Englishmen.

William — though perhaps he knew it not himself — had, in securing Sussex and Surrey, secured the then great iron-field of England, and an unlimited supply of weapons; and to that circumstance, it may be, as much as to any other, the success of his campaigns may be due.

It must have been in one of these December days that a handful of knights came through the Bruneswold, mud and blood bespattered, urging on tired horses, as men desperate and foredone. And the foremost of them all, when he saw Hereward at the gate of Bourne, leaped down, and threw his arms round his neck and burst into bitter weeping.

"Hereward, I know you, though you know me not. I am you nephew, Morcar Algarsson; and all is lost."

* * * * *

As the winter ran on, other fugitives came in, mostly of rank and family. At last Edwin himself came, young and fair, like Morcar; he who should have been the Conqueror's son-in-law; for whom his true-love pined, as he pined, in vain. Where were Sweyn and his Danes? Whither should they go till he came?

"To Ely," answered Hereward.

Whether or not it was his wit which first seized on the military capabilities of Ely is not told. Leofric the deacon, who is likely to know best, says that there were men there already holding theirs out against William, and that they sent for Hereward. But it is not clear from his words whether they were fugitives, or merely bold Abbot Thurstan and his monks.

It is but probable, nevertheless, that Hereward, as the only man among the fugitives who ever showed any ability whatsoever, and who was, also, the only leader (save Morcar) connected with the fen, conceived the famous " Camp of Refuge," and made it a formidable fact. Be that as it may, Edwin and Morcar went to Ely; and there joined them a Count Tosti (according to Leofric), unknown to history; a Siward Barn, or "the boy," who had been dispossessed of lands in Lincolnshire; and other valiant and noble gentlemen, — the last wrecks of the English aristocracy. And there they sat in Abbot Thurstan's hall, and waited for Sweyn and the Danes.

But the worst Job's messenger who, during that evil winter and spring, came into the fen, was Bishop Egelwin of Durham. He it was, most probably, who brought the news of Yorkshire laid waste with fire and sword. He it was, most certainly, who brought the worse news still, that Gospatrick and Waltheof were gone over to the king. He was at Durham, seemingly, when he saw that; and fled for his life ere evil overtook him: for to yield to William that brave bishop had no mind.

But when Hereward heard that Waltheof was married to the Conqueror's niece, he smote his hands together, and cursed him, and the mother who bore him to Siward the Stout.

"Could thy father rise from his grave, he would split thy craven head in the very lap of the Frenchwoman."

"A hard lap will he find it, Hereward," said Torfrida. "I know her, — wanton, false, and vain. Heaven grant he do not rue the day he ever saw her!"

"Heaven grant he may rue it! Would that her bosom were knives and fish-hooks, like that of the statue in the fairy-tale. See what he has done for us! He is Earl not only of his own lands, but he has taken poor Morcar's too, and half his earldom. He is Earl of Huntingdon, of Cambridge, they say, — of this ground on which we stand. What right have I here now? How can I call on a single man to arm, as I could in Morcar's name? I am an outlaw here and a robber; and so is every man with me. And do you think that William did not know that? He saw well enough what he was doing when he set up that great brainless idol as Earl again. He wanted to split up the Danish folk, and he has done it. The Northumbrians will stick to Waltheof. They think him a mighty hero, because he held York-gate alone with his own axe against all the French."

"Well, that was a gallant deed."

"Pish! we are all gallant men, we English. It is not courage that we want, it is brains. So the Yorkshire and Lindsay men, and the Nottingham men too, will go with Waltheof. And round here, and all through the fens, every coward, every prudent man even, — every man who likes to be within the law, and feel his head safe on his shoulders, — no blame to him, — will draw each from me for fear of this new Earl, and leave us to end as a handful of outlaws. I see it all. As William sees it all. He is wise enough, the Mamzer, and so is his father Belial, to whom he will go home some day. Yes, Torfrida," he went on after a pause, more gently, but in a tone of exquisite sadness, "you were right, as you always are. I am no match for that man. I see it now."

"I never said that. Only—"

"Only you told me again and again that he was the wisest man on earth."

"And yet, for that very reason, I bade you win glory without end, by defying the wisest man on earth."

"And do you bid me do it still?"

"God knows what I bid," said Torfrida, bursting into tears. "Let me go pray, for I never needed it more."

Hereward watched her kneeling, as he sat moody, all but desperate. Then he glided to her side, and said gently, —

"Teach me how to pray, Torfrida. I can say a pater or an ave. But that does not comfort a man's heart, as far as I could ever find. Teach me to pray, as you and my mother do."

And she put her arms round the wild man's neck, and tried to teach him, like a little child.

CHAPTER XXVI.

HOW HEREWARD FULFILLED HIS WORDS TO THE PRIOR OF THE GOLDEN BOROUGH.

IN the course of that winter died good Abbot Brand. Hereward went over to see him, and found him mumbling to himself texts of Isaiah, and confessing the sins of his people.

"' Woe to the vineyard that bringeth forth wild grapes. Woe to those that join house to house, and field to field,' — like us, and the Godwinssons, and every man that could, till we 'stood alone in the land.' 'Many houses, great and fair, shall be without inhabitants.' It is all foretold in Holy Writ, Hereward, my son. 'Woe to those who rise early to fill themselves with strong drink, and the tabret and harp are in their feasts; but they regard not the works of the Lord.' 'Therefore my people are gone into captivity, because they have no knowledge.' Ah, those Frenchmen have knowledge, and too much of it; while we have brains filled with ale instead of justice. 'Therefore hell hath enlarged herself, and opened her mouth without measure'; and all go down into it, one by one. And dost thou think thou shalt escape, Hereward, thou stout-hearted?"

"I neither know nor care; but this I know, that whithersoever I go, I shall go sword in hand."

"'They that take the sword shall perish by the sword,'" said Brand, and blessed Hereward, and died.

A week after came news that Thorold of Malmesbury was coming to take the Abbey of Peterborough, and had got as far as Stamford, with a right royal train.

Then Hereward sent Abbot Thorold word, that if he or his Frenchmen put foot into Peterborough, he, Hereward, would burn it over their heads. And that if he rode a mile beyond Stamford town, he should walk back into it barefoot in his shirt.

Whereon Thorold abode at Stamford, and kept up his spirits by singing the songs of Roland, — which some say he himself composed.

A week after that, and the Danes were come.

A mighty fleet, with Sweyn Ulfsson at their head, went up the Ouse toward Ely. Another, with Osbiorn at their head, having joined them off the mouth of the Humber, sailed (it seems) up the Nene. All the chivalry of Denmark and Ireland was come. And with it, all the chivalry and the unchivalry of the Baltic shores. Vikings from Jomsburg and Arkona, Gottlanders from Wisby; and with them savages from Esthonia, Finns from Åland, Letts who still offered in the forests of Rugen human victims to the four-headed Swantowit; foul hordes in sheep-skins and primeval filth, who might have been scented from Hunstanton Cliff ever since their ships had rounded the Skaw.

Hereward hurried to them with all his men. He was anxious, of course, to prevent their plundering the landsfolk as they went, — and that the savages from the Baltic shore would certainly do, if they could, however reasonable the Danes, Orkneymen, and Irish Ostmen might be.

Food, of course, they must take where they could find it; but outrages were not a necessary, though a too common, adjunct to the process of emptying a farmer's granaries.

He found the Danes in a dangerous mood, sulky, and disgusted, as they had good right to be. They had gone to the Humber, and found nothing but ruin; the land waste; the French holding both the shores of the Humber; and Osbiorn cowering in Humber-mouth, hardly able to feed his men. They had come to conquer England, and nothing was left for them to conquer, but a few peat-bogs. Then they would have what there was in them. Every one knew that gold grew up in England out of the ground, wherever a monk put his foot. And they would plunder Crowland. Their forefathers had done it, and had fared none the worse. English gold they would have, if they could not get fat English manors.

"No! not Crowland!" said Hereward; "any place but Crowland, endowed and honored by Canute the Great, — Crowland, whose abbot was a Danish nobleman, whose monks were Danes to a man, of their own flesh and blood. Canute's soul would rise up in Valhalla and curse them, if they took the value of a penny from St. Guthlac. St. Guthlac was their good friend. He would send them bread, meat, ale, all they needed. But woe to the man who set foot upon his ground."

Hereward sent off messengers to Crowland, warning all to be ready to escape into the fens; and entreating Ulfketyl to empty his storehouses into his barges, and send food to the Danes, ere a day was past. And Ulfketyl worked hard and well, till a string of barges wound its way through the fens, laden with beeves and bread, and ale-barrels in plenty, and with monks too, who welcomed the Danes as their brethren, talked to them in their own tongue, blessed them in St. Guthlac's name as the saviors of

England, and went home again, chanting so sweetly their thanks to Heaven for their safety, that the wild Vikings were awed, and agreed that St. Guthlac's men were wise folk and open-hearted, and that it was a shame to do them harm.

But plunder they must have.

"And plunder you shall have!" said Hereward, as a sudden thought struck him. 'I will show you the way to the Golden Borough,—the richest minster in England; and all the treasures of the Golden Borough shall be yours, if you will treat Englishmen as friends, and spare the people of the fens."

It was a great crime in the eyes of men of that time. A great crime, taken simply, in Hereward's own eyes. But necessity knows no law. Something the Danes must have, and ought to have; and St. Peter's gold was better in their purses than in that of Thorold and his French monks.

So he led them across the fens and side rivers, till they came into the old Nene, which men call Catwater and Muscal now.

As he passed Nomanslandhirne, and the mouth of the Crowland river, he trembled, and trusted that the Danes did not know that they were within three miles of St. Guthlac's sanctuary. But they went on ignorant, and up the Muscal till they saw St. Peter's towers on the wooded rise, and behind them the great forest which now is Milton Park.

There were two parties in Peterborough minster: a smaller faction of stout-hearted English, a larger one who favored William and the French customs, with Prior Herluin at their head. Herluin wanted not for foresight, and he knew that evil was coming on him. He knew that the Danes were in the fen. He knew that Hereward was with them. He knew that they had come to Crowland. Hereward could never mean to let them sack it. Peterborough must be their point. And Herluin set his teeth, like a bold man determined to abide the worst, and barred and barricaded every gate and door.

That night a hapless churchwarden, Ywar was his name, might have been seen galloping through Milton and Castor Hanglands, and on by Barnack quarries over Southorpe heath, with saddle-bags of huge size stuffed with 'gospels, mass-robes, cassocks, and other garments, and such other small things as he could carry away.' And he came before day to Stamford, where Abbot Thorold lay at his ease in his inn with his hommes d'armes asleep in the hall.

And the churchwarden knocked them up, and drew Abbot Thorold's curtains with a face such as his who

"drew Priam's curtains in the dead of night,
And would have told him, half his Troy was burned";

11   P

and told Abbot Thorold that the monks of Peterborough had sent him; and that unless he saddled and rode his best that night, with his meinie of men-at-arms, his Golden Borough would be even as Troy town by morning light.

"A moi hommes d'armes!" shouted Thorold, as he used to shout whenever he wanted to scourge his wretched English monks at Malmesbury into some French fashion.

The men leaped up, and poured in, growling.

"Take me this monk, and kick him into the street for waking me with such news."

"But, gracious lord, the outlaws will surely burn Peterborough; and folks said that you were a mighty man of war"

"So I am; but if I were Roland, Oliver, and Turpin rolled into one, how am I to fight Hereward and the Danes with forty men-at-arms? Answer me that, thou dunder-headed English porker. Kick him out."

And Ywar was kicked into the cold, while Thorold raged up and down his chamber in mantle and slippers, wringing his hands over the treasure of the Golden Borough, snatched from his fingers just as he was closing them upon it.

That night the monks of Peterborough prayed in the minster till the long hours passed into the short. The poor corrodiers, and other servants of the monastery, fled from the town outside into the Milton woods. The monks prayed on inside till an hour after matin. When the first flush of the summer's dawn began to show in the northeastern sky, they heard mingling with their own chant another chant, which Peterborough had not heard since it was Medehampstead, three hundred years ago, — the terrible Yuch-hey-saa-saa-saa, — the war-song of the Vikings of the north.

Their chant stopped of itself. With blanched faces and trembling knees they fled, regardless of all discipline, up into the minster tower, and from the leads looked out northeastward on the fen.

The first rays of the summer sun were just streaming over the vast sheet of emerald, and glittering upon the winding river; and on a winding line, too, seemingly endless, of scarlet coats and shields, black hulls, gilded poops and vanes and beak-heads, and the flash and foam of innumerable oars.

And nearer and louder came the oar-roll, like thunder working up from the northeast; and mingled with it that grim yet laughing Heysaa, which bespoke in its very note the revelry of slaughter.

The ships had all their sails on deck. But as they came nearer, the monks could see the banners of the two foremost vessels.

The one was the red and white of the terrible Dannebrog. The other, the scarcely less terrible white bear of Hereward.

"He will burn the minster! He has vowed to do it. As a child he vowed, and he must do it. In this very minster the fiend entered into him and possessed him; and to this minster has the fiend brought him back to do his will. Satan, my brethren, having a special spite (as must needs be) against St. Peter, rock and pillar of the Holy Church, chose out and inspired this man, even from his mother's womb, that he might be the foe and robber of St. Peter, and the hater of all who, like my humility, honor him, and strive to bring this English land into due obedience to that blessed apostle. Bring forth the relics, my brethren. Bring forth, above all things, those filings of St. Peter's own chains, — the special glory of our monastery, and perhaps its safeguard this day."

Some such bombast would any monk of those days have talked in like case. And yet, so strange a thing is man, he might have been withal, like Herluin, a shrewd and valiant man.

They brought out all the relics. They brought out the filings themselves, in a box of gold. They held them out over the walls at the ships, and called on all the saints to whom they belonged. But they stopped that line of scarlet, black, and gold as much as their spiritual descendants stop the lava-stream of Vesuvius, when they hold out similar matters at them, with a hope unchanged by the experience of eight hundred years. The Heysaa rose louder and nearer. The Danes were coming. And they came.

And all the while a thousand skylarks rose from off the fen, and chanted their own chant aloft, as if appealing to Heaven against that which man's greed and man's rage and man's superstition had made of this fair earth of God.

The relics had been brought out. But, as they would not work, the only thing to be done was to put them back again and hide them safe, lest they should bow down like Bel and stoop like Nebo, and be carried, like them, into captivity themselves, being worth a very large sum of money in the eyes of the more Christian part of the Danish host.

Then to hide the treasures as well as they could; which (says the Anglo-Saxon Chronicle) they hid somewhere in the steeple.

The Danes were landing now. The shout which they gave, as they leaped on shore, made the hearts of the poor monks sink low. Would they be murdered, as well as robbed? Perhaps not, — probably not. Hereward would see to that. And some wanted to capitulate.

Herluin would not hear of it. They were safe enough. St.

Peter's relic might not have worked a miracle on the spot; but it must have done something. St. Peter had been appealed to on his honor, and on his honor he must surely take the matter up. At all events, the walls and gates were strong, and the Danes had no artillery. Let them howl and rage round the holy place, till Abbot Thorold and the Frenchmen of the country rose and drove them to their ships.

In that last thought the cunning Norman was not so far wrong. The Danes pushed up through the little town, and to the minster gates : but entrance was impossible; and they prowled round and round like raging wolves about a winter steading; but found no crack of entry.

Prior Herluin grew bold; and coming to the leads of the gateway tower, looked over cautiously, and holding up a certain most sacred emblem,—not to be profaned in these pages,—cursed them in the name of his whole Pantheon.

"Aha, Herluin! Are you there?" asked a short, square man in gay armor. "Have you forgotten the peat-stack outside Bolldyke Gate, and how you bade light it under me thirty years since?"

"Thou art Winter?" and the Prior uttered what would be considered, from any but a churchman's lips, a blasphemous and bloodthirsty curse; but which was, as their writings sufficiently testify, merely one of the lawful weapons or "arts" of those Christians who were "forbidden to fight,"—the other weapon or art being that of lying.

"Aha! That goes like rain off a duck's back to one who has been a minster scholar in his time. You! Danes! Ostmen! down! If you shoot at that man I'll cut your heads off. He is the oldest foe I have in the world, and the only one who ever hit me without my hitting him again ; and nobody shall touch him but me. So down bows, I say."

The Danes — humorous all of them — saw that there was a jest toward, and perhaps some earnest too, and joined in jeering the Prior.

Herluin had ducked his head behind the parapet; not from cowardice, but simply because he had on no mail, and might be shot any moment. But when he heard Winter forbid them to touch him, he lifted up his head, and gave his old pupil as good as he brought.

With his sharp, swift Norman priest's tongue he sneered, he jeered, he scolded, he argued; and then threatened, suddenly changing his tone, in words of real eloquence He appealed to the superstitions of his hearers. He threatened them with supernatural vengeance.

Some of them began to slink away frightened. St. Peter was an ill man to have a blood feud with.

Winter stood, laughing and jeering again, for full ten minutes. At last: "I asked, and you have not answered: have you forgotten the peat-stack outside Bolldyke Gate? For if you have, Hereward has not. He has piled it against the gate, and it should be burnt through by this time. Go and see."

Herluin disappeared with a curse.

"Now, you sea-cocks," said Winter, springing up. "We'll to the Bolldyke Gate, and all start fair."

The Bolldyke Gate was on fire; and more, so were the suburbs. There was no time to save them, as Hereward would gladly have done, for the sake of the poor corrodiers. They must go, — on to the Bolldyke Gate. Who cared to put out flames behind him, with all the treasures of Golden Borough before him? In a few minutes all the town was alight. In a few minutes more, the monastery likewise.

A fire is detestable enough at all times, but most detestable by day. At night it is customary, a work of darkness which lights up the dark, picturesque, magnificent, with a fitness Tartarean and diabolic. But under a glaring sun, amid green fields and blue skies, all its wickedness is revealed without its beauty. You see its works, and little more. The flame is hardly noticed. All that is seen is a canker eating up God's works, cracking the bones of its prey, — for that horrible cracking is uglier than all stage-scene glares, — cruelly and shamelessly under the very eye of the great, honest, kindly sun.

And that felt Hereward, as he saw Peterborough burn. He could not put his thoughts into words, as men of this day can: so much the better for him, perhaps. But he felt all the more intensely — as did men of his day — the things he could not speak. All he said was aside to Winter, —

"It is a dark job. I wish it had been done in the dark." And Winter knew what he meant.

Then the men rushed into the Bolldyke Gate, while Hereward and Winter stood and looked with their men, whom they kept close together, waiting their commands. The Danes and their allies cared not for the great glowing heap of peat. They cared not for each other, hardly for themselves. They rushed into the gap; they thrust the glowing heap inward through the gateway with their lances; they thrust each other down into it, and trampled over them to fall themselves, rising scorched and withered, and yet struggling on toward the gold of the Golden Borough. One savage Lett caught another round the waist, and hurled him bodily into the fire, crying in his wild tongue: —

"You will make a good stepping-stone for me."

"That is not fair," quoth Hereward, and clove him to the chine.

It was wild work. But the Golden Borough was won.

"We must in now and save the monks," said Hereward, and dashed over the embers.

He was only just in time. In the midst of the great court were all the monks, huddled together like a flock of sheep, some kneeling, most weeping bitterly, after the fashion of monks.

Only Herluin stood in front of them, at bay, a lofty crucifix in his hand. He had no mind to weep. But with a face of calm and bitter wrath, he preferred words of peace and entreaty. They were what the time needed. Therefore they should be given. To-morrow he would write to Bishop Egelsine, to excommunicate with bell, book, and candle, to the lowest pit of Tartarus, all who had done the deed.

But to-day he spoke them fair. However, his fair speeches profited little, not being understood by a horde of Letts and Finns, who howled and bayed at him, and tried to tear the crucifix from his hands; but feared "the white Christ."

They were already gaining courage from their own yells; in a moment more blood would have been shed, and then a general massacre must have ensued.

Hereward saw it, and shouting, "After me, Hereward's men! a bear! a bear!" swung Letts and Finns right and left like corn-sheaves, and stood face to face with Herluin.

An angry Finn smote him on the hind-head full with a stone axe. He staggered, and then looked round and laughed.

"Fool! hast thou not heard that Hereward's armor was forged by dwarfs in the mountain-bowels? Off, and hunt for gold, or it will be all gone."

The Finn, who was astonished at getting no more from his blow than a few sparks, and expected instant death in return, took the hint and vanished jabbering, as did his fellows.

"Now, Herluin, the Frenchman!" said Hereward.

"Now, Hereward, the robber of saints!" said Herluin.

It was a fine sight. The soldier and the churchman, the Englishman and the Frenchman, the man of the then world, and the man of the then Church, pitted fairly, face to face.

Hereward tried, for one moment, to stare down Herluin. But those terrible eye-glances, before which Vikings had quailed, turned off harmless from the more terrible glance of the man who believed himself backed by the Maker of the universe, and all the hierarchy of heaven.

A sharp, unlovely face it was: though, like many a great

churchman's face of those days, it was neither thin nor haggard; but rather round, sleek, of a puffy and unwholesome paleness. But there was a thin lip above a broad square jaw, which showed that Herluin was neither fool nor coward.

"A robber and a child of Belial thou hast been from thy cradle; and a robber and a child of Belial thou art now. Dare thy last iniquity, and slay the servants of St. Peter on St. Peter's altar, with thy worthy comrades, the heathen Saracens,* and set up Mahound with them in the holy place."

Hereward laughed so jolly a laugh, that the Prior was taken aback.

"Slay St. Peter's rats? I kill men, not monks. There shall not a hair of your head be touched. Here! Hereward's men march these traitors and their French Prior safe out of the walls, and into Milton Woods, to look after their poor corrodiers, and comfort their souls, after they have ruined their bodies by their treason!"

"Out of this place I stir not. Here I am, and here I will live or die, as St. Peter shall send aid."

But as he spoke, he was precipitated rudely forward, and hurried almost into Hereward's arms. The whole body of monks, when they heard Hereward's words, cared to hear no more, but desperate between fear and joy, rushed forward, bearing away their Prior in the midst.

"So go the rats out of Peterborough, and so is my dream fulfilled. Now for the treasure, and then to Ely."

But Herluin burst himself clear of the frantic mob of monks, and turned back on Hereward.

"Thou wast dubbed knight in that church!"

"I know it, man; and that church and the relics of the saints in it are safe, therefore. Hereward gives his word."

"That, — but not that only, if thou art a true knight, as thou holdest, Englishman."

Hereward growled savagely, and made an ugly step toward Herluin. That was a point which he would not have questioned.

"Then behave as a knight, and save, save," — as the monks dragged him away, — "save the hospice! There are women, — ladies there!" shouted he, as he was borne off.

They never met again on earth; but both comforted themselves in after years, that two old enemies' last deed in common had been one of mercy.

Hereward uttered a cry of horror. If the wild Letts, even

* The Danes were continually mistaken, by Norman churchmen, for Saracens, and the Saracens considered to be idolaters. A maumeet, or idol, means a Mahomet.

the Jomsburgers, had got in, all was lost. He rushed to the door. It was not yet burst: but a bench, swung by strong arms, was battering it in fast.

"Winter! Geri! Siwards! To me, Hereward's men! Stand back, fellows. Here are friends here inside. If you do not, I'll cut you down."

But in vain. The door was burst, and in poured the savage mob. Hereward, unable to stop them, headed them, or pretended to do so, with five or six of his own men round him, and went into the hall.

On the rushes lay some half-dozen grooms. They were butchered instantly, simply because they were there. Hereward saw, but could not prevent. He ran as hard as he could to the foot of the wooden stair which led to the upper floor.

"Guard the stair-foot, Winter!" and he ran up.

Two women cowered upon the floor, shrieking and praying with hands clasped over their heads. He saw that the arms of one of them were of the most exquisite whiteness, and judging her to be the lady, bent over her. "Lady! you are safe. I will protect you. I am Hereward."

She sprang up, and threw herself with a scream into his arms.

"Hereward! Hereward! Save me. I am — "

"Alftruda!" said Hereward.

It was Alftruda; if possible more beautiful than ever.

"I have got you!" she cried. "I am safe now. Take me away, — out of this horrible place! Take me into the woods, — anywhere. Only do not let me be burnt here, — stifled like a rat. Give me air! Give me water!" And she clung to him so madly, that Hereward, as he held her in his arms, and gazed on her extraordinary beauty, forgot Torfrida for the second time.

But there was no time to indulge in evil thoughts, even had any crossed his mind. He caught her in his arms, and commanding the maid to follow, hurried down the stair.

Winter and the Siwards were defending the foot with swinging blades. The savages were howling round like curs about a bull; and when Hereward appeared above with the women, there was a loud yell of rage and envy.

He should not have the women to himself, — they would share the plunder equally, — was shouted in half a dozen barbarous dialects.

"Have you left any valuables in the chamber?" whispered he to Alftruda.

"Yes, jewels, — robes. Let them have all, only save me!"

"Let me pass!" roared Hereward. "There is rich booty in

the room above, and you may have it as these ladies' ransom. Them you do not touch. Back, I say, let me pass!"

And he rushed forward. Winter and the housecarles formed round him and the women, and hurried down the hall, while the savages hurried up the ladder, to quarrel over their spoil.

They were out in the court-yard, and safe for the moment. But whither should he take her?

"To Earl Osbiorn," said one of the Siwards. But how to find him?

"There is Bishop Christiern!" And the Bishop was caught and stopped.

"This is an evil day's work, Sir Hereward."

"Then help to mend it by taking care of these ladies, like a man of God." And he explained the case.

"You may come safely with me, my poor lambs," said the Bishop. "I am glad to find something to do fit for a churchman. To me, my housecarles."

But they were all off plundering.

"We will stand by you and the ladies, and see you safe down to the ships," said Winter, and so they went off.

Hereward would gladly have gone with them, as Alftruda piteously entreated him. But he heard his name called on every side in angry tones.

"Who wants Hereward?"

"Earl Osbiorn, — here he is."

"Those scoundrel monks have hidden all the altar furniture. If you wish to save them from being tortured to death, you had best find it."

Hereward ran with him into the Cathedral. It was a hideous sight; torn books and vestments, broken tabernacle work; foul savages swarming in and out of every dark aisle and cloister, like wolves in search of prey; five or six ruffians aloft upon the rood screen; one tearing the golden crown from the head of the crucifix, another the golden footstool from its feet.*

As Hereward came up, crucifix and man fell together, crashing upon the pavement, amid shouts of brutal laughter.

He hurried past them, shuddering, into the choir. The altar was bare, the golden pallium which covered it, gone.

"It may be in the crypt below. I suppose the monks keep their relics there," said Osbiorn.

"No! Not there. Do not touch the relics! Would you have the curse of all the saints? Stay! I know an old hiding-place. It may be there. Up into the steeple with me."

* The crucifix was probably of the Greek pattern, in which the figure stood upon a flat slab, projecting from the cross.

And in a chamber in the steeple they found the golden pall, and treasures countless and wonderful.

"We had better keep the knowledge of this to ourselves awhile," said Earl Osbiorn, looking with greedy eyes on a heap of wealth such as he had never beheld before.

"Not we! Hereward is a man of his word, and we will share and share alike." And he turned and went down the narrow winding stair.

Earl Osbiorn gave one look at his turned back; an evil spirit of covetousness came over him; and he smote Hereward full and strong upon the hind-head.

The sword turned upon the magic helm, and the sparks flashed out bright and wide.

Earl Osbiorn shrunk back, appalled and trembling.

"Aha!" said Hereward without looking round. "I never thought there would be loose stones in the roof. Here! Up here, Vikings, Berserker, and sea-cocks all! Here, Jutlanders, Jomsburgers, Letts, Finns, witches' sons and devils' sons all! Here!" cried he, while Osbiorn profited by that moment to thrust an especially brilliant jewel into his boot. "Here is gold, here is the dwarf's work! Come up and take your Polotaswarf! You would not get a richer out of the Kaiser's treasury. Here, wolves and ravens, eat gold, drink gold, roll in gold, and know that Hereward is a man of his word, and pays his soldiers' wages royally!"

They rushed up the narrow stair, trampling each other to death, and thrust Hereward and the Earl, choking, into a corner. The room was so full for a few moments, that some died in it. Hereward and Osbiorn, protected by their strong armor, forced their way to the narrow window, and breathed through it, looking out upon the sea of flame below.

"That was an unlucky blow," said Hereward, "that fell upon my head."

"Very unlucky. I saw it coming, but had no time to warn you. Why do you hold my wrist?"

"Men's daggers are apt to get loose at such times as these."

"What do you mean?" and Earl Osbiorn went from him, and into the now thinning press. Soon only a few remained, to search, by the glare of the flames, for what their fellows might have overlooked.

"Now the play is played out," said Hereward, "we may as well go down, and to our ships."

Some drunken ruffians would have burnt the church for mere mischief. But Osbiorn, as well as Hereward, stopped that. And gradually they got the men down to the ships; some drunk, some struggling under plunder; some cursing and quarrelling because nothing had fallen to their lot. It was a hideous scene; but one to which Hereward, as well as Osbiorn, was too well accustomed to see aught in it save an hour's inevitable trouble in getting the men on board.

The monks had all fled. Only Leofwin the long was left, and he lay sick in the infirmary. Whether he was burned therein, or saved by Hereward's men, is not told.

And so was the Golden Borough sacked and burnt. Now then, whither?.

The Danes were to go to Ely, and join the army there. Hereward would march on to Stamford; secure that town if he could; then to Huntingdon, to secure it likewise; and on to Ely afterwards.

"You will not leave me among these savages?" said Alftruda.

"Heaven forbid! You shall come with me as far as Stamford, and then I will set you on your way."

"My way?" said Alftruda, in a bitter and hopeless tone.

Hereward mounted her on a good horse, and rode beside her, looking — and he well knew it — a very perfect knight. Soon they began to talk. What had brought Alftruda to Peterborough, of all places on earth?

"A woman's fortune. Because I am rich, — and some say fair, — I am a puppet, and a slave, a prey. I was going back to my, — to Dolfin."

"Have you been away from him, then?"

"What! Do you not know?"

"How should I know, lady?"

"Yes, most true. How should Hereward know anything about Alftruda? But I will tell you. Maybe you may not care to hear?"

"About you? Anything. I have often longed to know how, — what you were doing."

"Is it possible? Is there one human being left on earth who cares to hear about Alftruda? Then listen. You know when Gospatrick fled to Scotland his sons went with him. Young Gospatrick, Waltheof,* and he,— Dolfin. Ethelreda, his girl, went too, — and she is to marry, they say, Duncan, Malcolm's eldest son by Ingebiorg. So Gospatrick will find himself, some day, father-in-law of the King of Scots."

"I will warrant him to find his nest well lined, wherever he be. But of yourself?"

* This Waltheof Gospatricksson must not be confounded with Waltheof Siwardsson, the young Earl. He became a wild border chieftain, then Baron of Atterdale, and then gave Atterdale to his sister Queen Ethelreda, and turned monk, and at last Abbot, of Crowland: crawling home, poor fellow, like many another, to die in peace in the sanctuary of the Danes.

"I refused to go. I could not face again that bleak black North. Beside — but that is no concern of Hereward's —"

Hereward was on the point of saying, "Can anything concern you, and not be interesting to me?"

But she went on, —

"I refused, and —"

"And he misused you?" asked he, fiercely.

"Better if he had. Better if he had tied me to his stirrup, and scourged me along into Scotland, than have left me to new dangers and to old temptations."

"What temptations?"

Alftruda did not answer; but went on, —

"He told me, in his lofty Scots' fashion, that I was free to do what I list. That he had long since seen that I cared not for him; and that he would find many a fairer lady in his own land."

"There he lied. So you did not care for him? He is a noble knight."

"What is that to me? Women's hearts are not to be bought and sold with their bodies, as I was sold. Care for him? I care for no creature upon earth. Once I cared for Hereward, like a silly child. Now I care not even for him."

Hereward was sorry to hear that. Men are vainer than women, just as peacocks are vainer than peahens; and Hereward was — alas for him! — a specially vain man. Of course, for him to fall in love with Alftruda would have been a shameful sin, — he would not have committed it for all the treasures of Constantinople; but it was a not unpleasant thought that Alftruda should fall in love with him. But he only said, tenderly and courteously, —

"Alas, poor lady!"

"Poor lady. Too true, that last. For whither am I going now? Back to that man once more."

"To Dolfin?"

"To my master, like a runaway slave. I went down South to Queen Matilda. I knew her well, and she was kind to me, as she is to all things that breathe. But now that Gospatrick is come into the king's grace again, and has bought the earldom of Northumbria, from Tweed to Tyne —"

"Bought the earldom?"

"That has he; and paid for it right heavily."

"Traitor and fool! He will not keep it seven years. The Frenchman will pick a quarrel with him, and cheat him out of earldom and money too."

The which William did, within three years.

"May it be so! But when he came into the king's grace, he must needs demand me back in his son's name."

"What does Dolfin want with you?"

"His father wants my money, and stipulated for it with the king. And beside, I suppose I am a pretty plaything enough still."

"You? You are divine, perfect. Dolfin is right. How could a man who had once enjoyed you live without you?"

Alftruda laughed, — a laugh full of meaning; but what that meaning was, Hereward could not divine.

"So now," she said, "what Hereward has to do, as a true and courteous knight, is to give Alftruda safe conduct, and, if he can, a guard; and to deliver her up loyally and knightly to his old friend and fellow-warrior, Dolfin Gospatricksson, earl of whatever he can lay hold of for the current month."

"Are you in earnest?"

Alftruda laughed one of her strange laughs, looking straight before her. Indeed, she had never looked Hereward in the face during the whole ride.

"What are those open holes? Graves?"

"They are Barnack stone-quarries, which Alfgar my brother gave to Crowland."

"So? That is pity. I thought they had been graves; and then you might have covered me up in one of them, and left me to sleep in peace."

"What can I do for you, Alftruda, my old play-fellow: Alftruda, whom I saved from the bear?"

"If she had foreseen the second monster into whose jaws she was to fall, she would have prayed you to hold that terrible hand of yours, which never since, men say, has struck without victory and renown. You won your first honor for my sake. But who am I now, that you should turn out of your glorious path for me?"

"I will do anything, — anything. But why miscall this noble prince a monster?"

"If he were fairer than St. John, more wise than Solomon, and more valiant than King William, he is to me a monster; for I loathe him, and I know not why. But do your duty as a knight, sir. Convey the lawful wife to her lawful spouse."

"What cares an outlaw for law, in a land where law is dead and gone? I will do what I — what you like. Come with me to Torfrida at Bourne; and let me see the man who dares try to take you out of my hand."

Alftruda laughed again.

"No, no. I should interrupt the little doves in their nest. Beside, the billing and cooing might make me envious. And I, alas! who carry misery with me round the land, might make your Torfrida jealous."

Hereward was of the same opinion, and rode silent and thoughtful through the great woods which are now the noble park of Burghley.

"I have found it!" said he at last. "Why not go to Gilbert of Ghent, at Lincoln?"

"Gilbert? Why should he befriend me?"

"He will do that, or anything else, which is for his own profit."

"Profit? All the world seems determined to make profit out of me. I presume you would, if I had come with you to Bourne."

"I do not doubt it. This is a very wild sea to swim in; and a man must be forgiven, if he catches at every bit of drift-timber."

"Selfishness, selfishness everywhere;—and I suppose you expect to gain by sending me to Gilbert of Ghent?"

"I shall gain nothing, Alftruda, save the thought that you are not so far from me—from us—but that we can hear of you,—send succor to you if you need."

Alftruda was silent. At last—

"And you think that Gilbert would not be afraid of angering the king?"

"He would not anger the king. Gilbert's friendship is more important to William, at this moment, than that of a dozen Gospatricks. He holds Lincoln town, and with it the key of Waltheof's earldom: and things may happen, Alftruda—I tell you; but if you tell Gilbert, may Hereward's curse be on you!"

"Not that! Any man's curse save yours!" said she in so passionate a voice that a thrill of fire ran through Hereward. And he recollected her scoff at Bruges,—"So he could not wait for me?" And a storm of evil thoughts swept through him. "Would to heaven!" said he to himself, crushing them gallantly down, "I had never thought of Lincoln. But there is no other plan."

But he did not tell Alftruda, as he meant to do, that she might see him soon in Lincoln Castle as its conqueror and lord. He half hoped that when that day came, Alftruda might be somewhere else.

"Gilbert can say," he went on, steadying himself again, "that you feared to go north on account of the disturbed state of the country; and that, as you had given yourself up to him of your own accord, he thought it wisest to detain you, as a hostage for Dolfin's allegiance."

"He shall say so. I will make him say so."

"So be it. Now, here we are at Stamford town; and I must to my trade. Do you like to see fighting, Alftruda,—the man's

game, the royal game, the only game worth a thought on earth?
For you are like to see a little in the next ten minutes."

"I should like to see you fight. They tell me none is so swift
and terrible in the battle as Hereward. How can you be otherwise, who slew the bear, — when we were two happy children together? But shall I be safe?"

"Safe? of course," said Hereward, who longed, peacock-like,
to show off his prowess before a lady who was — there was no
denying it — far more beautiful than even Torfrida.

But he had no opportunity to show off his prowess. For as
he galloped in over Stamford Bridge, Abbot Thorold galloped
out at the opposite end of the town through Casterton, and up the
Roman road to Grantham.

After whom Hereward sent Alftruda (for he heard that Thorold was going to Gilbert at Lincoln) with a guard of knights, bidding them do him no harm, but say that Hereward knew him
to be a *preux chevalier* and lover of fair ladies; that he had sent
him a right fair one to bear him company to Lincoln, and hoped
that he would sing to her on the way the song of Roland.

And Alftruda, who knew Thorold, went willingly, since it could
no better be.

After which, according to Gaimar, Hereward tarried three
days at Stamford, laying a heavy tribute on the burgesses for harboring Thorold and his Normans; and also surprised at a drinking-bout a certain special enemy of his, and chased him from room
to room sword in hand, till he took refuge shamefully in an outhouse, and begged his life.

And when his knights came back from Grantham, he marched
to Bourne.

"The next night," says Leofric the deacon, or rather the monk
who paraphrased his saga in Latin prose, — " Hereward saw in
his dreams a man standing by him of inestimable beauty, old of
years, terrible of countenance, in all the raiment of his body more
splendid than all things which he had ever seen, or conceived in
his mind; who threatened him with a great club which he carried
in his hand, and with a fearful doom, that he should take back to
his church all that had been carried off the night before, and
have them restored utterly, each in its place, if he wished to provide for the salvation of his soul, and escape on the spot a pitiable
death. But when awakened, he was seized with a divine terror,
and restored in the same hour all that he took away, and so departed, going onward with all his men."

So says Leofric, wishing, as may be well believed, to advance
the glory of St. Peter, and purge his master's name from the
stain of sacrilege. Beside, the monks of Peterborough no doubt

had no wish that the world should spy out their nakedness, and become aware that the Golden Borough was stript of all its gold.

Nevertheless, truth will out. Golden Borough was Golden Borough no more. The treasures were never restored; they went to sea with the Danes, and were scattered far and wide,— to Norway, to Ireland, to Denmark; "all the spoils," says the Anglo-Saxon Chronicle, "which reached the latter country, being the pallium and some of the shrines and crosses; and many of the other treasures they brought to one of the king's towns, and laid them up in the church. But one night, through their carelessness and drunkenness, the church was burned, with all that was therein. Thus was the minster of Peterborough burned and pillaged. May Almighty God have pity on it in His great mercy."

Hereward, when blamed for the deed, said always that he did it "because of his allegiance to the monastery." Rather than that the treasures gathered by Danish monks should fall into the hands of the French robbers, let them be given to their own Danish kinsmen, in payment for their help to English liberty.

But some of the treasure, at least, he must have surely given back, it so appeased the angry shade of St. Peter. For on that night, when marching past Stamford, they lost their way. "To whom, when they had lost their way, a certain wonder happened, and a miracle, if it can be said that such would be worked in favor of men of blood. For while in the wild night and dark they wandered in the wood, a huge wolf met them, wagging his tail like a tame dog, and went before them on a path. And they, taking the gray beast in the darkness for a white dog, cheered on each other to follow him to his farm, which ought to be hard by. And in the silence of the midnight, that they might see their way, suddenly candles appeared, burning, and clinging to the lances of all the knights,— not very bright, however; but like those which the folk call *candelæ nympharum*,— wills of the wisp. But none could pull them off, or altogether extinguish them, or throw them from their hands. And thus they saw their way, and went on, although astonished out of mind, with the wolf leading them, until day dawned, and they saw, to their great astonishment, that he was a wolf. And as they questioned among themselves about what had befallen, the wolf and the candles disappeared, and they came whither they had been minded,— beyond Stamford town,— thanking God, and wondering at what had happened."

After which Hereward took Torfrida, and his child, and all he had, and took ship at Bardeney, and went for Ely. Which when Earl Warrenne heard, he laid wait for him, seemingly near

Southery: but got nothing thereby, according to Leofric, but the pleasure of giving and taking a great deal of bad language; and (after his men had refused, reasonably enough, to swim the Ouse and attack Hereward) an arrow, which Hereward, "*modicum se inclinans*," stooping forward, says Leofric, — who probably saw the deed, — shot at him across the Ouse, as the Earl stood cursing on the top of the dike. Which arrow flew so stout and strong, that though it sprang back from Earl Warrenne's hauberk, it knocked him almost senseless off his horse, and forced him to defer his purpose of avenging Sir Frederic his brother.

After which Hereward threw himself into Ely, and assumed, by consent of all, the command of the English who were therein.

CHAPTER XXVII

HOW THEY HELD A GREAT MEETING IN THE HALL OF ELY

There sat round the hall of Ely all the magnates of the East land and East sea. The Abbot on his high seat; and on a seat higher than his, prepared specially, Sweyn Ulfsson, King of Denmark and England. By them sat the Bishops, Egelwin the Englishman and Christiern the Dane, Osbiorn, the young Earls Edwin and Morcar, and Sweyn's two sons; and, it may be, the sons of Tosti Godwinsson, and Arkill the great Thane, and Hereward himself. Below them were knights, vikings, captains, great holders from Denmark, and the Prior and inferior officers of Ely minster. And at the bottom of the misty hall, on the other side of the column of blue vapor which went trembling up from the great heap of burning turf amidst, were housecarles, monks, wild men from the Baltic shores, crowded together to hear what was done in that parliament of their betters.

They spoke like free Danes; the betters from the upper end of the hall, but every man as he chose. They were in full Thing; in parliament, as their forefathers had been wont to be for countless ages. Their House of Lords and their House of Commons were not yet defined from each other: but they knew the rules of the house, the courtesies of debate; and, by practice of free speech, had educated themselves to bear and forbear, like gentlemen.

But the speaking was loud and earnest, often angry, that day. "What was to be done?" was the question before the house.

"That depended," said Sweyn, the wise and prudent king, "on what could be done by the English to co-operate with them." And what that was has been already told.

"When Tosti Godwinsson, ye Bishops, Earls, Knights, and Holders, came to me five years ago, and bade me come and take the kingdom of England, I answered him, that I had not wit enough to do the deeds which Canute my uncle did; and so sat still in peace. I little thought that I should have lost in five years so much of those small wits which I confessed to, that I should come after all to take England, and find two kings in it already, both more to the English mind than me. While William the Frenchman is king by the sword, and Edgar the Englishman king by proclamation of Danish Earls and Thanes, there seems no room here for Sweyn Ulfsson."

"We will make room for you! We will make a rid road from here to Winchester!" shouted the holders and knights.

"It is too late. What say you, Hereward Leofricsson, who go for a wise man among men?"

Hereward rose, and spoke gracefully, earnestly, eloquently; but he could not deny Sweyn's plain words.

"Sir Hereward beats about the bush," said Earl Osbiorn, rising when Hereward sat down. "None knows better than he that all is over. Earl Edwin and Earl Morcar, who should have helped us along Watling Street, are here fugitives. Earl Gospatrick and Earl Waltheof are William's men now, soon to raise the landsfolk against us. We had better go home, before we have eaten up the monks of Ely."

Then Hereward rose again, and without an openly insulting word, poured forth his scorn and rage upon Osbiorn. Why had he not kept to the agreement which he and Countess Gyda had made with him through Tosti's sons? Why had he wasted time and men from Dover to Norwich, instead of coming straight into the fens, and marching inland to succor Morcar and Edwin? Osbiorn had ruined the plan, and he only, if it was ruined.

"And who was I, to obey Hereward?" asked Osbiorn, fiercely.

"And who wert thou, to disobey me?" asked Sweyn, in a terrible voice. "Hereward is right. We shall see what thou sayest to all this, in full Thing at home in Denmark."

Then Edwin rose, entreating peace. "They were beaten. The hand of God was against them. Why should they struggle any more? Or, if they struggled on, why should they involve the Danes in their own ruin?"

Then holder after holder rose, and spoke rough Danish common sense. They had come hither to win England. They had found it won already. Let them take what they had got from Peterborough, and go.

Then Winter sprang up. "Take the pay, and sail off with it, without having done the work? That would be a noble tale to carry home to your fair wives in Jutland. I shall not call you niddering, being a man of peace, as all know." Whereat all laughed; for the doughty little man had not a hand's breadth on head or arm without its scar. "But if your ladies call you so, you must have a shrewd answer to give, beside knocking them down."

Sweyn spoke without rising: "The good knight forgets that this expedition has cost Denmark already nigh as much as Harold Hardraade's cost Norway. It is hard upon the Danes, if they are to go away empty-handed as well as disappointed."

"The King has right!" cried Hereward. "Let them take the plunder of Peterborough as pay for what they have done, and what beside they would have done if Osbiorn the Earl — Nay, men of England, let us be just! — what they would have done if there had been heart and wit, one mind and one purpose, in England. The Danes have done their best. They have shown themselves what they are, our blood and kin. I know that some talk of treason, of bribes. Let us have no more such vain and foul suspicions. They came as our friends; and as our friends let them go, and leave us to fight out our own quarrel to the last drop of blood."

"Would God!" said Sweyn, "thou wouldest go too, thou good knight. Here, earls and gentlemen of England! Sweyn Ulfsson offers to every one of you, who will come to Denmark with him, shelter and hospitality till better times shall come."

Then arose a mixed cry. Some would go, some would not. Some of the Danes took the proposal cordially; some feared bringing among themselves men who would needs want land, of which there was none to give. If the English came, they must go up the Baltic, and conquer fresh lands for themselves from heathen Letts and Finns.

Then Hereward rose again, and spoke so nobly and so well, that all ears were charmed.

They were Englishmen; and they would rather die in their own merry England than conquer new kingdoms in the cold northeast. They were sworn, the leaders of them, to die or conquer, fighting the accursed Frenchman. They were bound to St. Peter, and to St. Guthlac, and to St. Felix of Ramsay, and St. Etheldreda the holy virgin, beneath whose roof they stood, to defend against Frenchmen the saints of England waom they despised and blasphemed, whose servants they cast out, thrust into prison, and murdered, that they might bring in Frenchmen from Normandy, Italians from the Pope of Rome. Sweyn Ulfsson spoke as became him, as a prudent and a generous prince; the man who alone of all kings defied and fought the great Hardraade till neither could fight more; the true nephew of Canute the king of kings: and they thanked him: but they would live and die Englishmen.

And every Englishman shouted, "Hereward has right! We will live and die fighting the French!"

And Sweyn Ulfsson rose again, and said with a great oath, "That if there had been three such men as Hereward in England, all would have gone well."

Hereward laughed. "Thou art wrong for once, wise king. We have failed, just because there were a dozen men in England as good as me, every man wanting his own way; and too many cooks have spoiled the broth. What we wanted is, not a dozen men like me, but one like thee, to take us all by the back of the neck and shake us soundly, and say, 'Do that, or die!'"

And so, after much talk, the meeting broke up. And when it broke up, there came to Hereward in the hall a noble-looking man of his own age, and put his hand within his, and said,—

"Do you not know me, Hereward Leofricsson?"

"I know thee not, good knight, more pity; but by thy dress and carriage, thou shouldest be a true Vikingsson."

"I am Sigtryg Ranaldsson, now King of Waterford. And my wife said to me, 'If there be treachery or faint-heartedness, remember this,— that Hereward Leofricsson slew the Ogre, and Hannibal of Gweek likewise, and brought me safe to thee. And, therefore, if thou provest false to him, niddering thou art; and no niddering is spouse of mine.'"

"Thou art Sigtryg Ranaldsson?" cried Hereward, clasping him in his arms, as the scenes of his wild youth rushed across his mind. "Better is old wine than new, and old friends likewise."

"And I, and my five ships, are thine to death. Let who will go back."

"They must go," said Hereward, half-peevishly. "Sweyn has right, and Osbiorn too. The game is played out. Sweep the chessmen off the board, as Earl Ulf did by Canute the king."

"And lost his life thereby. I shall stand by, and see thee play the last pawn."

"And lose thy life equally."

"What matter? I heard thee sing,—

'A bed-death, a priest death,
A straw death, a cow death,
Such death likes not me!'

Nor likes it me either, Hereward Leofricsson."

So the Danes sailed away: but Sigtryg Ranaldsson and his five ships remained.

Hereward went to the minster tower, and watched the Ouse flashing with countless oars northward toward Southrey Fen. And when they were all out of sight, he went back, and lay down on his bed and wept,— once and for all. Then he arose, and went down into the hall to abbots and monks, and earls and knights, and was the boldest, cheeriest, wittiest of them all.

"They say," quoth he to Torfrida that night, "that some men

have gray heads on green shoulders. I have a gray heart in a green body."

"And my heart is growing very gray, too," said Torfrida.

"Certainly not thy head." And he played with her raven locks.

"That may come, too; and too soon."

For, indeed, they were in very evil case.

CHAPTER XXVIII.

HOW THEY FOUGHT AT ALDRETH.

WHEN William heard that the Danes were gone, he marched on Ely, as on an easy prey.

Ivo Taillebois came with him, hungry after those Spalding lands, the rents whereof Hereward had been taking for his men for now twelve months. William de Warrenne was there, vowed to revenge the death of Sir Frederic, his brother. Ralph Guader was there, flushed with his success at Norwich. And with them all the Frenchmen of the east, who had been either expelled from their lands, or were in fear of expulsion.

With them, too, was a great army of mercenaries, ruffians from all France and Flanders, hired to fight for a certain term, on the chance of plunder or of fiefs in land. Their brains were all aflame with the tales of inestimable riches hidden in Ely. There were there the jewels of all the monasteries round; there were the treasures of all the fugitive English nobles; there were there — what was there not? And they grumbled, when William halted them and hutted them at Cambridge, and began to feel cautiously the strength of the place, — which must be strong, or Hereward and the English would not have made it their camp of refuge.

Perhaps he rode up to Madingley windmill, and saw fifteen miles away, clear against the sky, the long line of what seemed naught but a low upland park, with the minster tower among the trees; and between him and them, a rich champaign of grass, over which it was easy enough to march all the armies of Europe; and thought Ely an easy place to take. But men told him that between him and those trees lay a black abyss of mud and peat and reeds, Haddenham fen and Smithy fen, with the deep sullen West water or "Ald-reche" of the Ouse winding through them. The old Roman road was sunk and gone long since under the bog, whether by English neglect, or whether (as some think) by actual and bodily sinking of the whole land. The narrowest space between dry land and dry land was a full half-mile; and how to cross that half-mile, no man knew.

What were the approaches on the west? There were none.

Beyond Earith, where now run the great washes of the Bedford Level, was a howling wilderness of meres, seas, reed-ronds, and floating alder-beds, through which only the fen-men wandered, with leaping-pole and log canoe.

What in the east? The dry land neared the island on that side. And it may be that William rowed round by Burwell to Fordham and Soham, and thought of attempting the island by way of Barraway, and saw beneath him a labyrinth of islands, meres, fens, with the Ouse, now increased by the volume of the Cam, lying deep and broad between Barraway and Thetford-in-the-Isle; and saw, too, that a disaster in that labyrinth might be a destruction.

So he determined on the near and straight path, through Long Stratton and Willingham, down the old bridle-way from Willingham ploughed field, — every village there, and in the isle likewise, had and has still its "field," or ancient clearing of ploughed land, — and then to try that terrible half-mile, with the courage and wit of a general to whom human lives were as those of the gnats under the hedge.

So all his host camped themselves in Willingham field, by the old earthwork which men now call Belsar's Hills; and down the bridle-way poured countless men, bearing timber and fagots cut from all the hills, that they might bridge the black half-mile.

They made a narrow, firm path through the reeds, and down to the brink of the Ouse, if brink it could be called, where the water, rising and falling a foot or two each tide, covered the floating peat for many yards before it sunk into a brown depth of bottomless slime. They would make a bottom for themselves by driving piles.

The piles would not hold; and they began to make a floating bridge with long beams, says Leofric, and blown-up cattle-hides to float them.

Soon they made a floating sow, and thrust it on before them as they worked across the stream; for they were getting under shot from the island.

Meanwhile the besieged had not been idle. They had thrown up, says Leofric, a turf rampart on the island shore, and "antemuralia et propugnacula," — doubtless overhanging "hoardings," or scaffolds, through the floor of which they could shower down missiles. And so they awaited the attack, contenting themselves with gliding in and out of the reeds in their canoes, and anroying the builders with arrows and cross-bow bolts.

At last the bridge was finished, and the sow safe across the West water, and thrust in, as far as it would float, among the reeds on the high tide. They in the fort could touch it with a pole.

The English would have destroyed it if they could. But Hereward bade them leave it alone. He had watched all their work, and made up his mind to the event.

"The rats have set a trap for themselves," he said to his men, "and we shall be fools to break it up till the rats are safe inside.'

So there the huge sow lay, black and silent, showing nothing to the enemy but a side of strong plank, covered with hide to prevent its being burned. It lay there for three hours, and Hereward let it lie.

He had never been so cheerful, so confident. "Play the man this day, every one of you, and ere nightfall you will have taught the Norman once more the lesson of York. He seems to have forgotten that. It is me to remind him of it."

And he looked to his bow and to his arrows, and prepared to play the man himself, — as was the fashion in those old days, when a general proved his worth by hitting harder and more surely than any of his men.

At last the army was in motion, and Willingham field opposite was like a crawling ants' nest. Brigade after brigade moved down to the reed beds, and the assault began.

And now advanced along the causeway and along the bridge a dark column of men, surmounted by glittering steel. Knights in complete mail, footmen in leather coats and quilted jerkins; at first orderly enough, each under the banner of his lord; but more and more mingled and crowded as they hurried forward, each eager for his selfish share of the inestimable treasures of Ely. They pushed along the bridge. The mass became more and more crowded; men stumbled over each other, and fell off into the mire and the water, calling vainly for help, while their comrades hurried on unheeding, in the mad thirst for spoil.

On they came in thousands; and fresh thousands streamed out of the fields, as if the whole army intended to pour itself into the isle at once.

"They are numberless," said Torfrida, in a serious and astonished voice, as she stood by Hereward's side.

"Would they were!" said Hereward. ' Let them come on, thick and threefold. The more their numbers the fatter will the fish below be before to-morrow morning. Look there, already!"

And already the bridge was swaying, and sinking beneath their weight. The men in places were ankle deep in water. They rushed on all the more eagerly, and filled the sow, and swarmed up to its roof.

Then, what with its own weight, what with the weight of the laden bridge, — which dragged upon it from behind, — the huge sow began to tilt backwards, and slide down the slimy bank.

12

The men on the top tried vainly to keep their footing, to hurl grapnels into the rampart, to shoot off their quarrels and arrows.

"You must be quick, Frenchmen," shouted Hereward in derision, "if you mean to come on board here."

The Normans knew that well; and as Hereward spoke two panels in the front of the sow creaked on their hinges, and dropped landward, forming two draw-bridges, over which reeled to the attack a close body of knights, mingled with soldiers bearing scaling ladders.

They recoiled. Between the ends of the draw-bridges and the foot of the rampart was some two fathoms' depth of black ooze. The catastrophe which Hereward had foreseen was come, and a shout of derision arose from the unseen defenders above.

"Come on, — leap it like men! Send back for your horses, knights, and ride them at it like bold huntsmen!"

The front rank could not but rush on : for the pressure behind forced them forward, whether they would or not. In a moment they were wallowing waist deep, trampled on, and disappearing under their struggling comrades, who disappeared in their turn.

"Look, Torfrida! If they plant their scaling ladders, it will be on a foundation of their comrades' corpses." Torfrida gave one glance through the openings of the hoarding, upon the writhing mass below, and turned away in horror. The men were not so merciful. Down between the hoarding-beams rained stones, javelins, arrows, increasing the agony and death. The scaling ladders would not stand in the mire. If they had stood a moment, the struggles of the dying would have thrown them down; and still fresh victims pressed on from behind, shouting "Dex Aie! On to the gold of Ely!" And still the sow, under the weight, slipped further and further back into the stream, and the foul gulf widened between besiegers and besieged.

At last one scaling ladder was planted upon the bodies of the dead, and hooked firmly on the gunwale of the hoarding. Ere it could be hurled off again by the English, it was so crowded with men that even Hereward's strength was insufficient to lift it off. He stood at the top, ready to hew down the first comer; and he hewed him down.

But the Normans were not to be daunted. Man after man dropped dead from the ladder top, — man after man took his place; sometimes two at a time; sometimes scrambling over each other's backs.

The English, even in the insolence of victory, cheered them with honest admiration. "You are fellows worth fighting, you French!"

"So we are," shouted a knight, the first and last who crossed that parapet; for, thrusting Hereward back with a blow of his sword-hilt, he staggered past him over the hoarding, and fell on his knees.

A dozen men were upon him; but he was up again and shouting, —

"To me, men-at-arms! A Dade! a Dade!" But no man answered.

"Yield!" quoth Hereward.

Sir Dade answered by a blow on Hereward's helmet, which felled the chief to his knees, and broke the sword into twenty splinters.

"Well hit," said Hereward, as he rose. "Don't touch him, men! this is my quarrel now. Yield, sir! you have done enough for your honor. It is madness to throw away your life."

The knight looked round on the fierce ring of faces, in the midst of which he stood alone.

"To none but Hereward."

"Hereward am I."

"Ah," said the knight, "had I but hit a little harder!"

"You would have broke your sword into more splinters. My armor is enchanted. So yield like a reasonable and valiant man."

"What care I?" said the knight, stepping on to the earthwork, and sitting down quietly. "I vowed to St. Mary and King William that into Ely I would get this day; and in Ely I am; so I have done my work."

"And now you shall taste — as such a gallant knight deserves — the hospitality of Ely."

It was Torfrida who spoke.

"My husband's prisoners are mine; and I, when I find them such *prudhommes* as you are, have no lighter chains for them than that which a lady's bower can afford."

Sir Dade was going to make an equally courteous answer, when over and above the shouts and curses of the combatants rose a yell so keen, so dreadful, as made all hurry forward to the rampart.

That which Hereward had foreseen was come at last. The bridge, strained more and more by its living burden, and by the falling tide, had parted, — not at the Ely end, where the sliding of the sow took off the pressure, — but at the end nearest the camp. One sideway roll it gave, and then, turning over, engulfed in that foul stream the flower of Norman chivalry; leaving a line — a full quarter of a mile in length — of wretches drowning in the dark water, or, more hideous still, in the bottomless slime of peat and mud.

Thousands are said to have perished. Their armor and weapons were found at times, by delvers and dikers, for centuries after; are found at times unto this day, beneath the rich drained cornfields which now fill up that black half-mile, or in the bed of the narrow brook to which the Westwater, robbed of its streams by the Bedford Level, has dwindled down at last.

William, they say, struck his tents and departed forthwith, groaning from deep grief of heart; and so ended the first battle of Aldreth.

CHAPTER XXIX.

HOW SIR DADE BROUGHT NEWS FROM ELY.

A MONTH after the fight, there came into the camp at Cambridge, riding on a good horse, himself fat and well-liking, none other than Sir Dade.

Boisterously he was received, as one alive from the dead; and questioned as to his adventures and sufferings.

"Adventures I have had, and strange ones; but for sufferings, instead of fetter-galls, I bring back, as you see, a new suit of clothes; instead of an empty and starved stomach, a surfeit from good victuals and good liquor; and whereas I went into Ely on foot, I came out on a fast hackney."

So into William's tent he went; and there he told his tale.

"So, Dade, my friend?" quoth the Duke, in high good humor, for he loved Dade, "you seem to have been in good company?"

"Never in better, Sire, save in your presence. Of the earls and knights in Ely, all I can say is, God's pity that they are rebels, for more gallant and courteous knights or more perfect warriors never saw I, neither in Normandy nor at Constantinople, among the Varangers themselves."

"Eh! and what are the names of these gallants; for you have used your eyes and ears, of course?"

"Edwin and Morcar, the earls, — two fine young lads."

"I know it. Go on"; and a shade passed over William's brow, as he thought of his own falsehood, and his fair Constance, weeping in vain for the fair bridegroom whom he had promised to her.

"Siward Barn, as they call him, the boy Orgar, and Thurkill Barn. Those are the knights. Egelwin, bishop of Durham, is there too; and besides them all, and above them all, Hereward. The like of that knight I may have seen. His better saw I never."

"Sir fool!" said Earl Warrenne, who had not yet — small blame to him — forgotten his brother's death. "They have soused thy brains with their muddy ale, till thou knowest not friend from foe. What hast thou to come hither praising up to the King's Majesty such an outlawed villain as that, with whom no honest knight would keep company?"

"If you, Earl Warrenne, ever found Dade drunk or lying, it is more than the King here has done."

"Let him speak, Earl," said William. "I have not an honester man in my camp; and he speaks for my information, not for yours."

"Then for yours will I speak, Sir King. These men treated me knightly, and sent me away without ransom."

"They had an eye to their own profit, it seems," grumbled the Earl.

"But force me they did to swear on the holy Gospels that I should tell your Majesty the truth, the whole truth, and nothing but the truth. And I keep my oath," quoth Dade.

"Go on, then, without fear or favor. Are there any other men of note in the island?"

"No."

"Are they in want of provisions?"

"Look how they have fattened me."

"What do they complain of?"

"I will tell you, Sir King. The monks, like many more, took fright at the coming over of our French men of God to set right all their filthy, barbarous ways; and that is why they threw Ely open to the rebels."

"I will be even with the sots," quoth William.

"However, they think that danger blown over just now; for they have a story among them, which, as my Lord the King never heard before, he may as well hear now."

"Eh?"

"How your Majesty should have sent across the sea a whole shipload of French monks."

"That have I, and will more, till I reduce these swine into something like obedience to his Holiness of Rome."

"Ah, but your Majesty has not heard how one Bruman, a valiant English knight, was sailing on the sea and caught those monks. Whereon he tied a great sack to the ship's head, and cut the bottom out, and made every one of those monks get into that sack and so fall through into the sea; whereby he rid the monks of Ely of their rivals."

"Pish! why tell me such an old-wives' fable, knight?"

"Because the monks believe that old-wives' fable, and are stout-hearted and stiff-necked accordingly."

"The blood of martyrs is the seed of the Church," said William's chaplain, a pupil and friend of Lanfranc; "and if these men of Belial drowned every man of God in Normandy, ten would spring up in their places to convert this benighted and besotted land of Simonites and Balaamites, whose priests, like the brutes which perish, scruple not to defile themselves and the service of the altar with things which they impudently call their wives."

"We know that, good chaplain," quoth William, impatiently. He had enough of that language from Lanfranc himself; and, moreover, was thinking more of the Isle of Ely than of the celibacy of the clergy.

"Well, Sir Dade?"

"So they have got together all their kin; for among these monks every one is kin to a Thane, or Knight, or even an Earl. And there they are, brother by brother, cousin by cousin, knee to knee, and back to back, like a pack of wolves, and that in a hold which you will not enter yet awhile."

"Does my friend Dade doubt his Duke's skill at last?"

"Sir Duke, — Sir King I mean now, for King you are and deserve to be, — I know what you can do. I remember how we took England at one blow on Senlac field; but see you here, Sir King. How will you take an island where four kings such as you (if the world would hold four such at once) could not stop one churl from ploughing the land, or one bird-catcher from setting lime-twigs?"

"And what if I cannot stop the bird-catchers? Do they expect to lime Frenchmen as easily as sparrows?"

"Sparrows! It is not sparrows that I have been fattening on this last month. I tell you, Sire, I have seen wild-fowl alone in that island enough to feed them all the year round. I was there in the moulting-time, and saw them take, — one day one hundred, one two hundred; and once, as I am a belted knight, a thousand duck out of one single mere. There is a wood there, with herons sprawling about the tree-tops, — I did not think there were so many in the world, — and fish for Lent and Fridays in every puddle and leat, pike and perch, tench and eels, on every old-wife's table; while the knights think scorn of anything worse than smelts and burbot."

"Splendeur Dex!" quoth William, who, Normanlike, did not dislike a good dinner. "I must keep Lent in Ely before I die."

"Then you had best make peace with the burbot-eating knights, my lord."

"But have they flesh-meat?"

"The isle is half of it a garden, — richer land, they say, is none in these realms, and I believe it: but, besides that, there is a deer-park there with a thousand head in it, red and fallow; and plenty of swine in woods, and sheep, and cattle; and if they fail, there are plenty more to be got, they know where."

"They know where? Do you, Sir Knight?" asked William, keenly.

"Out of every little island in their fens, for forty miles on end. There are the herds fattening themselves on the richest pastures in the land, and no man needing to herd them, for they are all safe among dikes and meres."

"I will make my boats sweep their fens clear of every head—"

"Take care, my Lord King, lest never a boat come back from that errand. With their narrow flat-bottomed punts, cut out of a single log, and their leaping-poles, wherewith they fly over dikes of thirty feet in width,—they can ambuscade in those reed-beds and alder-beds, kill whom they will, and then flee away through the marsh like so many horse-flies. And if not, one trick have they left, which they never try save when driven into a corner: but from that, may all saints save us!"

"What then?"

"Firing the reeds."

"And destroying their own cover?"

"True: therefore they will only do it in despair."

"Then to despair will I drive them, and try their worst. So these monks are as stout rebels as the earls?"

"I only say what I saw. At the hall-table there dined each day maybe some fifty belted knights, with every one a monk next to him; and at the high table the abbot, and the three earls, and Hereward and his lady, and Thurkill Barn. And behind each knight, and each monk likewise, hung against the wall lance and shield, helmet and hauberk, sword and axe."

"To monk as well as knight?"

"As I am a knight myself; and were as well used, too, for aught I saw. The monks took turns with the knights as sentries, and as foragers, too; and the knights themselves told me openly, the monks were as good men as they."

"As wicked, you mean," groaned the chaplain. "O, accursed and bloodthirsty race, why does not the earth open and swallow you, with Korah, Dathan, and Abiram?"

"They would not mind," quoth Dade. "They are born and bred in the bottomless pit already. They would jump over, or flounder out, as they do to their own bogs every day."

"You speak irreverently, my friend," quoth William.

"Ask those who are in camp, and not me. As for whither they went, or how, the English were not likely to tell me. All I know is, that I saw fresh cattle come every few days, and fresh farms burnt, too, on the Norfolk side. There were farms burning last night only, between here and Cambridge. Ask your sentinels on he Rech-dike how that came about?"

"I can answer that," quoth a voice from the other end of the tent. "I was on the Rech-dike last night, close down to the fen, — worse luck and shame for me."

"Answer, then!" quoth William, with one of his horrible oaths, glad to have some one on whom he could turn his rage and disappointment.

"There came seven men in a boat up from Ely yestereven, and five of them were monks; they came up from Burwell fen, and plundered and burnt Burwell town."

"And where were all you mighty men of war?"

"Ten of us ran down to stop them, with Richard, Earl Osbern's nephew, at their head. The villains got to the top of the Rech-dike, and made a stand, and before we could get to them —"

"Thy men had run, of course."

"They were every one dead or wounded, save Richard; and he was fighting single-handed with an Englishman, while the other six stood around, and looked on."

"Then they fought fairly?" said William.

"As fairly, to do them justice, as if they had been Frenchmen, and not English churls. As we came down along the dike, a little man of them steps between the two, and strikes down their swords as if they had been two reeds. 'Come!' cries he, 'enough of this. You are two *prudhommes* well matched, and you can fight out this any other day'; and away he and his men go down the dike-end to the water."

"Leaving Richard safe?"

"Wounded a little, — but safe enough."

"And then?"

"We followed them to the boat as hard as we could; killed one with a javelin, and caught another."

"Knightly done!" and William swore an awful oath, "and worthy of valiant Frenchmen. These English set you the example of chivalry by letting your comrade fight his own battle fairly, instead of setting on him all together; and you repay them by hunting them down with darts, because you dare not go within sword's-stroke of better men than yourselves. Go. I am ashamed of you. No, stay. Where is your prisoner? For, Splendeur Dex! I will send him back safe and sound in return for Dade, to tell the knights of Ely that if they know so well the courtesies of war, William of Rouen does too."

"The prisoner, Sire," quoth the knight, trembling, "is — is —"

"You have not murdered him?"

"Heaven forbid! but —"

"He broke his bonds and escaped?"

"Gnawed them through, Sire, as we suppose, and escaped through the mire in the dark, after the fashion of those accursed frogs of Girvians."

"But did he tell you naught ere he bade you good morning?"

"He told us the names of all the seven. He that beat down the swords was Hereward himself."

"I thought as much. When shall I have that fellow at my side?"

"He that fought Richard was one Wenoch."

"I have heard of him."

"He that we slew was Siward, a monk."

"More shame to you."

"He that we took was Ayer the Hardy, a monk of Nicole — Licole," — the Normans could never say Lincoln.

"And the rest were Thurstan the Younger; Leofric the Deacon, Hereward's minstrel; and Boter, the traitor monk of St. Edmund's."

"And if I catch them," quoth William, "I will make an abbot of every one of them."

"Sire?" quoth the chaplain, in a deprecating tone.

CHAPTER XXX.

HOW HEREWARD PLAYED THE POTTER; AND HOW HE CHEATED THE KING.

They of Ely were now much straitened, being shut in both by land and water; and what was to be done, either by themselves or by the king, they knew not. Would William simply starve them; or at least inflict on them so perpetual a Lent, — for of fish there could be no lack, even if they ate or drove away all the fowl, — as would tame down their proud spirits; which a diet of fish and vegetables, from some ludicrous theory of monastic physicians, was supposed to do?* Or was he gathering vast armies, from they knew not whence, to try, once and for all, another assault on the island, — it might be from several points at once?

They must send out a spy, and find out news from the outer world, if news were to be gotten. But who would go?

So asked the bishop, and the abbot, and the earls, in council in the abbot's lodging.

Torfrida was among them. She was always among them now. She was their Alruna-wife, their Vala, their wise woman, whose counsels all received as more than human.

"I will go," said she, rising up like a goddess on Olympus. "I will cut off my hair, and put on boy's clothes, and smirch myself brown with walnut leaves; and I will go. I can talk their French tongue. I know their French ways; and as for a story to cover my journey and my doings, trust a woman's wit to invent that."

They looked at her, with delight in her courage, but with doubt.

"If William's French grooms got hold of you, Torfrida, it would not be a little walnut brown which would hide you," said Hereward. "It is like you to offer, — worthy of you, who have no peer."

"That she has not," quoth churchmen and soldiers alike.

"But — to send you would be to send Hereward's wrong half. The right half of Hereward is going; and that is, himself."

---

* The Cornish — the stoutest, tallest, and most prolific race of the South — live on hardly anything else but fish and vegetables.

"Uncle, uncle!" said the young earls, "send Winter, Geri, Leofwin Prat, any of your fellows: but not yourself. If we lose you, we lose our head and our king."

And all prayed Hereward to let any man go, rather than himself.

"I am going, lords and knights; and what Hereward says he does. It is one day to Brandon. It may be two days back; for if I miscarry, — as I most likely shall, — I must come home round about. On the fourth day, you shall hear of me or from me. Come with me, Torfrida."

And he strode out.

He cropped his golden locks, he cropped his golden beard; and Torfrida cried, as she cropped them, half with fear for him, half for sorrow over his shorn glories.

"I am no Samson, my lady; my strength lieth not in my locks. Now for some rascal's clothes, — as little dirty as you can get me, for fear of company."

And Hereward put on filthy garments, and taking mare Swallow with him, got into a barge and went across the river to Soham.

He could not go down the Great Ouse, and up the Little Ouse, which was his easiest way, for the French held all the river below the isle; and, beside, to have come straight from Ely might cause suspicion. So he went down to Fordham, and crossed the Lark at Mildenhall; and just before he got to Mildenhall, he met a potter carrying pots upon a pony.

"Halt, my stout fellow," quoth he, "and put thy pots on my mare's back."

"The man who wants them must fight for them," quoth that stout churl, raising a heavy staff.

"Then here is he that will," quoth Hereward; and, jumping off his mare, he twisted the staff out of the potter's hands, and knocked him down therewith.

"That will teach thee to know an Englishman when thou seest him."

"I have met my master," quoth the churl, rubbing his head. "But dog does not eat dog; and it is hard to be robbed by an Englishman, after being robbed a dozen times by the French."

"I will not rob thee. There is a silver penny for thy pots and thy coat, — for that I must have likewise. And if thou tellest to mortal man aught about this, I will find those who will cut thee to ribbons; and if not, then turn thy horse's head and ride back to Ely, if thou canst cross the water, and say what has befallen thee; and thou wilt find there an abbot who will give thee another penny for thy news."

So Hereward took the pots, and the potter's clay-greased coat, and went on through Mildenhall, "crying," saith the chronicler, "after the manner of potters, in the English tongue, 'Pots! pots! good pots and pans!'"

But when he got through Mildenhall, and well into the rabbit-warrens, he gave mare Swallow a kick, and went over the heath so fast northward, that his pots danced such a dance as broke half of them before he got to Brandon.

"Never mind," quoth he, "they will think that I have sold them." And when he neared Brandon he pulled up, sorted his pots, kept the whole ones, threw the sherds at the rabbits, and walked on into Brandon solemnly, leading the mare, and crying "Pots!"

So "semper marcida et deformis aspectu" — lean and ill-looking — was that famous mare, says the chronicler, that no one would suspect her splendid powers, or take her for anything but a potter's nag, when she was caparisoned in proper character. Hereward felt thoroughly at home in his part; as able to play the Englishman which he was by rearing, as the Frenchman which he was by education. He was full of heart, and happy. He enjoyed the keen fresh air of the warrens; he enjoyed the ramble out of the isle, in which he had been cooped up so long; he enjoyed the fun of the thing, — disguise, stratagem, adventure, danger. And so did the English, who adored him. None of Hereward's deeds is told so carefully and lovingly; and none, doubt it not, was so often sung in after years by farm-house hearths, or in the outlaws' lodge, as this. Robin Hood himself may have trolled out many a time, in doggrel strain, how Hereward played the potter.

And he came to Brandon, to the "king's court," — probably Weeting Hall, or castle, from which William could command the streams of Wissey and Little Ouse, with all their fens, — and cast about for a night's lodging, for it was dark.

Outside the town was a wretched cabin of mud and turf, — such a one as Irish folk live in to this day; and Hereward said to himself, "This is bad enough to be good enough for me."

So he knocked at the door, and knocked till it was opened, and a hideous old crone put out her head.

"Who wants to see me at this time of night?"

"Any one would, who had heard how beautiful you are. Do you want any pots?"

"Pots! What have I to do with pots, thou saucy fellow? I thought it was some one wanting a charm." And she shut the door.

"A charm?" thought Hereward. "Maybe she can tell me

news, if she be a witch. They are shrewd souls, these witches, and know more than they tell. But if I can get any news, I care not if Satan brings it in person."

So he knocked again, till the old woman looked out once more, and bade him angrily be off.

"But I am belated here, good dame, and afraid of the French. And I will give thee the best bit of clay on my mare's back, — pot, — pan, — pansion, — crock, — jug, or what thou wilt, for a night's lodging."

"Have you any little jars, — jars no longer than my hand?" asked she; for she used them in her trade, and had broken one of late: but to pay for one, she had neither money nor mind. So she agreed to let Hereward sleep there, for the value of two jars. "But what of that ugly brute of a horse of thine?"

"She will do well enough in the turf-shed."

"Then thou must pay with a pannikin."

"Ugh!" groaned Hereward; "thou drivest a hard bargain, for an Englishwoman, with a poor Englishman."

"How knowest thou that I am English?"

"So much the better if thou art not," thought Hereward; and bargained with her for a pannikin against a lodging for the horse in the turf-house, and a bottle of bad hay.

Then he went in, bringing his panniers with him with ostentatious care.

"Thou canst sleep there on the rushes. I have naught to give thee to eat."

"Naught needs naught," said Hereward; threw himself down on a bundle of rush, and in a few minutes snored loudly.

But he was never less asleep. He looked round the whole cabin; and he listened to every word.

The Devil, as usual, was a bad paymaster; for the witch's cabin seemed only somewhat more miserable than that of other old women. The floor was mud, the rafters unceiled; the stars shone through the turf roof. The only hint of her trade was a hanging shelf, on which stood five or six little earthen jars, and a few packets of leaves. A parchment, scrawled with characters which the owner herself probably did not understand, hung against the cob wall; and a human skull — probably used only to frighten her patients — dangled from the roof-tree.

But in a corner, stuck against the wall, was something which chilled Hereward's blood a little. A dried human hand, which he knew must have been stolen off the gallows, gripping in its fleshless fingers a candle, which he knew was made of human fat. That candle, he knew, duly lighted and carried, would enable the witch to walk unseen into any house on earth, yea, through the court of King William himself, while it drowned all men in preternatural slumber.

Hereward was very much frightened. He believed as devoutly in the powers of a witch as did then — and does now, for aught Italian literature, *e permissu superiorum,* shows — the Pope of Rome.

So he trembled on his rushes, and wished himself safe through that adventure, without being turned into a hare or a wolf.

"I would sooner be a wolf than a hare, of course, killing being more in my trade than being killed; but — who comes here?"

And to the first old crone, who sat winking her bleared eyes, and warming her bleared hands over a little heap of peat in the middle of the cabin, entered another crone, if possible uglier.

"Two of them! If I am not roasted and eaten this night, I am a lucky man."

And Hereward crossed himself devoutly, and invoked St. Ethelfrida of Ely, St. Guthlac of Crowland, St. Felix of Ramsey, — to whom, he recollected, he had been somewhat remiss; but, above all, St. Peter of Peterborough, whose treasures he had given to the Danes. And he argued stoutly with St. Peter and with his own conscience, that the means sanctify the end, and that he had done it all for the best.

"If thou wilt help me out of this strait, and the rest, blessed Apostle, I will give thee — I will go to Constantinople but what I will win it — a golden table twice as fine as those villains carried off, and one of the Bourne manors — Witham — or Toft — or Mainthorpe — whichever pleases thee best, in full fee; and a — and a — "

But while Hereward was casting in his mind what gewgaw further might suffice to appease the Apostle, he was recalled to business and common-sense by hearing the two old hags talk to each other in French.

His heart leapt for joy, and he forgot St. Peter utterly.

"Well, how have you sped? Have you seen the king?"

"No; but Ivo Taillebois. Eh! Who the foul fiend have you lying there?"

"Only an English brute. He cannot understand us. Talk on: only don't wake the hog. Have you got the gold?"

"Never mind."

Then there was a grumbling and a quarrelling, from which Hereward understood that the gold was to be shared between them.

"But it is a bit of chain. To cut it will spoil it."

The other insisted; and he heard them chop the gold chain in two.

"And is this all?"

"I had work enough to get that. He said, No play no pay; and he would give it me after the isle was taken. But I told him my spirit was a Jewish spirit, that used to serve Solomon the Wise; and he would not serve me, much less come over the sea from Normandy, unless he smelt gold; for he loved it like any Jew."

"And what did you tell him then?"

"That the king must go back to Aldreth again; for only from thence he would take the isle; for — and that was true enough — I dreamt I saw all the water of Aldreth full of wolves, clambering over into the island on each other's backs."

"That means that some of them will be drowned."

"Let them drown. I left him to find out that part of the dream for himself. Then I told him how he must make another causeway, bigger and stronger than the last, and a tower on which I could stand and curse the English. And I promised him to bring a storm right in the faces of the English, so that they could neither fight nor see."

"But if the storm does not come?"

"It will come. I know the signs of the sky, — who better? — and the weather will break up in a week. Therefore I told him he must begin his works at once, before the rain came on; and that we would go and ask the spirit of the well to tell us the fortunate day for attacking."

"That is my business," said the other; "and my spirit likes the smell of gold as well as yours. Little you would have got from me, if you had not given me half the chain."

Then the two rose.

"Let us see whether the English hog is asleep."

One of them came and listened to Hereward's breathing, and put her hand upon his chest. His hair stood on end; a cold sweat came over him. But he snored more loudly than ever.

The two old crones went out satisfied. Then Hereward rose, and glided after them.

They went down a meadow to a little well, which Hereward had marked as he rode thither, hung round with bits of rag and flowers, as similar " holy wells " are decorated in Ireland to this day.

He hid behind a hedge, and watched them stooping over the well, mumbling he knew not what of cantrips.

Then there was silence, and a tinkling sound as of water.

" Once — twice — thrice," counted the witches. Nine times he counted the tinkling sound.

" The ninth day, — the ninth day, and the king shall take Ely,' said one in a cracked scream, rising, and shaking her fist toward the isle.

Hereward was more than half-minded to have put his dagger — the only weapon which he had — into the two old beldames on the spot. But the fear of an outcry kept him still. He had found out already so much, that he was determined to find out more. So to-morrow he would go up to the court itself, and take what luck sent.

He slipt back to the cabin and lay down again; and as soon as he had seen the two old crones safe asleep, fell asleep himself, and was so tired that he lay till the sun was high.

"Get up!" screamed the old dame at last, kicking him, "or I shall make you give me another crock for a double night's rest."

He paid his lodging, put the panniers on the mare, and went on crying pots.

When he came to the outer gateway of the court he tied up the mare, and carried the crockery in on his own back boldly. The scullions saw him, and called him into the kitchen to see his crockery, without the least intention of paying for what they took.

A man of rank belonging to the court came in, and stared fixedly at Hereward.

"You are mightily like that villain Hereward, man," quoth he.

"Anon?" asked Hereward, looking as stupid as he could.

"If it were not for his brown face and short hair, he is as like the fellow as a churl can be to a knight."

"Bring him into the hall," quoth another, "and let us see if any man knows him."

Into the great hall he was brought, and stared at by knights and squires. He bent his knees, rounded his shoulders, and made himself look as mean as he could.

Ivo Taillebois and Earl Warrenne came down and had a look at him.

"Hereward!" said Ivo. "I will warrant that little slouching cur is not he. Hereward must be half as big again, if it be true that he can kill a man with one blow of his fist."

"You may try the truth of that for yourself some day," thought Hereward.

"Does any one here talk English? Let us question the fellow," said Earl Warrenne.

"Hereward? Hereward? Who wants to know about that villain?" answered the potter, as soon as he was asked in English. "Would to Heaven he were here, and I could see some of you noble knights and earls paying him for me; for I owe him more than ever I shall pay myself."

"What does he mean?"

"He came out of the isle ten days ago, nigh on to evening and drove off a cow of mine and four sheep, which was all my living, noble knights, save these pots."

"And where is he since?"

"In the isle, my lords, wellnigh starved, and his folk falling away from him daily from hunger and ague-fits. I doubt if there be a hundred sound men left in Ely."

"Have you been in thither, then, villain?"

"Heaven forbid! I in Ely? I in the wolf's den? If I went in with naught but my skin, they would have it off me before I got out again. If your lordships would but come down, and make an end of him once for all; for he is a great tyrant and terrible, and devours us poor folk like so many mites in cheese."

"Take this babbler into the kitchen, and feed him," quoth Earl Warrenne; and so the colloquy ended.

Into the kitchen again the potter went. The king's luncheon was preparing; and he listened to their chatter, and picked up this at least, which was valuable to him, — that the witches' story was true; that a great attack would be made from Aldreth; that boats had been ordered up the river to Cotinglade, and pioneers and entrenching tools were to be sent on that day to the site of the old causeway.

But soon he had to take care of himself. Earl Warrenne's commands to feed him were construed by the cook-boys and scullions into a command to make him drunk likewise. To make a laughing-stock of an Englishman was too tempting a jest to be resisted; and Hereward was drenched (says the chronicler) with wine and beer, and sorely baited and badgered. At last one rascal hit upon a notable plan.

"Pluck out the English hog's hair and beard, and put him blindfold in the midst of his pots, and see what a smash we shall have."

Hereward pretended not to understand the words, which were spoken in French; but when they were interpreted to him, he grew somewhat red about the ears.

Submit he would not. But if he defended himself, and made an uproar in the king's Court, he might very likely find himself riding Odin's horse before the hour was out. However, happily for him, the wine and beer had made him stout of heart, and when one fellow laid hold of his beard, he resisted sturdily.

The man struck him, and that hard. Hereward, hot of temper, and careless of life, struck him again, right under the ear.

The fellow dropped for dead.

Up leapt cook-boys, scullions, "lécheurs" (who hung about

the kitchen to "lécher," lick the platters), and all the foul-mouthed rascality of a great mediæval household; and attacked Hereward "cum furcis et tridentibus," with forks and flesh-hooks.

Then was Hereward aware of a great broach, or spit, before the fire; and recollecting how he had used such a one as a boy against the monks of Peterborough, was minded to use it against the cooks of Brandon; which he did so heartily, that in a few moments he had killed one, and driven the others backward in a heap.

But his case was hopeless. He was soon overpowered by numbers from outside, and dragged into the hall, to receive judgment for the mortal crime of slaying a man within the precincts of the Court.

He kept up heart. He knew that the king was there; he knew that he should most likely get justice from the king. If not, he could but discover himself, and so save his life: for that the king would kill him knowingly, he did not believe.

So he went in boldly and willingly, and up the hall, where, on the dais, stood William the Norman.

William had finished his luncheon, and was standing at the board side. A page held water in a silver basin, in which he was washing his hands. Two more knelt, and laced his long boots, for he was, as always, going a-hunting.

Then Hereward looked at the face of the great man, and felt at once that it was the face of the greatest man whom he had ever met.

"I am not that man's match," said he to himself. "Perhaps it will all end in being his man, and he my master."

"Silence, knaves!" said William, "and speak one of you at a time. How came this?"

"A likely story, forsooth!" said he, when he had heard. "A poor English potter comes into my court, and murders my men under my very eyes for mere sport. I do not believe you, rascals! You, churl," and he spoke through an English interpreter, "tell me your tale, and justice you shall have or take, as you deserve. I am the King of England, man, and I know your tongue, though I speak it not yet, more pity."

Hereward fell on his knees.

"If you are indeed my Lord the King, then I am safe; for there is justice in you, at least so all men say." And he told his tale, manfully.

"Splendeur Dex! but this is a far likelier story, and I believe it. Hark you, you ruffians! Here am I, trying to conciliate these English by justice and mercy whenever they will let me, and here are you outraging them, and driving them mad and desperate, just that you may get a handle against them, and thus rob the poor wretches and drive them into the forest. From the lowest to the highest, — from Ivo Taillebois there down to you cookboys, — you are all at the same game. And I will stop it! The next time I hear of outrage to unarmed man or harmless woman, I will hang that culprit, were he Odo my brother himself."

This excellent speech was enforced with oaths so strange and terrible, that Ivo Taillebois shook in his boots; and the chaplain prayed fervently that the roof might not fall in on their heads.

"Thou smilest, man?" said William, quickly, to the kneeling Hereward. "So thou understandest French?"

"A few words only, most gracious King, which we potters pick up, wandering everywhere with our wares," said Hereward, speaking in French; for so keen was William's eye, that he thought it safer to play no tricks with him.

Nevertheless, he made his French so execrable, that the very scullions grinned, in spite of their fear.

"Look you," said William, "you are no common churl; you have fought too well for that. Let me see your arm."

Hereward drew up his sleeve.

"Potters do not carry sword-scars like those; neither are they tattooed like English thanes. Hold up thy head, man, and let us see thy throat."

Hereward, who had carefully hung down his head to prevent his throat-patterns being seen, was forced to lift it up.

"Aha! So I expected. More fair ladies' work there. Is not this he who was said to be so like Hereward? Very good. Put him in ward till I come back from hunting. But do him no harm. For " — and William fixed on Hereward eyes of the most intense intelligence — " were he Hereward himself, I should be right glad to see Hereward safe and sound; my man at last, and earl of all between Humber and the Fens."

But Hereward did not rise at the bait. With a face of stupid and ludicrous terror, he made reply in broken French.

"Have mercy, mercy, Lord King! Make not that fiend earl over us. Even Ivo Taillebois there would be better than he. Send him to be earl over the imps in hell, or over the wild Welsh who are worse still: but not over us, good Lord King, whom he hath polled and peeled till we are —"

"Silence!" said William, laughing, as did all round him. "Thou art a cunning rogue enough, whoever thou art. Go into limbo, and behave thyself till I come back."

"All saints send your grace good sport, and thereby me a good deliverance," quoth Hereward, who knew that his fate might depend on the temper in which William returned. So he was thrust into an outhouse, and there locked up.

He sat on an empty barrel, meditating on the chances of his submitting to the king after all, when the door opened, and in strode one with a drawn sword in one hand, and a pair of leg-shackles in the other.

"Hold out thy shins, fellow! Thou art not going to sit at thine ease there like an abbot, after killing one of us grooms, and bringing the rest of us into disgrace. Hold out thy legs, I say!"

"Nothing easier," quoth Hereward, cheerfully, and held out a leg. But when the man stooped to put on the fetters, he received a kick which sent him staggering.

After which he recollected very little, at least in this world. For Hereward cut off his head with his own sword.

After which (says the chronicler) he broke away out of the house, and over garden walls and palings, hiding and running, till he got to the front gate, and leaped upon mare Swallow.

And none saw him, save one unlucky groom-boy, who stood yelling and cursing in front of the mare's head, and went to seize the bridle.

Whereon, between the imminent danger and the bad language, Hereward's blood rose, and he smote that unlucky groom-boy; but whether he slew him or not, the chronicler had rather not say.

Then he shook up mare Swallow, and rode for his life, with knights and squires (for the hue and cry was raised) galloping at her heels.

Who then were astonished but those knights, as they saw the ugly potter's garron gaining on them length after length, till she and her rider had left them far behind?

Who then was proud but Hereward, as the mare tucked her great thighs under her, and swept on over heath and rabbit burrow, over rush and fen, sound ground and rotten all alike to that enormous stride, to that keen bright eye which foresaw every footfall, to that raking shoulder which picked her up again at every stagger?

Hereward laid the bridle on her neck, and let her go. Fall she could not, and tire she could not; and he half wished she might go on forever. Where could a man be better than on a good horse, with all the cares of this life blown away out of his brains by the keen air which rushed around his temples? And he galloped on, as cheery as a boy, shouting at the rabbits as they scuttled from under his feet, and laughing at the dottrel as they postured and anticked on the mole-hills.

But think he must, at last, of how to get home. For to go through Mildenhall again would not be safe, and he turned over the moors to Icklingham; and where he went after, no man can tell.

Certainly not the chronicler; for he tells how Hereward got back by the Isle of Somersham. Which is all but impossible, for Somersham is in Huntingdonshire, many a mile on the opposite side of Ely Isle.

And of all those knights that followed him, none ever saw or heard sign of him save one, and his horse came to a standstill in "the aforesaid wood," which the chronicler says was Somersham; and he rolled off his horse, and lay breathless under a tree, looking up at his horse's heaving flanks and wagging tail, and wondering how he should get out of that place before the English found him and made an end of him.

Then there came up to him a ragged churl, and asked him who he was, and offered to help him.

"For the sake of God and courtesy," quoth he,—his Norman pride being wellnigh beat out of him,—"if thou hast seen or heard anything of Hereward, good fellow, tell me, and I will repay thee well."

"As thou hast asked me for the sake of God and of courtesy, Sir Knight, I will tell thee. I am Hereward. And in token thereof, thou shalt give me up thy lance and sword, and take instead this sword which I carried off from the king's court; and promise me, on the faith of a knight, to bear it back to King William; and tell him that Hereward and he have met at last, and that he had best beware of the day when they shall meet again."

So that knight, not having recovered his wind, was fain to submit, and go home a sadder and a wiser man. And King William laughed a royal laugh, and commanded his knights that they should in no wise harm Hereward, but take him alive, and bring him in, and they should have great rewards.

Which seemed to them more easily said than done.

CHAPTER XXXI.

HOW THEY FOUGHT AGAIN AT ALDRETH.

HEREWARD came back in fear and trembling, after all. He believed in the magic powers of the witch of Brandon; and he asked Torfrida, in his simplicity, whether she was not cunning enough to defeat her spells by counter spells.

Torfrida smiled, and shook her head.

"My knight, I have long since given up such vanities. Let us not fight evil with evil, but rather with good. Better are prayers than charms; for the former are heard in heaven above, and the latter only in the pit below. Let me and all the women of Ely go rather in procession to St. Etheldreda's well, there above the fort at Aldreth, and pray St. Etheldreda to be with us when the day shall come, and defend her own isle and the honor of us women who have taken refuge in her holy arms."

So all the women of Ely walked out barefoot to St. Etheldreda's well, with Torfrida at their head clothed in sackcloth, and with fetters on her wrists and waist and ankles; which she vowed, after the strange, sudden, earnest fashion of those times, never to take off again till she saw the French host flee from Aldreth before the face of St. Etheldreda. So they prayed, while Hereward and his men worked at the forts below. And when they came back, and Torfrida was washing her feet, sore and bleeding from her pilgrimage, Hereward came in.

"You have murdered your poor soft feet, and taken nothing thereby, I fear."

"I have. If I had walked on sharp razors all the way, I would have done it gladly, to know what I know now. As I prayed I looked out over the fen; and St. Etheldreda put a thought into my heart. But it is so terrible a one, that I fear to tell it to you. And yet it seems our only chance."

Hereward threw himself at her feet, and prayed her to tell. At last she spoke, as one half afraid of her own words,—

"Will the reeds burn, Hereward?"

Hereward kissed her feet again and again, calling her his prophetess, his savior.

"Burn! yes, like tinder, in this March wind, if the drought only holds. Pray that the drought may hold, Torfrida."

"There, there, say no more. How hard-hearted war makes even us women! There, help me to take off this rough sack-cloth, and dress myself again."

Meanwhile William had moved his army again to Cambridge, and on to Willingham-field, and there he began to throw up those "globos and montanas," of which Leofric's paraphraser talks, but of which now no trace remains. Then he began to rebuild his causeway, broader and stronger; and commanded all the fishermen of the Ouse to bring their boats to Cotinglade, and ferry over his materials. "Among whom came Hereward in his boat, with head and beard shaven lest he should be known, and worked diligently among the rest. But the sun did not set that day without mischief; for before Hereward went off, he finished his work by setting the whole on fire, so that it was all burnt, and some of the French killed and drowned."

And so he went on, with stratagems and ambushes, till "after seven days' continual fighting, they had hardly done one day's work; save four 'globos' of wood, in which they intended to put their artillery. But on the eighth day they determined to attack the isle, putting in the midst of them that pythoness woman on a high place, where she might be safe freely to exercise her art."

It was not Hereward alone who had entreated Torfrida to exercise her magic art in their behalf. But she steadily refused, and made good Abbot Thurstan support her refusal by a strict declaration, that he would have no fiends' games played in Ely, as long as he was abbot alive on land.

Torfrida, meanwhile, grew utterly wild. Her conscience smote her, in spite of her belief that St. Etheldreda had inspired her, at the terrible resource which she had hinted to her husband, and which she knew well he would carry out with terrible success. Pictures of agony and death floated before her eyes, and kept her awake at night. She watched long hours in the church in prayer; she fasted; she disciplined her tender body with sharp pains; she tried, after the fashion of those times, to atone for her sin, if sin it was. At last she had worked herself up into a religious frenzy. She saw St. Etheldreda in the clouds, towering over the isle, menacing the French host with her virgin palm-branch. She uttered wild prophecies of ruin and defeat to the French; and then, when her frenzy collapsed, moaned secretly of ruin and defeat hereafter to themselves. But she would be bold; she would play her part; she would encourage the heroes who looked to her as one inspired, wiser and loftier than themselves.

And so it befell, that when the men marched down to Haddenham that afternoon, Torfrida rode at their head on a white charger robed from throat to ankle in sackcloth, her fetters clanking on her limbs. But she called on the English to see in her the emblem of England, captive yet, unconquered, and to break her fetters and the worse fetters of every woman in England who was the toy and slave of the brutal invaders; and so fierce a triumph sparkled from her wild hawk-eyes that the Englishmen looked up to her weird beauty as to that of an inspired saint; and when the Normans came on to the assault there stood on a grassy mound behind the English fort a figure clothed in sackcloth, barefooted and bareheaded, with fetters shining on waist, and wrist, and ankle, — her long black locks streaming in the wind, her long white arms stretched crosswise toward heaven, in imitation of Moses of old above the battle with Amalek; invoking St. Etheldreda and all the powers of Heaven, and chanting doom and defiance to the invaders.

And the English looked on her, and cried: "She is a prophetess! We will surely do some great deed this day, or die around her feet like heroes!"

And opposite to her, upon the Norman tower, the old hag of Brandon howled and gibbered with filthy gestures, calling for the thunder-storm which did not come; for all above, the sky was cloudless blue.

And the English saw and felt, though they could not speak it, dumb nation as they were, the contrast between the spirit of cruelty and darkness and the spirit of freedom and light.

So strong was the new bridge, that William trusted himself upon it on horseback, with Ivo Taillebois at his side.

William doubted the powers of the witch, and felt rather ashamed of his new helpmate; but he was confident in his bridge, and in the heavy artillery which he had placed in his four towers.

Ivo Taillebois was utterly confident in his witch, and in the bridge likewise.

William waited for the rising of the tide; and when the tide was near its height, he commanded the artillery to open, and clear the fort opposite of the English. Then with crash and twang, the balistas and catapults went off, and great stones and heavy lances hurtled through the air.

"Back!" shouted Torfrida, raised almost to madness, by fasting, self-torture, and religious frenzy. "Out of yon fort, every man. Why waste your lives under that artillery? Stand still this day, and see how the saints of Heaven shall fight for you."

So utter was the reverence which she commanded for the moment, that every man drew back, and crowded round her feet outside the fort.

"The cowards are fleeing already. Let your men go, Sir King!" shouted Taillebois.

13

"On to the assault! Strike for Normandy!" shouted William
"I fear much," said he to himself, "that this is some stratagem
of that Hereward's. But conquered they must be."

The evening breeze curled up the reach. The great pike splashed out from the weedy shores, and sent the white-fish flying in shoals into the low glare of the setting sun: and heeded not, stupid things, the barges packed with mailed men, which swarmed in the reeds on either side the bridge, and began to push out into the river.

The starlings swung in thousands round the reed-ronds, looking to settle in their wonted place: but dare not; and rose and swung round again, telling each other, in their manifold pipings, how all the reed-ronds teemed with mailed men. And all above, the sky was cloudless blue.

And then came a trample, a roll of many feet on the soft spongy peat, a low murmur which rose into wild shouts of " Dex Aie!" as a human tide poured along the causeway, and past the witch of Brandon Heath.

"'Dex Aie?'" quoth William, with a sneer. "'Debbles Aie!' would fit better."

"If, Sire, the powers above would have helped us, we should have been happy enough to — But if they would not, it is not our fault if we try below," said Ivo Taillebois.

William laughed. "It is well to have two strings to one's bow, sir. Forward, men! forward!" shouted he, riding out to the bridge-end, under the tower.

"Forward!" shouted Ivo Taillebois.

"Forward!" shouted the hideous hag overhead. "The spirit of the well fights for you."

"Fight for yourselves," said William.

There was twenty yards of deep clear water between Frenchman and Englishman. Only twenty yards. Not only the arrows and arblast quarrels, but heavy hand-javelins, flew across every moment; every now and then a man toppled forward, and plunged into the blue depth among the eels and pike, to find his comrades of the summer before; then the stream was still once more. The coots and water-hens swam in and out of the reeds, and wondered what it was all about. The water-lilies flapped upon the ripple, as lonely as in the loneliest mere. But their floats were soon broken, their white cups stained with human gore.

Twenty yards of deep clear water. And treasure inestimable to win by crossing it.

They thrust out baulks, canoes, pontoons; they crawled upon them like ants, and thrust out more yet beyond, heedless of their comrades, who slipped, and splashed, and sank, holding out vain hands to hands too busy to seize them. And always the old witch jabbered overhead, with her cantrips, pointing, mumming praying for the storm; while all above, the sky was cloudless blue. And always on the mound opposite, while darts and quarrels whistled round her head, stood Torfrida, pointing with outstretched scornful finger at the strugglers in the river, and chanting loudly, what the Frenchmen could not tell; but it made their hearts, as it was meant to do, melt like wax within them.

"They have a counter witch to yours, Ivo, it seems; and a fairer one. I am afraid the devils, especially if Asmodeus be at hand, are more likely to listen to her than to that old broomstick-rider aloft."

"Fair is, that fair cause has, Sir King."

"A good argument for honest men, but none for fiends. What is the fair fiend pointing at so earnestly there?"

"Somewhat among the reeds. Hark to her now! She is singing, somewhat more like an angel than a fiend, I will say for her."

And Torfrida's bold song, coming clear and sweet across the water, rose louder and shriller till it almost drowned the jabbering of the witch.

"She sees more there than we do."

"I see it!" cried William, smiting his hand upon his thigh. "Par le splendeur Dex! She has been showing them where to fire the reeds; and they have done it!"

A puff of smoke; a wisp of flame; and then another and another; and a canoe shot out from the reeds on the French shore, and glided into the reeds of the island.

"The reeds are on fire, men! Have a care," shouted Ivo.

"Silence, fool! Frighten them once, and they will leap like sheep into that gulf. Men! right about! Draw off, — slowly and in order. We will attack again to-morrow."

The cool voice of the great captain arose too late. A line of flame was leaping above the reed bed, crackling and howling before the evening breeze. The column on the causeway had seen their danger but too soon, and fled. But whither?

A shower of arrows, quarrels, javelins, fell upon the head of the column as it tried to face about and retreat, confusing it more and more. One arrow, shot by no common aim, went clean through William's shield, and pinned it to the mailed flesh He could not stifle a cry of pain.

"You are wounded, Sire. Ride for your life! It is worth that of a thousand of these churls," and Ivo seized William's bridle and dragged him, in spite of himself, through the cowering, shrieking, struggling crowd.

On came the flames, leaping and crackling, laughing and shrieking, like a live fiend. The archers and slingers in the bouts cowered before it; and fell, scorched corpses, as it swept on. It reached the causeway, surged up, recoiled from the mass of human beings, then sprang over their heads and passed onwards, girding them with flame.

The reeds were burning around them; the timbers of the bridge caught fire; the peat and fagots smouldered beneath their feet. They sprang from the burning footway and plunged into the fathomless bog, covering their faces and eyes with scorched hands, and then sank in the black gurgling slime.

Ivo dragged William on, regardless of curses and prayers from his soldiery; and they reached the shore just in time to see between them and the water a long black smouldering writhing line; the morass to right and left, which had been a minute before deep reed, an open smutty pool, dotted with boatsful of shrieking and cursing men; and at the causeway-end the tower, with the flame climbing up its posts, and the witch of Brandon throwing herself desperately from the top, and falling dead upon the embers, a motionless heap of rags.

"Fool that you are! Fool that I was!" cried the great king, as he rolled off his horse at his tent door, cursing with rage and pain.

Ivo Taillebois sneaked off, sent over to Mildenhall for the second witch, and hanged her, as some small comfort to his soul. Neither did he forget to search the cabin till he found buried in a crock the bits of his own gold chain and various other treasures, for which the wretched old women had bartered their souls. All which he confiscated to his own use, as a much injured man.

The next day William withdrew his army. The men refused to face again that blood-stained pass. The English spells, they said, were stronger than theirs, or than the daring of brave men. Let William take Torfrida and burn her, as she had burned them, with reeds out of Willingham fen; then might they try to storm Ely again.

Torfrida saw them turn, flee, die in agony. Her work was done; her passion exhausted; her self-torture, and the mere weight of her fetters, which she had sustained during her passion, weighed her down; she dropped senseless on the turf, and lay in a trance for many hours.

Then she arose, and casting off her fetters and her sackcloth, was herself again: but a sadder woman till her dying day.

CHAPTER XXXII.

HOW KING WILLIAM TOOK COUNSEL OF A CHURCHMAN.

If Torfrida was exhausted, so was Hereward likewise. He knew well that a repulse was not a defeat. He knew well the indomitable persistence, the boundless resources, of the master-mind whom he defied; and he knew well that another attempt would be made, and then another, till — though it took seven years in the doing — Ely would be won at last. To hold out doggedly as long as he could was his plan: to obtain the best terms he could for his comrades. And he might obtain good terms at last. William might be glad to pay a fair price in order to escape such a thorn in his side as the camp of refuge, and might deal — or, at least, promise to deal — mercifully and generously with the last remnant of the English gentry. For himself, yield he would not: when all was over, he would flee to the sea, with Torfrida and his own housecarles, and turn Viking; or go to Sweyn Ulfsson in Denmark, and die a free man.

The English did not foresee these things. Their hearts were lifted up with their victory, and they laughed at William and his French, and drank Torfrida's health much too often for their own good. Hereward did not care to undeceive them. But he could not help speaking his mind in the abbot's chamber to Thurstan, Egelwin, and his nephews, and to Sigtryg Ranaldsson, who was still in Ely, not only because he had promised to stay there, but because he could not get out if he would.

Blockaded they were utterly, by land and water. The isle furnished a fair supply of food; and what was wanting, they obtained by foraging. But they had laid the land waste for so many miles round, that their plundering raids brought them in less than of old; and if they went far, they fell in with the French, and lost good men, even though they were generally successful. So provisions were running somewhat short, and would run shorter still.

Moreover, there was a great cause of anxiety. Bishop Egelwin, Abbot Thurstan, and the monks of Ely were in rebellion, not only against King William, but more or less against the Pope of Rome. They might be excommunicated. The minster lands might be taken away.

Bishop Egelwin set his face like a flint. He expected no mercy. All he had ever done for the French was to warn Robert Comyn that if he stayed in Durham, evil would befall him. But that was as little worth to him as it was to the said Robert. And no mercy he craved. The less a man had, the more fit he was for Heaven. He could but die; and that he had known ever since he was a chanter-boy. Whether he died in Ely, or in prison, mattered little to him, provided they did not refuse him the sacraments; and that they would hardly do. But call the Duke of Normandy his rightful sovereign he would not, because he was not, — nor anybody else just now, as far as he could see.

Valiant likewise was Abbot Thurstan, for himself. But he had — unlike Bishop Egelwin, whose diocese had been given to a Frenchman — an abbey, monks, and broad lands, whereof he was father and steward. And he must do what was best for the abbey, and also what the monks would let him do. For severe as was the discipline of a minster in time of peace, yet in time of war, when life and death were in question, monks had ere now turned valiant from very fear, like Cato's mouse, and mutinied: and so might the monks of Ely.

And Edwin and Morcar?

No man knows what they said or thought; perhaps no man cared much, even in their own days. No hint does any chronicler give of what manner of men they were, or what manner of deeds they did. Fair, gentle, noble, beloved even by William, they are mere names, and nothing more, in history: and it is to be supposed, therefore, that they were nothing more in fact. The race of Leofric and Godiva had worn itself out.

One night the confederates had sat late, talking over the future more earnestly than usual. Edwin, usually sad enough, was especially sad that night.

Hereward jested with him, tried to cheer him; but he was silent, would not drink, and went away before the rest.

The next morning he was gone, and with him half a dozen of his private housecarles.

Hereward was terrified. If defections once began, they would be endless. The camp would fall to pieces, and every man among them would be hanged, mutilated, or imprisoned, one by one, helplessly. They must stand or fall together.

He went raging to Morcar. Morcar knew naught of it. On the faith and honor of a knight, he knew naught. Only his brother had said to him a day or two before, that he must see his betrothed before he died.

"He is gone to William, then? Does he think to win her now, — an outcast and a beggar, — when he was refused her with broad lands and a thousand men at his back? Fool! See that thou play not the fool likewise, nephew, or —"

"Or what?" said Morcar, defiantly.

"Or thou wilt go, whither Edwin is gone,— to betrayal and ruin."

"Why so? He has been kind enough to Waltheof and Gospatrick, why not to Edwin?"

"Because," laughed Hereward, he wanted Waltheof, and he does not want you and Edwin. He can keep Mercia quiet without your help. Northumbria and the Fens he cannot without Waltheof's. They are a rougher set as you go east and north, as you should know already, and must have one of themselves over them to keep them in good humor for a while. When he has used Waltheof as his stalking-horse long enough to build a castle every ten miles, he will throw him away like a worn bowstring, Earl Morcar, nephew mine."

Morcar shook his head.

In a week more he was gone likewise. He came to William at Brandon.

"You are come in at last, young earl?" said William, sternly. "You are come too late."

"I throw myself on your knightly faith," said Morcar. But he had come in an angry and unlucky hour.

"How well have you kept your own, twice a rebel, that you should appeal to mine? Take him away."

"And hang him?" asked Ivo Taillebois.

"Pish! No,— thou old butcher. Put him in irons, and send him into Normandy."

"Send him to Roger de Beaumont, Sire. Roger's son is safe in Morcar's castle at Warwick, so it is but fair that Morcar should be safe in Roger's."

And to Roger de Beaumont he was sent, while young Roger was Lord of Warwick, and all around that once was Leofric and Godiva's.

Morcar lay in a Norman keep till the day of William's death. On his death-bed the tyrant's heart smote him, and he sent orders to release him. For a few short days, or hours, he breathed free air again. Then Rufus shut him up once more, and forever.

And that was the end of Earl Morcar.

A few weeks after, three men came to the camp at Brandon, and they brought a head to the king. And when William looked upon it, it was the head of Edwin.

The human heart must have burst up again in the tyrant, as he looked on the fair face of him he had so loved, and so wronged; for they say he wept.

The knights and earls stood round, amazed and awed, as they saw iron tears run down Pluto's cheek.

"How came this here, knaves?" thundered he at last.

They told a rambling story, how Edwin always would needs go to Winchester, to see the queen, for she would stand his friend, and do him right. And how they could not get to Winchester, for fear of the French, and wandered in woods and wolds; and how they were set upon, and hunted; and how Edwin still was mad to go to Winchester: but when he could not, he would go to Blethwallon and his Welsh; and how Earl Randal of Chester set upon them; and how they got between a stream and the tide-way of the Dee, and were cut off. And how Edwin would not yield. And how then they slew him in self-defence, and Randal let them bring the head to the king.

This, or something like it, was their story. But who could believe traitors? Where Edwin wandered, what he did during those months, no man knows. All that is known is, three men brought his head to William, and told some such tale. And so the old nobility of England died up and down the ruts and shaughs, like wounded birds; and, as of wounded birds, none knew or cared how far they had run, or how their broken bones had ached before they died.

"Out of their own mouths they are condemned, says Holy Writ," thundered William. "Hang them on high."

And hanged on high they were, on Brandon heath.

Then the king turned on his courtiers, glad to ease his own conscience by cursing them.

"This is your doing, sirs! If I had not listened to your base counsels, Edwin might have been now my faithful liegeman and my son-in-law; and I had had one more Englishman left in peace, and one less sin upon my soul."

"And one less thorn in thy side," quoth Ivo Taillebois.

"Who spoke to thee? Ralph Guader, thou gavest me the counsel: thou wilt answer it to God and his saints."

"That did I not. It was Earl Roger, because he wanted the man's Shropshire lands."

Whereon high words ensued; and the king gave the earl the lie in his teeth, which the earl did not forget.

"I think," said the rough, shrewd voice of Ivo, "that instead of crying over spilt milk, — for milk the lad was, and never would have grown to good beef, had he lived to my age — "

"Who spoke to thee?"

"No man, and for that reason I spoke myself. I have lands in Spalding, by your Majesty's grace, and wish to enjoy them in peace, having worked for them hard enough, — and how can I do that, as long as Hereward sits in Ely?"

"Splendeur Dex!" said William, "thou art right, old butcher." So they laid their heads together to slay Hereward. And after they had talked awhile, then spoke William's chaplain for the nonce, an Italian, a friend and pupil of Lanfranc of Pavia, an Italian also, then Archbishop of Canterbury, scourging and imprisoning English monks in the south. And he spoke like an Italian of those times, who knew the ways of Rome.

"If his Majesty will allow my humility to suggest—"

"What? Thy humility is proud enough under the rose, I will warrant: but it has a Roman wit under the rose likewise. Speak!"

"That when the secular and carnal arm has failed, as it is written,* He poureth contempt upon princes, and letteth them wander out of the way in the wilderness, or fens,—for the Latin word, and I doubt not the Hebrew, has both meanings."

"Splendeur Dex!" cried William, bitterly; "that hath he done with a vengeance! Thou art right so far, Clerk!"

"Yet helpeth He the poor, videlicet, his Church and the religious, who are vowed to holy poverty, out of misery, videlicet, the oppression of barbarous customs, and maketh them households like a flock of sheep."

"They do that for themselves already, here in England," said William, with a sneer at the fancied morals of the English monks and clergy.†

"But Heaven, and not the Church, does it for the true poor, whom your Majesty is bringing in, to your endless glory."

"But what has all this to do with taking Ely?" asked William, impatiently. "I asked thee for reason, and not sermons."

"This. That it is in the power of the Holy Father,—and that power he would doubtless allow you, as his dear son and most faithful servant, to employ for yourself, without sending to Rome, which might cause painful delays—to—"

It might seem strange that William, Taillebois, Guader, Warrenne, short-spoken, hard-headed, swearing warriors, could allow, complacently, a smooth churchman to dawdle on like this, count-

---

* I do not laugh at Holy Scripture myself. I only insert this as a specimen of the usual mediæval "cant,"—a name and a practice which are both derived, not from Puritans, but from monks.

† The alleged profligacy and sensuality of the English Church before the Conquest rests merely on a few violent and vague expressions of the Norman monks who displaced them. No facts, as far as I can find, have ever been alleged. And without facts on the other side, an impartial man will hold by the one fact which is certain, that the Church of England, popish as it was, was, unfortunately for it, not popish enough ; and from its insular freedom, obnoxious to the Church of Rome, and the ultramontane clergy of Normandy ; and was therefore to be believed capable—and therefore again accused—of any and every crime.

ing his periods on his fingers, and seemingly never coming to the point.

But they knew well, that the churchman was a far cunninger as well as a more learned, man than themselves. They knew well that they could not hurry him, and that they need not; that he would make his point at last, hunting it out step by step, and letting them see how he got thither, like a cunning hound. They knew that if he spoke, he had thought long and craftily, till he had made up his mind; and that, therefore, he would very probably make up their minds likewise. It was — as usual in that age — the conquest, not of a heavenly spirit, though it boasted itself such, but of a cultivated mind over brute flesh.

They might have said all this aloud, and yet the churchman would have gone on, as he did, where he left off, with unaltered blandness of tone.

"To convert to other uses the goods of the Church, — to convert them to profane uses would, I need not say, be a sacrilege as horrible to Heaven as impossible to so pious a monarch —"

Ivo Taillebois winced. He had just stolen a manor from the monks of Crowland, and meant to keep it.

"Church lands belonging to abbeys or sees, whose abbots or bishops are contumaciously disobedient to the Holy See, or to their lawful monarch, he being in the communion of the Church and at peace with the said Holy See. If, therefore, — to come to that point at which my incapacity, through the devious windings of my own simplicity, has been tending, but with halting steps, from the moment that your Majesty deigned to hear —"

"Put in the spur, man!" said Ivo, tired at last, "and run the deer to soil."

"Hurry no man's cattle, especially thine own," answered the churchman, with so shrewd a wink, and so cheery a voice, that Ivo, when he recovered from his surprise, cried, —

"Why, thou art a good huntsman thyself, I believe now."

"All things to all men, if by any means — But to return. If your Majesty should think fit to proclaim to the recalcitrants of Ely, that unless they submit themselves to your Royal Grace — and to that, of course, of His Holiness, our Father — within a certain day, you will convert to other uses — premising, to avoid scandal, that those uses shall be for the benefit of Holy Church — all lands and manors of theirs lying without the precincts of the Isle of Ely, — those lands being, as is known, large, and of great value, — Quid plura? Why burden your exalted intellect by detailing to you consequences which it has, long ere now, foreseen."

"* * * *" quoth William, who was as sharp as the Italian, and had seen it all. "I will make thee a bishop!"

"Spare to burden my weakness," said the chaplain; and slipt away into the shade.

"You will take his advice?" asked Ivo.

"I will."

"Then I shall see that Torfrida burn at last."

"Burn her?" and William swore.

"I promised my soldiers to burn the witch with reeds out of Haddenham fen, as she had burned them; and I must keep my knightly word."

William swore yet more. Ivo Taillebois was a butcher and a churl.

"Call me not butcher and churl too often, Lord King, ere thou hast found whether thou needest me or not. Rough I may be, false was I never."

"That thou wert not," said William, who needed Taillebois much, and feared him somewhat; and remarked something meaning in his voice, which made him calm himself, diplomat as he was, instantly. "But burn Torfrida thou shalt not."

"Well, I care not. I have seen a woman burnt ere now, and had no fancy for the screeching. Beside, they say she is a very fair dame, and has a fair daughter, too, coming on, and she may very well make a wife for a Norman."

"Marry her thyself."

"I shall have to kill Hereward first."

"Then do it, and I will give thee his lands."

"I may have to kill others before Hereward."

"You may?"

And so the matter dropped. But William caught Ivo alone after an hour, and asked him what he meant.

"No pay, no play. Lord King, I have served thee well, rough and smooth."

"Thou hast, and hast been well paid. But if I have said aught hasty—"

"Pish, Majesty. I am a plain-spoken man, and like a plain-spoken master. But, instead of marrying Torfrida or her daughter, I have more mind to her niece, who is younger, and has no Hereward to be killed first."

"Her niece? Who?"

"Lucia, as we call her,— Edwin and Morcar's sister,— Hereward's niece, Torfrida's niece."

"No pay, no play, saidst thou?— so say I. What meant you by having to kill others before Hereward?"

"Beware of Waltheof!" said Ivo.

"Waltheof? Pish! This is one of thy inventions for making me hunt every Englishman to death, that thou mayest gnaw their bones."

"Is it? Then this I say more. Beware of Ralph Guader!'

"Pish!"

"Pish on, Lord King." Etiquette was not yet discovered by Norman barons and earls, who thought themselves all but as good as their king, gave him their advice when they thought fit, and if he did not take it, attacked him with all their meinie. "Pish on, but listen. Beware of Roger!"

"And what more?"

"And give me Lucia. I want her. I will have her."

William laughed. "Thou of all men! To mix that ditch-water with that wine?"

"They were mixed in thy blood, Lord King, and thou art the better man for it, so says the world. Old wine and old blood throw any lees to the bottom of the cask; and we shall have a son worthy to ride behind —"

"Take care!" quoth William.

"The greatest captain upon earth."

William laughed again, like Odin's self.

"Thou shalt have Lucia for that word."

"And thou shalt have the plot ere it breaks. As it will."

"To this have I come at last," said William to himself, as they parted. "To murder these English nobles, to marry their daughters to my grooms. Heaven forgive me! They have brought it upon themselves by contumacy to Holy Church."

"Call my secretary, some one."

The Italian re-entered.

"The valiant and honorable and illustrious knight, Ivo Taillebois, Lord of Holland and Kesteven, weds Lucia, sister of the late earls' Edwin and Morcar, now with the queen; and with her, her manors. You will prepare the papers.

"I am yours to death," said Ivo.

"To do you justice, I think thou wert that already. Stay — here — Sir Priest — do you know any man who knows this Torfrida?"

"I do, Majesty," said Ivo. "There is one Sir Ascelin, a man of Gilbert's, in the camp."

"Send for him."

"This Torfrida," said William, "haunts me."

"Pray Heaven she have not bewitched your Majesty."

"Tut! I am too old a campaigner to take much harm by woman's sharpshooting at fifteen score yards off, beside a deep stream between. No. The woman has courage, — and beauty, too, you say?"

"What of that, O Prince?" said the Italian. "Who more beautiful — if report be true — than those lost women who dance nightly in the forests with Venus and Herodias, — as it may be this Torfrida has done many a time?"

"You priests are apt to be hard upon poor women."

"The fox found that the grapes were sour," said the Italian, laughing at himself and his cloth, or at anything else by which he could curry favor.

"And this woman was no vulgar witch. That sort of personage suits Taillebois's taste, rather than Hereward's."

"Hungry dogs eat dirty pudding," said Ivo, pertinently.

"The woman believed herself in the right. She believed that the saints of heaven were on her side. I saw it in her attitude, in her gestures. Perhaps she was right."

"Sire?" said both by-standers, in astonishment.

"I would fain see that woman, and see her husband too. They are folks after my own heart. I would give them an earldom to win them."

"I hope that in that day you will allow your faithful servant Ivo to retire to his ancestral manors in Anjou; for England will be too hot for him. Sire, you know not this man, — a liar, a bully, a robber, a swash-buckling ruffian, who — " and Ivo ran on with furious invective, after the fashion of the Normans, who considered no name too bad for an English rebel.

"Sir Ascelin," said William, as Ascelin came in, "you know Hereward?"

Ascelin bowed assent.

"Are these things true which Ivo alleges?"

"The Lord Taillebois may know best what manner of man he is since he came into this English air, which changes some folks mightily," with a hardly disguised sneer at Ivo; "but in Flanders he was a very perfect knight, beloved and honored of all men, and especially of your father-in-law, the great marquis."

"He is a friend of yours, then?"

"No man less. I owe him more than one grudge, though all in fair quarrel; and one, at least, which can only be wiped out in blood."

"Eh! What?"

Ascelin hesitated.

"Tell me, sir!" thundered William, "unless you have aught to be ashamed of."

"It is no shame, as far as I know, to confess that I was once a suitor, as were all knights for miles round, for the hand of the once peerless Torfrida. And no shame to confess, that when Hereward knew thereof, he sought me out at a tournament, and served me as he has served many a better man before and since."

"Over thy horse's croup, eh?" said William.

"I am not a bad horseman, as all know, Lord King. But Heaven save me, and all I love, from that Hereward. They say he has seven men's strength; and I verily can testify to the truth thereof."

"That may be by enchantment," interposed the Italian.

"True, Sir Priest. This I know, that he wears enchanted armor, which Torfrida gave him before she married him."

"Enchantments again," said the secretary.

"Tell me now about Torfrida," said William.

Ascelin told him all about her, not forgetting to say — what, according to the chronicler, was a common report — that she had compassed Hereward's love by magic arts. She used to practise sorcery, he said, with her sorceress mistress, Richilda of Hainault. All men knew it. Arnoul, Richilda's son, was as a brother to her. And after old Baldwin died, and Baldwin of Mons and Richilda came to Bruges, Torfrida was always with her while Hereward was at the wars.

"The woman is a manifest and notorious witch," said the secretary.

"It seems so indeed," said William, with something like a sigh. And so were Torfrida's early follies visited on her; as all early follies are. "But Hereward, you say, is a good knight and true?"

"Doubtless. Even when he committed that great crime at Peterborough —"

"For which he and all his are duly excommunicated by the Bishop," said the secretary.

"He did a very courteous and honorable thing." And Ascelin told how he had saved Alftruda, and instead of putting her to ransom, had sent her safe to Gilbert.

"A very knightly deed. He should be rewarded for it."

"Why not burn the witch, and reward him with Alftruda instead, since your Majesty is in so gracious a humor?" said Ivo.

"Alftruda! Who is she? Ay, I recollect her. Young Dolfin's wife. Why, she has a husband already."

"Ay, but his Holiness at Rome can set that right. What is there that he cannot do?"

"There are limits, I fear, even to his power. Eh, priest?"

"What his Holiness's powers as the viceroy of Divinity on earth might be, did he so choose, it were irreverent to inquire. But as he condescends to use that power only for the good of mankind, he condescends, like Divinity, to be bound by the very laws which he has promulgated for the benefit of his subjects; and to make himself only a life-giving sun, when he might be a destructive thunderbolt."

"He is very kind, and we all owe him thanks," said Ivo, who had a confused notion that the Pope might strike him dead with lightning, but was good-natured enough not to do so. "Still, he might think of this plan; for they say that the lady is an old friend of Hereward's, and not over fond of her Scotch husband."

"That I know well," said William.

"And beside — if aught untoward should happen to Dolfin and his kin —"

"She might, with her broad lands, be a fine bait for Hereward. I see. Now, do this, by my command. Send a trusty monk into Ely. Let him tell the monks that we have determined to seize all their outlying lands, unless they surrender within the week. And let him tell Hereward, by the faith and oath of William of Normandy, that if he will surrender himself to my grace, he shall have his lands in Bourne, and a free pardon for himself and all his comrades."

The men assented, much against their will, and went out on their errand.

"You have played me a scurvy trick, sir," said Ascelin, "in advising the king to give the Lady Alftruda to Hereward."

"What! Did you want her yourself? On my honor I knew not of it. But have patience. You shall have her yet, and all her lands, if you will hear my counsel, and keep it."

"But you would give her to Hereward!"

"And to you too. It is a poor bait, say these frogs of fenmen, that will not take two pike running. Listen to me. I must kill this Hereward. I hate him. I cannot eat my meat for thinking of him. Kill him I must."

"And so must I."

"Then we are both agreed. Let us work together, and never mind if one's blood be old and the other's new. I am neither fool nor weakly, as thou knowest."

Ascelin could not but assent.

"Then here. We must send the King's message. But we must add to it."

"That is dangerous."

"So is war; so is eating, drinking; so is everything. But we must not let Hereward come in. We must drive him to despair. Make the messenger add but one word, — that the king exempts from the amnesty Torfrida, on account of — You can put it into more scholarly shape than I can."

"On account of her abominable and notorious sorceries; and demands that she shall be given up forthwith to the ecclesiastical power, to be judged as she deserves."

"Just so. And then for a load of reeds out of Haddenham fen."

"Heaven forbid!" said Ascelin, who had loved her once. "Would not perpetual imprisonment suffice?"

"What care I? That is the churchmen's affair, not ours. But I fear we shall not get her. Even so Hereward will flee with her, — maybe escape to Flanders, or Denmark. He can escape through a rat's-hole if he will. And then we are at peace. I had sooner kill him and have done with it: but out of the way he must be put."

So they sent a monk in with the message, and commanded him to tell the article about the Lady Torfrida, not only to Hereward, but to the abbot and all the monks.

A curt and fierce answer came back, not from Hereward, but from Torfrida herself, — that William of Normandy was no knight himself, or he would not offer a knight his life, on condition of burning his lady.

William swore horribly. "What is all this about?" They told him — as much as they chose to tell him. He was very wroth. "Who was Ivo Taillebois, to add to his message? He had said that Torfrida should not burn." Taillebois was stout; for he had won the secretary over to his side meanwhile. He had said nothing about burning. He had merely supplied an oversight of the king's. The woman, as the secretary knew, could not, with all deference to his Majesty, be included in an amnesty. She was liable to ecclesiastical censure, and the ecclesiastical courts. William might exercise his influence on them in all lawful ways, and more, remit her sentence, even so far as to pardon her entirely, if his merciful temper should so incline him. But meanwhile, what better could he, Ivo, have done, than to remind the monks of Ely that she was a sorceress; that she had committed grave crimes, and was liable to punishment herself, and they to punishment also, as her shelterers and accomplices? What he wanted was to bring over the monks; and he believed that message had been a good stroke toward that. As for Hereward, the king need not think of him. He never would come in alive. He had sworn an oath, and he would keep it.

And so the matter ended.

CHAPTER XXXIII.

HOW THE MONKS OF ELY DID AFTER THEIR KIND.

WILLIAM'S bolt, or rather inextinguishable Greek fire, could not have fallen into Ely at a more propitious moment.

Hereward was away, with a large body of men, and many ships, foraging in the northeastern fens. He might not be back for a week.

Abbot Thurstan — for what cause is not said — had lost heart a little while before, and fled to "Angerhale, taking with him the ornaments and treasure of the church."

Hereward had discovered his flight with deadly fear: but provisions he must have, and forth he must go, leaving Ely in charge of half a dozen independent English gentlemen, each of whom would needs have his own way, just because it was his own.

Only Torfrida he took, and put her hand into the hand of Ranald Sigtrygsson, and said, " Thou true comrade and perfect knight, as I did by thy wife, do thou by mine, if aught befall."

And Ranald swore first by the white Christ, and then by the head of Sleipnir, Odin's horse, that he would stand by Torfrida till the last; and then, if need was, slay her.

"You will not need, King Ranald. I can slay myself," said she, as she took the Ost-Dane's hard, honest hand.

And Hereward went, seemingly by Mepal or Sutton. Then came the message; and all men in Ely knew it.

Torfrida stormed down to the monks, in honest indignation, to demand that they should send to William, and purge her of the calumny. She found the Chapter-door barred and bolted. They were all gabbling inside, like starlings on a foggy morning, and would not let her in. She hurried back to Ranald, fearing treason, and foreseeing the effect of the message upon the monks.

But what could Ranald do? To find out their counsels was impossible for him, or any man in Ely. For the monks could talk Latin, and the men could not. Torfrida alone knew the sacred tongue.

If Torfrida could but listen at the keyhole. Well, — all was fair in war. And to the Chapter-house door she went, guarded by Ranald and some of his housecarles, and listened, with a beating heart. She heard words now incomprehensible. That men

T

who most of them lived no better than their own serfs; who could have no amount of wealth, not even the hope of leaving that wealth to their children, — should cling to wealth, — struggle, forge, lie, do anything for wealth, to be used almost entirely not for themselves, but for the honor and glory of the convent, — indicates an intensity of corporate feeling, unknown in the outer world then, or now.

The monastery would be ruined! Without this manor, without that wood, without that stone quarry, that fishery, — what would become of them?

But mingled with those words were other words, unfortunately more intelligible to this day, — those of superstition.

What would St. Etheldreda say? How dare they provoke her wrath? Would she submit to lose her lands? She might do, — what might she not do? Her bones would refuse ever to work a miracle again. They had been but too slack in miracle-working for many years. She might strike the isle with barrenness, the minster with lightning. She might send a flood up the fens. She might —

William the Norman, to do them justice, those valiant monks feared not; for he was man, and could but kill the body. But St. Etheldreda, a virgin goddess, with all the host of heaven to back her, — might she not, by intercession with powers still higher than her own, destroy both body and soul in hell?

"We are betrayed. They are going to send for the Abbot from Angerhale," said Torfrida at last, reeling from the door. "All is lost."

"Shall we burst open the door and kill them all?" asked Ranald, simply.

"No, King, — no. They are God's men; and we have blood enough on our souls."

"We can keep the gates, lest any go out to the King."

"Impossible. They know the isle better than we, and have a thousand arts."

So all they could do was to wait in fear and trembling for Hereward's return, and send Martin Lightfoot off to warn him, wherever he might be.

The monks remained perfectly quiet. The organ droned, the chants wailed, as usual; nothing interrupted the stated order of the services; and in the hall, each day, they met the knights as cheerfully as ever. Greed and superstition had made cowards of them, — and now traitors.

It was whispered that Abbot Thurstan had returned to the minster: but no man saw him: and so three or four days went on.

Martin found Hereward after incredible labors, and told him all, clearly and shrewdly. The man's manifest insanity only seemed to quicken his wit, and increase his powers of bodily endurance.

Hereward was already on his way home; and never did he and his good men row harder than they rowed that day back to Sutton. He landed, and hurried on with half his men, leaving the rest to disembark the booty. He was anxious as to the temper of the monks. He foresaw all that Torfrida had foreseen. And as for Torfrida herself, he was half mad. Ivo Taillebois's addition to William's message had had its due effect. He vowed even deadlier hate against the Norman than he had ever felt before. He ascended the heights to Sutton. It was his shortest way to Ely. He could not see Aldreth from thence; but he could see Willingham field, and Belsar's hills, round the corner of Haddenham Hill.

The sun was setting long before they reached Ely; but just as he sank into the western fen, Winter stopped, pointing. "Was that the flash of arms? There, far away, just below Willingham town. Or was it the setting sun upon the ripple of some long water?"

"There is not wind enough for such a ripple," said one. But ere they could satisfy themselves, the sun was down, and all the fen was gray.

Hereward was still more uneasy. If that had been the flash of arms, it must have come off a very large body of men, moving in column, and on the old straight road between Cambridge and Ely. He hastened on his men. But ere they were within sight of the minster-tower, they were aware of a horse galloping violently towards them through the dusk. Hereward called a halt. He heard his own heart beat as he stopped. The horse was pulled up short among them, and a lad threw himself off.

"Hereward? Thank God, I am in time!"

The voice was the voice of Torfrida.

"Treason!" she gasped.

"I knew it."

"The French are in the island. They have got Aldreth. The whole army is marching from Cambridge. The whole fleet is coming up from Southrey. And you have time—"

"To burn Ely over the monks' heads. Men! Get bogwood out of yon cottage, make yourselves torches, and onward!"

Then rose a babel of questions, which Torfrida answered as she could. But she had nothing to tell. "Clerks' cunning," she said bitterly, "was an overmatch for woman's wit." She had sent out a spy: but he had not returned till an hour since. Then he came back breathless, with the news that the French army was on the march from Cambridge, and that, as he came over the water at Alrech, he found a party of French knights in the fort on the Ely side, talking peaceably with the monks on guard.

She had run up to the borough hill, — which men call Cherry Hill at this day, — and one look to the northeast had shown her the river swarming with ships. She had rushed home, put on men's clothes, hid a few jewels in her bosom, saddled Swallow, and ridden for her life thither.

"And King Ranald?"

He and his men had gone desperately out towards Haddenham, with what English they could muster; but all were in confusion. Some were getting the women and children into boats, to hide them in the reeds. Others battering the minster gates, vowing vengeance on the monks.

"Then Ranald will be cut off! Alas for the day that ever brought his brave heart hither!"

And when the men heard that, a yell of fury and despair burst from all throats.

Should they go back to their boats?

"No! onward," cried Hereward. "Revenge first, and safety after. Let us leave nothing for the accursed Frenchmen but smoking ruins, and then gather our comrades, and cut our way back to the north."

"Good counsel," cried Winter. "We know the roads, and they do not; and in such a dark night as is coming, we can march out of the island without their being able to follow us a mile."

They hurried on; but stopped once more, at the galloping of another horse.

"Who comes, friend or foe?"

"Alwyn, son of Orgar!" cried a voice under breath. "Don't make such a noise, men! The French are within half a mile of you."

"Then one traitor monk shall die ere I retreat," cried Hereward, seizing him by the throat.

"For Heaven's sake, hold!" cried Torfrida, seizing his arm. "You know not what he may have to say."

"I am no traitor, Hereward; I have fought by your side as well as the best; and if any but you had called Alwyn —"

"A curse on your boasting. Tell us the truth."

"The Abbot has made peace with the King. He would give up the island, and St. Etheldreda should keep all her lands and honors. I said what I could; but who was I to resist the whole chapter? Could I alone brave St. Etheldreda's wrath?"

"Alwyn, the valiant, afraid of a dead girl!"

"Blaspheme not, Hereward! She may hear you at this moment! Look there!" and pointing up, the monk cowered in terror, as a meteor flashed through the sky.

"That is St. Etheldreda shooting at us, eh? Then all I can say is, she is a very bad marksman. And the French are in the island?"

"They are."

"Then forward, men, for one half-hour's pleasure; and then to die like Englishmen."

"On?" cried Alwyn. "You cannot go on. The King is at Whichford at this moment with all his army, half a mile off! Right across the road to Ely!"

Hereward grew Berserk. "On! men!" shouted he, "we shall kill a few Frenchmen apiece before we die!"

"Hereward," cried Torfrida, "you shall not go on! If you go, I shall be taken. And if I am taken, I shall be burned. And I cannot burn, — I cannot! I shall go mad with terror before I come to the stake. I cannot go stript to my smock before those Frenchmen. I cannot be roasted piecemeal! Hereward, take me away! Take me away! or kill me, now and here!"

He paused. He had never seen Torfrida thus overcome.

"Let us flee! The stars are against us. God is against us! Let us hide, — escape abroad: beg our bread, go on pilgrimage to Jerusalem together, — for together it must be always: but take me away!"

"We will go back to the boats, men," said Hereward.

But they did not go. They stood there, irresolute, looking towards Ely.

The sky was pitchy dark. The minster roofs, lying northeast, were utterly invisible against the blackness.

"We may at least save some who escape out," said Hereward. "March on quickly to the left, under the hill to the ploughfield."

They did so.

"Lie down, men. There are the French, close on our right. Down among the bushes."

And they heard the heavy tramp of men within a quarter of a mile.

"Cover the mare's eyes, and hold her mouth, lest she neigh," said Winter.

Hereward and Torfrida lay side by side upon the heath. She was shivering with cold and horror. He laid his cloak over her; put his arm round her.

"Your stars did not foretell you this, Torfrida." He spoke not bitterly, but in utter sadness.

She burst into an agony of weeping.

"My stars at least foretold me nothing but woe, since first I saw your face."

"Why did you marry me, then?" asked he, half angrily.

"Because I loved you. Because I love you still."

"Then you do not regret?"

"Never, never, never! I am quite happy, — quite happy. Why not?"

A low murmur from the men made them look up. They were near enough to the town to hear, — only too much. They heard the tramp of men, shouts and yells. Then the shrill cries of women. All dull and muffled the sounds came to them through the still night; and they lay there spell-bound, as in a nightmare, as men assisting at some horrible tragedy, which they had no power to prevent. Then there was a glare, and a wisp of smoke against the black sky, and then a house began burning brightly, and then another.

"This is the Frenchman's faith!"

And all the while, as the sack raged in the town below, the minster stood above, dark, silent, and safe. The church had provided for herself, by sacrificing the children beneath her fostering shadow.

They waited nearly an hour: but no fugitives came out.

"Come, men," said Hereward, wearily, "we may as well to the boats."

And so they went, walking on like men in a dream, as yet too stunned to realize to themselves the hopeless horror of their situation. Only Hereward and Torfrida saw it all, looking back on the splendid past, — the splendid hopes for the future: glory, honor, an earldom, a free Danish England, — and this was all that was left!

"No it is not!" cried Torfrida suddenly, as if answering her own unspoken thoughts, and his. "Love is still left. The gallows and the stake cannot take that away." And she clung closer to her husband's side, and he again to hers.

They reached the shore, and told their tale to their comrades. Whither now?

"To Well. To the wide mere," said Hereward.

"But their ships will hunt us out there."

"We shall need no hunting. We must pick up the men at Cissham. You would not leave them to be murdered, too, as we have left the Ely men?"

No. They would go to Well. And then?

"The Bruneswald, and the merry greenwood," said Hereward.

"Hey for the merry greenwood!" shouted Leofric the Deacon.

And the men, in the sudden delight of finding any place, any purpose, answered with a lusty cheer.

"Brave hearts," said Hereward. "We will live and die together like Englishmen."

"We will, we will, Viking."

"Where shall we stow the mare?" asked Geri, "the boats are full already."

"Leave her to me. On board, Torfrida."

He got on board last, leading the mare by the bridle.

"Swim, good lass!" said he, as they pushed off; and the good lass, who had done it many a time before, waded in, and was soon swimming behind. Hereward turned, and bent over the side in the darkness. There was a strange gurgle, a splash, and a swirl. He turned round, and sat upright again. They rowed on.

"That mare will never swim all the way to Well," said one.

"She will not need it," said Hereward.

"Why," cried Torfrida, feeling in the darkness, "she is loose. What is this in your hand? Your dagger! And wet!"

"Mare Swallow is at the bottom of the reach. We could never have got her to Well."

"And you have—" cried a dozen voices.

"Do you think that I would let a cursed Frenchman — ay, even William's self — say that he had bestridden Hereward's mare?"

None answered: but Torfrida, as she laid her head upon her husband's bosom, felt the great tears running down from his cheek on to her own.

None spoke a word. The men were awe-stricken. There was something despairing and ill-omened in the deed. And yet there was a savage grandeur in it, which bound their savage hearts still closer to their chief.

And so mare Swallow's bones lie somewhere in the peat unto this day.

They got to Well; they sent out spies to find the men who had been "wasting Cissham with fire and sword"; and at last brought them in. Ill news, as usual, had travelled fast. They had heard of the fall of Ely, and hidden themselves "in a certain very small island which is called Stimtench," where, thinking that the friends in search of them were Frenchmen in pursuit, they hid themselves among the high reeds. There two of them — one Starkwolf by name, the other Broher — hiding near each other, "thought that, as they were monks, it might conduce to their safety if they had shaven crowns; and set to work with their swords to shave each other's heads as well as they could. But at last, by their war-cries and their speech, recognizing each other, they left off fighting," and went after Hereward.

So jokes, grimly enough, Leofric the Deacon, who must have seen them come in the next morning, with bleeding coxcombs, and could laugh over the thing in after years. But he was in no humor for jesting in the days in which they lay at Well. Nor was he in jesting humor when, a week afterwards, hunted by the Normans from Well, and forced too take to meres and waterways known only to them, and too shallow and narrow for the Norman ships, they found their way across into the old Nen, and so by Thorney on toward Crowland, leaving Peterborough far on the left. For as they neared Crowland, they saw before them, rowing slowly, a barge full of men. And as they neared that barge, behold, all they who rowed were blind of both their eyes; and all they who sat and guided them were maimed of both their hands. And as they came alongside, there was not a man in all that ghastly crew but was an ancient friend, by whose side they had fought full many a day, and with whom they had drunk deep full many a night. They were the first-fruits of William's vengeance; thrust into that boat, to tell the rest of the fen-men what those had to expect who dared oppose the Norman. And they were going, by some by-stream, to Crowland, to the sanctuary of the Danish fen-men, that they might cast themselves down before St. Guthlac, and ask of him that mercy for their souls which the conqueror had denied to their bodies. Alas for them! they were but a handful among hundreds, perhaps thousands, of mutilated cripples, who swarmed all over England, and especially in the north and east, throughout the reign of the Norman conqueror. They told their comrades' fate, slaughtered in the first attack, or hanged afterwards as rebels and traitors to a foreigner whom they had never seen, and to whom they owed no fealty by law of God or man.

" And Ranald Sigtrygsson ? "

None knew aught of him. He never got home again to his Irish princess.

" And the poor women ? " asked Torfrida.

But she received no answer.

And the men swore a great oath, and kept it, never to give quarter to a Norman, as long as there was one left on English ground.

Neither were the monks of Ely in jesting humor, when they came to count up the price of their own baseness. They had (as was in that day the cant of all cowardly English churchmen, as well as of the more crafty Normans) " obeyed the apostolic injunction, to submit to the powers that be, because they are ordained," &c. But they found the hand of the powers that be a very heavy one. Forty knights were billeted on them at free quarters with all their men. Every morning the butler had to distribute to them food and pay in the great hall; and in vain were their complaints of bad faith. William meanwhile, who loved money as well as he "loved the tall deer," had had 1,000 (another says 700) marks of them as the price of their church's safety, for the payment whereof, if one authority is to be trusted, they sold "all the furniture of gold and silver, crosses, altars, coffers, covers, chalices, platters, ewers, urnets, basons, cups, and saucers." Nay, the idols themselves were not spared, "for," beside that, "they sold a goodly image of our Lady with her little Son, in a throne wrought with marvellous workmanship, which Elsegus the abbot had made. Likewise, they stripped many images of holy virgins of much furniture of gold and silver."* So that poor St. Etheldreda had no finery in which to appear on festivals, and went in russet for many years after. The which money (according to another †) they took, as they had promised, to Picot the Viscount at Cambridge. He weighed the money; and finding it an ounce short, accused them of cheating the King, and sentenced them to pay 300 marks more. After which the royal commissioners came, plundered the abbey of all that was left, and took away likewise "a great mass of gold and silver found in Wentworth, wherewith the brethren meant to repair the altar vessels"; and also a "notable cope which Archbishop Stigand gave, which the church hath wanted to this day."

Thurstan, the traitor Abbot, died in a few months. Egelwin, the Bishop of Durham, was taken in the abbey. He was a bishop, and they dared not kill him. But he was a patriot, and must have no mercy. They accused him of stealing the treasures of Durham, which he had brought to Ely for the service of his country; and shut him up in Abingdon. A few months after, the brave man was found starved and dead, "whether of his own will or enforced"; and so ended another patriot prelate. But we do not read that the Normans gave back the treasure to Durham. And so, yielding an immense mass of booty, and many a fair woman, as the Norman's prey, ended the Camp of Refuge, and the glory of the Isle of Ely.

* These details are from a story found in the Isle of Ely, published by Dr. Giles. It seems a late composition, — probably of the sixteenth century, — and has manifest errors of fact; but *valeat quantum*.
† Stow's "Annals."

CHAPTER XXXIV.

HOW HEREWARD WENT TO THE GREENWOOD.

AND now is Hereward to the greenwood gone, to be a bold outlaw; and not only an outlaw himself, but the father of all outlaws, who held those forests for two hundred years, from the fens to the Scottish border. Utlages, forestiers, latrunculi (robberlets), sicarii, cutthroats, sauvages, who prided themselves upon sleeping on the bare ground; they were accursed by the conquerors, and beloved by the conquered. The Norman viscount or sheriff commanded to hunt them from hundred to hundred, with hue and cry, horse and bloodhound. The English yeoman left for them a keg of ale, or a basket of loaves, beneath the hollins green, as sauce for their meal of "nombles of the dere."

> " For hart and hind, and doe and roe,
> Were in that forest great plentie,"

> " Swannes and fesauntes they had full good
> And foules of the rivere.
> There fayled never so lytell a byrde,
> That ever was bred on brere."

With the same friendly yeoman "that was a good felawe," they would lodge by twos and threes during the sharp frosts of midwinter, in the lonely farm-house which stood in the "field" or forest-clearing; but for the greater part of the year their "lodging was on the cold ground" in the holly thickets, or under the hanging rock, or in a lodge of boughs.

And then, after a while, the life which began in terror, and despair, and poverty, and loss of land and kin, became not only tolerable, but pleasant. Bold men and hardy, they cared less and less for

> " The thornie wayes, the deep valleys,
> The snowe, the frost, the rayne,
> The colde, the hete ; for dry or wete
> We must lodge on the plaine,
> And us above, none other roofe,
> But a brake bushe, or twayne."

And they found fair lasses, too, in time, who, like Torfrida and Maid Marian, would answer to their warnings against the outlaw life, with the nut-browne maid, that —

> 'Amonge the wylde dere, such an archere
> As men say that ye be,
> He may not fayle of good intayle
> Where is so great plentè:
> And water clere of the rivere,
> Shall be full swete to me,
> With which in hele, I shall right wele,
> Endure, as ye may see.''

Then called they themselves "merry men," and the forest the "merry greenwood"; and sang, with Robin Hood,—

> " A merrier man than I, belyve
> There lives not in Christentie.''

They were coaxed back, at times, to civilized life; they got their grace of the king, and entered the king's service; but the craving after the greenwood was upon them. They dreaded and hated the four stone walls of a Norman castle, and, like Robin Hood, slipt back to the forest and the deer.

Gradually, too, law and order rose among them, lawless as they were; the instinct of discipline and self-government, side by side with that of personal independence, which is the peculiar mark and peculiar strength of the English character. Who knows not how, in the "Lytell Geste of Robin Hood," they shot at "pluck-buffet," the king among them, disguised as an abbot; and every man who missed the rose-garland, " his tackle he should tyne ";—

> " And bere a buffet on his head,
> I wys ryght all bare,
> And all that fell on Robyn's lote,
> He smote them wonder sair.
>
> " Till Robyn fayled of the garlonde,
> Three fyngers and mair.''

Then good Gilbert bids him in his turn

> " ' Stand forth and take his pay.'
>
> " ' If it be so,' sayd Robyn,
> ' That may no better be,
> Syr Abbot, I delyver thee myn arrowe,
> I pray thee, Syr, serve thou me.'
>
> " ' It falleth not for myne order,' saith oc kynge,
> ' Robyn, by thy leve,
> For to smyte no good yeman,
> For doute I should hym greve.'
>
> " ' Smyte on boldly,' sayd Robyn,
> ' I give thee large leve.'
> Anon our kynge, with that word,
> He folde up his sleve.
>
> " And such a buffet he gave Robyn,
> To grounde he yode full nere.
> ' I make myn avowe,' sayd Robyn,
> ' Thou art a stalwarte frere.

"'There is pyth in thyn arme,' sayd Robyn,
'I trowe thou canst well shoote.'
Thus our kynge and Robyn Hode
Together they are met.'"

Hard knocks in good humor, strict rules, fair play, and equal justice, for high and low; this was the old outlaw spirit, which has descended to their inlawed descendants; and makes, to this day, the life and marrow of an English public school.

One fixed idea the outlaw had, — hatred of the invader. If "his herde were the king's deer," "his treasure was the earl's purse"; and still oftener the purse of the foreign churchman, Norman or Italian, who had expelled the outlaw's English cousins from their convents; shamefully scourged and cruelly imprisoned them, as the blessed Archbishop Lanfranc did at Canterbury, because they would not own allegiance to a French abbot; or murdered them at the high altar, as did the new abbot of Glastonbury, because they would not change their old Gregorian chant for that of William of Fescamp.*

On these mitred tyrants the outlaw had no mercy, as far as their purses were concerned. Their persons, as consecrated, were even to him sacred and inviolable, — at least, from wounds and death; and one may suppose Hereward himself to have been the first author of the laws afterward attributed to Robin Hood. As for "robbing and reving, beting and bynding," free warren was allowed against the Norman.

"'Thereof no foors,' said Robyn,
'We shall do well enow.
But look ye do no housbonde harme,
That tilleth wyth his plough.

"'No more ye shall no good yemàn,
That walketh by grene wood shawe;
Ne no knyght, ne no squyer,
That will be good felàwe.

"'These bysshoppes, and these archbysshoppes,
Ye shall them bete and binde;
The hye sheryff of Nottingham,
Hym holde in your mynde.'
        *   *   *
"Robyn loved our dere Ladye.
For doubt of dedely synne,
Wolde he never do company harme
That any woman was ynne."

And even so it was with Hereward in the Bruneswald, if the old chroniclers, Leofric especially, are to be believed.

And now Torfrida was astonished. She had given way utterly at Ely, from woman's fear, and woman's disappoint-

* See the Anglo-Saxon Chronicle.

ment. All was over. All was lost. What was left, save to lie?

But — and it was a new and unexpected fact to one of her excitable Southern blood, easily raised, and easily depressed — she discovered that neither her husband, nor Winter, nor Geri, nor Wenoch, nor Ranald of Ramsey, nor even the romancing harping Leofric, thought that all was lost. She argued it with them, not to persuade them into base submission, but to satisfy her own surprise.

"But what will you do?"

"Live in the greenwood."

"And what then?"

"Burn every town which a Frenchman holds, and kill every Frenchman we meet."

"But what plan have you?"

"Who wants a plan, as you call it, while he has the green hollies overhead, the dun deer on the lawn, bow in his hand, and sword by his side?"

"But what will be the end of it all?"

"We shall live till we die."

"But William is master of all England."

"What is that to us? He is not our master."

"But he must be some day. You will grow fewer and fewer. His government will grow stronger and stronger."

"What is that to us? When we are dead, there will be brave yeomen in plenty to take our place. You would not turn traitor?"

"I? never! never! I will live and die with you in your greenwood, as you call it. Only — I did not understand you English."

Torfrida did not. She was discovering the fact, which her nation have more than once discovered since, that the stupid valor of the Englishman never knows when it is beaten; and sometimes, by that self-satisfied ignorance, succeeds in not being beaten after all.

So Hereward — if the chronicles speak truth — assembled a formidable force, wellnigh, at last, four hundred men. Winter, Geri, Wenoch, Grogan, one of the Azers of Lincoln, were still with him. Ranald the butler still carried his standard. Of Duti and Outi, the famous brothers, no more is heard. A valiant Matelgar takes their place; Alfric and Sexwold and many another gallant fugitive cast up, like scattered hounds, at the sound of "The Wake's" war-horn. There were those among them (says Gaimar) who scorned to fight single-handed less than three Normans. As for Hereward, he would fight seven.

"Les quatre oscist, les treis fuirent:
Naffrez, sanglant, cil s'en partirent
En plusurs lius issi avrit,
K'encontre seit très bien se tuit
De seit hommes avait vertu,
Un plus hardi ne fu veu."

They ranged up the Bruneswald, dashing out to the war-cry of "A Wake! a Wake!" laying all waste with fire and sword, that is, such towns as were in the hands of Normans. And a noble range they must have had for gallant sportsmen. Away south, between the Nene and Welland, stretched from Stamford and Peterborough the still vast forests of Rockingham, nigh twenty miles in length as the crow flies, down beyond Rockingham town, and Geddington Chase. To the west, they had the range of the "hunting counties," dotted still, in the more eastern part, with innumerable copses and shaughs, the remnants of the great forest, out of which, as out of Rockinghamshire, have been cut those fair parks and

"Handsome houses,
Where the wealthy nobles dwell";

past which the Lord of Burleigh led his Welsh bride to that Burghley House by Stamford town, wellnigh the noblest of them all, which was, in Hereward's time, deep wood, and freestone down. Round Exton, and Normanton, and that other Burley on the Hill; on through those Morkery woods, which still retain the name of Hereward's ill-fated nephew; north by Irnham and Corby; on to Belton and Syston (par nobile), and southwest again to those still wooded heights, whence all-but-royal Belvoir looks out over the rich green vale below, did Hereward and his men range far and wide, harrying the Frenchman, and hunting the dun deer. Stags there were in plenty. There remain to this day, in Grimsthorpe Park by Bourne, the descendants of the very deer which Earl Leofric and Earl Algar, and after them Hereward the outlaw, hunted in the Bruneswald.

Deep-tangled forest filled the lower claylands, swarming with pheasant, roe, badger, and more wolves than were needed. Broken, park-like glades covered the upper freestones, where the red deer came out from harbor for their evening graze, and the partridges and plovers whirred up, and the hares and rabbits loped away, innumerable; and where hollies and ferns always gave dry lying for the night. What did men need more, whose bodies were as stout as their hearts?

They were poachers and robbers; and why not? The deer had once been theirs, the game, the land, the serfs; and if Godric of Corby slew the Irnham deer, burned Irnham Hall over the head of the new Norman lord, and thought no harm, he did but what he would with that which had been once his own.

Easy it was to dash out by night and make a raid; to harry the places which they once had owned themselves, in the vale of Belvoir to the west, or to the east in the strip of fertile land which sloped down into the fen, and levy black-mail in Rippinghale, or Folkingham, or Aslackby, or Sleaford, or any other of the " Vills " (now thriving villages) which still remain in Domesday-book, and written against them the ugly and significant, —

" In Tatenai habuerunt Turgisle et Suen IIII. Carrucæ træ," &c. " Hoc Ivo Taillebosc ibi habet in dominio," — all, that is, that the wars had left of them.

The said Turgisle (Torkill or Turketil misspelt by Frenchmen) and Sweyn, and many a good man more, — for Ivo's possessions were enormous, — were thorns in the sides of Ivo and his men which must be extracted, and the Bruneswald a nest of hornets, which must be smoked out at any cost.

Wherefore it befell, that once upon a day there came riding to Hereward in the Bruneswald a horseman all alone.

And meeting with Hereward and his men he made signs of amity, and bowed himself low, and pulled out of his purse a letter, protesting that he was an Englishman and a " good felawe. and that, though he came from Lincoln town, a friend to the English had sent him.

That was believable enough, for Hereward had his friends and his spies far and wide.

And when he opened the letter, and looked first, like a wary man, at the signature, a sudden thrill went through him.

It was Alftruda's.

If he was interested in her, considering what had passed between them from her childhood, it was nothing to be ashamed of. And yet somehow he felt ashamed of that same sudden thrill.

And Hereward had reason to be ashamed. He had been faithful to Torfrida, — a virtue most rare in those days. Few were faithful then, save, it may be, Baldwin of Mons to his tyrant and idol, the sorceress Richilda; and William of Normandy, — whatever were his other sins, — to his wise and sweet and beautiful Matilda. The stories of his coldness and cruelty to her seem to rest on no foundation. One need believe them as little as one does the myth of one chronicler, that when she tried to stop him from some expedition, and clung to him as he sat upon his horse, he smote his spur so deep into her breast that she fell dead. The man had self-control, and feared God in his own wild way, — therefore it was, perhaps, that he conquered.

And Hereward had been faithful likewise to Torfrida, and loved her with an overwhelming adoration, as all true men love. And for that very reason he was the more aware that his feeling for Alftruda was strangely like his feeling for Torfrida, and yet strangely different.

There was nothing in the letter that he should not have read. She called him her best and dearest friend, twice the savior of her life. What could she do in return, but, at any risk to herself, try and save his life? The French were upon him. The posse comitatus of seven counties was raising. "Northampton, Cambridge, Lincoln, Holland, Leicester, Huntingdon, Warwick," were coming to the Bruneswald to root him out.

"Lincoln?" thought Hereward. "That must be Gilbert of Ghent, and Ogor the Breton. No! Gilbert is not coming, Sir Ascelin is coming for him. Holland? That is my friend Ivo Taillebois. Well, we shall have the chance of paying off old scores. Northampton? The earl thereof just now is the pious and loyal Waltheof, as he is of Huntingdon and Cambridge. Is he going to join young Fitz-Osbern from Warwick and Leicester, to root out the last Englishman? Why not? That would be a deed worthy of the man who married Judith, and believes in the powers that be, and eats dirt daily at William's table."

Then he read on.

Ascelin had been mentioned, he remarked, three or four times in the letter, which was long, as from one lingering over the paper, wishing to say more than she dared. At the end was a hint of the reason:—

"O, that having saved me twice, you could save me once more. Know you that Gospatrick has been driven from his earldom on charge of treason, and that Waltheof has Northumbria in his place, as well as the parts round you? And that Gospatrick is fled to Scotland again, with his sons,— my man among them? And now the report comes, that my man is slain in battle on the Border; and that I am to be given away,— as I have been given away twice before,— to Ascelin. This I know, as I know all, not only from him of Ghent, but from him of Peterborough, Ascelin's uncle."

Hereward laughed a laugh of cynical triumph,— pardonable enough in a broken man.

"Gospatrick! the wittol! the woodcock! looking at the springe, and then coolly putting his head therein. Throwing the hatchet after the helve! selling his soul and never getting the price of it! I foresaw it, foretold it, I believe to Alftruda herself,— foretold that he would not keep his bought earldom three years. What a people we are, we English, if Gospatrick is,— as he is,— the shrewdest man among us, with a dash of canny Scots blood too. 'Among the one-eyed, the blind is king,' says Torfrida, out of her wise ancients, and blind we are, if he is our best. No. There is one better man left I trust, one that will never be fool enough to put his head into the wolf's mouth, and trust the Norman, and that is Hereward the outlaw."

And Hereward boasted to himself, at Gospatrick's expense, of his own superior wisdom, till his eye caught a line or two, which finished the letter.

"O that you would change your mind, much as I honor you for it. O that you would come in to the king, who loves and trusts you, having seen your constancy and faith, proved by so many years of affliction. Great things are open to you, and great joys;—I dare not tell you what : but I know them, if you would come in. You, to waste yourself in the forest, an outlaw and a savage! Opportunity once lost, never returns; time flies fast, Hereward, my friend, and we shall all grow old,—I think at times that I shall soon grow old. And the joys of life will be impossible, and nothing left but vain regrets."

"Hey?" said Hereward, "a very clerkly letter. I did not think she was so good a scholar. Almost as good a one as Torfrida."

That was all he said ; and as for thinking, he had the posse comitatus of seven counties to think of. But what could those great fortunes and joys be, which Alftruda did not dare to describe?

She growing old, too? Impossible, that was woman's vanity. It was but two years since she was as fair as a saint in a window. "She shall not marry Ascelin. I will cut his head off. She shall have her own choice for once, poor child."

And Hereward found himself worked up to a great height of paternal solicitude for Alftruda, and righteous indignation against Ascelin. He did not confess to himself that he disliked much, in his selfish vanity, the notion of Alftruda's marrying any one at all. He did not want to marry her himself,—of course not. But there is no dog in the manger so churlish on such points as a vain man. There are those who will not willingly let their own sisters, their own daughters, their own servants marry. Why should a woman wish to marry any one but them?

But Hereward, however vain, was no dreamer or sluggard. He set to work, joyfully, cheerfully, scenting battle afar off, like Job's war-horse, and pawing for the battle. He sent back Alftruda's messenger, with this answer: —

"Tell your lady that I kiss her hands and feet. That I cannot write, for outlaws carry no pen and ink. But that what she has commanded, that will I perform."

It is noteworthy, that when Hereward showed Torfrida (which he did frankly) Alftruda's letter, he did not tell her the exact words of his answer, and stumbled and varied much, vexing her thereby, when she, naturally, wished to hear them word for word.

Then he sent out spies to the four airts of heaven. And his spies, finding a friend and a meal in every hovel, brought home all the news he needed.

He withdrew Torfrida and his men into the heart of the forest, — no hint of the place is given by the chronicler, — cut down trees, formed an abattis of trunks and branches, and awaited the enemy.

CHAPTER XXXV.

HOW ABBOT THOROLD WAS PUT TO RANSOM.

Though Hereward had as yet no feud against "Bysshopp s and Archbysshoppes," save Egelsin of Selsey, who had excommunicated him, but who was at the other end of England, he had feud, as may be supposed, against Thorold, Abbot of Peterborough, and Thorold feud likewise against him. When Thorold had entered the "Golden Borough," hoping to fatten himself with all its treasures, he had found it a smoking ruin, and its treasures gone to Ely to pay Sweyn and his Danes. And such a "sacrilege," especially when he was the loser thereby, was the unpardonable sin itself in the eyes of Thorold, as he hoped it might be in the eyes of St. Peter. Joyfully therefore he joined his friend Ivo Taillebois, when, "with his usual pompous verbosity," saith Peter of Blois, writing on this very matter, he asked him to join in destroying Hereward.

Nevertheless, with all the Norman chivalry at their back, it behooved them to move with caution; for (so says the chronicler) "Hereward had in these days very many foreigners, as well as landsfolk, who had come to him to practise and learn war, and fled from their masters and friends when they heard of his fame; and some of them the king's courtiers, who had come to see whether those things which they heard were true, whom Hereward nevertheless received cautiously, on plighted troth and oath."

So Ivo Taillebois summoned all his men, and all other men's men who would join him, and rode forth through Spalding and Bourne, having announced to Lucia his bride that he was going to slay her one remaining relative; and when she wept, cursed and kicked her, as he did once a week. After which he came to Thorold of Peterborough.

So on the two worthies rode from Peterborough to Stamford, and from Stamford into the wilderness, no man knows whither.

"And far they rode by bush and shaugh,
And far by moss and mire," —

but never found a track of Hereward or his men. And Ivo

Taillebois left off boasting how he would burn Torfrida over a slow fire, and confined himself to cursing; and Abbot Thorold left off warbling the song of Roland as if he had been going to a second battle of Hastings, and wished himself in warm bed at Peterborough.

But at the last they struck upon a great horse-track, and followed it at their best pace for several miles, and yet no sign of Hereward.

"Catch an Englishman," quoth the abbot.

But that was not so easy. The poor folk had hidden themselves, like Israel of old, in thickets and dens and caves of rocks, at the far-off sight of the Norman tyrants, and not a living soul had appeared for twenty miles. At last they caught a ragged wretch herding swine, and haled him up to Ivo.

"Have you seen Hereward, villain?" asked he, through an interpreter.

"Nay."

"You lie. These are his fresh horse-tracks, and you must have seen him pass."

"Eh?"

"Thrust out one of his eyes, and he will find his tongue."

It was done.

"Will you answer now?"

The poor wretch only howled.

"Thrust out the other."

"No, not that! Mercy: I will tell. He is gone by this four hours. How have you not met him?"

"Fool! The hoofs point onward there."

"Ay,"—and the fellow could hardly hide a grin,—"but he had shod all his horses backwards."

A storm of execration followed. They might be thrown twenty miles out of their right road by the stratagem.

"So you had seen Hereward, and would not tell. Put out his other eye," said Taillebois, as a vent to his own feelings.

And they turned their horses' heads, and rode back, leaving the man blind in the forest.

The day was waning now. The fog hung heavy on the treetops, and dripped upon their heads. The horses were getting tired, and slipped and stumbled in the deep clay paths. The footmen were more tired still, and, cold and hungry, straggled more and more. The horse-tracks led over an open lawn of grass and fern, with here and there an ancient thorn, and round it on three sides thick wood of oak and beech, with under copse of holly and hazel. Into that wood the horse-tracks led, by a path on which there was but room for one horse at a time.

"Here they are at last!" cried Ivo. "I see the fresh footmarks of men, as well as horses. Push on, knights and men at-arms."

The Abbot looked at the dark, dripping wood, and meditated.

"I think that it will be as well for some of us to remain here; and, spreading our men along the woodside, prevent the escape of the villains. *A moi, hommes d'armes!*"

"As you like. I will go in and bolt the rabbit; and you shall snap him up as he comes out."

And Ivo, who was as brave as a bull-dog, thrust his horse into the path, while the Abbot sat shivering outside. "Certain nobles of higher rank," says Peter de Blois, "followed his example, not wishing to rust their armor, or tear their fine clothes, in the dank copse."

The knights and men-at-arms straggled slowly into the forest, some by the path, some elsewhere, grumbling audibly at the black work before them. At last the crashing of the branches died away, and all was still.

Abbot Thorold sat there upon his shivering horse, shivering himself as the cold pierced through his wet mail; and as near an hour past, and no sign of foe or friend appeared, he cursed the hour in which he took off the beautiful garments of the sanctuary to endure those of the battle-field. He thought of a warm chamber, warm bath, warm footcloths, warm pheasant, and warm wine. He kicked his freezing iron feet in the freezing iron stirrup. He tried to blow his nose with his freezing iron hand; but dropt his handkerchief into the mud, and his horse trod on it. He tried to warble the song of Roland; but the words exploded in a cough and a sneeze. And so dragged on the weary hours, says the chronicler, nearly all day, till the ninth hour. But never did they see coming out of the forest the men who had gone in.

A shout from his nephew, Sir Ascelin, made all turn their heads. Behind them, on the open lawn, in the throat between the woods by which they had entered, were some forty knights, galloping toward them.

"Ivo?"

"No!" almost shrieked the Abbot. "There is the white-bear banner. It is Hereward."

"There is Winter on his left," cried one. "And there, with the standard, is the accursed monk, Ranald of Ramsey."

And on they came, having debouched from the wood some two hundred yards off, behind a roll in the lawn, just far enough off to charge as soon as they were in line.

On they came, two deep, with lances high over their shoulders, heads and heels well down, while the green tufts flew behind them. "*A moi, hommes d'armes!*" shouted the Abbot. But too late. The French turned right and left. To form was impossible, ere the human whirlwind would be upon them.

Another half-minute and with a shout of "A bear! a bear The Wake! the Wake!" they were struck, ridden through, hurled over, and trampled into the mud.

"I yield. Grace! I yield!" cried Thorold, struggling from under his horse; but there was no one to whom to yield. The knights' backs were fifty yards off, their right arms high in the air, striking and stabbing.

The battle was "*à l'outrance.*" There was no quarter given that day.

"And he that came live out thereof
Was he that ran away."

The Abbot tried to make for the wood, but ere he could gain it, the knights had turned, and one rode straight at him, throwing away a broken lance, and drawing his sword.

Abbot Thorold may not have been the coward which Peter of Blois would have him, over and above being the bully which all men would have him; but if so, even a worm will turn; and so did the Abbot: he drew sword from thigh, got well under his shield, his left foot forward, and struck one blow for his life, and at the right place, — his foe's bare knee.

But he had to do with a warier man than himself. There was a quick jerk of the rein; the horse swerved round, right upon him, and knocked him head over heels; while his blow went into empty air.

"Yield or die!" cried the knight, leaping from his horse, and kneeling on his head.

"I am a man of God, an abbot, churchman, Thorold."

"Man of all the devils!" and the knight lugged him up, and bound his arms behind him with the abbot's own belt.

"Ahoi! Here! I have caught a fish. I have got the Golden Borough in my purse!" roared he. "How much has St. Peter gained since we borrowed of him last, Abbot? He will have to pay out the silver pennies bonnily, if he wishes to get back thee."

"Blaspheme not, godless barbarian!" Whereat the knight kicked him.

"And you have Thorold the scoundrel, Winter?" cried Hereward, galloping up. "And we have three or four more dainty French knights, and a viscount of I know not where among them. This is a good day's work. Now for Ivo and his tail."

And the Abbot, with four or five more prisoners, were hoisted on to their own horses, tied firmly, and led away into the forest path.

"Do not leave a wounded man to die," cried a knight who lay on the lawn.

"Never we. I will come back and put you out of your pain," quoth some one.

"Siward! Siward Le Blanc! Are you in this meinie?" cried the knight in French.

"That am I. Who calls?"

"For God's sake save him!" cried Thorold. "He is my own nephew, and I will pay —"

"You will need all your money for yourself," said Siward the White, riding back.

"Are you Sir Ascelin of Ghent?"

"That am I, your host of old."

"I wish I had met you in better company. But friends we are, and friends must be."

And he dismounted, and did his best for the wounded man, promising to return and fetch him off before night, or send yeomen to do so.

As he pushed on through the wood, the Abbot began to see signs of a fight; riderless horses crashing through the copse, wounded men straggling back, to be cut down without mercy by the English. The war had been "*à l'outrance*" for a long while. None gave or asked quarter. The knights might be kept for ransom: they had money. The wretched men of the lower classes, who had none, were slain : as they would have slain the English.

Soon they heard the noise of battle; and saw horsemen and footmen pellmell, tangled in an abattis, from behind which archers and cross-bowmen shot them down in safety.

Hereward dashed forward, with the shout of Torfrida; and at that the French, taken in the flank, fled, and were smitten as they fled, hip and thigh.

Hereward bade them spare a fugitive, and bring him to him.

"I give you your life; so run, and carry my message. That is Taillebois's banner there forward, is it not?"

"Yes."

"Then go after him, and tell him, — Hereward has the Abbot of Burgh, and half a dozen knights, safe by the heels. And unless Ivo clears the wood of his men by nightfall, I will hang every one of them up for the crows before morning."

Ivo got the message, and having had enough fighting for the day, drew off, says the chronicler, for the sake of the Abbot and his fellow-captives.

Two hours after the Abbot and the other prisoners were sitting, unbound, but unarmed, in the forest encampment, waiting for a right good meal, with Torfrida bustling about them, after binding up the very few wounded among their own men.

Every courtesy was shown them; and their hearts were lifted up, as they beheld approaching among the trees great caldrons of good soup; forest salads; red deer and roe roasted on the wood embers; spits of pheasants and partridges, larks and buntings, thrust off one by one by fair hands into the burdock leaves which served as platters; and last, but not least, jacks of ale and wine, appearing mysteriously from a cool old stone quarry. Abbot Thorold ate to his heart's content, complimented every one, vowed he would forswear all Norman cooks and take to the greenwood himself, and was as gracious and courtly as if he had been at the new palace at Winchester.

And all the more for this reason, — that he had intended to overawe the English barbarians by his polished Norman manners. He found those of Hereward and Torfrida, at least, as polished as his own.

"I am glad you are content, Lord Abbot," said Torfrida; "I trust you prefer dining with me to burning me, as you meant to do."

"I burn such peerless beauty! I injure a form made only for the courts of kings! Heaven and all saints, knighthood and all chivalry, forbid. What Taillebois may have said, I know not! I am no more answerable for his intentions than I am for his parentage, — or his success this day. Let churls be churls, and wood-cutters wood-cutters. I at least, thanks to my ancestors, am a gentleman."

"And, as a gentleman, will of course contribute to the pleasure of your hosts. It will surely please you to gratify us with one stave at least of that song, which has made your name famous among all knights," holding out a harp.

"I blush: but obey. A harp in the greenwood? A court in the wilderness! What joy!"

And the vain Abbot took the harp, and said, — "These, if you will allow my modesty to choose, are the staves on which I especially pride myself. The staves which Taillefer — you will pardon my mentioning him — "

"Why pardon? A noble minstrel he was, and a brave warrior, though our foe. And often have I longed to hear him, little thinking that I should hear instead the maker himself."

So said Hereward; and the Abbot sang — those wondrous staves, where Roland, left alone of all the Paladins, finds death come on him fast. And on the Pyrenæan peak, beneath the pine, he lays himself, his "face toward the ground, and under him his sword and magic horn, that Charles, his lord, may say and all his folk, The gentle count, he died a conqueror"; and then "turns his eyes southward toward Spain, betakes himself to remember many things; of so many lands which he conquered valiantly; of pleasant France; of the men of his lineage; of Charlemagne, his lord, who brought him up. He could not help to weep and sigh, but yet himself he would not forget. He bewailed his sins, and prayed God's mercy:—True Father, who ne'er yet didst lie, who raised St. Lazarus from death, and guarded Daniel from the lions, guard my soul from all perils, for the sins which in my life I did! His right glove then he offered to God; St. Gabriel took it from his hand; on his arm the chief bowed down, with joined hands he went unto his end. God sent down his angel Cherubim and St. Michael, whom men call 'del peril.' Together with them, St. Gabriel, he came; the soul of the count they bore to Paradise."

And the Abbot ended, sadly and gently, without that wild "Aoi!" the war-cry with which he usually ends his staves. And the wild men of the woods were softened and saddened by the melody; and as many as understood French, said, when he finished, "Amen! so may all good knights die!"

"Thou art a great maker, Abbot! They told truths of thee. Sing us more of thy great courtesy."

And he sang them the staves of the Olifant, the magic horn,—how Roland would not sound it in his pride, and sounded it at Turpin's bidding, but too late; and how his temples burst with that great blast, and Charles and all his peers heard it through the gorges, leagues away in France. And then his "Aoi" rang forth so loud and clear, like any trumpet blast, under the oaken glades, that the wild men leaped to their feet, and shouted, "Health to the gleeman! Health to the Abbot Thorold!"

"I have won them," thought the Abbot to himself. Strange mixture that man must have been, if all which is told of him is true; a very typical Norman, compact of cunning and ferocity, chivalry and poetry, vanity and superstition, and yet able enough to help to conquer England for the Pope.

Then he pressed Hereward to sing, with many compliments; and Hereward sang, and sang again, and all his men crowded round him as the outlaws of Judæa may have crowded round David in Carmel or Hebron, to hear, like children, old ditties which they loved the better the oftener they heard them.

"No wonder that you can keep these knights together, if you can charm them thus with song. Would that I could hear you singing thus in William's hall."

"No more of that, Sir Abbot. The only music which I have for William is the music of steel on steel.".

Hereward answered sharply, because he was half of Thorold's mind.

"Now," said Torfrida, as it grew late, "we must ask our noble guest for what he can give us as easily and well as he can song, — and that is news. We hear naught here in the greenwood, and must throw one's self on the kindness of a chance visitor."

The Abbot leapt at the bait, and told them news, court gossip, bringing in great folks' names and his own, as often and as familiarly mingled as he could.

"What of Richilda?" asked Torfrida.

"Ever since young Arnoul was killed at Cassel —"

"Arnoul killed?" shrieked Terfrida.

"Is it possible that you do not know?"

"How should I know, shut up in Ely for — years it seems."

"But they fought at Cassel three months before you went to Ely."

"Be it so. Only tell me. Arnoul killed!"

Then the Abbot told, not without feeling, a fearful story.

Robert the Frison and Richilda had come to open war, and Gerbod the Fleming, Earl of Clucter, had gone over from England to help Robert. William had sent Fitz Osbern, Earl of Hereford, the scourge and tyrant of the Welsh, to help Richilda. Fitz Osbern had married her, there and then. She had asked help of her liege lord, the King of France, and he had sent her troops. Robert and Richilda had fought on St. Peter's day, 1071, — nearly two years before, at Bavinchorum, by Cassel.

Richilda had played the heroine, and routed Robert's left wing, taken him prisoner, and sent him off to St. Omer. Men said that she had done it by her enchantments. But her enchantments betrayed her nevertheless. Fitz Osbern, her bridegroom, fell dead. Young Arnoul had two horses killed under him. Then Gerbod smote him to the ground, and Richilda and her troops fled in horror. Richilda was taken, and exchanged for the Frison; at which the King of France, being enraged, had come down and burnt St. Omer. Then Richilda, undaunted, had raised fresh troops to avenge her son. Then Robert had met them at Broqueroie by Mons, and smote them with a dreadful slaughter.* Then Richilda had turned and fled wildly into a convent; and, so men said, tortured herself night and day with fearful penances, if by any means she might atone for her great sins.

Torfrida heard, and laid her head upon her knees, and wept so bitterly, that the Abbot entreated pardon for having pained her so much.

* The place was called till late, and may be now, "The Hedges of Death."

The news had a deep and lasting effect on her. The thought of Richilda shivering and starving in the squalid darkness of a convent, abode by her thenceforth. Should she ever find herself atoning in like wise for her sorceries, — harmless as they had been; for her ambitions, — just as they had been; for her crimes? But she had committed none. No, she had sinned in many things: but she was not as Richilda. And yet in the loneliness and sadness of the forest, she could not put Richilda from before the eyes of her mind.

It saddened Hereward likewise. For Richilda he cared little. But that boy. How he had loved him! How he had taught him to ride, and sing, and joust, and handle sword, and all the art of war. How his own rough soul had been the better for that love. How he had looked forward to the day when Arnoul should be a great prince, and requite him with love. Now he was gone. Gone? Who was not gone, or going? He seemed to himself the last tree in the forest. When should his time come, and the lightning strike him down to rot beside the rest? But he tost the sad thoughts aside. He could not afford to nourish them. It was his only chance of life, to be merry and desperate.

"Well!" said Hereward, ere they hapt themselves up for the night. "We owe you thanks, Abbot Thorold, for an evening worthy of a king's court, rather than a holly-bush."

"I have won him over," thought the Abbot.

"So charming a courtier, — so sweet a minstrel, — so agreeable a newsmonger, — could I keep you in a cage forever, and hang you on a bough, I were but too happy: but you are too fine a bird to sing in captivity. So you must go, I fear, and leave us to the nightingales. And I will take for your ransom — "

Abbot Thorold's heart beat high.

"Thirty thousand silver marks."

"Thirty thousand fiends!"

"My beau Sire, will you undervalue yourself? Will you degrade yourself? I took Abbot Thorold, from his talk, to be a man who set even a higher value on himself than other men set on him. What higher compliment can I pay to your vast worth, than making your ransom high accordingly, after the spirit of our ancient English laws? Take it as it is meant, beau Sire; be proud to pay the money; and we will throw you Sir Ascelin into the bargain, as he seems a friend of Siward's."

Thorold hoped that Hereward was drunk, and might forget, or relent; but he was so sore at heart that he slept not a wink that night. But in the morning he found, to his sorrow, that Hereward had been as sober as himself.

In fine, he had to pay the money; and was a poor man all his days.

"Aha! Sir Ascelin," said Hereward apart, as he bade them all farewell with many courtesies. "I think I have put a spoke in your wheel about the fair Alftruda."

"Eh? How? Most courteous victor?"

"Sir Ascelin is not a very wealthy gentleman."

Ascelin laughed assent.

"Nudus intravi, nudus exeo — England; and I fear now, this mortal life likewise."

"But he looked to his rich uncle the Abbot, to further a certain marriage-project of his. And, of course, neither my friend Gilbert of Ghent, nor my enemy William of Normandy, are likely to give away so rich an heiress without some gratification in return."

"Sir Hereward knows the world, it seems."

"So he has been told before. And, therefore, having no intention that Sir Ascelin, however worthy of any and every fair lady, should marry this one; he took care to cut off the stream at the fountain-head. If he hears that the suit is still pushed, he may cut off another head beside the fountain's."

"There will be no need," said Ascelin, laughing again. "You have very sufficiently ruined my uncle, and my hopes."

"My head?" said he, as soon as Hereward was out of hearing. "If I do not cut off thy head ere all is over, there is neither luck nor craft left among Normans. I shall catch the Wake sleeping some day, let him be never so Wakeful."

CHAPTER XXXVI.

HOW ALFTRUDA WROTE TO HEREWARD.

THE weary months ran on, from summer into winter, and winter into summer again, for two years and more, and neither Torfrida nor Hereward were the better for them. Hope deferred maketh the heart sick: and a sick heart is but too apt to be a peevish one. So there were fits of despondency, jars, mutual recriminations. "If I had not taken your advice, I should not have been here." "If I had not loved you so well, I might have been very differently off," — and so forth. The words were wiped away the next hour, perhaps the next minute, by sacred kisses; but they had been said, and would be recollected, and perhaps said again.

Then, again, the "merry greenwood" was merry enough in the summer tide, when shaughs were green, and

"The woodwele sang, and would not cease,
   Sitting upon the spray,
So loud, it wakened Robin Hood
   In the greenwood where he lay."

But it was a sad place enough, when the autumn fog crawled round the gorse, and dripped off the hollies, and choked alike the breath and the eyesight; when the air sickened with the graveyard smell of rotting leaves, and the rain-water stood in the clay holes over the poached and sloppy lawns.

It was merry enough, too, when they were in winter quarters in friendly farm-houses, as long as the bright sharp frosts lasted, and they tracked the hares and deer merrily over the frozen snows; but it was doleful enough in those same farm-houses in the howling wet weather, when wind and rain lashed in through unglazed window, and ill-made roof, and there were coughs and colds and rheumatisms, and Torfrida ached from head to foot, and once could not stand upright for a whole month together, and every cranny was stuffed up with bits of board and rags, keeping out light and air as well as wind and water; and there was little difference between the short day and the long night; and the men gambled and wrangled amid clouds of peat-reek, over draughtboards and chessmen which they had carved for themselves, and Torfrida sat stitching and sewing, making and mending, her eyes bleared with peat-smoke, her hands sore and coarse from continual labor, her cheek bronzed, her face thin and hollow, and all her beauty worn away for very trouble. Then sometimes there was not enough to eat, and every one grumbled at her; or some one's clothes were not mended, and she was grumbled at again. And sometimes a foraging party brought home liquor, and all who could got drunk to drive dull care away; and Hereward, forgetful of all her warnings, got more than was good for him likewise; and at night she coiled herself up in her furs, cold and contemptuous; and Hereward coiled himself up, guilty and defiant, and woke her again and again with startings and wild words in his sleep. And she felt that her beauty was gone, and that he saw it; and she fancied him (perhaps it was only fancy) less tender than of yore; and then in very pride disdained to take any care of her person, and said to herself, though she dare not say it to him, that if he only loved her for her face, he did not love her at all. And because she fancied him cold at times, she was cold likewise, and grew less and less caressing, when for his sake, as well as her own, she should have grown more so day by day.

Alas for them! there are many excuses. Sorrow may be a softening medicine at last, but at first it is apt to be a hardening one; and that savage outlaw life which they were leading can never have been a wholesome one for any soul of man, and its graces must have existed only in the brains of harpers and gleemen. Away from law, from self-restraint, from refinement, from elegance, from the very sound of a church-going bell, they were sinking gradually down to the level of the coarse men and women whom they saw; the worse and not the better parts of both their characters were getting the upper hand; and it was but too possible that after a while the hero might sink into the ruffian, the lady into a slattern and a shrew.

But in justice to them be it said, that neither of them had complained of the other to any living soul. Their love had been as yet too perfect, too sacred, for them to confess to another (and thereby confess to themselves) that it could in any wise fail. They had each idolized the other, and been too proud of their idolatry to allow that their idol could crumble or decay.

And yet at last that point, too, was reached. One day they were wrangling about somewhat, as they too often wrangled, and Hereward in his temper let fall the words, "As I said to Winter the other day, you grow harder and harder upon me."

Torfrida started and fixed on him wide, terrible, scornful eyes "So you complain of me to your boon companions?"

And she turned and went away without a word. A gulf had opened between them. They hardly spoke to each other for a week.

Hereward complained of Torfrida? What if Torfrida should complain of Hereward? But to whom? Not to the coarse women round her; her pride revolted from that thought;— and yet she longed for counsel, for sympathy,—to open her heart but to one fellow-woman. She would go to the Lady Godiva at Crowland, and take counsel of her, whether there was any method (for so she put it to herself) of saving Hereward; for she saw but too clearly that he was fast forgetting all her teaching, and falling back to a point lower than that even from which she had raised him up.

To go to Crowland was not difficult. It was mid-winter. The dikes were all frozen. Hereward was out foraging in the Lincolnshire wolds. So Torfrida, taking advantage of his absence, proposed another foraging party to Crowland itself. She wanted stuff for clothes, needles, thread, what not. A dozen stout fellows volunteered at once to take her. The friendly monks of Crowland would feast them royally, and send them home heaped with all manner of good things; while as for meeting Ivo Taillebois's men, if they had but three to one against them, there was a fair chance of killing a few, and carrying off their clothes and weapons, which would be useful. So they made a sledge, tied beef-bones underneath it, put Torfrida thereon, well wrapped in deer and fox and badger skin, and then putting on their skates, swept her over the fen to Crowland, singing like larks along the dikes.

And Torfrida went in to Godiva, and wept upon her knees; and Godiva wept likewise, and gave her such counsel as she could,— how if the woman will keep the men heroic, she must keep herself not heroic only, but devout likewise; how she herself, by that one deed which had rendered her name famous then, and famous (though she never dreamt thereof) now, and it may be to the end of time,— had once for all, tamed, chained, and as it were converted, the heart of her fierce young lord; and enabled her to train him in good time into the most wise, most just, most pious, of all King Edward's earls.

And Torfrida said yes, and yes, and yes, and felt in her heart that she knew all that already. Had not she, too, taught, entreated, softened, civilized? Had not she, too, spent her life upon a man, and that man a wolf's-head and a landless outlaw, more utterly than Godiva could ever have spent hers on one who lived lapped in luxury and wealth and power? Torfrida had done her best, and she had failed, or at least fancied in her haste that she had failed.

What she wanted was, not counsel, but love. And she clung round the Lady Godiva, till the broken and ruined widow opened all her heart to her, and took her in her arms, and fondled her as if she had been a babe. And the two women spoke few words after that, for indeed there was nothing to be said. Only at last, "My child, my child," cried Godiva, "better for thee, body and soul, to be here with me in the house of God, than there amid evil spirits and deeds of darkness in the wild woods."

"Not a cloister, not a cloister," cried Torfrida, shuddering, and half struggling to get away.

"It is the only place, poor wilful child, the only place this side the grave, in which we wretched creatures, who for our sins are women born, can find aught of rest or peace. By us sin came into the world, and Eve's curse lies heavy on us to this day, and our desire is to our lords, and they rule over us; and when the slave can work for her master no more, what better than to crawl into the house of God, and lay down our crosses at the foot of His cross and die? You too will come here, Torfrida, some day, I know it well. You too will come here to rest."

"Never, never," shrieked Torfrida, "never to these horrid vaults. I will die in the fresh air! I will be buried under the green hollies; and the nightingales as they wander up from my own Provence, shall build and sing over my grave. Never, never!" murmured she to herself all the more eagerly, because something within her said that it would come to pass.

The two women went into the church to Matins, and prayed long and fervently. And at the early daybreak the party went back laden with good things and hearty blessings, and caught one of Ivo Taillebois's men by the way, and slew him, and got off him a new suit of clothes in which the poor fellow was going courting; and so they got home safe into the Bruneswald.

But Torfrida had not found rest unto her soul. For the first time in her life since she became the bride of Hereward, she had had a confidence concerning him and unknown to him. It was to his own mother,—true. And yet she felt as if she had betrayed him: but then had he not betrayed her? And to Winter of all men?

It might have been two months afterwards that Martin Lightfoot put a letter into Torfrida's hand.

The letter was addressed to Hereward; but there was nothing strange in Martin's bringing it to his mistress. Ever since their marriage, she had opened and generally answered the very few epistles with which her husband was troubled.

She was going to open this one as a matter of course, when glancing at the superscription she saw, or fancied she saw, that it was in a woman's hand. She looked at it again. It was sealed plainly with a woman's seal; and she looked up at Martin Lightfoot. She had remarked as he gave her the letter a sly significant look in his face.

"What doest thou know of this letter?" she inquired sharply.

"That it is from the Countess Alftruda, whomsoever she may be."

A chill struck through her heart. True, Alftruda had written before, only to warn Hereward of danger to his life, — and hers. She might be writing again, only for the same purpose. But still, she did not wish that either Hereward, or she, should owe Alftruda their lives, or anything. They had struggled on through weal and woe without her, for many a year. Let them do so without her still. That Alftruda had once loved Hereward she knew well. Why should she not? The wonder was to her that every woman did not love him. But she had long since gauged Alftruda's character, and seen in it a persistence like her own, yet as she proudly hoped of a lower temper; the persistence of the base weasel, not of the noble hound: yet the creeping weasel might endure, and win, when the hound was tired out by his own gallant pace. And there was a something in the tone of Alftruda's last letter which seemed to tell her that the weasel was still upon the scent of its game. But she was too proud to mistrust Hereward, or rather, to seem to mistrust him. And yet — how dangerous Alftruda might be as a rival, if rival she choose to be. She was up in the world now, free, rich, gay, beautiful, a favorite at Queen Matilda's court, while she —

"How came this letter into thy hands?" asked she as carelessly as she could.

"I was in Peterborough last night," said Martin, "concerning little matters of my own, and there came to me in the street a bonny young page with smart jacket on his back, smart cap on his head, and smiles and bows, and 'You are one of Hereward's men,' quoth he."

"'Say that again, young jackanapes,' said I, 'and I'll cut your tongue out,' whereat he took fright and all but cried. He was very sorry, and meant no harm, but he had a letter for my master, and he heard I was one of his men.

"Who told him that?"

"Well, one of the monks, he could not justly say which, or would n't, and I, thinking the letter of more importance than my own neck, ask him quietly into my friend's house. There he pulls out this and five silver pennies, and I shall have five more if I bring an answer back: but to none than Hereward must I give it. With that I calling my friend, who is an honest woman, and nigh as strong in the arms as I am, ask her to clap her back against the door, and pull out my axe."

"'Now,' said I, 'I must know a little more about this letter Tell me, knave, who gave it thee, or I'll split thy skull.'

"The young man cries and blubbers; and says that it is the Countess Alftruda, who is staying in the monastery, and that he is her serving man, and that it is as much as my life is worth to touch a hair of his head, and so forth, — so far so good.

"Then I asked him again, who told him I was my master's man? — and he confessed that it was Herluin the prior, — he that was Lady Godiva's chaplain of old, whom my master robbed of his money when he had the cell of Bourne years agone. Very well, quoth I to myself, that's one more count on our score against Master Herluin. Then I asked him how Herluin and the Lady Alftruda came to know aught of each other? and he said that she had been questioning all about the monastery without Abbot Thorold's knowledge, for one that knew Hereward and favored him well. That was all I could get from the knave, he cried so for fright. So I took his money and his letter, warning him that if he betrayed me, there were those would roast him alive before he was done with me. And so away over the town wall, and ran here five-and-twenty miles before breakfast, and thought it better as you see to give the letter to my lady first."

"You have been officious," said Torfrida, coldly. "'T is addressed to your master. Take it to him. Go."

Martin Lightfoot whistled and obeyed, while Torfrida walked away proudly and silently with a beating heart.

Again Godiva's words came over her. Should she end in the convent of Crowland? And suspecting, fearing, imagining all sorts of baseless phantoms, she hardened her heart into a great hardness.

Martin had gone with the letter, and Torfrida never heard any more of it.

So Hereward had secrets which he would not tell to her. At last!

That, at least, was a misery which she would not confide to Lady Godiva, or to any soul on earth.

But a misery it was. Such a misery as none can delineate, save those who have endured it themselves, or had it confided to them by another. And happy are they to whom neither has befallen.

She wandered on and into the wild-wood, and sat down by a spring. She looked in it — her only mirror — at her wan, coarse face, with wild black elf-locks hanging round it, and wondered whether Alftruda, in her luxury and prosperity, was still so very beautiful. Ah, that that fountain were the fountain of Jouvence, the spring of perpetual youth, which all believed in those days to exist somewhere, — how would she plunge into it, and be young and fair once more!

No! she would not! She had lived her life, and lived it well, gallantly, lovingly, heroically. She had given that man her youth, her beauty, her wealth, her wit. He should not have them a second time. He had had his will of her. If he chose to throw her away when he had done with her, to prove himself base at last, unworthy of all her care, her counsels, her training, — dreadful thought! To have lived to keep that man for her own, and just when her work seemed done, to lose him! No, there was worse than that. To have lived that she might make that man a perfect knight, and just when her work seemed done, to see him lose himself!

And she wept till she could weep no more. Then she washed away her tears in that well. Had it been in Greece of old, that well would have become a sacred well thenceforth, and Torfrida's tears have changed into forget-me-nots, and fringed its marge with azure evermore.

Then she went back, calm, all but cold: but determined not to betray herself, let him do what he would. Perhaps it was all a mistake, a fancy. At least she would not degrade him, and herself, by showing suspicion. It would be dreadful, shameful to herself, wickedly unjust to him, to accuse him, were he innocent after all.

Hereward, she remarked, was more kind to her now. But it was a kindness which she did not like. It was shy, faltering, as of a man guilty and ashamed; and she repelled it as much as she dared, and then, once or twice, returned it passionately, madly, in hopes —

But he never spoke a word of that letter.

After a dreadful month, Martin came mysteriously to her again. She trembled, for she had remarked in him lately a strange change. He had lost his usual loquacity and quaint humor; and had fallen back into that sullen taciturnity, which, so she heard, he had kept up in his youth. He, too, must know evil which he dared not tell.

"There is another letter come. It came last night," said he.

"What is that to thee or me? My lord has his state secrets. Is it for us to pry into them? Go!"

"I thought — I thought —"

"Go, I say!"

"That your ladyship might wish for a guide to Crowland."

"Crowland?" almost shrieked Torfrida, for the thought of Crowland had risen in her own wretched mind instantly and involuntarily. "Go, madman!"

Martin went. Torfrida paced madly up and down the farm-house. Then she settled herself into fierce despair.

There was a noise of trampling horses outside. The men were arming and saddling, seemingly for a raid.

Hereward hurried in for his armor. When he saw Torfrida, he blushed scarlet.

"You want your arms," said she, quietly; "let me fetch them."

"No, never mind. I can harness myself; I am going south-west, to pay Taillebois a visit. I am in a great hurry. I shall be back in three days. Then — good by."

He snatched his arms off a perch, and hurried out again, dragging them on. As he passed her, he offered to kiss her; she put him back, and helped him on with his armor, while he thanked her confusedly.

"He was as glad not to kiss me, after all!"

She looked after him as he stood, his hand on his horse's withers. How noble he looked! And a great yearning came over her. To throw her arms round his neck once, and then to stab herself, and set him free, dying, as she had lived, for him.

Two bonny boys were wrestling on the lawn, young outlaws who had grown up in the forest with ruddy cheeks and iron limbs.

"Ah, Winter!" she heard him say, "had I had such a boy as that! —"

She heard no more. She turned away, her heart dead within her. She knew all that these words implied, in days when the possession of land was everything to the free man; and the possession of a son necessary, to pass that land on in the ancestral line. Only to have a son; only to prevent the old estate passing, with an heiress, into the hands of strangers, what crimes did not men commit in those days, and find themselves excused for them by public opinion. And now, — her other children (if she ever had any) had died in childhood; the little Torfrida, named after herself, was all that she had brought to Hereward; and he was the last of his house. In him the race of Leofric, of Godiva, of Earl Oslae, would become extinct; and that girl would marry — whom? Whom but some French conqueror, — or at best some English outlaw. In either case Hereward would have no descendants for whom it was worth his while to labor or to fight. What wonder if he longed for a son, — and not a son of hers, the barren tree, — to pass his name down to future generations? It might be worth while, for that, to come in to the king, to recover his lands, to — She saw it all now, and her heart was dead within her.

She spent that evening neither eating nor drinking, but sitting over the log embers, her head upon her hands, and thinking over all her past life and love, since she saw him, from the gable window, ride the first time into St. Omer. She went through it all, with a certain stern delight in the self-torture, deliberately day by day, year by year, — all its lofty aspirations, all its blissful passages, all its deep disappointments, and found in it — so she chose to fancy in the wilfulness of her misery — nothing but cause for remorse. Self in all, vanity, and vexation of spirit; for herself she had loved him; for herself she had tried to raise him; for herself she had set her heart on man, and not on God. She had sown the wind: and behold, she had reaped the whirlwind. She could not repent; she could not pray. But oh! that she could die.

She was unjust to herself, in her great nobleness. It was not true, not half, not a tenth part true.

But perhaps it was good for her that it should seem true, for that moment; that she should be emptied of all earthly things for once, if so she might be filled from above. At last she went into the inner room to lie down and try to sleep. At her feet, under the perch where Hereward's armor had hung, lay an open letter.

She picked it up, surprised at seeing such a thing there, and kneeling down, held it eagerly to the wax candle which was on a spike at the bed's head.

She knew the handwriting in a moment. It was Alftruda's.

This, then, was why Hereward had been so strangely hurried. He must have had that letter, and dropped it.

Her eye and mind took it all in, in one instant, as the lightning flash reveals a whole landscape. And then her mind became as dark as that landscape, when the flash is past.

It congratulated Hereward on having shaken himself free from the fascination of that sorceress. It said that all was settled with King William. Hereward was to come to Winchester. She had the King's writ for his safety ready to send to him. The King would receive him as his liegeman. Alftruda would receive him as her husband. Archbishop Lanfranc had made difficulties about the dissolution of the marriage with Torfrida: but gold would do all things at Rome; and Lanfranc was her very good friend, and a reasonable man, — and so forth.

Men, and beasts likewise, when stricken with a mortal wound, will run, and run on, blindly, aimless, impelled by the mere instinct of escape from intolerable agony. And so did Torfrida. Half undrest as she was, she fled forth into the forest, she knew not whither, running as one does wrapt in fire: but the fire was not without her, but within.

She cast a passing glance at the girl who lay by her, sleeping a pure and gentle sleep —"

"O that thou hadst but been a boy!" Then she thought no more of her, not even of Hereward: but all of which she was conscious was a breast and brain bursting; an intolerable choking, from which she must escape.

She ran, and ran on, for miles. She knew not whether the night was light or dark, warm or cold. Her tender feet might have been ankle deep in snow. The branches over her head might have been howling in the tempest, or dripping with rain. She knew not, and heeded not. The owls hooted to each other under the staring moon, but she heard them not. The wolves glared at her from the brakes, and slunk off appalled at the white ghostly figure: but she saw them not. The deer stood at gaze in the glades till she was close upon them, and then bounded into the wood. She ran right at them, past them, heedless. She had but one thought. To flee from the agony of a soul alone in the universe with its own misery.

At last she was aware of a man close beside her. He had been following her a long way, she recollected now; but she had not feared him, even heeded him. But when he laid his hand upon her arm, she turned fiercely, but without dread.

She looked to see if it was Hereward. To meet him would be death. If it were not he, she cared not who it was. It was not Hereward; and she cried angrily, "Off! off!" and hurried on.

"But you are going the wrong way! The wrong way!" said the voice of Martin Lightfoot.

"The wrong way! Fool, which is the right way for me, save the path which leads to a land where all is forgotten?"

"To Crowland! To Crowland! To the minster! To the monks! That is the only right way for poor wretches in a world like this. The Lady Godiva told you you must go to Crowland. And now you are going. I too, I ran away from a monastery when I was young; and now I am going back. Come along!"

"You are right! Crowland, Crowland; and a nun's cell till death. Which is the way, Martin?"

"O a wise lady! A reasonable lady! But you will be cold before you get thither. There will be a frost ere morn. So, when I saw you run out, I caught up something to put over you."

Torfrida shuddered, as Martin wrapped her in the white bearskin.

"No! Not that! Anything but that!" and she struggled to shake it off.

"Then you will be dead ere dawn. Folks that run wild in the forest thus, for but one night, die!"

" Would God I could die!"

" That shall be as He wills; you do not die while Martin can keep you alive. Why, you are staggering already."

Martin caught her up in his arms, threw her over his shoulder as if she had been a child, and hurried on, in the strength of madness.

At last he stopped at a cottage door, set her down upon the turf, and knocked loudly.

" Grimkel Tolison! Grimkel, I say!"

And Martin burst the door open with his foot.

" Give me a horse, on your life," said he to the man inside. " I am Martin, Hereward's man, upon my master's business."

" What is mine is Hereward's, God bless him," said the man, struggling into a garment, and hurrying out to the shed.

" There is a ghost against the gate!" cried he, recoiling.

" That is my matter, not yours. Get me a horse to put the ghost upon."

Torfrida lay against the gate-post, exhausted now; but quite unable to think. Martin lifted her on to the beast, and led her onward, holding her up again and again.

" You are tired. You had run four miles before I could make you hear me."

" Would I had run four thousand." And she relapsed into stupor.

They passed out of the forest, across open wolds, and at last down to the river. Martin knew of a boat there. He lifted her from the horse, turned him loose, put Torfrida into the boat, and took the oars.

She looked up, and saw the roofs of Bourne shining white in the moonlight.

And then she lifted up her voice, and shrieked three times: " Lost! Lost! Lost!" with such a dreadful cry, that the starlings whirred up from the reeds, and the wild-fowl rose clanging off the meres, and the watch-dogs in Bourne and Mainthorpe barked and howled, and folk told fearfully next morning how a white ghost had gone down from the forest to the fen, and wakened them with its unearthly cry.

The sun was high when they came to Crowland minster. Torfrida had neither spoken nor stirred; and Martin, who in the midst of his madness kept a strange courtesy and delicacy, had never disturbed her, save to wrap the bear-skin more closely over her.

When they came to the bank, she rose, stepped out without his help, and drawing the bear-skin closely round her, and over her head, walked straight up to the gate of the house of nuns.

All men wondered at the white ghost; but Martin walked behind her, his left finger on his lips, his right hand grasping his little axe, with such a stern and serious face, and so fierce an eye, that all drew back in silence, and let her pass.

The portress looked through the wicket.

"I am Torfrida," said a voice of terrible calm. "I am come to see the Lady Godiva. Let me in."

The portress opened, utterly astounded.

"Madam?" said Martin eagerly, as Torfrida entered.

"What? What?" She seemed to waken from a dream. "God bless thee, thou good and faithful servant"; and she turned again.

"Madam? Say!"

"What?"

"Shall I go back and kill him?" And he held out the little axe.

Torfrida snatched it from his grasp with a shriek, and cast it inside the convent door.

"Mother Mary and all saints!" cried the portress, "your garments are in rags, madam!"

"Never mind. Bring me garments of yours. I shall need none other till I die!" and she walked in and on.

"She is come to be a nun!" whispered the portress to the next sister, and she again to the next; and they all gabbled, and lifted up their hands and eyes, and thanked all the saints of the calendar, over the blessed and miraculous conversion of the Lady Torfrida, and the wealth which she would probably bring to the convent.

Torfrida went straight on, speaking to no one, not even to the prioress; and into Lady Godiva's chamber.

There she dropped at the countess's feet, and laid her head upon her knees.

"I am come, as you always told me I should do. But it has been a long way hither, and I am very tired."

"My child! What is this? What brings you here?"

"I am doing penance for my sins."

"And your feet all cut and bleeding."

"Are they?" said Torfrida, vacantly. "I will tell you all about it when I wake."

And she fell fast asleep, with her head in Godiva's lap.

The countess did not speak or stir. She beckoned the good prioress, who had followed Torfrida in, to go away. She saw that something dreadful had happened; and prayed as she awaited the news.

Torfrida slept for a full hour. Then she woke with a start.

"Where am I? Hereward!"

Then followed a dreadful shriek, which made every nun in that quiet house shudder, and thank God that she knew nothing of those agonies of soul, which were the lot of the foolish virgins who married and were given in marriage themselves, instead of waiting with oil in their lamps for the true bridegroom.

"I recollect all now," said Torfrida. "Listen!" And she told the countess all, with speech so calm and clear, that Godiva was awed by the power and spirit of that marvellous woman.

But she groaned in bitterness of soul. "Anything but this. Rather death from him than treachery. This last, worst woe had God kept in his quiver for me most miserable of women. And now his bolt has fallen! Hereward! Hereward! That thy mother should wish her last child laid in his grave!"

"Not so," said Torfrida, "it is well as it is. How better? It is his only chance for comfort, for honor, for life itself. He would have grown a — I was growing bad and foul myself in that ugly wilderness. Now he will be a knight once more among knights, and win himself fresh honor in fresh fields. Let him marry her. Why not? He can get a dispensation from the Pope, and then there will be no sin in it, you know. If the Holy Father cannot make wrong right, who can? Yes. It is very well as it is. And I am very well where I am. Women! bring me scissors, and one of your nun's dresses. I am come to be a nun like you."

Godiva would have stopped her. But Torfrida rose upon her knees, and calmly made a solemn vow, which, though canonically void without her husband's consent, would, she well knew, never be disputed by any there: and as for him, — "He has lost me; and forever. Torfrida never gives herself away twice."

"There's carnal pride in those words, my poor child," said Godiva.

"Cruel!" said she, proudly. "When I am sacrificing myself utterly for him."

"And thy poor girl?"

"He will let her come hither," said Torfrida with forced calm. "He will see that it is not fit that she should grow up with — yes, he will send her to me — to us. And I shall live for her — and for you. If you will let me be your bower woman, dress you, serve you, read to you. You know that I am a pretty scholar. You will let me, mother? I may call you mother, may I not?" And Torfrida fondled the old woman's thin hands. "For I do want so much something to love."

"Love thy heavenly bridegroom, the only love worthy of woman!" said Godiva, as her tears fell fast on Torfrida's head.

She gave a half-impatient toss.

"That may come, in good time. As yet it is enough to do, if I can keep down this devil here in my throat. Women, bring me the scissors."

And Torfrida cut off her raven locks, now streaked with gray, and put on the nun's dress, and became a nun thenceforth.

On the second day there came to Crowland Leofric the priest, and with him the poor child.

She had woke in the morning and found no mother. Leofric and the other men searched the woods round, far and wide. The girl mounted her horse, and would go with them. Then they took a bloodhound, and he led them to Grimkel's hut. There they heard of Martin. The ghost must have been Torfrida. Then the hound brought them to the river. And they divined at once that she was gone to Crowland, to Godiva; but why, they could not guess.

Then the girl insisted, prayed, at last commanded them to take her to Crowland. And to Crowland they came.

Leofric left the girl at the nun's house door, and went into the monastery, where he had friends enow, runaway and renegade as he was. As he came into the great court, whom should he meet but Martin Lightfoot, in a lay brother's frock.

"Aha? And are you come home likewise? Have you renounced the Devil and this last work of his?"

"What work? What devil?" asked Leofric, who saw method in Martin's madness. "And what do you here, in a long frock?"

"Devil? Hereward the devil. I would have killed him with my axe; but she got it from me, and threw it in among the holy sisters, and I had work to get it again. Shame on her, to spoil my chance of heaven! For I should have surely won heaven, you know, if I had killed the devil."

After much beating about, Leofric got from Martin the whole tragedy.

And when he heard it, he burst out weeping.

"O Hereward, Hereward! O knightly honor! O faith and troth and gratitude, and love in return for such love as might have tamed lions, and made tyrants mild! Are they all carnal vanities, works of the weak flesh, bruised reeds which break when they are leaned upon? If so, you are right, Martin, and there is naught left, but to flee from a world in which all men are liars."

And Leofric, in the midst of Crowland Yard, tore off his belt and trusty sword, his hauberk and helm also, and letting down his monk's frock, which he wore trussed to the mid-knee, he went to the Abbot's lodgings, and asked to see old Ulfketyl.

"Bring him up," said the good abbot, "for he is a valiant man and true, in spite of all his vanities; and may be he brings news of Hereward, whom God forgive."

And when Leofric came in, he fell upon his knees, bewailing and confessing his sinful life; and begged the abbot to take him back again into Crowland minster, and lay upon him what penance he thought fit, and put him in the lowest office, because he was a man of blood; if only he might stay there, and have a sight at times of his dear Lady Torfrida, without whom he should surely die.

So Leofric was received back, in full chapter, by abbot and prior and all the monks. But when he asked them to lay a penance upon him, Ulfketyl arose from his high chair and spoke.

"Shall we, who have sat here at ease, lay a penance on this man, who has shed his blood in fifty valiant fights for us, and for St. Guthlac, and for this English land? Look at yon scars upon his head and arms. He has had sharper discipline from cold steel than we could give him here with rod; and has fasted in the wilderness more sorely, many a time, than we have fasted here."

And all the monks agreed, that no penance should be laid on Leofric. Only that he should abstain from singing vain and carnal ballads, which turned the heads of the young brothers, and made them dream of naught but battles, and giants, and enchanters, and ladies' love.

Hereward came back on the third day, and found his wife and daughter gone. His guilty conscience told him in the first instant why. For he went into the chamber, and there, upon the floor, lay the letter which he had looked for in vain.

No one had touched it where it lay. Perhaps no one had dared to enter the chamber. If they had, they would not have dared to meddle with writing, which they could not read, and which might contain some magic spell. Letters were very safe in those old days.

There are moods of man which no one will dare to describe, unless, like Shakespeare, he is Shakespeare, and like Shakespeare knows it not.

Therefore what Hereward thought and felt will not be told. What he did was this.

He raged and blustered. He must hide his shame. He must justify himself to his knights; and much more to himself; or if not justify himself, must shift some of the blame over to the opposite side. So he raged and blustered. He had been robbed of his wife and daughter. They had been cajoled away by the monks of Crowland. What villains were those, to rob an honest man of his family while he was fighting for his country?

So he rode down to the river, and there took two great barges, and rowed away to Crowland, with forty men-at-arms.

And all the while he thought of Alftruda, as he had seen her at Peterborough.

And of no one else?

Not so. For all the while he felt that he loved Torfrida's little finger better than Alftruda's whole body, and soul into the bargain.

What a long way it was to Crowland. How wearying were the hours through mere and sea. How wearying the monotonous pulse of the oars. If tobacco had been known then, Hereward would have smoked all the way, and been none the wiser, though the happier, for it; for the herb that drives away the evil spirits of anxiety, drives away also the good, though stern, spirits of remorse.

But in those days a man could only escape facts by drinking; and Hereward was too much afraid of what he should meet in Crowland, to go thither drunk.

Sometimes he hoped that Torfrida might hold her purpose, and set him free to follow his wicked will. All the lower nature in him, so long crushed under, leapt up chuckling and grinning and tumbling head over heels, and cried, — Now I shall have a holiday!

Sometimes he hoped that Torfrida might come out to the shore, and settle the matter in one moment, by a glance of her great hawk's eyes. If she would but quell him by one look; leap on board, seize the helm, and assume without a word the command of his men and him; steer them back to Bourne, and sit down beside him with a kiss, as if nothing had happened. If she would but do that, and ignore the past, would he not ignore it? Would he not forget Alftruda, and King William, and all the world, and go up with her into Sherwood, and then north to Scotland and Gospatrick, and be a man once more?

No. He would go with her to the Baltic or the Mediterranean. Constantinople and the Varangers would be the place and the men. Ay, there to escape out of that charmed ring into a new life!

No. He did not deserve such luck; and he would not get it. She would talk it all out. She must, for she was a woman. She would blame, argue, say dreadful words, — dreadful, because true and deserved. Then she would grow angry, as women do when they are most in the right, and say too much, — dreadful words, which would be untrue and undeserved. Then he should resist, recriminate. He would not stand it. He could not stand it. No. He could never face her again.

And yet if he had seen a man insult her, — if he had seen her at that moment in peril of the slightest danger, the slightest bruise, he would have rushed forward like a madman, and died, saving her from that bruise. And he knew that: and with the strange self-contradiction of human nature, he soothed his own conscience by the thought that he loved her still; and that, therefore — somehow or other, he cared not to make out how — he had done her no wrong. Then he blustered again, for the benefit of his men. He would teach these monks of Crowland a lesson. He would burn the minster over their heads.

"That would be pity, seeing they are the only Englishmen left in England," said Siward the White, his nephew, very simply.

"What is that to thee? Thou hast helped to burn Peterborough at my bidding; and thou shalt help to burn Crowland."

"I am a free gentleman of England; and what I choose, I do. I and my brother are going to Constantinople to join the Varanger guard, and shall not burn Crowland, or let any man burn it."

"Shall not let?"

"No," said the young man, so quietly, that Hereward was cowed.

"I — I only meant — if they did not do right by me."

"Do right thyself," said Siward.

Hereward swore awfully, and laid his hand on his sword-hilt. But he did not draw it; for he thought he saw overhead a cloud which was very like the figure of St. Guthlac in Crowland window, and an awe fell upon him from above.

So they came to Crowland; and Hereward landed and beat upon the gates, and spoke high words. But the monks did not open the gates for a while. At last the gates creaked, and opened; and in the gateway stood Abbot Ulfketyl in his robes of state, and behind him Prior, and all the officers, and all the monks of the house.

"Comes Hereward in peace or in war?"

"In war!" said Hereward.

Then that true and trusty old man, who sealed his patriotism, if not with his blood, — for the very Normans had not the heart to take that, — still with long and bitter sorrows, lifted up his head, and said, like a valiant Dane, as his name bespoke him:

"Against the traitor and the adulterer — "

"I am neither," roared Hereward.

"Thou wouldst be, if thou couldst. Whoso looketh upon a woman to — "

"Preach me no sermons, man! Let me in to seek my wife."

"Over my body," said Ulfketyl, and laid himself down across the threshold.

Hereward recoiled. If he had dared to step over that sacred body, there was not a blood-stained ruffian in his crew who dared to follow him.

"Rise, rise! for God's sake, Lord Abbot," said he. "Whatever I am, I need not that you should disgrace me thus. Only let me see her, — reason with her."

"She has vowed herself to God, and is none of thine henceforth."

"It is against the canons. A wrong and a robbery."

Ulfketyl rose, grand as ever.

"Hereward Leofricsson, our joy and our glory once. Hearken to the old man who will soon go whither thine Uncle Brand is gone, and be free of Frenchmen, and of all this wicked world. When the walls of Crowland dare not shelter the wronged woman, fleeing from man's treason to God's faithfulness, then let the roofs of Crowland burn till the flame reaches heaven, for a sign that the children of God are as false as the children of this world, and break their faith like any belted knight."

Hereward was silenced. His men shrunk back from him. He felt as if God, and the Mother of God, and St. Guthlac, and all the host of heaven, were shrinking back from him likewise. He turned to supplications, compromises, — what else was left.

"At least you will let me have speech of her, or of my mother?"

"They must answer that, not I."

Hereward sent in, entreating to see one, or both.

"Tell him," said Lady Godiva, "who calls himself my son, that my sons were men of honor, and that he must have been changed at nurse."

"Tell him," said Torfrida, "that I have lived my life, and am dead. Dead. If he would see me, he will only see my corpse."

"You would not slay yourself?"

"What is there that I dare not do? You do not know Torfrida. He does."

And Hereward did; and went back again like a man stunned.

After a while there came by boat to Crowland all Torfrida's wealth: clothes, jewels: not a shred had Hereward kept. The magic armor came with them.

Torfrida gave all to the abbey, there and then. Only the armor she wrapped up in the white bear's skin, and sent it back to Hereward, with her blessing, and entreaty not to refuse that, her last bequest.

Hereward did not refuse, for very shame. But for very shame he never wore that armor more. For very shame he never slept again upon the white bear's skin, on which he and his true love had lain so many a year.

And Torfrida turned herself utterly to serve the Lady Godiva, and to teach and train her child as she had never done before, while she had to love Hereward, and to work day and night, with her own fingers, for all his men. All pride, all fierceness, all care of self, had passed away from her. In penitence, humility, obedience, and gentleness, she went on; never smiling; but never weeping. Her heart was broken; and she felt it good for herself to let it break.

And Leofric the priest, and mad Martin Lightfoot, watched like two dogs for her going out and coming in; and when she went among the poor corrodiers, and nursed the sick, and taught the children, and went to and fro upon her holy errands, blessing and blessed, the two wild men had a word from her mouth, or a kiss of her hand, and were happy all the day after. For they loved her with a love mightier than ever Hereward had heaped upon her; for she had given him all: but she had given those two wild men naught but the beatific vision of a noble woman.

CHAPTER XXXVII.

HOW HEREWARD LOST SWORD BRAIN-BITER.

"On account of which," says the chronicler, "many troubles came to Hereward: because Torfrida was most wise, and of great counsel in need. For afterwards, as he himself confessed, things went not so well with him as they did in her time."

And the first thing that went ill was this. He was riding through the Bruneswald, and behind him Geri, Wenoch, and Matelgar, these three. And there met him in an open glade a knight, the biggest man he had ever seen, on the biggest horse, and five knights behind him. He was an Englishman, and not a Frenchman, by his dress; and Hereward spoke courteously enough to him. But who he was, and what his business was in the Bruneswald, Hereward thought that he had a right to ask.

"Tell me who thou art, who askest, before I tell thee who I am who am asked, riding here on common land," quoth the knight, surlily enough.

"I am Hereward, without whose leave no man has ridden the Bruneswald for many a day."

"And I am Letwold the Englishman, who rides whither he will in merry England, without care for any Frenchman upon earth."

"Frenchman? Why callest thou me Frenchman, man? I am Hereward."

"Then thou art, if tales be true, as French as Ivo Taillebois. I hear that thou hast left thy true lady, like a fool and a churl, and goest to London, or Winchester, or the nether pit, — I care not which, — to make thy peace with the Mamzer."

The man was a surly brute: but what he said was so true, that Hereward's wrath arose. He had promised Torfrida many a time, never to quarrel with an Englishman, but to endure all things. Now, out of very spite to Torfrida's counsel, because it was Torfrida's, and he had promised to obey it, he took up the quarrel.

"If I am a fool and a churl, thou art a greater fool, to provoke thine own death; and a greater — "

"Spare your breath," said the big man, "and let me try Hereward, as I have many another."

Whereon they dropped their lance-points, and rode at each other like two mad bulls. And, by the contagion of folly common in the middle age, at each other rode Hereward's three knights and Letwold's five. The two leaders found themselves both rolling on the ground; jumped up, drew their swords, and hewed away at each other. Geri unhorsed his man at the first charge, and left him stunned. Then he turned on another, and did the same by him. Wenoch and Matelgar each upset their man. The fifth of Letwold's knights threw up his lance-point, not liking his new company. Geri and the other two rode in on the two chiefs, who were fighting hard, each under shield.

"Stand back!" roared Hereward, "and give the knight fair play! When did any one of us want a man to help him? Kill or die single, has been our rule, and shall be."

They threw up their lance-points, and stood round to see that great fight. Letwold's knight rode in among them, and stood likewise; and friend and foe looked on, as they might at a pair of game-cocks.

Hereward had, to his own surprise and that of his fellows, met his match. The sparks flew, the iron clanged; but so heavy were the stranger's strokes, that Hereward reeled again and again. So sure was the guard of his shield, that Hereward could not wound him, hit where he would. At last he dealt a furious blow on the stranger's head.

"If that does not bring your master down!" quoth Geri.

"By —, Brain-biter is gone!"

It was too true. Sword Brain-biter's end was come. The Ogre's magic blade had snapt off short by the handle.

"Your master is a true Englishman, by the hardness of his brains," quoth Wenoch, as the stranger, reeling for a moment, lifted up his head, and stared at Hereward in the face, doubtful what to do.

"Will you yield, or fight on?" cried he.

"Yield?" shouted Hereward, rushing upon him, as a mastiff might on a lion, and striking at his helm, though shorter than him by a head and shoulders, such swift and terrible blows with the broken hilt, as staggered the tall stranger.

"What are you at, forgetting what you have at your side?" roared Geri.

Hereward sprang back. He had, as was his custom, a second sword on his right thigh.

"I forget everything now," said he to himself angrily.

And that was too true. But he drew the second sword, and sprang at his man once more.

The stranger tried, according to the chronicler, who probably had it from one of the three by-standers, a blow which has cost many a brave man his life. He struck right down on Hereward's head. Hereward raised his shield, warding the stroke, and threw in that *coup de jarret*, which there is no guarding, after the downright blow has been given. The stranger dropped upon his wounded knee.

"Yield," cried Hereward in his turn.

"That is not my fashion." And the stranger fought on, upon his stumps, like Witherington in Chevy Chase.

Hereward, mad with the sight of blood, struck at him four or five times. The stranger's shield was so quick that he could not hit him, even on his knee. He held his hand, and drew back, looking at his new rival.

"What the murrain are we two fighting about?" said he at last.

"I know not; neither care," said the other, with a grim chuckle. "But if any man will fight me, him I fight, ever since I had beard to my chin."

"Thou art the best man that ever I faced."

"That is like enough."

"What wilt thou take, if I give thee thy life?"

"My way on which I was going. For I turn back for no man alive on land."

"Then thou hast not had enough of me?"

"Not by another hour."

"Thou must be born of fiend, and not of man."

"Very like. It is a wise son knows his own father."

Hereward burst out laughing.

"Would to heaven I had had thee for my man this three years since."

"Perhaps I would not have been thy man."

"Why not?"

"Because I have been my own man ever since I was born, and am well content with myself for my master."

"Shall I bind up thy leg?" asked Hereward, having no more to say, and not wishing to kill the man.

"No. It will grow again, like a crab's claw."

"Thou art a fiend." And Hereward turned away, sulky, and half afraid.

"Very like. No man knows what a devil he is, till he tries."

"What dost mean?" and Hereward turned angrily back.

"Fiends we are all, till God's grace comes."

"Little grace has come to thee yet, by thy ungracious tongue."

"Rough to men, may be gracious to women."

"What hast thou to do with women?" asked Hereward, fiercely.

"I have a wife, and I love her."

"Thou art not like to get back to her to-day."

"I fear not, with this paltry scratch. I had looked for a cut from thee, would have saved me all fighting henceforth."

"What dost mean?" asked Hereward, with an oath.

"That my wife is in heaven, and I would needs follow her."

Hereward got on his horse, and rode away. Never could he find out who that Sir Letwold was, or how he came into the Bruneswald. All he knew was, that he never had had such a fight since he wore beard; and that he had lost Sword Brainbiter: from which his evil conscience augured that his luck had turned, and that he should lose many things beside.

CHAPTER XXXVIII.

HOW HEREWARD CAME IN TO THE KING.

AFTER these things Hereward summoned all his men, and set before them the hopelessness of any further resistance, and the promises of amnesty, lands, and honors which William had offered him, and persuaded them — and indeed he had good arguments enough and to spare — that they should go and make their peace with the King.

They were so accustomed to look up to his determination, that when it gave way theirs gave way likewise. They were so accustomed to trust his wisdom, that most of them yielded at once to his arguments.

That the band should break up, all agreed. A few of the more suspicious, or more desperate, said that they could never trust the Norman; that Hereward himself had warned them again and again of his treachery. That he was now going to do himself what he had laughed at Gospatrick and the rest for doing; what had brought ruin on Edwin and Morcar; what he had again and again prophesied would bring ruin on Waltheof himself ere all was over.

But Hereward was deaf to their arguments. He had said as little to them as he could about Alftruda, for very shame; but he was utterly besotted on her. For her sake, he had determined to run his head blindly into the very snare of which he had warned others. And he had seared — so he fancied — his conscience. It was Torfrida's fault now, not his. If she left him, — if she herself freed him of her own will, — why, he was free, and there was no more to be said about it.

And Hereward (says the chronicler) took Gwenoch, Geri, and Matelgar, and rode south to the King.

Where were the two young Siwards? It is not said. Probably they, and a few desperadoes, followed the fashion of so many English in those sad days, — when, as sings the Norse skald,

"Cold heart and bloody hand
Now rule English land," —

and took ship for Constantinople, and enlisted in the Varanger guard, and died full of years and honors, leaving fair-haired children behind them, to become Varangers in their turn.

Be that as it may, Hereward rode south. But when he had gotten a long way upon the road, a fancy (says the chronicler) came over him. He was not going in pomp and glory enough. It seemed mean for the once great Hereward to sneak into Winchester with three knights. Perhaps it seemed not over safe for the once great Hereward to travel with only three knights. So he went back all the way to camp, and took (says the chronicler) "forty most famous knights, all big and tall of stature, and splendid, — if from nothing else, from their looks and their harness alone."

So Hereward and those forty knights rode down from Peterborough, along the Roman road. For the Roman roads were then, and for centuries after, the only roads in this land; and our forefathers looked on them as the work of gods and giants, and called them after the names of their old gods and heroes, — Irmen Street, Watling Street, and so forth.

And then, like true Englishmen, our own forefathers showed their respect for the said divine works, not by copying them, but by picking them to pieces to pave every man his own court-yard. Be it so. The neglect of new roads, the destruction of the old ones, was a natural evil consequence of local self-government. A cheap price, perhaps, after all, to pay for that power of local self-government which has kept England free unto this day.

Be that as it may, down the Roman road Hereward went; past Alconbury Hill, of the old posting days; past Wimpole Park, then deep forest; past Hatfield, then deep forest likewise; and so to St. Alban's. And there they lodged in the minster; for the monks thereof were good English, and sang masses daily for King Harold's soul. And the next day they went south, by ways which are not so clear.

Just outside St. Alban's — Verulamium of the Romans (the ruins whereof were believed to be full of ghosts, demons, and magic treasures) — they turned, at St. Stephen's, to the left, off the Roman road to London; and by another Roman road struck into the vast forest which ringed London round from northeast to southwest. Following the upper waters of the Colne, which ran through the woods on their left, they came to Watford, and then turned probably to Rickmansworth. No longer on the Roman paved ways, they followed horse-tracks, between the forest and the rich marsh-meadows of the Colne, as far as Denham, and then struck into a Roman road again at the north end of Langley Park. From thence, over heathy commons, — for that western part of Buckinghamshire, its soil being light and some gravel, was little cultivated then, and hardly all cultivated now,— they held on straight by Langley town into the Vale of Thames.

Little they dreamed, as they rode down by Ditton Green, off the heathy commons, past the poor, scattered farms, on to the vast rushy meadows, while upon them was the dull weight of disappointment, shame, all but despair; their race enslaved, their country a prey to strangers, and all its future, like their own, a lurid blank,— little they dreamed of what that vale would be within eight hundred years,— the eye of England, and it may be of the world; a spot which owns more wealth and peace, more art and civilization, more beauty and more virtue, it may be, than any of God's gardens which make fair this earth. Windsor, on its crowned steep, was to them but a new hunting palace of the old miracle-monger Edward, who had just ruined England.

Runnymede, a mile below them down the broad stream, was but a horse-fen fringed with water-lilies, where the men of Wessex had met of old to counsel, and to bring the country to this pass. And as they crossed, by ford or ferry-boat, the shallows of old Windsor, whither they had been tending all along, and struck into the moorlands of Wessex itself, they were as men going into an unknown wilderness: behind them ruin, and before them unknown danger.

On through Windsor Forest, Edward the Saint's old hunting-ground; its bottoms choked with beech and oak, and birch and alder scrub; its upper lands vast flats of level heath; along the great trackway which runs along the lower side of Chobham Camp, some quarter of a mile broad, every rut and trackway as fresh at this day as when the ancient Briton, finding that his neighbor's essedum — chariot, or rather cart — had worn the ruts too deep, struck out a fresh wandering line for himself across the dreary heath.

Over the Blackwater by Sandhurst, and along the flats of Hartford Bridge, where the old furze-grown ruts show the trackway to this day. Down into the clayland forests of the Andredsweald, and up out of them again at Basing, on to the clean crisp chalk turf; to strike at Popham Lane the Roman road from Silchester, and hold it over the high downs, till they saw far below them the royal city of Winchester.

Itchen, silver as they looked on her from above, but when they came down to her, so clear that none could see where water ended and where air began, hurried through the city in many a stream. Beyond it rose the "White Camp," the "Venta Belgarum," the circular earthwork of white chalk on the high down. Within the city rose the ancient minster church, built by Ethelwold, — ancient even then, — where slept the ancient kings; Kennulf, Egbert, and Ethelwulf the Saxons; and by them the Danes, Canute the Great, and Hardacanute his son, and Norman Emma his wife, and Ethelred's before him; and the great Earl Godwin, who seemed to Hereward to have died, not twenty, but two hundred years ago; — and it may be an old Saxon hall upon the little isle whither Edgar had bidden bring the heads of all the wolves in Wessex, where afterwards the bishops built Wolvesey Palace. But nearer to them, on the down which sloped up to the west, stood an uglier thing, which they saw with curses deep and loud, — the keep of the new Norman castle by the west gate.

Hereward halted his knights upon the down outside the northern gate. Then he rode forward himself. The gate was open wide; but he did not care to go in.

So he rode into the gateway, and smote upon that gate with his lance-but. But the porter saw the knights upon the down, and was afraid to come out; for he feared treason.

Then Hereward smote a second time; but the porter did not come out.

Then he took the lance by the shaft, and smote a third time. And he smote so hard, that the lance-but flew to flinders against Winchester Gate.

And at that started out two knights, who had come down from the castle, seeing the meinie on the down, and asked, —

"Who art thou who knockest here so bold?"

"Who I am any man can see by those splinters, if he knows what men are left in England this day."

The knights looked at the broken wood, and then at each other. Who could the man be who could beat an ash stave to flinders at a single blow?

"You are young, and do not know me; and no shame to you. Go and tell William the King, that Hereward is come to put his hands between the King's, and be the King's man henceforth."

"You are Hereward?" asked one, half awed, half disbelieving at Hereward's short stature.

"You are — I know not who. Pick up those splinters, and take them to King William; and say, 'The man who broke that lance against the gate is here to make his peace with thee,' and he will know who I am."

And so cowed were these two knights with Hereward's royal voice, and royal eye, and royal strength, that they went simply, and did what he bade them.

And when King William saw the splinters, he was as joyful as man could be, and said, —

"Send him to me, and tell him, Bright shines the sun to me that lights Hereward into Winchester."

"But, Lord King, he has with him a meinie of full forty knights."

"So much the better. I shall have the more valiant Englishmen to help my valiant French."

So Hereward rode round, outside the walls, to William's new entrenched palace, outside the west gate, by the castle.

And then Hereward went in, and knelt before the Norman, and put his hands between William's hands, and swore to be his man.

"I have kept my word," said he, "which I sent to thee at Rouen seven years agone. Thou art King of all England; and I am the last man to say so."

"And since thou hast said it, I am King indeed. Come with me, and dine; and to-morrow I will see thy knights."

And William walked out of the hall leaning on Hereward's shoulder, at which all the Normans gnashed their teeth with envy.

"And for my knights, Lord King? Thine and mine will mix, for a while yet, like oil and water; and I fear lest there be murder done between them."

"Likely enough."

So the knights were bestowed in a "vill" near by; "and the next day the venerable king himself went forth to see those knights, and caused them to stand, and march before him, both with arms, and without. With whom being much delighted, he praised them, congratulating them on their beauty and stature, and saying that they must all be knights of fame in war." After which Hereward sent them all home except two; and waited till he should marry Alftruda, and get back his heritage.

"And when that happens," said William, "why should we not have two weddings, beausire, as well as one? I hear that you have in Crowland a fair daughter, and marriageable."

Hereward bowed.

"And I have found a husband for her suitable to her years, and who may conduce to your peace and serenity."

Hereward bit his lip. To refuse was impossible in those days. But —

"I trust that your Grace has found a knight of higher lineage than him, whom, after so many honors, you honored with the hand of my niece."

William laughed. It was not his interest to quarrel with Hereward. "Aha! Ivo, the wood-cutter's son. I ask your pardon for that, Sir Hereward. Had you been my man then, as you are now, it might have been different."

"If a king ask my pardon, I can only ask his in return."

"You must be friends with Taillebois. He is a brave knight, and a wise warrior."

"None ever doubted that."

"And to cover any little blots in his escutcheon, I have made him an earl, as I may make you some day."

"Your Majesty, like a true king, knows how to reward. Who is this knight whom you have chosen for my lass?"

"Sir Hugh of Evermue, a neighbor of yours, and a man of blood and breeding."

"I know him, and his lineage; and it is very well. I humbly thank your Majesty."

"Can I be the same man?" said Hereward to himself, bitterly.

And he was not the same man. He was besotted on Alftruda, and humbled himself accordingly.

CHAPTER XXXIX.

HOW TORFRIDA CONFESSED THAT SHE HAD BEEN INSPIRED BY THE DEVIL.

AFTER a few days, there came down a priest to Crowland, and talked with Torfrida, in Archbishop Lanfranc's name.

Whether Lanfranc sent him, or merely (as is probable) Alftruda, he could not have come in a more fit name. Torfrida knew (with all the world) how Lanfranc had arranged William the Norman's uncanonical marriage, with the Pope, by help of Archdeacon Hildebrand (afterwards Pope himself); and had changed his mind deftly to William's side when he saw that William might be useful to Holy Church, and could enslave, if duly managed, not only the nation of England to himself, but the clergy of England to Rome. All this Torfrida, and the world, knew. And therefore she answered: —

"Lanfranc? I can hardly credit you: for I hear that he is a good man, though hard. But he has settled a queen's marriage suit; so he may very well settle mine."

After which they talked together; and she answered him, the priest said, so wisely and well, that he never had met with a woman of so clear a brain, or of so stout a heart.

At last, being puzzled to get that which he wanted, he touched on the matter of her marriage with Hereward.

She wished it, he said, dissolved. She wished herself to enter religion.

Archbishop Lanfranc would be most happy to sanction so holy a desire, but there were objections. She was a married woman; and her husband had not given his consent.

"Let him give it, then."

There were still objections. He had nothing to bring against her, which could justify the dissolution of the holy bond: unless — "

"Unless I bring some myself?"

"There have been rumors — I say not how true — of magic and sorcery! — "

Torfrida leaped up from her seat, and laughed such a laugh, that the priest said in after years, it rung through his head as if it had arisen out of the pit of the lost.

"So that is what you want, Churchman! Then you shall have it. Bring me pen and ink. I need not to confess to you. You shall read my confession when it is done. I am a better scribe, mind you, than any clerk between here and Paris."

She seized the pen and ink, and wrote; not fiercely, as the priest expected, but slowly and carefully. Then she gave it the priest to read.

"Will that do, Churchman? Will that free my soul, and that of your French Archbishop?"

And the priest read to himself.

How Torfrida of St. Omer, born at Arles in Provence, confest that from her youth up she had been given to the practice of diabolic arts, and had at divers times and places used the same, both alone and with Richilda, late Countess of Hainault. How, wickedly, wantonly, and instinct with a malignant spirit, she had compassed, by charms and spells, to win the love of Hereward. How she had ever since kept in bondage him, and others whom she had not loved with the same carnal love, but only desired to make them useful to her own desire of power and glory, by the same magical arts; for which she now humbly begged pardon of Holy Church, and of all Christian folk; and, penetrated with compunction, desired only that she might retire into the convent of Crowland. She asserted the marriage which she had so unlawfully compassed to be null and void; and prayed to be released therefrom, as a burden to her conscience and soul, that she might spend the rest of her life in penitence for her many enormous sins. She submitted herself to the judgment of Holy Church, only begging that this her free confession might be counted in her favor and that she might not be put to death, as she deserved, nor sent into perpetual imprisonment; because her mother-in-law according to the flesh, the Countess Godiva, being old and infirm, had daily need of her; and she wished to serve her menially as long as she lived. After which, she put herself utterly upon the judgment of the Church. And meanwhile, she desired and prayed that she might be allowed to remain at large in the said monastery of Crowland, not leaving the precincts thereof, without special leave given by the Abbot and prioress in one case between her and them reserved; to wear garments of hair-cloth; to fast all the year on bread and water; and to be disciplined with rods or otherwise, at such times as the prioress should command, and to such degree as her body, softened with carnal luxury, could reasonably endure. And beyond — that, being dead to the world, God might have mercy on her soul.

And she meant what she said. The madness of remorse and disappointment, so common in the wild middle age, had come over her; and with it the twin madness of self-torture.

The priest read, and trembled; not for Torfrida: but for himself, lest she should enchant him after all.

"She must have been an awful sinner," said he to the monks when he got safe out of the room; "comparable only to the witch of Endor, or the woman Jezebel, of whom St. John writes in the Revelations."

"I do not know how you Frenchmen measure folks, when you see them; but to our mind she is,—for goodness, humility, and patience comparable only to an angel of God," said Abbot Ulfketyl.

"You Englishmen will have to change your minds on many points, if you mean to stay here."

"We shall not change them, and we shall stay here," quoth the Abbot.

"How? You will not get Sweyn and his Danes to help you a second time."

"No, we shall all die, and give you your wills, and you will not have the heart to cast our bones into the fens?"

"Not unless you intend to work miracles, and set up for saints, like your Alphege Edmund."

"Heaven forbid that we should compare ourselves with them! Only let us alone till we die."

"If you let us alone, and do not turn traitor meanwhile."

Abbot Ulfketyl bit his lip, and kept down the rising fiend.

"And now," said the priest, "deliver me over Torfrida the younger, daughter of Hereward and this woman, that I may take her to the King, who has found a fit husband for her."

"You will hardly get her."

"Not get her?"

"Not without her mother's consent. The lass cares for naught but her."

"Pish! that sorceress? Send for the girl."

Abbot Ulfketyl, forced in his own abbey, great and august lord though he was, to obey any upstart of a Norman priest who came backed by the King and Lanfranc, sent for the lass.

The young outlaw came in,—hawk on fist, and its hood off, for it was a pet,—short, sturdy, upright, brown-haired, blue-eyed, ill-dressed, with hard hands and sun-burnt face, but with the hawk-eye of her father, and her mother, and the hawks among which she was bred. She looked the priest over from head to foot, till he was abashed.

"A Frenchman!" said she, and she said no more.

The priest looked at her eyes, and then at the hawk's eyes. They were disagreeably like each other. He told his errand as courteously as he could, for he was not a bad-hearted man for a Norman priest.

The lass laughed him to scorn. The King's commands? She never saw a king in the greenwood, and cared for none. There was no king in England now, since Sweyn Ulfsson sailed back to Denmark. Who was this Norman William, to sell a free English lass like a colt or a cow? The priest might go back to the slaves of Wessex, and command them if he could; but in the fens, men were free, and lasses too.

The priest was piously shocked and indignant; and began to argue.

She played with her hawk, instead of listening, and then was marching out of the room.

"Your mother," said he, " is a sorceress."

"You are a knave, or set on by knaves. You lie, and you know you lie." And she turned away again.

"She has confessed it."

"You have driven her mad between you, till she will confess anything. I presume you threatened to burn her, as some of you did awhile back." And the young lady made use of words equally strong and true.

The priest was not accustomed to the direct language of the greenwood, and indignant on his own account, threatened, and finally offered to use, force. Whereon there looked up into his face such a demon (so he said) as he never had seen or dreamed of, and said: "If you lay a finger on me, I will brittle you like any deer." And therewith pulled out a saying-knife, about half as long again as the said priest's hand, being very sharp, so he deposed, down the whole length of one edge, and likewise down his little finger's length of the other.

Not being versed in the terms of English venery, he asked Abbot Ulfketyl what brittling of a deer might mean; and being informed that it was that operation on the carcass of a stag which his countrymen called eventrer, and Highland gillies now "gralloching," he subsided, and thought it best to go and consult the young lady's mother.

She, to his astonishment, submitted at once and utterly. The King, and he whom she had called her husband, were very gracious. It was all well. She would have preferred, and the Lady Godiva too, after their experience of the world and the flesh, to have devoted her daughter to Heaven in the minster there. But she was unworthy. Who was she, to train a bride for Him who died on Cross? She accepted this as part of her penance, with thankfulness and humility. She had heard that Sir Hugh of Evermue was a gentleman of ancient birth and good prowess, and she thanked the King for his choice. Let the priest tell her daughter that she commanded her to go with him to Winchester. She did not wish to see her. She was stained with many crimes, and unworthy to approach a pure maiden. Besides, it would only cause misery and tears. She was trying to die to the world and to the flesh; and she did not wish to reawaken their power within her. Yes. It was very well. Let the lass go with him."

"Thou art indeed a true penitent," said the priest, his human heart softening him.

"Thou art very much mistaken," said she, and turned away.

The girl, when she heard her mother's command, wept, shrieked, and went. At least she was going to her father. And from wholesome fear of that same saying-knife, the priest left her in peace all the way to Winchester.

After which, Abbot Ulfketyl went into his lodgings, and burst, like a noble old nobleman as he was, into bitter tears of rage and shame.

But Torfrida's eyes were as dry as her own sackcloth.

The priest took the letter back to Winchester, and showed it — it may be to Archbishop Lanfranc. But what he said, this chronicler would not dare to say. For he was a very wise man, and a very stanch and strong pillar of the Holy Roman Church. Meanwhile, he was man enough not to require that anything should be added to Torfrida's penance; and that was enough to prove him a man in those days, — at least for a churchman, — as it proved Archbishop or St. Ailred to be, a few years after, in the case of the nun of Watton, to be read in Gale's "Scriptores Anglicania." Then he showed the letter to Alftruda.

And she laughed one of her laughs, and said, "I have her at last!"

Then, as it befell, he was forced to show the letter to Queen Matilda; and she wept over it human tears, such as she, the noble heart, had been forced to keep many a time before, and said, "The poor soul!— You, Alftruda, woman! does Hereward know of this?"

"No, madam," said Alftruda, not adding that she had taken good care that he should not know.

"It is the best thing which I have heard of him. I should tell him, were it not that I must not meddle with my lord's plans. God grant him a good delivery, as they say of the poor souls in jail. Well, madam, you have your will at last. God give you grace thereof, for you have not given Him much chance as yet."

"Your majesty will honor us by coming to the wedding?" asked Alftruda, utterly unabashed.

Matilda the good looked at her with a face of such calm, childlike astonishment, that Alftruda dropped her "fairy neck" at last, and slunk out of the presence like a beaten cur.

William went to the wedding; and swore horrible oaths that they were the handsomest pair he had ever seen. And so Here ward married Alftruda. How Holy Church settled the matter is not said. But that Hereward married Alftruda, under these very circumstances, may be considered a "historic fact," being vouched for by Gaimar, and by the Peterborough Chronicler. And doubtless Holy Church contrived that it should happen without sin, if it conduced to her own interest.

And little Torfrida — then, it seems, some sixteen years of age — was married to Hugh of Evermue. She wept and struggled as she was dragged into the church.

"But I do not want to be married. I want to go back to my mother."

"The diabolic instinct may have descended to her," said the priests, "and attracts her to the sorceress. We had best sprinkle her with holy water."

So they sprinkled her with holy water, and used exorcisms. Indeed, the case being an important one, the personages of rank, they brought out from their treasures the apron of a certain virgin saint, and put it round her neck, in hopes of driving out the hereditary fiend.

"If I am led with a halter, I must needs go," said she, with one of her mother's own flashes of wit, and went. "But Lady Alftruda," whispered she, half-way up the church, "I never loved him."

"Behave yourself before the King, or I will whip you till the blood runs."

And so she would, and no one would have wondered in those days.

"I will murder you if you do. But I never even saw him."

"Little fool! And what are you going through, but what I went through before you?"

"You to say that?" gnashed the girl, as another spark of her mother's came out. "And you gaining what —"

"What I waited for for fifteen years," said Alftruda, coolly. "If you have courage and cunning, like me, to wait for fifteen years, you too may have your will likewise."

The pure child shuddered, and was married to Hugh of Evermue, who is not said to have kicked her; and was, according to them of Crowland, a good friend to their monastery, and therefore, doubtless, a good man. Once, says wicked report, he offered to strike her, as was the fashion in those chivalrous days. Whereon she turned upon him like a tigress, and bidding him remember that she was the daughter of Hereward and Torfrida, gave him such a beating that he, not wishing to draw sword upon her, surrendered at discretion; and they lived all their lives afterwards as happily as most other married people in those times.

CHAPTER XL.

HOW HEREWARD BEGAN TO GET HIS SOUL'S PRICE.

AND now behold Hereward at home again, fat with the wages of sin, and not knowing that they are death.

He is once more " Dominus de Brunune cum Marisco," " Lord of Bourne with the fen, with all returns and liberties and all other things adjacent to the same vill which are now held as a barony from the Lord King of England." He has a fair young wife, and with her farms and manors, even richer than his own. He is still young, hearty, wise by experience, high in the king's favor, and deservedly so.

Why should he not begin life again?

Why not? Unless it be true that the wages of sin are, not a new life, but death.

And yet he has his troubles. Hardly a Norman knight or baron round but has a blood-feud against him, for a kinsman slain. Sir Aswart, Thorold the abbot's man, was not likely to forgive him for turning him out of the three Mainthorpe manors, which he had comfortably held for two years past, and sending him back to lounge in the abbot's hall at Peterborough, without a yard of land he could call his own. Sir Ascelin was not likely to forgive him for marrying Alftruda, whom he had intended to marry himself. Ivo Taillebois was not likely to forgive him for existing within a hundred miles of Spalding, any more than the wolf would forgive the lamb for fouling the water below him. Beside, had he (Ivo) not married Hereward's niece? and what more grievous offence could Hereward commit, than to be her uncle, reminding Ivo of his own low birth by his nobility, and too likely to take Lucia's part, whenever it should please Ivo to beat or kick her? Only " Gilbert of Ghent," the pious and illustrious earl, sent messages of congratulation and friendship to Hereward, it being his custom to sail with the wind, and worship the rising sun — till it should decline again.

But more: hardly one of the Normans round, but, in the conceit of their skin-deep yesterday's civilization, look on Hereward as a barbarian Englishman, who has his throat tattooed, and wears a short coat, and prefers — the churl — to talk Eng lish in his own hall, though he can talk as good French as they when he is with them, beside three or four barbarian tongues if he has need.

But more still: if they are not likely to bestow their love on Hereward, Hereward is not likely to win love from them of his own will. He is peevish, and wrathful, often insolent and quarrelsome; and small blame to him. The Normans are invaders and tyrants, who have no business there, and should not be there, if he had his way. And they and he can no more amalgamate than fire and water. Moreover, he is a very great man, or has been such once, and he thinks himself one still. He has been accustomed to command men, whole armies; and he will no more treat these Normans as his equals, than they will treat him as such. His own son-in-law, Hugh of Evermue, has to take hard words, — thoroughly well deserved, it may be; but all the more unpleasant for that reason.

The truth was, that Hereward's heart was gnawed with shame and remorse; and therefore he fancied, and not without reason, that all men pointed at him the finger of scorn.

He had done a bad, base, accursed deed. And he knew it. Once in his life — for his other sins were but the sins of his age — the Father of men seems (if the chroniclers say truth) to have put before this splendid barbarian good and evil, saying, Choose! And he knew that the evil was evil, and chose it nevertheless.

Eight hundred years after, a still greater genius and general had the same choice — as far as human cases of conscience can be alike — put before him. And he chose as Hereward chose.

But as with Napoleon and Josephine, so it was with Hereward and Torfrida. Neither throve after.

It was not punished by miracle. What sin is? It worked out its own punishment; that which it merited, deserved, or earned, by its own labor. No man could commit such a sin without shaking his whole character to the root. Hereward tried to persuade himself that his was not shaken; that he was the same Hereward as ever. But he could not deceive himself long. His conscience was evil. He was discontented with all mankind, and with himself most of all. He tried to be good, — as good as he chose to be. If he had done wrong in one thing, he might make up for it in others; but he could not.

All his higher instincts fell from him one by one. He did not like to think of good and noble things; he dared not think of them. He felt, not at first, but as the months rolled on, that he was a changed man; that God had left him. His old bad habits began to return to him. Gradually he sank back into the very vices from which Torfrida had raised him sixteen years before. He took to drinking again, to dull the malady of thought; he excused himself to himself; he wished to forget his defeats, his disappointment, the ruin of his country, the splendid past which lay behind him like a dream. True: but he wished to forget likewise Torfrida fasting and weeping in Crowland. He could not bear the sight of Crowland tower on the far green horizon, the sound of Crowland bells booming over the flat on the south-wind. He never rode down into the fens; he never went to see his daughter at Deeping, because Crowland lay that way. He went up into the old Bruneswald, hunted all day long through the glades where he and his merry men had done their doughty deeds, and came home in the evening to get drunk.

Then he lost his sleep. He sent down to Crowland, to Leofric the priest, that he might come to him, and sing his sagas of the old heroes, that he might get rest. But Leofric sent back for answer that he would not come.

That night Alftruda heard him by her side in the still hours, weeping silently to himself. She caressed him: but he gave no heed to her.

"I believe," said she bitterly at last, "that you love Torfrida still better than you do me."

And Hereward answered, like Mahomet in like case, "That do I, by heaven. She believed in me when no one else in the world did."

And the vain, hard Alftruda answered angrily; and there was many a fierce quarrel between them after that.

With his love of drinking, his love of boasting came back. Because he could do no more great deeds — or rather had not the spirit left in him to do more — he must needs, like a worn-out old man, babble of the great deeds which he had done; insult and defy his Norman neighbors; often talk what might be easily caricatured into treason against King William himself.

There were great excuses for his follies, as there are for those of every beaten man; but Hereward was spent. He had lived his life, and had no more life which he could live; for every man, it would seem, brings into the world with him a certain capacity, a certain amount of vital force, in body and in soul; and when that is used up, the man must sink down into some sort of second childhood, and end, like Hereward, very much where he began; unless the grace of God shall lift him up above the capacity of the mere flesh, into a life literally new, ever-renewing, ever-expanding, and eternal.

But the grace of God had gone away from Hereward, as it goes away from all men who are unfaithful to their wives.

It was very pitiable. Let no man judge him. Life, to most, is very hard work. There are those who endure to the end, and are saved; there are those, again, who do not endure : upon whose souls may God have mercy.

So Hereward soon became as intolerable to his Norman neighbors as they were intolerable to him.

Whereon, according to the simple fashion of those primitive times, they sought about for some one who would pick a quarrel with Hereward, and slay him in fair fight. But an Archibald Bell-the-Cat was not to be found on every hedge.

But it befell that Oger the Breton, he who had Morcar's lands round Bourne, came up to see after his lands, and to visit his friend and fellow-robber, Ivo Taillebois.

Ivo thought the hot-headed Breton, who had already insulted Hereward with impunity at Winchester, the fittest man for his purpose; and asked him, over his cups, whether he had settled with that English ruffian about the Docton land?

Now, King William had judged that Hereward and Oger should hold that land between them, as he and Toli had done. But when "two dogs," as Ivo said, "have hold of the same bone, it is hard if they cannot get a snap at each other's noses."

Oger agreed to that opinion; and riding into Bourne, made inquisition into the doings at Docton. And — scandalous injustice!— he found that an old woman had sent six hens to Hereward, whereof she should have kept three for him.

So he sent to demand formally of Hereward those three hens; and was unpleasantly disappointed when Hereward, instead of offering to fight him, sent him them in an hour, and a lusty young cock into the bargain, with this message, — That he hoped they might increase and multiply; for it was a shame of an honest Englishman if he did not help a poor Breton churl to eat roast fowls for the first time in his life, after feeding on nothing better than furze-toppings, like his own ponies.

To which Oger, who, like a true Breton, believed himself descended from King Arthur, Sir Tristram, and half the knights of the Round Table, replied that his blood was to that of Hereward as wine to peat-water; and that Bretons used furze-toppings only to scourge the backs of insolent barbarians.

To which Hereward replied, that there were gnats enough pestering him in the fens already, and that one more was of no consequence.

Wherefrom the Breton judged, as at Winchester, that Hereward had no lust to fight.

The next day he met Hereward going out to hunt, and was confirmed in his opinion when Hereward lifted his cap to him most courteously, saying that he was not aware before that his neighbor was a gentleman of such high blood.

"Blood? Better at least than thine, thou bare-legged Saxon, who has dared to call me churl. So you must needs have your throat cut? I took you for a wiser man."

"Many have taken me for that which I am not. If you will harness yourself, I will do the same; and we will ride up into the Bruneswald, and settle this matter in peace."

"Three men on each side to see fair play," said the Breton.

And up into the Bruneswald they rode; and fought long without advantage on either side.

Hereward was not the man which he had been. His nerve was gone, as well as his conscience; and all the dash and fury of his old onslaughts gone therewith.

He grew tired of the fight, not in body, but in mind; and more than once drew back.

"Let us stop this child's play," said he, according to the chronicler; "what need have we to fight here all day about nothing?'

Whereat the Breton fancied him already more than half-beaten, and attacked more furiously than ever. He would be the first man on earth who ever had had the better of the great outlaw. He would win himself eternal glory, as the champion of all England.

But he had mistaken his man, and his indomitable English pluck. "It was Hereward's fashion, in fight and war," says the chronicler, "always to ply the man most at the last." And so found the Breton; for Hereward suddenly lost patience, and rushing on him with one of his old shouts, hewed at him again and again, as if his arm would never tire.

Oger gave back, would he or not. In a few moments his sword-arm dropt to his side, cut half through.

"Have you had enough, Sir Tristram the younger?" quoth Hereward, wiping his sword, and walking moodily away.

Oger went out of Bourne with his arm in a sling, and took counsel with Ivo Taillebois. Whereon they two mounted, and rode to Lincoln, and took counsel with Gilbert of Ghent.

The fruit of which was this. That a fortnight after Gilbert rode into Bourne with a great meinie, full a hundred strong, and with him the sheriff and the king's writ; and arrested Hereward on a charge of speaking evil of the king, breaking his peace, compassing the death of his faithful lieges, and various other wicked, traitorous, and diabolical acts.

Hereward was minded at first to fight and die. But Gilbert, who — to do him justice — wished no harm to his ancient squire, reasoned with him. Why should he destroy not only himself, but perhaps his people likewise? Why should he throw away his last chance? The king was not so angry as he seemed; and if Hereward would but be reasonable, the matter might be arranged As it was, he was not to be put to strong prison. He was to be in the custody of Robert of Herepol, Chatelain of Bedford, who, Hereward knew, was a reasonable and courteous man. The king had asked him, Gilbert, to take charge of Hereward.

"And what said you?"

"That I had rather have in my pocket the seven devils that came out of St. Mary Magdalene; and that I would not have thee within ten miles of Lincoln town, to be Earl of all the Danelagh. So I begged him to send thee to Sir Robert, just because I knew him to be a mild and gracious man."

A year before, Hereward would have scorned the proposal; and probably, by one of his famous stratagems, escaped there and then out of the midst of all Gilbert's men. But his spirit was broken; indeed, so was the spirit of every Englishman; and he mounted his horse sullenly, and rode alongside of Gilbert, unarmed for the first time for many a year.

"You had better have taken me," said Sir Ascelin aside to the weeping Alftruda.

"I? helpless wretch that I am! What shall I do for my own safety, now he is gone?"

"Let me come and provide for it."

"Out! wretch! traitor!" cried she.

"There is nothing very traitorous in succoring distressed ladies," said Ascelin. "If I can be of the least service to Alftruda the peerless, let her but send, and I fly to do her bidding."

So they rode off.

Hereward went through Cambridge and Potton like a man stunned, and spoke never a word. He could not even think, till he heard the key turned on him in a room — not a small or doleful one — in Bedford keep, and found an iron shackle on his leg, fastened to the stone bench on which he sat.

Robert of Herepol had meant to leave his prisoner loose. But there were those in Gilbert's train who told him, and with truth, that if he did so, no man's life would be safe. That to brain the jailer with his own keys, and then twist out of his bowels a line wherewith to let himself down from the top of the castle, would be not only easy, but amusing, to the famous "Wake."

So Robert consented to fetter him so far, but no further; and begged his pardon again and again as he did it, pleading the painful necessities of his office.

But Hereward heard him not. He sat in stupefied despair. A great black cloud had covered all heaven and earth, and entered into his brain through every sense, till his mind, as he said afterwards, was like hell, with the fire gone out.

A jailer came in, he knew not how long after, bringing a good meal, and wine. He came cautiously toward the prisoner, and when still beyond the length of his chain, set the food down, and thrust it toward him with a stick, lest Hereward should leap on him and wring his neck.

But Hereward never even saw him or the food. He sat there all day, all night, and nearly all the next day, and hardly moved hand or foot. The jailer told Sir Robert in the evening that he thought the man was mad, and would die.

So good Sir Robert went up to him, and spoke kindly and hopefully. But all Hereward answered was, that he was very well. That he wanted nothing. That he had always heard well of Sir Robert. That he should like to get a little sleep: but that sleep would not come.

The next day Sir Robert came again early, and found him sitting in the same place.

"He was very well," he said. "How could he be otherwise? He was just where he ought to be. A man could not be better than in his right place."

Whereon Sir Robert gave him up for mad.

Then he bethought of sending him a harp, knowing the fame of Hereward's music and singing. "And when he saw the harp," the jailer said, "he wept; but bade take the thing away. And so sat still where he was."

In this state of dull despair he remained for many weeks. At last he woke up.

There passed through and by Bedford large bodies of troops, going as it were to and from battle. The clank of arms stirred Hereward's heart as of old, and he sent to Sir Robert to ask what was toward.

Sir Robert, "the venerable man," came to him joyfully and at once, glad to speak to an illustrious captive, whom he looked on as an injured man; and told him news enough.

Taillebois's warning about Ralph Guader and Waltheof had not been needless. Ralph, as the most influential of the Bretons, was on no good terms with the Normans, save with one, and that one of the most powerful,— Fitz-Osbern, Earl of Hereford. His sister Ralph was to have married; but William, for reasons unknown, forbade the match. The two great earls celebrated the wedding in spite of William, and asked Waltheof as a guest. And at Exning, between the fen and Newmarket Heath,—

"Was that bride-ale
Which was man's bale."

For there was matured the plot which Ivo and others had long seen brewing. William had made himself hateful to all men by his cruelties and tyrannies; and indeed his government was growing more unrighteous day by day. Let them drive him out of England, and part the land between them. Two should be dukes, the third king paramount.

"Waltheof, I presume, plotted drunk, and repented sober, when too late. The wittol! He should have been a monk."

"Repented he has, if ever he was guilty. For he fled to Archbishop Lanfranc, and confessed to him so much, that Lanfranc declares him innocent, and has sent him on to William in Normandy."

"O kind priest! true priest! To send his sheep into the wolf's mouth."

"You forget, dear sire, that William is our king."

"I can hardly forget that, with this pretty ring upon my ankle. But after my experience of how he has kept faith with me, what can I expect for Waltheof the wittol, save that which I have foretold many a time?"

"As for you, dear sire, the king has been misinformed concerning you. I have sent messengers to reason with him again and again; but as long as Taillebois, Warrenne, and Robert Malet had his ear, of what use were my poor words?"

"And what said they?"

"That there would be no peace in England if you were loose."

"They lied. I am no boy, like Waltheof. I know when the game is played out. And it is played out now. The Frenchman is master, and I know it well. Were I loose to-morrow, and as great a fool as Waltheof, what could I do, with, it may be, some forty knights and a hundred men-at-arms, against all William's armies? But how goes on this fool's rebellion? If I had been loose I might have helped to crush it in the bud."

"And you would have done that against Waltheof?"

"Why not against him? He is but bringing more misery on England. Tell that to William. Tell him that if he sets me free, I will be the first to attack Waltheof, or whom he will. There are no English left to fight against," said he, bitterly, "for Waltheof is none now."

"He shall know your words when he returns to England."

"What, is he abroad, and all this evil going on?"

"In Normandy. But the English have risen for the King in Herefordshire, and beaten Earl Roger; and Odo of Bayeux and Bishop Mowbray are on their way to Cambridge, where they hope to give a good account of Earl Ralph; and that the English may help them there."

"And they shall! They hate Ralph Guader as much as I do. Can you send a message for me?"

"Whither?"

"To Bourne in the Bruneswald; and say to Hereward's men, wherever they are, Let them rise and arm, if they love Hereward, and down to Cambridge, to be the foremost at Bishop Odo's side against Ralph Guader, or Waltheof himself. Send! send! O that I were free!"

"Would to Heaven thou wert free, my gallant sir!" said the good man.

From that day Hereward woke up somewhat. He was still a broken man, querulous, peevish; but the hope of freedom and the hope of battle woke him up. If he could but get to his men! But his melancholy returned. His men — some of them at least — went down to Odo at Cambridge, and did good service. Guader was utterly routed, and escaped to Norwich, and thence to Brittany, — his home. The bishops punished their prisoners, the rebel Normans, with horrible mutilations.

"The wolves are beginning to eat each other," said Hereward to himself. But it was a sickening thought to him, that his men had been fighting and he not at their head.

After a while there came to Bedford Castle two witty knaves. One was a cook, who "came to buy milk," says the chronicler; the other seemingly a gleeman. They told stories, jested, harped, sang, drank, and pleased much the garrison and Sir Robert, who let them hang about the place.

They asked next, whether it were true that the famous Hereward was there? If so, might a man have a look at him?

The jailer said that many men might have gone to see him, so easy was Sir Robert to him. But he would have no man; and none dare enter save Sir Robert and he, for fear of their lives. But he would ask him of Herepol.

The good knight of Herepol said, "Let the rogues go in; they may amuse the poor man."

So they went in, and as soon as they went, he knew them. One was Martin Lightfoot, the other Leofric the Unlucky.

"Who sent you?" asked he surlily, turning his face away.

"She."

"Who?"

"We know but one she, and she is at Crowland."

"She sent you? and wherefore?"

"That we might sing to you, and make you merry."

Hereward answered them with a terrible word, and turned his face to the wall, groaning, and then bade them sternly to go.

So they went, for the time.

The jailer told this to Sir Robert, who saw all, being a kind-hearted man.

"From his poor first wife, eh? Well, there can be no harm in that. Nor if they came from this Lady Alftruda either, for that matter; let them go in and out when they will."

"But they may be spies and traitors."

"Then we can but hang them."

Robert of Herepol, it would appear from the chronicle, did not much care whether they were spies or not.

So the men went to and fro, and often sat with Hereward. But he forbade them sternly to mention Torfrida's name.

Alftruda sent to him meanwhile, again and again, messages of passionate love and sorrow, and he listened to them as sullenly as he did to his two servants, and sent no answer back. And so sat more weary months, in the very prison, it may be in the very room, in which John Bunyan sat nigh six hundred years after: but in a very different frame of mind.

One day Sir Robert was going up the stairs with another knight, and met the two coming down. He was talking to that knight earnestly, indignantly: and somehow, as he passed Leofric and Martin he thought fit to raise his voice, as if in a great wrath.

"Shame to all honor and chivalry! good saints in heaven, what a thing is human fortune! That this man, who had once a gallant army at his back, should be at this moment going like a sheep to the slaughter, to Buckingham Castle, at the mercy of his worst enemy, Ivo Taillebois, of all men in the world. If there were a dozen knights left of all those whom he used to heap with wealth and honor, worthy the name of knights, they would catch us between here and Stratford, and make a free man of their lord."

So spake — or words to that effect, according to the Latin chronicler, who must have got them from Leofric himself — the good knight of Herepol.

"Hillo, knaves!" said he, seeing the two, "are you here eavesdropping? out of the castle this instant, on your lives."

Which hint those two witty knaves took on the spot.

A few days after, Hereward was travelling toward Buckingham, chained upon a horse, with Sir Robert and his men, and a goodly company of knights belonging to Ivo. Ivo, as the story runs, seems to have arranged with Ralph Pagnel at Buckingham to put him into the keeping of a creature of his own. And how easy it was to put out a man's eyes, or starve him to death, in a Norman keep, none knew better than Hereward.

But he was past fear or sorrow. A dull heavy cloud of despair had settled down upon his soul. Black with sin, his heart could not pray. He had hardened himself against all heaven and earth, and thought, when he thought at all, only of his wrongs: but never of his sins.

They passed through a forest, seemingly somewhere near what is Newport Pagnel, named after Ralph, his would-be jailer.

Suddenly from the trees dashed out a body of knights, and at their head the white-bear banner, in Ranald of Ramsey's hand.

"Halt!" shouted Sir Robert; "we are past the half-way stone. Earl Ivo's and Earl Ralph's men are answerable now for the prisoner."

"Treason!" shouted Ivo's men, and one would have struck Hereward through with his lance; but Winter was too quick for him, and bore him from his saddle; and then dragged Hereward out of the fight.

The Normans, surprised while their helmets were hanging at their saddles, and their arms not ready for battle, were scattered at once. But they returned to the attack, confident in their own numbers.

They were over confident. Hereward's fetters were knocked off; and he was horsed and armed, and, mad with freedom and battle, fighting like himself once more.

Only as he rode to and fro, thrusting and hewing, he shouted to his men to spare Sir Robert, and all his meinie, crying that he was the savior of his life; and when the fight was over, and all Ivo's and Ralph's men who were not slain had ridden for their lives into Stratford, he shook hands with that venerable knight, giving him innumerable thanks and courtesies for his honorable keeping; and begged him to speak well of him to the king.

And so these two parted in peace, and Hereward was a free man.

CHAPTER XLI.

HOW EARL WALTHEOF WAS MADE A SAINT.

A FEW months after, there sat in Abbot Thorold's lodgings in Peterborough a select company of Normans, talking over affairs of state after their supper.

"Well, earls and gentlemen," said the Abbot, as he sipped his wine, "the cause of our good king, which is happily the cause of Holy Church, goes well, I think. We have much to be thankful for when we review the events of the past year. We have finished the rebels; Roger de Breteuil is safe in prison, Ralph Guader unsafe in Brittany, and Waltheof more than unsafe in — the place to which traitors descend. We have not a manor left which is not in loyal Norman hands; we have not an English monk left who has not been scourged and starved into holy obedience; not an English saint for whom any man cares a jot, since Guerin de Lire preached down St. Adhelm, the admirable primate disposed of St. Alphege's martyrdom, and some other wise man — I am ashamed to say that I forget who — proved that St. Edmund of Suffolk was merely a barbarian knight, who was killed fighting with Danes only a little more heathen than himself. We have had great labors and great sufferings since we landed in this barbarous isle upon our holy errand ten years since; but, under the shadow of the gonfalon of St. Peter, we have conquered, and may sing 'Dominus Illuminatio mea,' with humble and thankful hearts."

"I don't know that," said Ascelin, "my Lord Uncle; I shall never sing 'Dominus Illuminatio' till I see your coffers illuminated once more by those thirty thousand marks."

"Or I," said Oger le Breton, "till I see myself safe in that bit of land which Hereward holds wrongfully of me in Locton."

"Or I," said Ivo Taillebois, "till I see Hereward's head on Bourne gable, where he stuck up those Norman's heads seven years ago. But what the Lord Abbot means by saying that we have done with English saints I do not see, for the villains of Crowland have just made a new one for themselves"

"A new one?"

"I tell you truth and fact; I will tell you all, Lord Abbot; and you shall judge whether it is not enough to drive an honest man mad to see such things going on under his nose. Men say of me that I am rough, and swear and blaspheme. I put it to you, Lord Abbot, if Job would not have cursed if he had been Lord of Spalding? You know that the king let these Crowland monks have Waltheof's body?"

"Yes, I thought it an unwise act of grace. It would have been wiser to leave him, as he desired, out on the down, in ground unconsecrate."

"Of course, of course; for what has happened?"

"That old traitor, Ulfketyl, and his monks bring the body to Crowland, and bury it as if it had been the Pope's. In a week they begin to spread their lies, — that Waltheof was innocent; that Archbishop Lanfranc himself said so."

"That was the only act of human weakness which I have ever known the venerable prelate commit," said Thorold.

"That these Normans at Winchester were so in the traitor's favor, that the king had to have him out and cut off his head in the gray of the morning, ere folks were up and about; that the fellow was so holy that he past all his time in prison in weeping and praying, and said over the whole Psalter every day, because his mother had taught it him, — I wish she had taught him to be an honest man; — and that when his head was on the block he said all the Paternoster, as far as Lead us not into temptation, and then off went his head; whereon, his head being off, finished the prayer with — you know best what comes next, Abbot?"

"Deliver us from evil, Amen! What a manifest lie! The traitor was not permitted, it is plain, to ask for that which could never be granted to him, but his soul, unworthy to be delivered from evil, entered instead into evil, and howls forever in the pit."

"But all the rest may be true," said Oger; "and yet that be no reason why these monks should say it."

"So I told them, and threatened them too; for, not content with making him a martyr, they are making him a saint."

"Impious! Who can do that, save the Holy Father?" said Thorold.

"You had best get your bishop to look to them, then, for they are carrying blind beggars and mad girls by the dozen to be cured at the man's tomb, that is all. Their fellows in the cell at Spalding went about to take a girl that had fits off one of my manors, to cure her; but that I stopped with a good horsewhip."

"And rightly."

"And gave the monks a piece of my mind, and drove them clean out of their cell home to Crowland."

What a piece of Ivo's mind on this occasion might be, let Ingulf describe.

"Against our monastery and all the people of Crowland he was, by the instigation of the Devil, raised to such an extreme pitch of fury, that he would follow their animals in the marshes with his dogs, drive them to a great distance down in the lakes, mutilate some in the tails, others in the ears, while often, by breaking the backs and legs of the beasts of burden, he rendered them utterly useless. Against our cell also (at Spalding) and our brethren, his neighbors, the prior and monks, who dwelt all day within his presence, he rages with tyrannical and frantic fury, lamed their oxen and horses, daily impounded their sheep and poultry, striking down, killing, and slaying their swine and pigs; while at the same time the servants of the prior were oppressed in the Earl's court with insupportable exactions, were often assaulted in the highways with swords and staves, and sometimes killed."

"Well," went on the injured Earl, "this Hereward gets news of me, — and news too, I don't know whence, but true enough it is, — that I had sworn to drive Ulfketyl out of Crowland by writ from king and bishop, and lock him up as a minister at the other end of England."

"You will do but right. I will send a knight off to the king this day, telling him all, and begging him to send us up a trusty Norman as abbot of Crowland, that we may have one more gentleman in the land fit for our company."

"You must kill Hereward first. For, as I was going to say, he sent word to me 'that the monks of Crowland were as the apple of his eye, and Abbot Ulfketyl to him as more than a father; and that if I dared to lay a finger on them or their property, he would cut my head off.'"

"He has promised to cut my head off likewise," said Ascelin. "Earl, knights, and gentlemen, do you not think it wiser that we should lay our wits together once and for all, and cut off his."

"But who will catch the Wake sleeping?" said Ivo, laughing.

"That will I. I have my plans, and my intelligencers."

And so those wicked men took counsel together to slay Hereward.

CHAPTER XLII.

HOW HEREWARD GOT THE REST OF HIS SOUL'S PRICE.

IN those days a messenger came riding post to Bourne. The Countess Judith wished to visit the tomb of her late husband, Earl Waltheof; and asked hospitality on her road of Hereward and Alftruda.

Of course she would come with a great train, and the trouble and expense would be great. But the hospitality of those days, when money was scarce, and wine scarcer still, was unbounded, and a matter of course; and Alftruda was overjoyed. No doubt, Judith was the most unpopular person in England at that moment; called by all a traitress and a fiend. But she was an old acquaintance of Alftruda's; she was the king's niece; she was immensely rich, not only in manors of her own, but in manors, as Domesday-book testifies, about Lincolnshire and the counties round, which had belonged to her murdered husband, — which she had too probably received as the price of her treason. So Alftruda looked to her visit as to an honor which would enable her to hold her head high among the proud Norman dames, who despised her as the wife of an Englishman.

Hereward looked on the visit in a different light. He called Judith ugly names, not undeserved; and vowed that if she entered his house by the front door he would go out at the back. "Torfrida prophesied," he said, "that she would betray her husband, and she had done it."

"Torfrida prophesied? Did she prophesy that I should betray you likewise?" asked Alftruda, in a tone of bitter scorn.

"No, you handsome fiend: will you do it?"

"Yes; I am a handsome fiend, am I not?" and she bridled up her magnificent beauty, and stood over him as a snake stands over a mouse.

"Yes; you are handsome, — beautiful: I adore you."

"And yet you will not do what I wish?"

"What you wish? What would I not do for you? what have I not done for you?"

"Then receive Judith. And now, go hunting, and bring me in game. I want deer, roe, fowls; anything and everything from the greatest to the smallest. Go and hunt."

And Hereward trembled, and went.

There are flowers whose scent is so luscious that silly children will plunge their heads among them, drinking in their odor, to the exclusion of all fresh air. On a sudden sometimes comes a revulsion of the nerves. The sweet odor changes in a moment to a horrible one; and the child cannot bear for years after the scent which has once disgusted it by over-sweetness.

And so had it happened to Hereward. He did not love Alftruda now: he loathed, hated, dreaded her. And yet he could not take his eyes for a moment off her beauty. He watched every movement of her hand, to press it, obey it. He would have preferred instead of hunting, simply to sit and watch her go about the house at her work. He was spell-bound to a thing which he regarded with horror.

But he was told to go and hunt; and he went, with all his men, and sent home large supplies for the larder. And as he hunted, the free, fresh air of the forest comforted him, the free forest life came back to him, and he longed to be an outlaw once more, and hunt on forever. He would not go back yet, at least to face that Judith. So he sent back the greater part of his men with a story. He was ill; he was laid up at a farm-house far away in the forest, and begged the countess to excuse his absence. He had sent fresh supplies of game, and a goodly company of his men, knights and housecarles, who would escort her royally to Crowland.

Judith cared little for his absence; he was but an English barbarian. Alftruda was half glad to have him out of the way, lest his now sullen and uncertain temper should break out; and bowed herself to the earth before Judith, who patronized her to her heart's content, and offered her slyly insolent condolences on being married to a barbarian. She herself could sympathize, — who more?

Alftruda might have answered with scorn that she was an Adeliza, and of better English blood than Judith's Norman blood; but she had her ends to gain, and gained them.

For Judith was pleased to be so delighted with her that she kissed her lovingly, and said with much emotion that she required a friend who would support her through her coming trial; and who better than one who herself had suffered so much? Would she accompany her to Crowland?

Alftruda was overjoyed, and away they went.

And to Crowland they came; and to the tomb in the minster, whereof men said already that the sacred corpse within worked miracles of healing.

And Judith, habited in widow's weeds, approached the tomb.

and laid on it, as a peace-offering to the manes of the dead, a splendid pall of silk and gold.

A fierce blast came howling off the fen, screeched through the minster towers, swept along the dark aisles; and then, so say the chroniclers, caught up the pall from off the tomb, and hurled it far away into a corner.

"A miracle!" cried all the monks at once; and honestly enough, like true Englishmen as they were.

"The Holy heart refuses the gift, Countess," said old Ulfketyl in a voice of awe.

Judith covered her face with her hands, and turned away trembling, and walked out, while all looked upon her as a thing accursed.

Of her subsequent life, her folly, her wantonness, her disgrace, her poverty, her wanderings, her wretched death, let others tell.

But these Normans believed that the curse of Heaven was upon her from that day. And the best of them believed likewise that Waltheof's murder was the reason that William, her uncle, prospered no more in life.

"Ah, saucy sir," said Alftruda to Ulfketyl, as she went out, "there is one waiting at Peterborough now who will teach thee manners, — Ingulf of Fontenelle, Abbot, in thy room."

"Does Hereward know that?" asked Ulfketyl, looking keenly at her.

"What is that to thee?" said she, fiercely, and flung out of the minster. But Hereward did not know. There were many things abroad of which she told him nothing.

They went back and were landed at Deeping town, and making their way along the King Street, or old Roman road, to Bourne. Thereon a man met them, running. They had best stay where they were. The Frenchmen were out, and there was fighting up in Bourne.

Alftruda's knights wanted to push on, to see after the Bourne folk; Judith's knights wanted to push on to help the French: and the two parties were ready to fight each other. There was a great tumult. The ladies had much ado to still it.

Alftruda said that it might be but a countryman's rumor; that, at least, it was shame to quarrel with their guests. At last it was agreed that two knights should gallop on into Bourne, and bring back news.

But those knights never came back. So the whole body moved on Bourne, and there they found out the news for themselves.

Hereward had gone home as soon as they had departed, and sat down to eat and drink. His manner was sad and strange.

He drank much at the midday meal, and then lay down to sleep, setting guards as usual.

After a while he leapt up with a shriek and a shudder. They ran to him, asking whether he was ill.

"Ill? No. Yes. Ill at heart. I have had a dream,—an ugly dream. I thought that all the men I ever slew on earth came to me with their wounds all gaping, and cried at me, Our luck then, thy luck now.' Chaplain! is there not a verse somewhere,—Uncle Brand said it to me on his deathbed,—'Whoso sheddeth man's blood, by man shall his blood be shed'?"

"Surely the master is fey," whispered Guenock in fear to the chaplain. "Answer him out of Scripture."

"Text? None such that I know of," quoth Priest Ailward, a graceless fellow who had taken Leofric's place. "If that were the law, it would be but few honest men that would die in their beds. Let us drink, and drive girls' fancies out of our heads."

So they drank again; and Hereward fell asleep once more.

"It is thy turn to watch, Priest," said Guenock to Ailward. "So keep the door well, for I am worn out with hunting," and so fell asleep.

Ailward shuffled into his harness, and went to the door. The wine was heady; the sun was hot. In a few minutes he was asleep likewise.

Hereward slept, who can tell how long? But at last there was a bustle, a heavy fall; and waking with a start, he sprang up. He saw Ailward lying dead across the gate, and above him a crowd of fierce faces, some of which he knew too well. He saw Ivo Taillebois; he saw Óger; he saw his fellow-Breton, Sir Raoul de Dol; he saw Sir Ascelin; he saw Sir Aswa, Thorold's man; he saw Sir Hugh of Evermue, his own son-in-law; and with them he saw, or seemed to see, the Ogre of Cornwall, and O'Brodar of Ivark, and Dirk Hammerhand of Walcheren, and many another old foe long underground; and in his ear rang the text,—"Whoso sheddeth man's blood, by man shall his blood be shed." And Hereward knew that his end was come.

There was no time to put on mail or helmet. He saw the old sword and shield hang on a perch, and tore them down. As he girded the sword on Winter sprang to his side.

"I have three lances,—two for me and one for you, and we can hold the door against twenty."

"Till they fire the house over our heads. Shall Hereward die like a wolf in a cave? Forward, all Hereward's men!"

And he rushed out upon his fate. No man followed him, save

Winter. The rest, disperst, unarmed, were running hither and thither helplessly.

"Brothers in arms, and brothers in Valhalla!" shouted Winter as he rushed after him.

A knight was running to and fro in the Court, shouting Hereward's name. "Where is the villain? Wake! We have caught thee asleep at last."

"I am out," quoth Hereward, as the man almost stumbled against him; "and this is in."

And through shield, hauberk, and body, as says Gaima, went Hereward's javelin, while all drew back, confounded for the moment at that mighty stroke.

"Felons!" shouted Hereward, "your king has given me his truce; and do you dare break my house, and kill my folk? Is that your Norman law? And is this your Norman honor? — To take a man unawares over his meat? Come on, traitors all, and get what you can of a naked man;* you will buy it dear — Guard my back, Winter!"

And he ran right at the press of knights; and the fight began.

"He gored them like a wood-wild boar,
As long as that lance might endure,"

says Gaimar.

"And when that lance did break in hand,
Full fell enough he smote with brand."

And as he hewed on silently, with grinding teeth and hard, glittering eyes, of whom did he think? Of Alftruda?

Not so. But of that pale ghost, with great black hollow eyes, who sat in Crowland, with thin bare feet, and sackcloth on her tender limbs, watching, praying, longing, loving, uncomplaining. That ghost had been for many a month the background of all his thoughts and dreams. It was so clear before his mind's eye now, that, unawares to himself, he shouted Torfrida! as he struck, and struck the harder at the sound of his old battle-cry.

And now he is all wounded and be-bled; and Winter, who has fought back to back with him, has fallen on his face; and Hereward stands alone, turning from side to side, as he sweeps his sword right and left till the forest rings with the blows, but staggering as he turns. Within a ring of eleven corpses he stands. Who will go in and make the twelfth?

A knight rushes in, to fall headlong down, cloven through the helm: but Hereward's blade snaps short, and he hurls it away as his foes rush in with a shout of joy. He tears his shield from his left arm, and with it, says Gaimar, brains two more.

* I. e. without armor.

But the end is come. Taillebois and Evermue are behind him now; four lances are through his back, and bear him down to his knees.

"Cut off his head, Breton!" shouted Ivo. Raoul de Dol .ushed forward, sword in hand. At that cry Hereward lifted up his dying head. One stroke more ere it was all done forever.

And with a shout of "Torfrida!" which made the Bruneswald ring, he hurled the shield full in the Breton's face, and fell forward dead.

The knights drew their lances from that terrible corpse slowly and with caution, as men who have felled a bear, yet dare not step within reach of the seemingly lifeless paw.

"The dog died hard," said Ivo. "Lucky for us that Sir Ascelin had news of his knights being gone to Crowland. If he had had them to back him, we had not done this deed to-day."

"I will make sure," said Ascelin, as he struck off the once fair and golden head.

"Ho, Breton," cried Ivo, "the villain is dead. Get up, man, and see for yourself. What ails him?"

But when they lifted up Raoul de Dol his brains were running down his face; and all men stood astonished at that last mighty stroke.

"That blow," said Ascelin, "will be sung hereafter by minstrel and maiden as the last blow of the last Englishman. Knights, we have slain a better knight than ourselves. If there had been three more such men in this realm, they would have driven us and King William back again into the sea."

So said Ascelin; those words of his, too, were sung by many a jougleur, Norman as well as English, in the times that were to come.

"Likely enough," said Ivo; "but that is the more reason why we should set that head of his up over the hall-door, as a warning to these English churls that their last man is dead, and their last stake thrown and lost."

So perished "the last of the English."

It was the third day. The Normans were drinking in the hall of Bourne, casting lots among themselves who should espouse the fair Alftruda, who sat weeping within over the headless corpse; when in the afternoon a servant came in, and told them how a barge full of monks had come to the shore, and that they seemed to be monks from Crowland. Ivo Taillebois bade drive them back again into the barge with whips. But Hugh of Evermue spoke up.

"I am lord and master in Bourne this day, and if Ivo have a quarrel against St. Guthlac, I have none. This Ingulf of Fontenelle, the new abbot who has come thither since old Ulfketyl was sent to prison, is a loyal man, and a friend of King William's, and my friend he shall be till he behaves himself as my foe. Let them come up in peace."

Taillebois growled and cursed: but the monks came up, and .no the hall; and at their head Ingulf himself, to receive whom all men rose, save Taillebois.

"I come," said Ingulf, in most courtly French, "noble knights, to ask a boon and in the name of the Most Merciful, on behalf of a noble and unhappy lady. Let it be enough to have avenged yourself on the living. Gentlemen and Christians war not against the dead."

"No, no, Master Abbot!" shouted Taillebois; "Waltheof is enough to keep Crowland in miracles for the present. You shall not make a martyr of another Saxon churl. He wants the barbarian's body, knights, and you will be fools if you let him have it."

"Churl? barbarian?" said a haughty voice; and a nun stepped forward who had stood just behind Ingulf. She was clothed entirely in black. Her bare feet were bleeding from the stones; her hand, as she lifted it, was as thin as a skeleton's.

She threw back her veil, and showed to the knights what had been once the famous beauty of Torfrida.

But the beauty was long past away. Her hair was white as snow; her cheeks were fallen in. Her hawk-like features were all sharp and hard. Only in their hollow sockets burned still the great black eyes, so fiercely that all men turned uneasily from her gaze.

"Churl? barbarian?" she said, slowly and quietly, but with an intensity which was more terrible than rage. "Who gives such names to one who was as much better born and better bred than those who now sit here, as he was braver and more terrible than they? The base wood-cutter's son? The upstart who would have been honored had he taken service as yon dead man's groom?"

"Talk to me so, and my stirrup leathers shall make acquaintance with your sides," said Taillebois.

"Keep them for your wife. Churl? Barbarian? There is not a man within this hall who is not a barbarian compared with him. Which of you touched the harp like him? Which of you, like him, could move all hearts with song? Which of you knows all tongues from Lapland to Provence? Which of you has been the joy of ladies' bowers, the counsellor of earls and heroes, the rival of a mighty king? Which of you will compare yourself with him, — whom you dared not even strike, you and your robber crew, fairly in front, but skulked round him till he fell pecked to death by you, as Lapland Skratlings peck to death the bear. Ten years ago he swept this hall of such as you, and I ung their heads upon yon gable outside; and were he alive but one five minutes again, this hall would be right cleanly swept again! Give me his body, — or bear forever the name of cowards, and Torfrida's curse."

And she fixed her terrible eyes first on one, and then on another, calling them by name.

"Ivo Taillebois, — basest of all — "

"Take the witch's accursed eyes off me!" and he covered his face with his hands. "I shall be overlooked, — planet struck. Hew the witch down! Take her away!"

"Hugh of Evermue, — the dead man's daughter is yours, and the dead man's lands. Are not these remembrances enough of him? Are you so fond of his memory that you need his corpse .kewise?"

"Give it her! Give it her!" said he, hanging down his head like a rated cur.

"Ascelin of Lincoln, once Ascelin of Ghent, — there was a time when you would have done — what would you not? — for one glance of Torfrida's eyes. — Stay. Do not deceive yourself, fair sir, Torfrida means to ask no favor of you, or of living man. But she commands you. Do the thing she bids, or with one glance of her eye she sends you childless to your grave."

"Madam! Lady Torfrida! What is there I would not do for you? What have I done now, save avenge your great wrong?"

Torfrida made no answer, but fixed steadily on him eyes which widened every moment.

"But, madam," — and he turned shrinking from the fancied spell, — "what would you have? The — the corpse? It is in the keeping of — of another lady."

"So?" said Torfrida, quietly. "Leave her to me"; and she swept past them all, and flung open the bower door at their backs, discovering Alftruda sitting by the dead.

The ruffians were so utterly appalled, not only by the false powers of magic, but by veritable powers of majesty and eloquence, that they let her do what she would.

"Out!" cried she, using a short and terrible epithet. "Out, siren, with fairy's face and tail of fiend, and leave the husband with his wife!"

Alftruda looked up, shrieked; and then, with the sudden passion of a weak nature, drew a little knife, and sprang up.

Ivo made a coarse jest. The Abbot sprang in: "For the sake of all holy things, let there be no more murder here!"

Torfrida smiled, and fixed her snake's eye upon her wretched rival.

"Out! woman, and choose thee a new husband among these French gallants, ere I blast thee from head to foot with the leprosy of Naaman the Syrian."

Alftruda shuddered, and fled shrieking into an inner room.

"Now, knights, give me — that which hangs outside."

Ascelin hurried out, glad to escape. In a minute he returned. The head was already taken down. A tall lay brother, the moment he had seen it, had climbed the gable, snatched it away, and now sat in a corner of the yard, holding it on his knees, talking to it, chiding it, as if it had been alive. When men had offered to take it, he had drawn a battle-axe from under his frock, and threatened to brain all comers. And the monks had warned off Ascelin, saying that the man was mad, and had Berserk fits of superhuman strength and rage.

"He will give it me!" said Torfrida, and went out.

"Look at that gable, foolish head," said the madman. "Ten years agone, you and I took down from thence another head. O foolish head, to get yourself at last up into that same place! Why would you not be ruled by her, you foolish golden head?"

"Martin!" said Torfrida.

"Take it and comb it, mistress, as you used to do. Comb out the golden locks again, fit to shine across the battle-field. She has let them get all tangled into elf-knots, that lazy slut within."

Torfrida took it from his hands, dry-eyed, and went in.

Then the monks silently took up the bier, and all went forth, and down the hill toward the fen. They laid the corpse within the barge, and slowly rowed away.

> And on by Porsand and by Asendyke,
> By winding reaches on, and shining meres
> Between gray reed-ronds and green alder-beds,
> A dirge of monks and wail of women rose
> In vain to Heaven for the last Englishman;
> Then died far off within the boundless mist,
> And left the Norman master of the land.

So Torfrida took the corpse home to Crowland, and buried it in the choir, near the blessed martyr St. Waltheof; after which she did not die, but lived on many years,* spending all day in nursing and feeding the Countess Godiva, and lying all night on Hereward's tomb, and praying that he might find grace and mercy in that day.

And at last Godiva died; and they took her away and buried her with great pomp in her own minter church of Coventry.

---

* If Ingulf can be trusted, Torfrida died about A D. 1085.

And after that Torfrida died likewise; because she had nothing left for which to live. And they laid her in Hereward's grave, and their dust is mingled to this day.

And Leofric the priest lived on to a good old age, and above all things he remembered the deeds and the sins of his master, and wrote them in a book, and this is what remains thereof.

But when Martin Lightfoot died, no man has said; for no man in those days took account of such poor churls and running serving-men.

And Hereward's comrades were all scattered abroad, some maimed, some blinded, some with tongues cut out, to beg by the wayside, or crawl into convents, and then die; while their sisters and daughters, ladies born and bred, were the slaves of grooms and scullions from beyond the sea.

And so, as sang Thorkel Skallason, —

"Cold heart and bloody hand *
Now rule English land."

And after that things waxed even worse and worse, for sixty years and more; all through the reigns of the two Williams, and of Henry Beauclerc, and of Stephen; till men saw visions and portents, and thought that the foul fiend was broken loose on earth. And they whispered oftener and oftener that the soul of Hereward haunted the Bruneswald, where he loved to hunt the dun deer and the roe. And in the Bruneswald, when Henry of Poitou was made abbot,† men saw — let no man think lightly of the marvel which we are about to relate, for it was well known all over the country — upon the Sunday, when men sing, "Exsurge quare, O Domine," many hunters hunting, black, and tall, and loathly, and their hounds were black and ugly with wide eyes, and they rode on black horses and black bucks. And they saw them in the very deer-park of the town of Peterborough, and in all the woods to Stamford; and the monks heard the blasts of the horns which they blew in the night. Men of truth kept watch upon them, and said that there might be well about twenty or thirty horn-blowers. This was seen and heard all that Lent until Easter, and the Norman monks of Peterborough said how it was Hereward, doomed to wander forever with Apollyon and all his crew, because he had stolen the riches of the Golden Borough: but the poor folk knew better, and said that the mighty outlaw was rejoicing in the chase, blowing his horn for Englishmen to rise against the French; and therefore it was that he was seen first on "Arise, O Lord" Sunday.

But they were so sore trodden down that they could never

* Laing's Heimskringla.
† Anglo-Saxon Chronicle, A. D. 1127.

rise; for the French* had filled the land full of castles. "They greatly oppressed the wretched people by making them work at these castles; and when the castles were finished, they filled them with devils and evil men. They took those whom they suspected of having any goods, both men and women, and they put them in prison for their gold and silver, and tortured them with pains unspeakable, for never were any martyrs tormented as these were. They hung some by their feet, and smoked them with foul smoke; some by the thumbs, or by the head, and put burning things on their feet. They put a knotted string round their heads, and twisted it till it went into the brain. They put them in dungeons wherein were adders, and snakes, and toads, and thus wore them out. Some they put into a crucet-house, — that is, into a chest that was short and narrow, and they put sharp stones therein, and crushed the man so that they broke all his bones. There were hateful and grim things called Sachenteges in many of the castles, which two or three men had enough to do to carry. This Sachentege was made thus: It was fastened to a beam, having a sharp iron to go round a man's throat and neck, so that he might no ways sit, nor lie, nor sleep, but he must bear all the iron. Many thousands they wore out with hunger.... They were continually levying a tax from the towns, which they called Truserie, and when the wretched townsfolk had no more to give, then burnt they all the towns, so that well mightest thou walk a whole day's journey or ever thou shouldest see a man settled in a town, or its lands tilled....

"Then was corn dear, and flesh, and cheese, and butter, for there was none in the land. Wretched men starved with hunger. Some lived on alms who had been once rich. Some fled the country. Never was there more misery, and never heathens acted worse than these."

For now the sons of the Church's darlings, of the Crusaders whom the Pope had sent, beneath a gonfalon blessed by him, to destroy the liberties of England, turned, by a just retribution, upon that very Norman clergy who had abetted all their iniquities in the name of Rome. "They spared neither church nor churchyard, but took all that was valuable therein, and then burned the church and all together. Neither did they spare the lands of bishops, nor of abbots, nor of priests; but they robbed the monks and clergy, and every man plundered his neighbor as much as he could. If two or three men came riding to a town, all the townsfolk fled before them, and thought that they were robbers. The bishops and clergy were forever cursing them but this to them was nothing, for they were all accursed and for-

* Anglo-Saxon Chronicle, A. D. 1137.

sworn and reprobate. The earth bare no corn: you might as well have tilled the sea, for all the land was ruined by such deeds, and it was said openly that Christ and his saints slept."

And so was avenged the blood of Harold and his brothers, of Edwin and Morcar, of Waltheof and Hereward.

And those who had the spirit of Hereward in them fled to the merry greenwood, and became bold outlaws, with Robin Hood, Scarlet, and John, Adam Bell, and Clym of the Cleugh, and William of Cloudeslee; and watched with sullen joy the Norman robbers tearing in pieces each other, and the Church who had blest their crime.

And they talked and sung of Hereward, and all his doughty deeds, over the hearth in lone farm-houses, or in the outlaw's lodge beneath the hollins green; and all the burden of their song was, "Ah that Hereward were alive again!" for they knew not that Hereward was alive forevermore; that only his husk and shell lay mouldering there in Crowland choir; that above them, and around them, and in them, destined to raise them out of that bitter bondage, and mould them into a great nation, and the parents of still greater nations in lands as yet unknown, brooded the immortal spirit of Hereward, now purged from all earthly dross, even the spirit of Freedom, which can never die.

CHAPTER XLIII.

HOW DEEPING FEN WAS DRAINED.

ILL war and disorder, ruin and death, cannot last forever They are by their own nature exceptional and suicidal, and spend themselves with what they feed on. And then the true laws of God's universe, peace and order, usefulness and life, will reassert themselves, as they have been waiting all along to do, hid in God's presence from the strife of men.

And even so it was with Bourne.

Nearly eighty years after, in the year of Grace 1155, there might have been seen sitting, side by side and hand in hand, upon a sunny bench on the Bruneswald slope, in the low December sun, an old knight and an old lady, the master and mistress of Bourne.

Much had changed since Hereward's days. The house below had been raised a whole story. There were fresh herbs and flowers in the garden, unknown at the time of the Conquest. But the great change was in the fen, especially away toward Deeping on the southern horizon.

Where had been lonely meres, foul watercourses, stagnant slime, there were now great dikes, rich and fair corn and grass lands, rows of pure white cottages. The newly-drained land swarmed with stocks of new breeds: horses and sheep from Flanders, cattle from Normandy; for Richard de Rulos was the first — as far as history tells — of that noble class of agricultural squires, who are England's blessing and England's pride.

"For this Richard de Rulos," says Ingulf, or whoever wrote in his name, "who had married the daughter and heiress of Hugh of Evermue, Lord of Bourne and Deeping, being a man of agricultural pursuits, got permission from the monks of Crowland, for twenty marks of silver, to enclose as much as he would of the common marshes. So he shut out the Welland by a strong embankment, and building thereon numerous tenements and cottages, in a short time he formed a large 'vill,' marked out gardens, and cultivated fields; while, by shutting out the river, he found in the meadow land, which had been lately deep lakes and impassable marshes (wherefore the place was called Deeping, the deep meadow), most fertile fields and desirable lands, and out of sloughs and bogs accursed made quiet a garden of pleasaunce."

So there the good man, the beginner of the good work of centuries, sat looking out over the fen, and listening to the music which came on the southern breeze — above the low of the kine, and the clang of the wild-fowl settling down to rest — from the bells of Crowland minster far away.

They were not the same bells which tolled for Hereward and Torfrida. Those had run down in molten streams upon that fatal night when Abbot Ingulf leaped out of bed to see the vast wooden sanctuary wrapt in one sheet of roaring flame, from the carelessness of a plumber who had raked the ashes over his fire in the bell-tower, and left it to smoulder through the night.

Then perished all the riches of Crowland; its library too, of more than seven hundred volumes, with that famous Nadir or Orrery, the like whereof was not in all England, wherein the seven planets were represented, each in their proper metals. And even worse, all the charters of the monastery perished, a loss which involved the monks thereof in centuries of lawsuits, and compelled them to become as industrious and skilful forgers of documents as were to be found in the minsters of the middle age.

But Crowland minster had been rebuilt in greater glory than ever, by the help of the Norman gentry round. Abbot Ingulf, finding that St. Guthlac's plain inability to take care of himself had discredited him much in the fen-men's eyes, fell back, Norman as he was, on the virtues of the holy martyr, St. Waltheof, whose tomb he opened with due reverence, and found the body as whole and uncorrupted as on the day on which it was buried: and the head united to the body, while a fine crimson line around the neck was the only sign remaining of his decollation.

On seeing which Ingulf "could not contain himself for joy: and interrupting the response which the brethren were singing, with a loud voice began the hymn 'Te Deum Laudamus,' on which the chanter taking it up, enjoined the rest of the brethren to sing it." After which Ingulf — who had never seen Waltheof in life, discovered that it was none other than he whom he had seen in a vision at Fontenelle, as an earl most gorgeously arrayed, with a torc of gold about his neck, and with him an abbot, two bishops, and two saints, the two former being Usfran and Ausbert, the abbots, St. Wandresigil of Fontenelle, and the two saints, of course St. Guthlac and St. Neot.

Whereon, crawling on his hands and knees, he kissed the face of the holy martyr, and "perceived such a sweet odor proceeding from the holy body, as he never remembered to have smelt, either in the palace of the king, or in Syria with all its aromatic herbs."

Quid plura? What more was needed for a convent of burnt-out monks? St. Waltheof was translated in state to the side of St. Guthlac; and the news of this translation of the holy martyr being spread throughout the country, multitudes of the faithful flocked daily to the tomb, and offering up their vows there, tended in a great degree " to resuscitate our monastery."

But more. The virtues of St. Waltheof were too great not to turn themselves, or be turned, to some practical use. So if not in the days of Ingulf, at least in those of Abbot Joffrid who came after him, St. Waltheof began, says Peter of Blois. to work wonderful deeds. " The blind received their sight, the deaf their hearing, the lame their power of walking, and the dumb their power of speech; while each day troops innumerable of other sick persons were arriving by every road, as to the very fountain of their safety, ... and by the offerings of the pilgrims who came flocking in from every part, the revenues of the monastery were increased in no small degree."

Only one wicked Norman monk of St. Alban's, Audwin by name, dared to dispute the sanctity of the martyr, calling him a wicked traitor who had met with his deserts. In vain did Abbot Joffrid, himself a Norman from St. Evroult, expostulate with the inconvenient blasphemer. He launched out into invective beyond measure; till on the spot, in presence of the said father, he was seized with such a stomach-ache, that he went home to St. Alban's, and died in a few days; after which all went well with Crowland, and the Norman monks who worked the English martyr to get money out of the English whom they had enslaved.

And yet,— so strangely mingled for good and evil are the works of men,— that lying brotherhood of Crowland set up, in those very days, for pure love of learning and of teaching learning, a little school of letters in a poor town hard by, which became, under their auspices, the University of Cambridge.

So the bells of Crowland were restored, more melodious than ever; and Richard of Rulos doubtless had his share in their restoration. And that day they were ringing with a will, and for a good reason; for that day had come the news, that Henry Plantagenet was crowned king of England.

"' Lord,'" said the good old knight, "' now lettest thou thy servant depart in peace.' This day, at last, he sees an English king head the English people."

" God grant," said the old lady, " that he may be such a lord to England as thou hast been to Bourne."

" If he will be,— and better far will he be, by God's grace, from what I hear of him, than ever I have been,-- he must learn that which I learnt from thee, — to understand these Englishmen, and know what stout and trusty prudhommes they are all, down to the meanest serf, when once one can humor their sturdy independent tempers."

"And he must learn, too, the lesson which thou didst teach me, when I would have had thee, in the pride of youth, put on the magic armor of my ancestors, and win me fame in every tournament and battle-field Blessed be the day when Richard of Rulos said to me, 'If others dare to be men of war, I dare more; for I dare to be a man of peace. Have patience with me, and I will win for thee and for myself a renown more lasting, before God and man, than ever was won with lance!' Do you remember those words, Richard mine?"

The old man leant his head upon his hands. "It may be that not those words, but the deeds which God has caused to follow them, may, by Christ's merits, bring us a short purgatory and a long heaven."

"Amen. Only whatever grief we may endure in the next life for our sins, may we endure it as we have the griefs of this life, hand in hand."

"Amen, Torfrida. There is one thing more to do before we die. The tomb in Crowland. Ever since the fire blackened it, it has seemed to me too poor and mean to cover the dust which once held two such noble souls. Let us send over to Normandy for fair white stone of Caen, and let carve a tomb worthy of thy grandparents."

"And what shall we write thereon?"

"What but that which is there already? 'Here lies the last of the English.'"

"Not so. We will write, — 'Here lies the last of the old English.' But upon thy tomb, when thy time comes, the monks of Crowland shall write, — 'Here lies the first of the new English; who, by the inspiration of God, began to drain the Fens.'"

EXPLICIT.

Novels by F. Marion Crawford.

Just Published. 12mo, extra cloth, $1.25.
A CIGARETTE-MAKER'S ROMANCE.

12mo, extra cloth, $1.25.

MR. ISAACS.

A Tale of Modern India. 12mo, $1.50.

If considered only as a semi-love story it is exceptionally fascinating, but when judged as a literary effort it is truly great.—*Home Journal.*

Under an unpretentious title we have here the most brilliant novel, or rather romance, that has been given to the world for a very long time.—*The American.*

DOCTOR CLAUDIUS.

A True Story. 12mo, $1.50.

An interesting and attractive story, and in some directions a positive advance upon "Mr. Isaacs."—*New York Tribune.*

"Doctor Claudius" is surprisingly good, coming after a story of so much merit as "Mr. Isaacs." The hero is a magnificent specimen of humanity, and sympathetic readers will be fascinated by his chivalrous wooing of the beautiful American countess.—*Boston Traveller.*

ZOROASTER.

12mo, $1.50.

The novel opens with a magnificent description of the march of the Babylonian court to Belshazzar's feast, with the sudden and awful ending of the latter by the marvelous writing on the wall which Daniel is called to interpret. From that point the story moves on in a series of grand and dramatic scenes and incidents which will not fail to hold the reader fascinated and spellbound to the end.
—*Christian at Work.*

A TALE OF A LONELY PARISH.

12mo, $1.50.

It is a pleasure to have anything so perfect of its kind as this brief and vivid story. . . . It is doubly a success, being full of human sympathy, as well as thoroughly artistic in its nice balancing of the unusual with the commonplace, the clever juxtaposition of innocence and guilt, comedy and tragedy, simplicity and intrigue.—*Critic.*

Mr. Crawford's management of this stock personage is highly effective, all the situations in which he figures are dramatic, the difficult scene of his first meeting with the wife is admirably done, and the closing chapter is one of the strongest, and at the same time one of the most natural, pieces of writing that any author has given us.—*New York Tribune.*

MACMILLAN & CO.,
112 Fourth Avenue, New York.

Novels by F. Marion Crawford.

SARACINESCA. 12mo, cloth, $1.50.

His highest achievement, as yet, in the realms of fiction. The work has two distinct merits, either of which would serve to make it great—that of telling a perfect story in a perfect way, and of giving a graphic picture of Roman society in the last days of the Pope's temporal power. . . . The story is exquisitely told.—*Boston Traveller.*

One of the most engrossing novels we have ever read.—*Boston Times.*

Will add greatly to his reputation as a novelist. . . . If "Saracinesca" receives its deserts from the reading public, it will be the most popular, as it is the most admirable, of its author's works. The interest of the story is kept up from its beginning to its close.—*Mail and Express.*

MARZIO'S CRUCIFIX. 12mo, cloth, $1.50.

Mr. Crawford is a thorough artist, and he has here given a masterly tale, full of the most delicate and truthful character drawing, and with exquisite coloring. In the midst of the feverish and morbid novels of the day, it is a genuine relief to come upon such a sweet and wholesome story as this.—*Albany Argus.*

Now this is brought out in this little story with a firmness of touch, a power and skill which belong to the first rank in art. . . . we take the liberty of saying that this work belongs to the highest department of character painting in words.
—*Churchman.*

WITH THE IMMORTALS. 12mo, cloth, $2.00.

Altogether an admirable piece of art worked in the spirit of a thorough artist. Every reader of cultivated tastes will find it a book prolific in entertainment of the most refined description, and to all such we commend it heartily.
—*Boston Saturday Evening Gazette.*

There is enough food for many a day, even for many a year in Cæsar's sad reflections, in Heine's cynical tenderness, Johnson's rugged, simple, overbearing goodness, Da Vinci's scholarly majesty, and even in the coarser nature of Francis . . . this book will live long, and be more and more cherished; may, indeed, find itself with the immortals in reality as well as in name.—*Boston Herald.*

GREIFENSTEIN. 12mo, cloth, $1.50.

"Greifenstein" is a very strong and well-written story, full of dramatic situations, fine scenic description, subtle argument, and succinct narrative. . . . It is evident that the conception upon which he has worked took strong hold upon him, and that the sense of the play of destiny in the development of the career and its counteraction by the purity and high vitality of Hilda was as present to him as is the story. Hilda is, indeed, a remarkable character. . . . But there are really no dummies in this novel, which is no less original and fresh than powerful and interesting, and which we are inclined to rank as the best piece of work the author has yet done.—*New York Tribune.*

SANT' ILARIO. 12mo, cloth, $1.50.

The author shows steady and constant improvement in his art. "Sant' Ilario" is a continuation of the chronicles of the Saracinesca family. . . . A singularly powerful and beautiful story. . . . Admirably developed, with a naturalness beyond praise. . . . It must rank with "Greifenstein" as the best work the author has produced. It fulfils every requirement of artistic fiction. It brings out what is most impressive in human character, and what is most interesting in human action, without owing any of its effectiveness to sensationalism or artifice. It is natural, fluent in evolution, accordant with experience, graphic in description, penetrating in analysis, and absorbing in interest.—*New York Tribune.*

It is unique in style, intensely dramatic in composition, and certain to hold the attention of the reader from the beginning to the end.—*Journal of Commerce.*

MACMILLAN & CO.,
112 Fourth Avenue, New York.

NEW UNIFORM EDITION OF

CHARLOTTE M. YONGE'S NOVELS AND TALES.

12mo. $1.00 each volume.

———•———

THE HEIR OF REDCLYFFE. Illustrated.
HEARTSEASE. Illustrated.
HOPES AND FEARS. Illustrated.
DYNEVOR TERRACE. Illustrated.
THE DAISY CHAIN. Illustrated.
THE TRIAL: More Links of the Daisy Chain. Illustrated.
PILLARS OF THE HOUSE; or, Under Wode Under Rode. 2 vols. Illustrated.
THE YOUNG STEPMOTHER. Illustrated.
THE CLEVER WOMAN OF THE FAMILY. Illustrated.
THE THREE BRIDES. Illustrated.
MY YOUNG ALCIDES. Illustrated.
THE CAGED LION. Illustrated.
THE DOVE IN THE EAGLE'S NEST. Illustrated.
THE CHAPLET OF PEARLS. Illustrated.
LADY HESTER, AND THE DANVERS PAPERS. Illustrated.
MAGNUM BONUM. Illustrated.
LOVE AND LIFE. Illustrated.
UNKNOWN TO HISTORY. A Story of the Captivity of Mary of Scotland.
STRAY PEARLS. Memoirs of Margaret de Ribaumont, Viscountess of Belaise.
THE ARMOURER'S 'PRENTICES.
THE TWO SIDES OF THE SHIELD.
NUTTIE'S FATHER.
SCENES AND CHARACTERS; or, Eighteen Months at Beechcroft.
CHANTRY HOUSE.
A MODERN TELEMACHUS.
BEECHCROFT AT ROCKSTONE.
WOMANKIND. A Book for Mothers and Daughters.
A REPUTED CHANGELING; or, Three Seventh Years, Two Centuries Ago.

———

MACMILLAN & CO.,

112 FOURTH AVENUE, NEW YORK.

NEW UNIFORM EDITION

OF THE COLLECTED

WORKS OF CHARLES KINGSLEY.

In 12mo, cloth extra, price $1.25 each.

Westward Ho!
Hypatia.
Yeast.
Alton Locke.
Two Years Ago.
Hereward the Wake.
Poems.
The Heroes.
The Water-Babies.
Madame How and Lady Why.
At Last.
Prose Idylls.
Plays and Puritans, and Other Historical Essays.
The Roman and the Teuton.

Sanitary and Social Lectures and Essays.
Historical Lectures and Essays.
Scientific Lectures and Essays.
Literary and General Lectures.
The Hermits. Illustrated.
Glaucus, or the Wonders of the Shore. With Colored Illustrations.
Village Sermons and Town and Country Sermons.
The Good News of God.
Sermons on National Subjects.
Sermons for the Times.
Discipline and other Sermons.
Water of Life and other Sermons.
Pentateuch and David.

A TWENTY-FIVE CENT EDITION

OF

CHARLES KINGSLEY'S NOVELS.

In 8vo. Paper Covers.

Westward Ho!
Hypatia.
Yeast.

Alton Locke.
Two Years Ago.
Hereward the Wake.

MACMILLAN & CO.,
112 Fourth Avenue, New York.

Popular Books for the Young.

BY CHARLES KINGSLEY.

MADAM HOW AND LADY WHY: First Lessons in Earth Lore for Children. $1.00.

THE HEROES; or, Greek Fairy Tales for My Children. With Illustrations. $1.00.

This lovely version of three of the most famous folk-stories of the old Greeks. — *Mail and Express.*

Ought to be in the hands of every child in the country. — *Christian Union.*

THE WATER-BABIES: A Fairy Tale for a Land-Baby. Illustrated. $1.00.

One of the best children's stories ever written. "Water-Babies" is deservedly an English classic. — *Christian Union.*

GLAUCUS; or, The Wonders of the Sea-Shore. With numerous colored Illustrations. Cloth, extra, $2.00.

BY CHARLOTTE M. YONGE,

Author of "The Heir of Redclyffe."

THE LITTLE DUKE. Richard the Fearless. With Illustrations. 16mo, $1.00.

THE PRINCE AND THE PAGE. A Story of the Last Crusade. With Illustrations. 16mo, $1.00.

LITTLE LUCY'S WONDERFUL GLOBE. With Illustrations by L. Frölich. 16mo, $1.25.

THE LANCES OF LYNWOOD. With Illustrations. 16mo, $1.25.

A BOOK OF GOLDEN DEEDS OF ALL TIMES AND ALL LANDS. 16mo, $1.25.

THE STORY OF THE CHRISTIANS AND MOORS OF SPAIN. 16mo, $1.25.

A STOREHOUSE OF STORIES. Storehouse the First. 16mo, $1.00.

A STOREHOUSE OF STORIES. Storehouse the Second. 16mo, $1.00.

THE POPULATION OF AN OLD PEAR TREE; or, Stories of Insect Life. From the French of E. Van Bruysel. With Illustrations. 16mo, $1.00.

MACMILLAN & CO.,
112 Fourth Avenue, New York.

WORKS OF LEWIS CARROLL.

Published by Macmillan & Co.

ALICE'S ADVENTURES IN WONDERLAND.

With 42 Illustrations by TENNIEL. 12mo, cloth, gilt, $1.00.

Lewis Carroll's immortal story.—*Academy.*

That most delightful of children's stories.—*Saturday Review.*

THROUGH THE LOOKING-GLASS AND WHAT ALICE FOUND THERE.

With 50 Illustrations by TENNIEL. 12mo, cloth, gilt, $1.00.

Will fairly rank with the tale of her previous experience.—*Daily Telegraph.*

Many of Mr. Tenniel's designs are masterpieces of wise absurdity.—*Athenæum.*

ALICE'S ADVENTURES IN WONDERLAND, and THROUGH THE LOOKING-GLASS AND WHAT ALICE FOUND THERE.

Printed in one volume, with all the Illustrations. 12mo, cloth, plain, $1.25.

THE NURSERY "ALICE." Containing 20 Colored Enlargements from Tenniel's Illustrations to "Alice's Adventures in Wonderland," with Text adapted to Nursery Readers.

Cover designed and colored by E. GERTRUDE THOMSON. 4to, $1.50.

Let the little people rejoice! The most charming book in the world has appeared for them. The "Nursery Alice," by Lewis Carroll, with its wealth of colored illustrations from Tenniel's pictures, is certainly the most artistic juvenile that has been seen for many and many a day.—*Boston Budget.*

MACMILLAN & CO.,
112 Fourth Avenue, New York.

WORKS OF LEWIS CARROLL.

Published by Macmillan & Co.

SYLVIE AND BRUNO.
With 46 Illustrations by HARRY FURNISS. 12mo, cloth, gilt, $1.50.

RHYME? AND REASON?
With 65 Illustrations by ARTHUR B. FROST, and 9 by HENRY HOLIDAY. 12mo, cloth, gilt, $1.50.

This book is a reprint, with additions, of the comic portions of "Phantasmagoria, and other Poems," and of the "Hunting of the Snark."

A TANGLED TALE.
Reprinted from the *Monthly Packet*, with Illustrations. $1.50.

ALICE'S ADVENTURES UNDERGROUND.
Being a fac-simile of the original MS. Book, afterward developed into "Alice's Adventures in Wonderland." With 37 Illustrations by the author. 12mo, cloth, gilt, $1.50.

THE GAME OF LOGIC.
With envelope containing card and counters. 12mo, cloth, $1.00.

MACMILLAN & CO.,
112 FOURTH AVENUE, NEW YORK.

MRS. MOLESWORTH'S
Story Books for Children.

Published by Macmillan & Co.

THE CHILDREN OF THE CASTLE.

With Illustrations by WALTER CRANE. 16mo, cloth extra, $1.25.

NEW EDITION OF MRS. MOLESWORTH'S WORKS.

With Illustrations by WALTER CRANE. 16mo, cloth, extra, $1.00 each.

THE RECTORY CHILDREN.

A delightful Christmas book for children : a racy, charming home story, full of good impulses and bright suggestions.—*Boston Traveller.*

Quiet, sunny, interesting, and thoroughly winning and wholesome.
—*Boston Journal.*

FOUR WINDS FARM.	"CARROTS."
"US." An Old-Fashioned Story.	THE CUCKOO CLOCK.
CHRISTMAS TREE LAND.	TELL ME A STORY.
TWO LITTLE WAIFS.	THE ADVENTURES OF HERR BABY.
THE TAPESTRY ROOM.	ROSY.
A CHRISTMAS CHILD.	LITTLE MISS PEGGY.
GRANDMOTHER DEAR.	A CHRISTMAS POSY.

There is no more acceptable writer for children than Mrs. Molesworth.
—*Literary World.*

No English writer of stories for children has a better reputation than Mrs. Molesworth, and none whose stories we are familiar with deserves it better.
—*New York Mail and Express.*

Mistress of the art of writing for children.—*Spectator.*

MACMILLAN & CO.,
112 Fourth Avenue, New York.

www.ingramcontent.com/pod-product-compliance
Lightning Source LLC
Chambersburg PA
CBHW022114290426
44112CB00008B/671